ONE GOD

ONE GOD

The Political and Moral Philosophy
of Western Civilization

Ernesto Lorca

Montréal/New York/London

Black Rose Books No. FF314

Hardcover ISBN: 1-55164-211-5 (bound) Paperback ISBN: 1-55164-210-7 (pbk.)

Canadian Cataloguing in Publication Data

Lorca, Ernesto (1923-2002)

One God : the political and moral philosophy of western civilization / Ernesto Lorca

Includes bibliographical references.

1. Violence--Religious aspects--Christianity. 2. Violence--Religious aspects--Judaism.
3. Violence--Religious aspects--Islam. I. Title.

BL221.L67 2002   291.5'697   C2002-903113-3

Cover design: Associés libres

C.P. 1258	2250 Military Road	99 Wallis Road
Succ. Place du Parc	Tonawanda, NY	London, E9 5LN
Montréal, H2X 4A7	14150	England
Canada	USA	UK

To order books:

In Canada: (phone) 1-800-565-9523 (fax) 1-800-221-9985
email: utpbooks@utpress.utoronto.ca

In United States: (phone) 1-800-283-3572 (fax) 1-651-917-6406

In the UK & Europe: (phone) London 44 (0)20 8986-4854 (fax) 44 (0)20 8533-5821
email: order@centralbooks.com

Our Web Site address: http://www.web.net/blackrosebooks

A publication of the Institute of Policy Alternatives of Montréal (IPAM)

Printed in Canada

TABLE OF CONTENTS

PREFACE

What follows is the sort of work which I thought was needed to be done some time by some one—for understanding the world, and changing it, for the better.

No book is complete. Each book is a beginning, an invitation to, or occasion for, conversation and re-thinking. This one is no exception. I offer it most humbly, even pleadingly: Let us please re-examine the idea and phenomenon of religion, and re-evaluate our values.

This manuscript was submitted for publication before the unfolding of the momentous events of September 2001. The "problem of religion" that is put forth here, therefore, did not need for its argument the further evidence, or wisdom of hindsight, that we might have gained from those developments. It was all there to be discerned before September 2001.

Religious freedom, tolerance, and pluralism are of course better than their opposites. But the former are too temporary, if not illusory and artificial, for religions are by definition, and in essence, exclusive and explosive, exclusionary and destructive. Internally, they justify class societies, with all their attendant inequalities and injustices; externally, they reproduce a world of war of all against all, with all the atrocities committed in the name of their respective gods.

THE ABSOLUTE TEXT AS THE
INALTERABLE, INDIVISIBLE, INCONTROVERTIBLE SOVEREIGN

Hear now, O Israel, the decrees and laws I am about to teach you. Follow them so that you may live.... Do not add to what I command you and do not subtract from it, but keep the commands of the LORD your God that I give you. —Deuteronomy 4:1-2

See that you do all I command you; do not add to it or take away from it.
—Deuteronomy 12:32

It is easier for heaven and earth to disappear than for the least stroke of a pen to drop out of the Law. —Luke 16:17

I warn everyone who hears the words of the prophecy of this book: If anyone adds anything to them, God will add to him the plagues described in this book. And if anyone takes words away from this book of prophecy, God will take away from him his share in the tree of life and in the holy city, which are described in this book.
—Revelation 22:18-19

No man can change the words of God. —Enam 6:34

Your Lord's word has been completed in terms of truth and justice. There is no one to change his words. —Enam 6:115

✳✳✳✳

Above all, you must understand that no prophecy of Scripture came about by the prophet's own interpretation. For prophecy never had its origin in the will of man, but men spoke from God as they were carried along by the Holy Spirit.
—2 Peter 1:20-21

If we annul a verse or wish it to be overlooked, we definitely bring a similar or better one.
—Bakara 2:106

God has revealed the Book as the true book. Those who fall into disagreement as regards the Book have certainly fallen into profound conflict. —Bakara 2:176

The law for the prophets we sent before you is the same as this one. You cannot find any change whatsever in our law.
                                                                        —İsrâ 17:77

God revealed to his servant the truest of true books, this Book, which contains no contradiction or fault.
                                                                        —Kehf 18:1-3

God erases whatever he wishes and leaves intact whatever he wills. The original of all books is with him.
                                                                        —Rad 13:39

∗∗∗∗

For whoever keeps the whole law and yet stumbles at just one point is guilty of breaking all of it.
                                                                        —James 2:10

Do you, then, believe in some part of the Book and reject others?   —Bakara 2:85

We torment those who divide Koran into parts.   —Hicr:15-90

Except for infidels, no one contests God's verses.   —Mümin 40:4

Those who contest God's verses without having any proof revealed to them are received with great hatred in the sight of God and his faithful. God seals off the heart of every presumptuous thug.
                                                                        —Mümin 40:35

When prophets brought men self-evident divine knowledge, they trusted in their own (human) knowledge and mocked it. And that which they mocked, immediately strangled them.
                                                                        —Mümin 40:83

∗∗∗∗

Of course there have been additions and subtractions—by prophets and the powers that be—but how can one deny the fact that religious texts are the ones that are least amenable to interpretation and change?

That is, indeed, a fact which gives all the more reason for taking religion and God more seriously as something not much reformable, secularizable, rationalizable, humanizable…

INTRODUCTION

This is a book on *the* Books: the books of the "peoples of the Book,"[1] that is, the *Old Testament* (*Torah*) of the Jewish people, the *Old* and *New Testaments* (*Bible*) of the Christian peoples, and the *Koran* of the Muslim peoples; the last consisting, on its own account, of all the three at once but superseding the first two by way of sublation, whereas the first, historically and ideationally, is the main source of the two later derivatives. Subsequent geographical, cultural, ethnic-national, and denominational-theological differentiation and intra-controversy notwithstanding, all three are Middle Eastern Abrahamic monotheisms that constitute the religious bases of the moral and political theory of Western civilization, eclipsing in major respects the other source of this civilization—the ancient (pre-Platonic) Greek philosophy of nature, man, and society.

The three books constitute a triad, or a trilogy. Without the *Old Testament*, the source of all, neither the *New Testament* nor the *Koran* can be understood. And it is with the *Koran*, "the last and the most developed" chapter, that a better illuminating projector can be held onto the *Old* and *New Testaments*. For, despite Christian-Western-centric clamor as to the alienness of the *Koran* and Islam (and vice versa), the latter is, doctrinally, the third legitimate "seed" of Abrahamic monotheism, let alone being a step-child. As we shall see ample evidence especially in the Third Part, Koranic Islam, both objectively and self-professedly, is an offspring and a not too original derivative of Judeo-Christianity, and much more "ecumenical" than the first two creeds, and not any more totalitarian within or any more aggressive outwardly than its elders brothers. This study hopes, among other things, to correct certain misplaced causalities as to the relationship between the historical development of the three great religions and the allegedly different, antagonistic "nature" or "essence" thereof. Similarities and differences, continuities and discontinuities between these religions is a subject I will pull together in the conclusion after we deal at length with each scripture, indicating in the process, however, local intertextual relationships between them.

The subject of the study thus stated, I should make haste to clarify several points concerning what there is, and what there is not, in it regarding its scope and material, intellectual or research problem, genre and method, intended or hoped for audience, and, of course, its conductor's theoretical and philosophical position or perspective.

What I have done, concerning the scope and the material, is an analysis of the political and moral theory of the three sacred books—the *Old* and *New Testaments* and the *Koran*—and not of the whole, or most/many, of these religions' other important scriptural documents, for the three Books *are* the most canonical, central, and authoritative texts of these religions. That they do have a privileged and higher determinative position over others will, I think, be readily conceded. I have simply focused on them. Doing a more comprehensive job is neither within the range of my learning, nor has it been among my intentions for the simple reason that such is not necessary for my purpose and argument.

Conversely, "political and moral theory" may well be an understatement. Although that is my focus, I frequently make so bold as to enlarge the conventional definitions thereof by foraying into ethical, epistemological and ontological matters, not to mention the crossing over of the boundaries of more mundane disciplines of political economy, sociology and psychology, philosophical anthropology, and so forth. The three texts are so invitingly and temptingly rich in all those respects that one might not always be self-restrained enough to abruptly stop at those boundaries. Nevertheless, I have not been so presumptuous as to go a long way in those directions, either. Others have done that, and will do more, and I hope more critical work in those disciplines, bringing out the abundantly problematic aspects of religions that await further non-theological, rational-critical treatment.

At any rate, I consider political theory as something larger than, say, history of political thought (in this case religio-political thought) or reductively empirical or positivistic political scientific theory. Nor do I think that any empathic-relativistic, Verstehen-like understanding must be the final station of theoretical inquiry; previous political theories should be examined also from the vantage point of our later theoretical acquisitions. Wisdom of retrospect or hindsight ceases to be pejorative in this kind of endeavor.

Of course religion *is* ideology. Analyzing it as such, however, merely from the standpoint of sociology or politics of religion is a necessary but not sufficient enterprise and bears the risk of being arrested at functionalist apologetics. A critical examination of exactly what kind of an ideology it is and a normative evaluation of its functions, of what it disguises as well as what it brings to the fore, as all ideologies do, has been my predominant concern. What partial representations of reality it postulates as the whole reality and what partial interests it advances as the general interest of humankind deserve more critical and normative scrutiny than those undertaken by the empiricist and value-free kinds of "social scientific" sociologies and politics of religion. For, more than any other kind of ideology, religion deals in basic human values, morals, and political matters. Hence the double-focus on the "political" and "moral" theories of Western monotheistic civilization. There is an organic relationship, or a dialectical interrelationship, if you will, between morals and politics. Moral values and rules shape politics and/or politics create and use moral precepts as handmaidens of political legitimation of certain social-political orders. Nowhere is this relationship clearer and more vital than that which obtains in our present subject.

However widened a definition I may confer on political theory in general, and however rich the Books are, I should further specify some other absences or non-agenda in this study. Absences not only, again, because of my lack of competence, but also because they are unnecessary for my purpose and argument at this time—although they are very legitimate and fruitful kinds and sites of research and expertise in themselves. Thus, there is, here, no history of religion, sociology of religion, psychology of religion (individual or social), anthropology of religion, philosophy of religion, politics of religion and state or society or law, and so forth. What I am looking at here is not the genesis, development, institutional organization, theory-practice discrepancies, local variations, denominations, schisms, wars, homicides, psychological (placebo) functions of religions, let alone their theological and exegetical intricacies. What I am looking at here is the political and moral theory contained in the Book(s) as *the* normative text(s) that has shaped and continues to constitute and reproduce, and constrain, the basic moral values and political orders of human society in their essentials—rather than the plethora of theological and institutional variations in time and space. Religion has been the oldest and most powerful ideology and institution of socialization in human history, and it has not yet ceased to be so.

Restated, my aim is not to describe, understand or explain (or predict) religion(s) either from a structural-functional point of view or from an historical-institutional standpoint, let alone from a non-critical theological hermeneutical-exegetical vantage point. Without reducing political theory to normative theory, my aim is to understand, analyze, expose, interpret, *and* to critically evaluate the Book(s) from a logical-normative standpoint. After all, or rather first and foremost, these texts themselves are normative texts: the Book(s), the Command(s), the Law(s), the "true"/"trustworthy"/"scientific" Word(s) of God. (And of prophets, of priests, of redactors, of other called-chosen-elect Few—to be absolutely obeyed by the faithful Multitude, without adding or subtracting a letter.) Self-profession of normativity, in itself and needing nothing else, invites and legitimates normative critique—academic, popular, and theological (as the theological history of religion itself attests). Of course, in descending order, the range of interpretation and critique narrows down from the academic to the theological, provided that the former be not overtly or covertly theological, as has been the case with many "secular" academics in all disciplines.

To inquire into the reasonableness, goodness, justness, intentions and consequences of such normative texts that purport to regulate morals and politics in society—and our knowledge of reality—is an undertaking the legitimacy of which no sane person with good faith can contest from a moral or academic social scientific standpoint. This is in the nature, and laws, of rational human reasoning, discourse, debate, and action. And it should be done properly: procedure-wise and respect-wise. The subject is an immensely important and exceptionally delicate one. Perhaps, more so than any other imaginable, or rather, so far imagined ones. For roughly 2500 years many peoples have believed in and acted according to these Books, and today 2.5-3 billions of the world's population (half of it) continue to do so in differing degrees of loyalty to the letter(s) of the Word(s) of the Western God. Basic precepts of these books continue to lurk behind the moral and political theories of many communities (and persons), however secularized or laicized they may have, or said to have, become in terms of the institutional and external aspects of religion, and its relation to society and the State.

The residues, in fact continuities, of monotheism in the West are much greater than are usually perceived or admitted. The church (or the synagogue or the mosque) and the clergy of various types may be said to have receded in social and political, that is, public life, but the hold of the Books, and especially of the "idea of God," that ingenuous human construct, on individual consciences and epistemologies is mostly intact: The God, the Creator-, the Chooser/Blesser-, the Curser/Punisher-God, who is at the Beginning, in the Middle (this world), and at the End (the other world) still has a firm grip on the minds and hearts of many people, shaping their view of the world, of nature, of society, of their individual selves, and—very significantly—their interpersonal relations with their fellow members of the species. In short, epistemology, psychology, morality, *and* politics, are all still awash with the idea of God, if not with institutional religion.

The political relevance of religion may be overlooked if one reduces it to the contemporary arrangements of institutional religion. Divine right of kings or the church as the second "sword" may be passé, but the "idea of God" and his "Words"/Book(s) are still very much with us. They still determine, underlie, legitimate many things in private political philosophies (in addition to basic values and morals) and, more indirectly and in mediated ways, our public political philosophy and practices. This, I believe, will come out clearly, in the textual body and the conclusion of this study, with implications for our arrested development on the path of egalitarian, free, democratic polities and of dignified interpersonal human relations.

In this study, I do not propose or pretend to disprove or argue against the existence of God(s). That has already been done by a host of philosophical atheists and by scientific human thought decisively for the past, at least, two centuries. Like religion, the *idea* of God "exists" sociologically and historically and as an ideational figment of human imagination, with nevertheless immense consequences in reality; but God as an entity, a fact, a thing, a relation, does not. It is a mere mental construct, unlike, for example, mathematical constructs, without a material referent in nature. It is a name, it is a bundle of attributed properties, for a non-being.

What I am doing here is an analysis of the political and moral theory of the three great religions, with their mono-God at the helm. This analysis would stand even if that God did exist and put forth that theory. And it is bad political and moral theory, not only because that God is a bad one, which he is (theodicy is a totally redundant discipline), but precisely because the *idea* of god(s) is a bad idea to start with. The very fact that God is thought to exist or made out to exist has crippled humanity's cultural potential for developing better politics and morals. There can be no "good" God, a contradiction in terms, and therefore, no good religion. Religion without god(s) cannot be, and vice versa.

In undertaking this logico-normative critique, I have imposed upon myself the following procedural and methodological constraints. I closely read the books twice in their entirety to arrive at a decision as to which passages would exhaustively represent what is strictly political and moral in them. I reread the selected passages thrice with a view to better understand, expose, and comment upon them. Upon this textual research and preliminary workmanship, I tried to perform a four-layered task, not always neatly and mechanically delineated: (1) I presented substantial excerpts to let the text speak for itself and to serve as documentary evidence for what is to follow; (2) I made an exposition of them within the vocabulary of their own discourses, in order to elucidate their intended meaning; (3) I gave a running commentary on them with a view to further interpret what that discourse and content means, including the implications and objective consequences of those intended meanings. Thus, I have, in a sense, done some hermeneutics and exposition, if not exegesis, of these grand, or better the grandest, religious narratives. But, of course, not in the theological tradition. I have employed some empathic understanding. But without, I think, falling into empathic fallacies. I have, in a sense, "walked with the text" (but not walked in the way of the text), without going faster than the text itself, that is, up to station (4) and as a restraint against the risk of proffering unfounded or stretched judgments that did not inhere in the text.

It is only after (1) and (2) and starting with (3) and continuing in (4) that I put forth my further and farther-reaching interpretations, based both on my own theoretical baggage and our contemporary, and therefore retrospective, perspectives. In other words, I took care that my selectivity is sufficiently exhaustive and representative and not biased, arbitrary, and inadequate. That is, I proceeded dialogically and in a moving-equilibrium with the text. Not to agree with it, to be sure, but to understand it judiciously before disagreeing with its moral and political norms. I made a sort of participant reading, and even observed the reader itself (myself), without, however, "going native" at the end. I shall soon explicate all this, lest it may be perceived as hypocritical premeditation, or foregone conclusion, in the guise of disinterested objective inquiry.

I humbly presume that I am rendering a certain service to the reader. These three books are very lengthy ones, and this is among the reasons why they are not read widely and fully by believers and nonbelievers alike, who suffice with second-hand narrations, which are often arbitrarily or manipulatively selective. One of the things I have done here is to adequately abridge them for the impatient or the put-off reader at least in so far as their political and moral content is concerned, through the device of presenting lengthy excerpts throughout. Such full quotations both enable the text to speak for itself and constitute direct evidence for what I subsequently say in my basic running commentary.

At times, I do not even comment on the excerpted text, or I just emphatically underline its crucial section, the underlining becoming, in itself, my commentary. This is closely related to my main objective in doing this work: I am eliciting and commenting upon what the Book(s) themselves say and not the shape they have taken in the hands of intermediary theologians or reciters.

This is also the reason why I confine myself to the primary texts and do not take issue with secondary sources or any part of the (vast) theological literature on them. And: "primary text" means the central, canonical, holy Book(s), *the* Book(s), *Bible* and *Koran*, not other biblical scriptures or "tefsir," not even "hadis." Thus, there is no foray into even, say, different interpretations of the *Bible* according to Catholics and Protestants, let alone those of divers denominations of lower order. What they all believe in common as the basics suffices for the purpose at hand. The former are but minor differences, and the "narcissism of minor differences," to adapt Freud's expressive phrase.

The genre of this study is criticism, not scholarship, to revive that old distinction, and it is not theological criticism but anti-theological critique, or rather just critical commentary, or an analytical essay based on the method of close textual analysis—a normative analysis of a text made up of the *Old Testament*, the *New Testament*, and the *Koran*. The *Old Testament* does most of the story-telling and historical narration and performs the parallel task of normative legislation, and it is the longest. Through the *New Testament* to the *Koran*, the narrative text shortens, common history is referred to with necessary contemporary additions, and the normative text is repeated, refined, and basically upheld with certain immanent critiques.

I embarked on this project with no stronger prejudice than that of a philosophical atheist, finding the idea of God logically and epistemologically wrong, inconsistent, and unpersuasive and the phenomenon of religion obsolete and naive, but in its time a source of well-meaning rules for moral and political conduct. And my initial research question was: "What political and moral theory exactly, is there in the Books?" I admit that this was not maximum sympathy, but it was not maximum antipathy either. (In the conclusion, after the textual analysis—which took me three years—I shall say that this moderately biased atheist has now become a philosophical *anti*-theist.)

A corollary to my auto-limitation of doing a logico-normative study is the lack of "context" herein, in the historicist, relativist sense of that term. Although I have provided some contextual fluidity to the basically normative text, that has been for purposes less of analysis than of presentation. Although these grand/grandest narratives are richly historical as they are literary, and are therefore major sources of much world history and literature, they are, as I said above, first and foremost law-books, books of normative rules. Some of these are of course context-bound and have been subject to change in time and space as regards those elements which are of a lower level of abstraction; major precepts, however, those that are of a higher level of abstraction and are the apex of the Books' hierarchy of norms, the idea of God being the first but not the only one, are and have been trans-contextual and trans-historical. The context of today is not much different than the context of, say, 500 A.D., with regard to fundamental epistemological, moral, and political religiosity—certainly in the individual psyche and also significantly in the public one.

In this study, which is about the trans-contextual normative principles of the grand religious narratives, the literary merits and meanings of the texts are not on board either. Not that I could have done it but chose otherwise. I couldn't have. But, again, they are not directly relevant. There is much literary merit in these normative narratives, but I have to control for the narrative to elucidate the norms, unless they have direct bearing on the latter. Thus go overboard symbols, myths, metaphors, allegories, *and* miracles, wonders, signs. The former list falls within the jurisdiction of literature, high or low; the latter cluster within that of theologians and, unfortunately, the faithful—whom the miracles are for. I am concerned with hard worldly human politics and ethics.

As for the 4th layer mentioned above, I have in mind something like the following. Although, through (2) to (3), and especially in (3), I criticize the ideas of God and religion, I still raise in (4) the question, "Isn't there in religion, or haven't religions contributed to, any body of good normative rules, some good first principles, for our morals and politics?" (My answer, at the end, shall be no. Not anything beyond some very rudimentary principles of basic human morality such as the undesirability of murder, theft, etc., which could have been achieved anyway within the course of human history without the aid of these religions, which I do think have, in net balance, immoralized humankind. Their "good sides" are overwhelmed and outweighed by their harmful teachings, their bad morals and bad politics.) I also try to tackle the question/argument that religions reflect human nature and/or that human nature is so "crooked a timber" that religions had to come to straighten it out. No, I will say, at the end, it has been the other way around: human nature is not as bad as religions portray it, nor should social relations and politics be as inegalitarian and homophobic in the older dictionary meaning as religions posit it. It is the religions and the idea of God that have worsened human nature (historical-cultural human nature, that is, and our assumptions and actions about it) and have preempted or impeded a better "human nature" and more humane politics. It is not human nature and the nature of human society that has necessitated such religions; it is such religions that have brought about such people and politics.

To my knowledge, this study is the first of its kind in that: (1) it is a critical study of all the three Books within one cover; (2) it is a nearly exhaustive textual analysis of their political and moral theory from a non-theological point of view; and (3) it sheds, I hope some new light, on the unfortunate religious bases of the moral, political, and epistemological theories of Western civilization. (*And* on the Eastern ones, to the extent of the expansion of Islam in the East beyond the Middle East and also to the extent of the influence of Western-Christian imperialism and colonialism in the whole world.)

I am well aware that a work's being the first of its kind is not sufficient ground for its being a worthy one. There are at least three minimal requirements. The subject or problem should be interesting and important. (Which is the case here.) It should be untouched, or overtouched erroneously. (The latter is the case here.) The task should be performed well in terms of labor and procedure. (The reader will decide that.) Mine has been, I am confident, an elementary but responsible one. It will, I hope, suggest the possibility and necessity of a distinct brand of religion-critique that will receive much better treatment in the hands of wiser and more sophisticated examiners. I hereby make only an initial statement on the subject and most probably will not devote more time to it. But I do expect to see better examples of this approach and method forthcoming. Needless to say, I am ready to stand corrected on matters of the logic of textual analysis.

I write this essay from the standpoint of a naturalist humanist and rationalist, with all due humility and fallibility and with full respect to good people who are believers. But I also want to make it clear that this is a book that tries to show that the Books are not good books, morally and politically. They are not good particularly for women, children, workers, and most men. They are not good even for the chosen few, who have been their historical beneficiaries. They may have gained might, wealth, status (along with illusions and delusions), but they have lost the chance of being rational and just human beings in their relations with other human beings (however well-intending persons some may have been).

I submit this analysis mainly to the consideration of the general reader, "everyman" and "everywoman," and only then to that of particularly four categories of potential readers: (1) women, workers, and youth (who are not yet entrenched in any one establishment); (2) honest theologians and believers, from whom I expect rational argumentation instead of fideistic emotional condemnation; (3) relatively secularist academics and intellectuals, with the expectation that they reevaluate their weak laicist, deist or agnostic positions; (4) philosophical atheists, to whom I would like to convey the idea that anti-theism is the logically more consistent and morally more compelling stance. From the second I would not accept as reasonable the response that our approach and language are incommensurable, or that the Books, like miracles, are for the believer or the faithful. Human reason and lives do not allow such a luxurious leeway. Human conscience should not permit such an alibi for acts harmful to other human beings, acts that are legitimized by religious commands and the idea of God. From the third I would not accept as convincing the differentiation that institutional religion has become obsolete and/but that the idea of God is tenable and can be personal and publicly harmless. The latter remains the axiomatic pinnacle of the former. From the fourth, I expect nothing less than philosophical and praxiological anti-theism. From the first I expect the most, for they are the ones who have suffered most and have lost most because of God and religion and who will lose least but gain worlds from the overthrow of religious and Godly fetters, shackles, yokes.

I spoke and acted, not with the word and the sword of God, but only with human words and no sword at all. I require the same. No more hatred toward, and murdering and exploitation of, other human beings—willfully or as a consequence of illusioned indifference or passive approval—in the guise and name of holiness and Godly truth. The last are mere human untruths. Untruths for oppressing, exploiting, and dehumanizing the majority of men and the entirety of women.

Two final introductory remarks. I am advancing the necessity of anti-theism not as an imposition but as a suggestion. When I say philosophical *and* praxiological anti-theism, I mean not a political program or regime that excludes or prohibits all other kinds of belief but a process of rational discursive program of religion-critique in the intellectual, educational, academic, and philosophical spheres, which includes demonstration of the inadequacy *and* unintended harmful consequences of not confronting the evils of even the best of liberal/liberation theology, secularism, deism, "personal-God" theism, agnosticism, polite and hands-off philosophical atheism as public positions, as distinct from individually held worldviews. The latter may be relatively progressive personal gestures but do not absolve their owners from negative responsibility as citizens and members of the species. They may not be perpetrators of religious evil, but remaining an indifferent spectator thereof can hardly be said to be a very meritorious ethical stance.

I am not making these statements from within a certain religious community against that community or against other religious communities, either to disparage the former or to deprecate the latter from the vantage point of any (other) religious belief or faith. This is not criticism of a certain religion; it is a critique of all religion(s) and God(s) from the standpoint of human reason and dignity. Nor is any disrespect meant toward the believers or the faithful of religions, the "God-fearing peoples." Neither am I taking literary liberties with their sacred, sacrosanct books. I have very seriously, and for quite a long time, studied their texts, and what I am trying to say is very simple and pedantically sober: I am not "abhorring" or "scoffing at" their persons or communities as religions do; I am trying to tell them, on the evidence of their own scriptures, that their books are not as good as they think they are or were led to believe by their selectively quoting preachers and theologians.

I think what follows is one plausible and legitimate reading of the scriptures of Western monotheistic civilization, and I hope it may be received as one which is a little more than just another reading.

Notes

1. Please note that the usage is "peoples of the Book" (peoples as the object of the subject Book) and not "the Book of peoples" (the Book as the object of the subject peoples). The vital point, in these religions, that human beings are for the Book and God and not vice versa, is a theme to which we shall recurrently return. Human beings are the instrument of God, prophets, rulers, books, to be commanded and governed; they are not the authors of their own lives and social arrangements. All sorts of profound moral and political consequences follow from the basic postulate embedded in this usage.

PART ONE

THE OLD TESTAMENT

GENESIS

1. The Beginning: Creation of the Universe

> In the beginning God created the heavens and the earth. (1:1)
> And God said, "Let there be…"(1:3) …and there was…(1:3)
> God saw that the…was good. (1:4)
> God saw all that he had made [including "man, male and female"], and it was very good. (1:31)

God creates everything; he creates by saying and naming, willing into existence creatures; he likes what he creates. A creator, through constitutive speech acts, creates all things. The willful word of God has creative, constitutive power. This is reported/narrated by an authorial voice, one which frequently employs quotations from God.[1]

The original, fundamental question of the short cosmology of the *Old Testament* (one page out of 714 pages in the IBS's 1984 edition), also adopted by the other two monotheistic Abrahamic religions of Christianity and Islam, is not "how did all this happen? or came to be?" but "who created all this?" (and it is immediately answered in the very first sentence of the scripture as God). "All that" are not beings, existences, phenomena to be understood and explained; they are creatures made—for certain purposes—by a/the creator who makes (and can unmake) them. The scripture does not ask questions; it proceeds with statements.

No assumption, philosophical questioning or reflection, hypothetical or argumentative reasoning is involved; the scripture is declarative, descriptive, enumerative, and imperative on the issues of the causes, state, and purposes of existence. It is not philosophy; it is dogmatics and didactics concerning the sources of our knowledge of reality, of the meaning and purpose of life. This is the indubitable ontology and epistemology that the Book gives us.

God creates by willing, saying, naming as well as by filling,[2] shaping, and differentiating in binary oppositions the creatures called day and light, sky and earth, land and sea, plants and animals, sun and moon and stars; and he likes what he creates as a self-congratulatory artist. Similarly, man:

Then God said, "Let us make man in our image, in our likeness, and let them rule over the fish of the sea and the birds of the air, over the livestock, over all the earth, and over all the creatures that move along the ground."

So God created man in his own image, in the image of God he created him; male and female he created them.

God blessed them and said to them, "Be fruitful and increase in number; fill the earth and subdue it. Rule over the fish of the sea and the birds of the air and over every living creature that moves on the ground."

Then God said, "I give you every seed-bearing plant on the face of the whole earth and every tree that has fruit with seed in it. They will be yours for food. (1:26-30)

So God creates man:
- "in his own image"
- "male and female"
- and "bless(es) them"
- to "subdue" and "rule over" nature

In other words, man is like God and is blessed to reproduce, and to master and exploit nature. This is not a nature-friendly Book; it posits a hierarchy of subjection and exploitation from the very beginning: God → man → nature. And: "God saw all that he had made [including him (man), male and female], and it was very good" (1:31, 1:27). So far so good; God contentedly goes to rest on the seventh day, after six days of creative work.

2. Adam and Eve: Creation of Man—Male and Female

God provides man with food ("gives" all plants and animals to him who stands highest in the hierarchy of creation because of his likeness to God[3]) and with the first basic values/purposes of human life: eating (food) and reproducing (increase in numbers) and, as a corollary of the latter, multitude and plentitude and high quantities (first of population and then, as we shall see, of power, wealth, status, and fame—the threesome or foursome of all ancient tales as well as of all dominant contemporary/secular(!) moral systems).

God creates non-human nature in five and a half days and in less than one page, so the narrative cosmology of the *Old Testament* is very short, though its approach permeates the whole text. And God is satisfied with his non-human creation once and for all (1:3, 10, 12, 18, 21, 25, ff.). Not so with his human creation.

Although God creates human nature in his own image and likeness (in one day—the sixth—and in a little more than two pages), he is happy with it for the first and the last time on the day of creation (1:28 and 1:31). The remaining 712 pages of the *Old Testament* is a voluminous monument to the displeasure of God with his own human creation. In contradistinction to the very short cosmology of the book, its adversarial anthropology, history, and philosophical anthropology is very, very long.

Why? What happened beginning with the eighth day? Or wasn't the sixth day's art as faultless as God thought?

> The LORD God made [nature]…And there was no man to work the ground…the LORD God formed the man from the dust of the ground…(2:4-7)

Man, apparently made by God (now Lord God) for the purpose of working the ground (exploiting nature), is formed not from the earth or soil or ground but from the "dust" thereof. Despite all image-talk, likeness-talk, this is the first instance of the book giving away the low value placed upon man, the low worth assigned to him from the very beginning. His substance is not earth, the productive earth that gives life and to which life may return, even if speaking figuratively; his substance is "dust," mere dust. The scripture has God make man from the basest of matter. So that he doesn't think he is something; he is literally nothing, naught—that is, man in general. (Only God's chosen ones will be allowed to become somebodies, even God-like, as we shall see, for whom the rest will "work the ground.")

Man's value (and destiny) thus decided on the sixth day, the scripture needs nothing but to produce a convenient pretext on the eighth day or the following days for man to actually deserve his dust-like status and existence. For that pretext, in turn, the scripture needs the good offices of a midwife, yet to be created. The former makes its entry in the form of "sin and fall," the latter in the form of "woman," that is, the "female" term of the equation "him (man), male and female" (1:27).

God gives man the authority to "name" all creatures: "…and whatever the man called each living creature, that was its name" (2:19). Then he "make(s) a helper suitable for him" (2:18) from the latter's rib, who is to be called "woman" (2:23), or "part" of man, "for she was taken out of man" (2:23). Thus, woman is a derivative of man, a derivative helper, an organically united subordinate. ("Bone of my bones and flesh of my flesh" 2:23.) She, Eve, too, is named by him, Adam (3:20).

God takes man and puts him in the garden of Eden "to work it" (2:15) and commands him not to "eat from the tree of knowledge of good and evil" (2:17) if he is not to die. We may note in passing that some worldly goods, as high values for man, make their appearance quite early in the sacred text: "The gold of that land is good…and onyx (is) also there." (2:12).

3. The Fall of Man: By the Hand of Woman

The helper prepares man's fall. The serpent, Satan, who apparently cannot lead astray the strong man, advises the weak woman to eat the fruit of the forbidden tree without fear of death, which is "good for food and pleasing to the eye, and also desirable for gaining wisdom" (3:6). "(Y)ou will be like God, knowing good and evil" (3:5).

Woman eats and makes man eat, too. The eyes of both of them are opened, God holds court, the man gives away the woman ("The woman you put here with me—she gave me some fruit from the tree" 3:12). God punishes the woman by increasing her pains in childbearing and by making the man "rule over" her (3:16). The yielding *and* seductive woman is put under the rule of the innocent and seduced man. The misogyny of the book(s) is inaugurated.

God punishes Adam for having listened to his wife, curses the ground because of him (which "will produce thorn and thistles" (3:18) for him), and makes man (and woman) mortal: "…for dust you are/and to dust you will return" (3:19). As if there were any other normal natural alternative to death, and for that matter, painful childbirth. And, also, to increasing in number by sexual intercourse.

Had it not been intended punitively, all of this could have been interpreted as a realistic or even philosophical portrayal of the mortality of humankind and the hardships of life, e.g., "…through painful toil you will eat of it (ground) all the days of your life" (3:17). But it is willed as a curse; realities of life are presented as the result of God's curse upon humankind's sinful behavior. Life becomes something to be endured rather than lived. Enjoyment of life is ruled out (for most, not all, men) by an anti-life dictum. (Here, Adam and Eve are condemned for a life time; later, as we shall see, humankind will be condemned for generations and generations to come.)

The reinforcement (on the eighth day) of the debasement (on the sixth day) of God's most-favored creature is ostensibly predicated on the twin facts of being from "dust" (6th day) and committing "sin" (8th day). But what is the sin? Eating the fruit of the tree of the knowledge of good and evil? Or, as a result of that, Adam and Eve's realizing their nakedness because of the opening of their eyes and thus becoming like God(s) (3:5, 3:22), knowing good and evil? Or their sleeping together, etc?

No myth can explain, or explain away, the utter illogicalities of Genesis 3: God creates man (male and female) in his own image (the former more so than the latter), throughout the Book(s) he commands man and woman to learn of good and evil and to practice the former and avoid the latter, he orders them to increase in number and become man and wife and one "flesh" (2:24), and so forth. If evil/sin is having sexual intercourse, the scripture's argument is logically inconsistent and unconvincing.

Not the meaningfulness, but the intended/alluded meaning of the whole thing, however, may become somewhat understandable if and only if God or the Book(s) or the authors of both are imputed with a predetermination or premeditation to posit "man" as worthless and sinful from the very beginning and deserving of punishment and pain and oppression forever. "Man, male and female," are predestined for eternal curse and pain, and "man, female" furnishes the convenient pretext in taking the initiative and seducing "man, male." In a sense, the first historical "sacred (man)-profane (woman)" pair is thereby introduced.

The message, motivation, interest, and the expected gain of the male authors of the sacred text is, in net balance, to establish the control and domination of man over woman by announcing the opposite as "sinful" and chronologically more original than "original sin."

Original sin, in fact, is not a collaborative act; it is firstly and primarily committed by the female "man." Transformation of sexual difference and complementarity into gender discrimination and inequality is what Genesis is mainly about. Authors of Genesis are among the earliest patent-holders of patriarchal gender oppression; in consonance with the basic story of creation of Genesis establishing a primal hierarchy, in which each echelon is derived from the one above. God from God, man (male man) from God's breath, woman (female man) from man's rib. A veritable hierarchy, however alike or intimate each echelon may be. But all hierarchies are organic in the final analysis.

Sexual intercourse in itself is not the sin/evil. The sin/evil is eating from the tree of the knowledge of good and evil—whatever that may be—and woman's taking the initiative. But is it wholly disconnected with sex? It doesn't appear so: "The man and his wife were both naked, and they felt no shame" (2:25) before they ate the fruit, but they did feel ashamed after they ate the fruit. Their eyes were opened, they realized they were naked, they covered themselves, etc. What can be made of all this?

Sexual intercourse for procreation, reproduction, for increasing in number is okay. What seems not to be okay is the visual and physical pleasures of sex, consciousness and free pursuit of sexual pleasure by man, that is, by "female man," and her seeking this on equal footing with "male man," let alone initiating the proceedings. In his triple curse to the serpent, woman, and man, God says to the woman: "Your desire will be for your husband/and he will rule over you" (3:16). (To be repeated in the *New Testament*.) Woman's sexual desire is restricted to her husband, and man will lord it over woman. Basically, it is the woman who gets punished. Paternalistic, domineering monogamy for woman, all degrees of polygamy for man are thus divinely legislated on the flimsy pretext of original sin/temptation/seduction on the part of woman as the primary culprit. Man on this account is but a secondary culprit; his sin consists in listening to woman—something he shouldn't do from now on. The authors of the Book(s) hit two birds with one stone: They will subordinate most men to some men, as we shall see, and they subordinate all women to all men at the very outset. (Most men can't win, but it is an absolute no-win situation for all women. Some men, in lording over most men, give the latter a domain/subjects (women) in which they, too, can lord it over. The Book(s)'s inegalitarianism is both homophobic, as we shall see, and misogynist at the same time.)

God expels his most-favored creature from the Garden of Eden, saying: "The man has now become like one of us, knowing good and evil. He must not be allowed to reach out his hand and take also from the tree of life and eat, and live forever" (3:22). Likeness and docility of inferiors is okay, but competition from equals is barred.

4. Cain and Abel: Fraternal Strife Initiated

God, rhetorically pleased with all that he has created—most of all with man, male and female—decides for rather unconvincing reasons to become displeased with man. No theodicical manoeuver has been able to reasonably answer the simple questions of "How can man be defective if he is created in the image of (perfect) God?" or, conversely, "If man is defective but, all the same, created in the image of God, how can God be imperfect?" But the more interesting question is the following: After committing his/her first sin, why doesn't God correct man but, not only holding him perpetually responsible for one (dubious) sin, also keep trapping him into ever new sins as we shall see?

In accordance with the Godly command to increase in number Adam lies with his wife Eve, and she gives birth to the brothers Cain and Abel. God (Adam) decides not only to prefer the younger Abel's meat offering over the older Cain's fruit offering for not readily understandable or justifiable reasons[4] again but also, on this pretext, plants seeds of rivalry and enmity between human brothers at the very dawn of their history. Why offering fruit is "not right" and "sinful" is not explained (4:7). Not given any chance to express his indignation upon rejection or non-recognition, the "angry" and "downcast" Cain (4:6) is made to kill his brother Abel. (In the future, this fraternal enmity will recur, among others, between Jacob and Esau.)

God punishes Cain more severely than Adam. Not even condemned to hard labor on an unproductive land, he is cursed to become a restless wanderer. Thus, fratricide is punished; but, as we shall see, fraternal strife will be instigated throughout. Yet God does not condone vengeance: "…if anyone kills Cain, he will suffer vengeance seven times over" (4:15). (Monopoly of vengeance belongs to God?)

Cain goes away, he lies with his wife, they have a son, the son has a son, and so forth. The fifth in line marries two women (names mentioned), each gives birth to sons (ancestors of livestock breeding, of harp and flute playing, of forging tools out of bronze and iron). The sister of one of these sons is mentioned by name. Otherwise, presence and names of mothers, sisters, wives, daughters—sometimes in more than one of these roles—are not usually mentioned in the text.

In the meantime Adam, too, lies with his wife, they have a third son, Seth ("in his own likeness, in his own image," 5:3), Seth has a son, Enosh, and man begins "to call on the name of the LORD" (4:26).

Thus, it is Cain's and Seth's sons who lie with the women around to "increase in number." Who was Cain's wife? Whose daughters and sisters were the partners of the aforementioned sons in each line? Given the available, arithmetically limited pool of childbearable females around, it must have been a process of incestuous, in-family breeding to a certain extent. Perhaps, that is one reason for the omission of women's names.

5. From Adam to Noah: Long Live the Patriarchs

The "written account of Adam's line" is given (5:1). Only men are mentioned. Adam lives 930 years, Seth 912, Enosh 905, Kenan 910, Mahalalel 895, Jared 962, Enoch 365, Methuselah 969, Lamech 777, and Noah 500 until he has three sons (Shem, Ham, Japheth) and another 450 afterwards. All these men "walk with God"; then they "are no more" because

God "takes them away." In due course, God will reduce patriarchs' lives to "hundred and twenty years" (6:3).

6,7,8. The Flood (and "Human Nature")
God's displeasure with his own creation (if not image) continues:

> The LORD saw how great man's wickedness on the earth had become, and that every inclination of the thoughts of his heart was only evil all the time. The LORD was grieved that he had made man on the earth, and his heart was filled with pain. So the LORD said, I will wipe mankind, whom I have created, from the face of the earth...(6:5-7)

Why "wipe out" man and not, instead, "correct" him, if he is so powerful a God? Or is it that this God, or authors thereof, have a vested interest in continuing to have an incorrigible man, sinning perpetually in the absence of prior Godly advice and corrective intervention? And what exactly is this "great wickedness" of man and the always evil "inclination(s) of the thoughts of his heart?"

The sacred text offers but the following clue for this supposed profanity:

> When men began to increase in number on the earth and daughters were born to them, the sons of God saw that the daughters of men were beautiful, and *they married any of them they chose*. (6: 1-2) (Emphasis mine.)

And:

> ...sons of God went to the daughters of men and had children by them. They were the heroes of old, men of renown. (6:4)

If the "sons of God," the "heroes of old," the "men of renown" are other from mere "men," the former marrying (probably forcefully) the beautiful daughters of the latter, there should have arisen no problem within the inner logic of the patriarchal and autocratic context then at hand. The clause which I have underlined in the first excerpt, however, may be suggestive of the probability that the two have been the same: men marrying any of the girls and women *they chose*, that is, marrying some daughters (in the generic sense) that should not have been chosen for marriage or intercourse, namely sisters, daughters (in the narrow sense), and other close female kin.

If the particular "wickedness" in question seems to be incestuous behavior (above all, father-daughter and brother-sister incest), which is to be curtailed, at least from now on; it is at the same time somewhat rationalized on the grounds that the actors have been prominent, heroic men of yore, not only attracted by the irresistible beauty of women but also impelled by the requirements of reproduction and multiplication given an initially limited pool of females.[5]

But the alleged wickedness is not restricted to the foregoing: "...and that every [not only sexual] inclination of the thoughts of his heart was only evil all the time" (6:5). Closely related as it is to incestuous sexuality, man, in this account, is also essentially evil. Not generally, not most of the time; essentially: "only evil" and "all the time." Here we have a very early, formative and determinative codification of our monotheistic civilization's underlying assumption about human nature—that man is bad. (Once you postulate it as bad, it cannot develop or improve; it can only be curbed. And, what are religions for?)

Only Noah finds favor in the eyes of God: "Noah [comfort] was a righteous man, blameless among the people of his time" (6:9), who "would comfort us in the labor and painful toil of our hands caused by the ground the LORD has cursed" (5:29). Noah is the first agriculturalist.

God repeats his dissatisfaction with the world and its people, who are "corrupt" and "violent" and gives Noah detailed, precise instructions for the building of the ark, which is going to house two of all living creatures, along with Noah & wife and 3 sons & wives. "Everything on earth will perish. But I will establish my covenant with you" (6:17-18).

When the flood was over "Noah built an alter to the LORD and, taking some of all the clean animals and clean birds, he sacrificed burnt offerings on it. The LORD smelled the pleasing aroma and said in his heart" (8:20-21):

> Never again will I curse the ground because of man, even though every inclination of his heart is evil from childhood. And never again will I destroy all living creatures, as I have done. (8:21)

To the evilness of men is now added the phrase "from childhood." As for God's promises, he will, as we shall see, not keep the first and abide by the second only partially.

9. God's Covenant With Noah

God blesses Noah & Sons and says to them:

> Be fruitful and increase in number and fill the earth. The fear and dread of you will fall upon...every creature; they are given into your hands...I now give you everything. (9:1-3)

And God, somewhat inconsistently with his previous stricture against vengeance, adds:

> Whoever sheds the blood of man, by man shall his blood be shed. (9:6)

And he establishes his covenant with Noah & Sons for all generations to come:

> Never again will all life be cut off by the waters of a flood; never again will there be a flood to destroy the earth. (9:11)

Just as God had driven a wedge between the brothers Cain and Abel, Noah, "a man of the soil" and God's chosen one, discriminates between his sons. He drinks wine, he lies uncovered in his tent, Ham sees his father's nakedness and tells his two brothers, Shem and Japheth, to cover Noah, and Noah's anger for Ham falls upon Ham's son, Canaan—a totally innocent third party. Noah curses Canaan for his father Ham's deed, a dubious misdeed in itself. Canaan is to be not only a slave to his uncles but also to be the "lowest of slaves" to his brothers (9:25-27).

10. The Table of Nations

A list of the "clans of Noah's sons" is given, "according to their lines of descent, within their nations. From these the nations spread out over the earth after the flood" (10:32). "Those are the sons[6] of …by their clans and languages, in their territories and nations" (10:31). In this historical-geographical account of lineages, women are not mentioned, and the characteristics of some clans singled out for mention are being "maritime peoples" (10:5), a "mighty warrior on the earth" (10:8), a "mighty hunter before the LORD" (10:9)—all signifying expansion and aggression as laudable deeds.

11. The Tower of Babel: "Others" Are First Created by God

In the previous chapter, each nation/tribe had "its own language" (10:5). "Now the whole world had one language and a common speech" (11:1). They settle in Babylonia, they use brick instead of stone, tar for mortar, and plan to build a city:

> Come, let us build ourselves a city, with a tower that reaches to the heavens, so that we may make a name for ourselves and not be scattered over the face of the whole earth. (11:4)

God does not like the idea of "united nations" with one language, living together peacefully:

> If as one people speaking the same language they have began to do this, then nothing they plan to do will be impossible for them. Come, let us go down and confuse their language so they will not understand each other. (11:6-7)

This is reminiscent of God's unwillingness to have man acquire knowledge of good and evil (problematic in itself as indicated above); just as he does not want men to know (in contradistinction to believe and obey), he does not want men to understand each other and cooperate among themselves, for this might pose a threat to their individual submission to God. So, as scheming as a "divide and rule" colonialist, he not only confuses ("Babelizes") their language but also "scatter(s) them over the face of the earth" (11:9). He doesn't want rivals, let alone a united front of mankind.

Another family/tribal lineage is given, in which the phrase "he had sons" is now replaced by "he had sons and daughters." One son, Terah, takes his son Abram, his grandson Lot son of Haran, and his daughter-in-law Sarai wife of Abram to Haran, where they settle. Whose daughter Sarai was, we shall learn only later, unlike the case of Milcah, who married the third son Nahor. Milcah was the daughter of Haran (11:29); the uncle married his niece.

12. The Call of Abram (and the Duty of Sarai)

God tells Abram to leave his "country," his "people," and his "father's household," in yet another instance of choosing and favouring "one man" as worthy.

God will:

- bless Abram
- make him into "a great nation"

- make his "name great"
- bless those who bless Abram
- curse those who curse Abram
- bless (or curse) all peoples on earth "through" Abram (12:2-3)

Through this one chosen man, his nation, too, is to be favored over other peoples. In the eyes of God, not all but only one or few or some men are worthy.

Abram takes "his wife Sarai, his nephew Lot, all the possessions they had accumulated and the people they had acquired in Haran" (12:5), and they go to Canaan. At Shechem, God "appears" to Abram and promises this land to his offspring. The latter builds an altar to God. (Note the concept of "acquiring people.")

Because of famine Abram goes down to Egypt for a while and tells Sarai the following:

I know what a beautiful woman you are. When the Egyptians see you, they will say, "This is his wife." Then they will kill me but will let you live. Say you are my sister, so that I will be treated well for your sake and my life will be spared because of you. (12:11-13)

Abram's prediction comes true, Sarai is "taken into" Pharaoh's palace as a wife, Abram is treated well, he acquires "sheep and cattle, male and female donkeys, menservants and maidservants, and camels" (12:16 and 19), that is, a lot of possessions, animal and human.

God, instead of warning Abram—before or after the fact—against his dishonourable scheme, not only rewards him but also "inflict(s) serious diseases on Pharaoh and his household" (12:17). For Abram, (and for his God), security of life and property—*and* aggrandizement thereof—by any means and at any cost, including using his wife as chattel, is permissible, even laudable. Note that Abram is not solely after his life, he is from the very beginning, at least equally, after "good treatment" for his wife's sake.

God's punishing Pharaoh for lying with another man's wife is not a convincing moral. Moreover, it is at least in this case unfair; he didn't know the facts of the case; he was misled and lied to. God has punished the wrong man, but he is a partisan God, and an opportunistic one: worldly riches is what matters; the means for that end do not matter. That's the prime value he teaches his chosen ones:

Abram had become very wealthy in livestock and in silver and gold. (13:2)

13,14,15. Abram, Lot, God's Covenant with Abram

Since "the land could not support them [Abram and Lot] while they stayed together, for their possessions were so great that they were not able to stay together" (13:6), they decide not to quarrel but to part company. Possesive individualism starts much earlier than Christian capitalism, Protestant or otherwise.

The warring kings of the region, in shifting alliances, eventually conquer and loot Sodom and Gomorrah, also carrying off Lot and his possessions. Abram the Hebrew (first mention of Hebrew), with "318 trained men born in his household" (14:14), (showing the size of a patriarchal household), recovers Lot and "his possessions, together with the women and the other people" (14:16). Melchizedek king of Salem, priest of God Most High, brings bread and wine and blesses Abram. Abram gives him a tenth of everything.

God promises Abram sons as his rightful heirs and also the "land, from the river of Egypt to the great river, the Euphrates" (15:5 and 19).

16. Hagar and Ishmael ("A Wild Donkey of a Man")

In due course, Sarai's (who is barren) maidservant Hagar, upon Sarai's suggestion, sleeps with Abram and conceives. Hagar despises Sarai, Sarai disposes her off upon Abram's advice, the angel of God persuades Hagar to go back, Hagar gives birth to Ishmael in Abram's household. However, the angel of God had already prescribed a lowly status for the child:

He will be a wild donkey of a man; his hand will be against everyone and everyone's hand against him, and he will live in hostility toward all his brothers. (16:12)

Why? Just because he was born of a maidservant?

17. The Covenant of Circumcision: Control of Minds Through Control of Bodies

"God Almighty" (first mention of almighty) confirms his covenant with Abram:

You will be the father of many nations. No longer will you be called Abram;[7] your name will be Abraham,[8] for I have made you a father of many nations...and kings will come from you...an everlasting covenant between me and you and your descendants after you for the generations to come, to be your God and...their God. (17:4-8)

After this embryonic promise of transition from local patriarchy to imperial monarchy, God stipulates the bodily sign, proof, or precondition of his covenant: circumcision. A physical sign of distinction inscribed on the body, and for that matter, on a particular part of the male body. "My covenant in your flesh is to be an everlasting covenant" (17:13). Every male who is eight years old, born in the household or bought with money from a foreigner is to be circumcised. Religion involves, among other things, control of bodies.

Sarai from now on is to be called Sarah, and with the blessing of God she will give a son to Abraham, who shall be called Isaac.

18. The Three Visitors

God visits Abraham and says: "For I have chosen him...to keep the way of the LORD by doing what is right and just" (18:19). During this visit Abraham pleads with God concerning Sodom and Gomorrah's sins. "Will you sweep away the righteous with the wicked? What if there are fifty righteous people in the city?" (18:23-24) From 50, they go down to 45, 40, 30, 20, and finally to 10, at which number God says, if he were to find it, he would not destroy the city.

19. Homosexual Sodom and Gomorrah Destroyed; Father-Daughter Incest Vindicated

The two angels of God who had proceeded to the city, stopped at Lot's house; "all the men from every part of the city of Sodom—both young and old—surrounded the house. They called to Lot, 'where are the men who came to you tonight? Bring them out to us so that we can have sex with them' " (19:4-5). The sacred text that forbids homosexuality permits heterosexuality—even in the following form. Lot says:

> No, my friends. Don't do this wicked thing. Look, I have two daughters who have never slept with men. Let me bring them out to you, and you can do what you like with them. But don't do anything to these men, for they have come under the protection of my roof. (19:8)

Apparently, for Lot, the honor of two men, two strangers at that, is more important and valuable than the honor of his two daughters, who, too, ought to be considered "under the protection of (his) roof." The two men strike the crowd with blindness, they urge him to get out of the city with his belongings, God destroys the cities by raining down burned sulphur, "smoke rising from the land, like smoke from a furnace" (19:28).

In their place of flight, Lot gets raped by his daughters. The elder says to the younger:

> ...there is no man around here to lie with us.... Let's get our father to drink wine and then lie with him and preserve our family line through our father. (19:31-32)

The honorable Lot "was not aware of it when she lay down or when she got up" (19:33). Same with the younger. Both get pregnant and have sons: Moab (cf. Moabites) and Ben-Ammi (cf. Ammonites). Again, the innocent man and the wicked woman; and this time in the context of father-daughter incest, with no sanction accruing to Lot, one of the chosen ones of God and one of the favorite prophets of the three Abrahamic patriarchal religions of Judaism, Christianity, and Islam.

20. Abraham and Abimelech: Abraham Capitalizes on Sarah Again

In Gerar, Abraham, although powerful and wealthy[9] by now, repeats his lucrative trick, the one he played on Pharaoh. He introduces Sarah as her sister again, Abimelech king of Gerar takes her, but this time the deceived is not severely punished (just temporary illness for himself and barrenness for his wife and his slave girls) by God for he does not "go near her" upon God's warning, and God instructs him to return her to Abraham "for he is a prophet" (20:7). All ends up well: Abraham is given "sheep and cattle and male and female slaves" and "a thousand shekels of silver" (25 pounds of silver) (20:14 and 16). The first prophet of the first mono-God is thus awarded; *he* was chosen because he is the one who first totally obeyed.

We also learn that Abraham's lies are only half-lies: "...she [Sarah] really is my sister, the daughter of my father though not of my mother; and she became my wife" (20:12), that is, a sister-wife, or, better, a half-sister-wife. (All the same, she is a wife, isn't she?) Abraham is so unscrupulously egocentric that he thinks that having Sarah lie, as well, is right: "This is how you can show your love to me" (20:13), says the polygamous, sister-incestuous, and greedy Abraham, *the* chosen of chosen.

21. The Birth of Isaac

The God-promised son, Isaac, is born to the no longer barren Sarah, Sarah wants to expel Hagar and Ishmael ("that slave woman and her son" who "will never share in the inheritance with...Isaac," 21:10). God comforts Abraham by saying that, although his offspring will be reckoned through Isaac, he will make his other son from the maidservant into a nation also—a second-rate nation, to be sure. However, "God was with the boy as he grew up" (21:20).

Abraham makes a treaty with Abimelech, in whose land he is living, and swears that he "will not deal falsely with" the latter.

22, 23. Abraham Tested; Sarah Dies

God asks Abraham to sacrifice his only son Isaac as a burnt offering to God, Abraham complies to the last minute when the angel of God stops him from slaying and burning his boy: "Now I know that you fear God..." (22:12). "Fear," and not even "love," of God is what makes this man ready to kill his own son, as he was ready to market his wife. Thus is the power of fear and belief and thus are the rewards thereof. Satisfied, God rewards Abraham with promises:

Your descendants will take possession of the cities of their enemies...(22:17)

Sarah dies, and Abraham buys a burial place for her from the Hittites.

24. Isaac and Rebekah

Endogamous and scornful of other nations, Abraham wills to his chief servant not to get a wife for his son from the daughters of the Canaanites but from his own father's family (living in the town of Nahor) and bring her to this promised land. The envoy meets the beautiful and virgin Rebekah, daughter of Bethuel son of Milcah wife of Abraham's brother Nahor. He gives her a gold nose ring weighing a beka (1/5 ounce) and two gold bracelets weighing ten shekels (4 ounces). The polite and hospitable Rebekah leads the envoy to the family house.

Father Bethuel and brother Laban, without asking Rebekah, give her away: "Here is Rebekah; take her and go, and let her become the wife of your master's son" (24:51). Rebekah is not unwilling; but if she were, she wasn't going to be asked anyway. "Then the servant brought out gold and silver jewelry and articles of clothing and gave them to Rebekah; he also gave costly gifts to her brother and to her mother" (24:52-53). Rebekah and her maids are seen off with the wish: "...may your offspring possess the gates of their enemies" (24:60).

25. The Death of Abraham and Hierarchy of Sons

Abraham, after marrying a second time and having more sons, dies and is buried with his first wife, Sarah. "Abraham left everything he owned to Isaac. But while he was still living, he gave gifts to the sons of his concubines and sent them away from his son Isaac to the land of the east" (25:5-6).

A summary list, or account, of Ishmael and his sons are given, who "lived in hostility toward all their brothers" (25:18). (Cf. supra.)

Isaac's wife Rebekah is also barren, like Sarah. But Isaac prays to the Lord, God answers his prayer, and Rebekah gives birth to twin boys, first to the (the marginally older) Esau (red and hairy), then to the (the marginally younger) Jacob (grasping the heel or, literally, deceiving).

Esau, the physically stronger one, "became a skillful hunter, a man of the open country" while Jacob, the physically weaker but mentally abler(?) one, "was a quiet man, staying among the tents" (25:27-28).

Even before the birth, God had (self-fulfillingly) prophesied to Rebekah that:

Two nations are in your womb, and two peoples from within you will be separated: one people will be stronger than the other. And the older will serve the younger. (25:23)

God once again implants fraternal strife and domination/subordination relationships into human history, something that will later and to date be attributed to human nature. And why should one brother (in the strict or the general sense of the word) necessarily "serve" or "be enslaved to" or "live in hostility with" the other brother?

The above premonition (or intention?) is indeed affirmed. Esau asks for some stew from Jacob; the latter instantly, and out of the blue (or of commercial acumen), demands his brother's birthright in return for this service.

26. Isaac and Abimelech: Lucrative Trick Repeated

Famine sets in. Isaac, unlike Abraham, does not go to Egypt upon God's instructions but stays in Gerar and, like Abraham, declares his wife Rebekah to be his sister. But King Abimelech chances to see him caressing Rebekah, Isaac confesses his fright, the former proves to be more judicious than Isaac himself: "One of the men might well have slept with your wife, and you would have brought guilt upon us" (26:10). The King is motivated by self-interest. Interests of the woman are again a non-agenda. And: Rebekah, like Sarah, is again in dutiful submission. This time God does not intervene, but as a result of Abimelech's leniency, "Isaac planted crops in that land and the same year reaped a hundredfold, because the LORD blessed him: The man became rich, and his wealth continued to grow until he became very wealthy" (26:12-13). (The time-honored trick, in a sense, pays again, although it isn't even a half-lie this time.)

Abimelech tells Isaac to move away because he has become too powerful. Isaac digs earth, finds water, builds an altar, God appears to him and tells him not to be afraid, Isaac makes a treaty with Abimelech not to molest each other (the initiative coming from the latter). God continues to make prosperous his chosen ones.

27. Jacob Gets Isaac's Blessing, Esau His Curse (Fraternal Strife Institutionalized)
The aged Isaac wants some wild game from Esau, Rebekah conspires against his older son and tells Jacob to do this before his brother in order to get his father's blessing, a blessing intended for Esau. Jacob debates the idea not on principle but in its pragmatics: "What if my father touches me? I would appear to be tricking him…" (27:12). But Rebekah persuades him and dresses him up like Esau. Jacob pretends to be Esau, lies repeatedly to dispell Isaac's suspicions, and gets his unearned blessing from his father, which includes:

• richness and abundance
• nations serving and peoples bowing
• lording over brothers (27:28-29)

Esau returns, Isaac sees the deceit but refuses to give him a blessing too and curses him. Rebekah, apprehensive of Esau's intentions to kill his deceitful brother, persuades Jacob to flee to her brother Laban. A motherly love which privileges one son and persecutes the other. This episode, one of the most dramatic and unjust episodes in the whole *Old Testament*, deserves full quotation:

> When Esau heard his father's words, he burst out with a loud and bitter cry and said to his father, "Bless me–me too, my father!"
> But he said, "Your brother came deceitfully and took your blessing."
> Esau said, "Isn't he rightly named Jacob? He has deceived me these two times: He took my birthright, and now he's taken my blessing!" Then he asked, "Haven't you reserved any blessing for me?"
> Isaac answered Esau, "I have made him lord over you and have made all his relatives his servants, and I have sustained him with grain and new wine. So what can I possibly do for you, my son?"
> Esau said to his father, "Do you have only one blessing, my father? Bless me too, my father!" Then Esau wept aloud. (27:34-38)

The unfair and obstinate Isaac insists on his erroneous course and witholds his blessing from his other son. The justification or purpose seems to be to propagate fraternal strife at any cost—and the award going to the deceiver.

The *New Testament* and the *Koran* shall approve of this story.

28, 29, 30, 31. The Irresistible Rise of Jacob's House
On his way to Laban, Jacob the deceiver has a dream in which God says to him what he already has said and promised to Abraham and Isaac.

Jacob sees Rachel, daughter of Laban, kisses her, weeps aloud, tells her who he is, he is welcomed to Laban's house. Laban offers wages for Jacob's work; Jacob names it: "I'll work for you seven years in return for your younger daughter Rachel" (29:18), who was lovely in form and beautiful, whereas the older daughter Leah had weak (or delicate) eyes. At the end of seven years Jacob asks for his wife, but Laban gives him Leah, and Jacob unwittingly lies with her. Laban also gives his servant girl Zilpah to his daughter Leah.

Jacob asks: "Why have you deceived me?" (29:25) Laban belatedly answers: "It is not our custom here to give the younger daughter in marriage before the older one" (29:26). Jacob is to work for another seven years for Laban for Rachel, but she is given as a wife to Jacob within a week's time, together with Laban's other servant girl, Bilhah, as a maidservant. Now Jacob has two wives and two concubines.

Leah gives birth, upon God's opening her womb, to four sons. Rachel is barren, so she gives Bilhah to Jacob, who gives him two sons. Leah, too, gives Zilpah to Jacob, who also bears two sons. Hostility and jealousy between two sisters escalate.

Rachel asks for some mandrake roots from Leah, in return for the latter's sleeping again with Jacob. "You must sleep with me. I have hired you with my son's mandrakes" (30:16). She bears a fifth and a sixth son, and also a daughter named Dinah. Rachel, too, gives birth to a fifth (Joseph) and, later, a sixth son.

Jacob wants to go back to his homeland. Laban asks him to name his wages to stay. Jacob deceives (or outsmarts?) Laban (as to how, the reader is referred to 30:31-42). "So the weak animals went to Laban and the strong ones to Jacob. In this way the man grew exceedingly prosperous and came to own large flocks, and maidservants and menservants, and camels and donkeys" (30:42-43).

Laban's sons complain: "Jacob has taken everything our father owned and has gained all this wealth…" (31:1). Then God says to Jacob: "Go back to the land of your fathers and to your relatives, and I will be with you" (31:3). Jacob tells Rachel and Leah how Laban "cheated (him) by changing (his) wages ten times(!)" (31:7) and how the angel of God, in his dream, showed him how to outcheat Laban and go back to his father's home.

Rachel and Leah bring up the matter of inheritance. "Not only has he [Laban] sold us, but he has used up what was paid for us. Surely all the wealth that God took away from our father belongs to us and our children. So do whatever God has told you" (31:15-16). So, Jacob "drove all his livestock ahead of him, along with all the goods he had accumulated" (31:18). Before starting on their journey, Rachel steals her father's household gods. "Moreover, Jacob deceived Laban…by not telling him he was running away" (31:20). (From amoral familism to in-family immorality?)

Laban pursues Jacob, but God comes to Laban in his dream and says to him: "Be careful not to say anything to Jacob, either good or bad" (31:24). Laban overtakes Jacob, Rachel hides the stolen objects and sits on them and lies: "Don't be angry, my lord, that I cannot stand up in your presence; I'm having my period" (31:35). In the end, Laban and Jacob reach an understanding and part.

32, 33. Jacob and Esau Meet: Prophet's Indignity vs. Human Dignity

On his way, Jacob sends word to Esau and asks to "find favor in (his) eyes" (32:5) and prepares to meet him:

> In great fear and distress Jacob divided the people who were with him into two groups, and the flocks and herds and camels as well. He thought, "If Esau comes and attacks one group, the group that is left may escape."
>
> Then Jacob prayed, "O God of my father Abraham, god of my father Isaac, O LORD, who said to me, 'Go back to your country and your relatives, and I will make you prosper,' I am unworthy of all the kindness and faithfulness you have shown your servant. I had only my staff when I crossed this Jordan, but now I have become two groups. Save me, I pray, from the hand of my brother Esau, for I am afraid he will come and attack me, and also the mothers with their children. But you have said, 'I will surely make you prosper and will make your descendants like the sand of the sea, which cannot be counted.' " (32:7-12)

Sheer fright or also pangs of conscience? Prosperity at any rate!

He also selects a substantial gift from his livestock for his brother and waits. At night he wrestles with God, who does not overpower him but gives him a limp. ("Croaked timber of humanity" or man crippled by God?) God changes his name from Jacob to Israel (meaning: he struggles with God). Physical proximity to God is a distinction of the father of Israel.

Jacob sees Esau coming. "He put the maidservants and their children in front, Leah and her children next, and Rachel and Joseph in the rear" (33:2). Prudence *and* hierarchy of worth among the members of the patriarchal household.

Contrary to Jacob's apprehensions, "Esau ran to meet Jacob and embraced him; he threw his arms around his neck and kissed him. And they wept" (33:4). Time has removed Esau's anger, and brotherly love has gotten the upper hand in him, while Jacob was still harboring bad faith.

Esau accepts Jacob's gifts reluctantly ("I already have plenty" [33:8], meaning: maximization of goods is not my main goal), and they part peacefully. When Jacob approached the city of Shecheim in Canaan, he bought a plot, set up an altar, and called it El Elohe Israel (meaning: the God of Israel or mighty is the God of Israel).

34. Dinah and the Shechemites

Leah's daughter from Jacob, Dinah, is taken and violated by the son of the local ruler, but the ruler and son ask for her as a wife. They are prepared to pay any price and give any gift, they offer intermarriage and their land for settlement, trade, and acquiring property. "Jacob's sons reply deceitfully" and put forth the condition of circumcision for all males of the area. The others agree and act accordingly, but three days later, "while all of them were still in pain, two of Jacob's sons, Simeon and Levi, Dinah's brothers, took their swords and attacked the unsuspecting city, killing every male" (34:25-26). No observance of pacta sunt servanda.

> The sons of Jacob came upon the dead bodies and looted the city where their sister had been defiled. They seized their flocks and herds and donkeys and everything else of theirs in the city and out in the fields. They carried off all their wealth and all their women and children, taking as plunder everything in the houses. (34:27-29)

The ever-duplicitous and opportunistically pragmatic Jacob admonishes his two sons, not on principle, not on the ground that they did not honor their word, but in view of the risk of retaliation their act might have caused.

35. Jacob Returns to Bethel

Jacob tells his household to jettison all foreign gods they have with them, and they come to Bethel. An altar is built, God reappears and repeats that Jacob's name from now on is not Jacob ("he grasps the heel" or, figuratively, "he deceives") but Israel ("he struggles with God").[10] He again promises population, nations, kings, land.

Rachel gives birth to another son, Ben-Oni/Benjamin ("Don't be afraid, for you have another son," [35:17]), she dies, she is buried. Jacob returns to his father's homeland, Isaac dies, he is buried. (Meanwhile, Reuben, Jacob's firstborn, "went in and slept with his father's concubine Bilhah, and Israel heard of it," [35:22]).

36. Esau's Descendants

Despite ancestral advice, Esau takes his wives (3) from the women of Canaan and has many sons, descendants, and chiefs. His lineage is given, in which some wives and daughters are also mentioned by name. Another list is given of kings who reigned in Edom before any Israelite king reigned.

37. Joseph's Dreams

Fraternal hostility is once more kindled by (1) Israel's favoritism for Joseph and (2) by the latter's condescending attitude toward his 11 brothers: "Do you intend to reign over us?" (37:8) First, they plan to kill Joseph, but, upon Reuben's intervention, they throw him into a dry cistern, and then they sell him to merchants headed for Egypt. They lie to their father to the effect that a ferocious animal devoured him.

38. Judah and Tamar

Another son of Israel, Judah, marries his first son to Tamar, than his second son to her upon the firstborn's death; God kills the first because he is wicked and the second who lay with Tamar but did not impregnate her because he spilled his semen on the ground ("Onan-ism?"); Judah sends Tamar away ostensibly until his third son grows up to marry her; Tamar deceives him in the guise of a prostitute and gets pregnant by Judah (because she had not been given to the third son!); when Judah decides to "have her burned to death" (35:24) because she is guilty of prostitution, Tamar reveals who the impregnator is; Judah does not proceed further and does not "sleep with her again" (38:26). (Women are guilty of prostitution; men, who uphold that institution, have no responsibility. This is not only unfair; it is also illogical.)

Twin boys from Tamar (who lies with her father-in-law *because* she is not given to the third son!): the first comer "puts out his hand" and a scarlet thread is tied to his wrist; the second comer "breaks out" and is the real first comer for the scarlet-marked one (Zerah) is actually delivered after the breaker-out (Perez), upon the former's drawing his hand back.

39, 40, 41, 42, 43, 44, 45, 46, 47. Joseph in Egypt: From Rags to Riches
The merchants sell Joseph in Egypt to Potiphar, an important official of Pharaoh. "The LORD was with Joseph and he prospered" (39:2). The main result and, perhaps, purpose of God's being with his chosen persons is their prospering, before all other successes. Potiphar also prospers because of Joseph.

The master's wife invites Joseph to her bed, Joseph refuses this wicked offer, she traps and slanders him, Joseph is imprisoned unjustly. "…the LORD was with Joseph and gave him success in whatever he did" (39:23)—in the prison, too.

Joseph interprets dreams correctly in the prison as an agent of God ("Do not interpretations belong to God? Tell me your dreams," [40:8]).

Joseph's prowess in dream interpretation is belatedly reported to Pharaoh. He sends for Joseph, Joseph interprets his dreams ("I cannot do it, but God will give Pharaoh the answer he desires," [41:16]) as meaning seven years of abundance to be followed by seven years of famine.

The Godly agent Joseph ventriloquises God:

"And now let Pharaoh look for a discerning and wise man and put him in charge of the land of Egypt. Let Pharaoh appoint commissioners over the land to take a fifth of the harvest of Egypt during the seven years of abundance. They should collect all the food of these good years that are coming and store up the grain under the authority of Pharaoh, to be kept in the cities for food. This food should be held in reserve for the country, to be used during the seven years of famine that will come upon Egypt, so that the country may not be ruined by the famine." (41:33-36)

Joseph is put in charge of Egypt:

Then Pharaoh took his signet ring from his finger and put it on Joseph's finger. He dressed him in robes of fine linen and put a gold chain around his neck. He had him ride in a chariot as his second-in-command, and men shouted before him, "Make way!" Thus he put him in charge of the whole land of Egypt. (41:42-43)

Joseph, rewarded with power, wealth, status-fame, acts with high business acumen:

> During the seven years of abundance the land produced plentifully. Joseph collected
> all the food produced in those seven years of abundance in Egypt and stored it in the
> cities. In each city he put the food grown in the fields surrounding it. Joseph stored
> up huge quantities of grain, like the sand of the sea; it was so much that he stopped
> keeping records because it was beyond measure. (41:47-49)

Then:

> The seven years of abundance in Egypt came to an end, and the seven years of fam-
> ine began, just as Joseph had said. There was famine in all the other lands, but in the
> whole land of Egypt there was food. When all Egypt began to feel the famine, the
> people cried to Pharaoh for food. Then Pharaoh told all the Egyptians, "Go to Jo-
> seph and do what he tells you." When the famine had spread over the whole coun-
> try, Joseph opened the storehouses and sold grain to the Egyptians, for the famine
> was severe throughout Egypt. And all the countries came to Egypt to buy grain from
> Joseph, because the famine was severe in all the world. (41:53-57)

Joseph, one of the favorite prophets of *Koran*, too, makes windfall commercial profits from
conditions of famine.

Jacob/Israel, too, sends his 10 sons to Egypt to buy grain. Jacob does not send
Benjamin, Joseph's brother, "because he was afraid that harm might come to him" (42:4).
Jacob does not trust his own sons—after what befell on Joseph.

Joseph recognizes them, accuses them of being spies, keeps one of them (Simeon) as
hostage until they bring their youngest, Benjamin, sends back the rest filling their bags with
grain and putting each man's silver back in his sack.

More grain is needed, Jacob gives in and reluctantly agrees to send Benjamin along, tells
his sons to take double the amount of silver along with some gifts. They are taken into Joseph's house, and food is served (Egyptians and Hebrews eat separately). Then they are sent
back with grain and silver pouches again, plus Joseph's silver cup cached in the mouth of the
youngest one's sack.

Joseph's man catches up with them and says: "Why have you repaid good with evil..."
(44:4). They defend themselves; Benjamin is found out to have the cup and is, therefore, to
become a slave of Joseph. The brothers return to offer themselves all as slaves, Joseph says
only Benjamin is going to be one, Judah further implores with Joseph offering himself in
lieu of Benjamin, and Joseph finally gives in and reveals himself.

Joseph weeps, brothers are terrified, Joseph tells them not to be distressed for "God sent
me ahead of you to preserve for you a remnant on earth and to save your lives by a great deliverance" (45:7). "So then, it was not you who sent me here, but God" (45:8). And he tells
them to come back with their father and all his household to live near him for the remaining
five years of famine. Brothers part amicably.

Jacob/Israel agrees to go to Egypt with all his sons and grandsons and his daughters and granddaughters—all his offspring. However, the ensuing list mentions only the sons by name. 32 (6+26) sons from Leah and 1 daughter, Dinah, are named; 16 (2+14) sons from Zilpah; 14 (2+12) sons from Rachel; 7 (2+5) sons from Bilhah—70 in all, "not counting his (Jacob's) son's wives," (46:26).

The party, who are "shepherds; they tend livestock" (46:32), settle in Goshen, "for all shepherds are detestable to the Egyptians" (46:34).

When the money of the people of Egypt and Canaan is gone (all the existing money was already collected by Joseph and brought to Pharaoh's palace), all Egypt comes to Joseph and wants more food: Joseph sells them food in exchange for their livestock. Next year he buys all their land (except that of priests) in exchange for more food, also "reduc(ing) the people to servitude" (47:21). "Now that I have bought you and your land..." (47:23). And Joseph establishes the rule that one fifth of the produce belongs to Pharaoh. The same Joseph who eventually bestows love on his blood-brothers has no compassion for other human brothers. The Book affirms his reducing the people to servitude.

48. Manasseh and Ephraim: Fraternal Strife Again
Joseph brings his two sons to Israel; Israel blesses the younger more strongly than the older despite Joseph's intervention, merely saying that "his younger brother will be greater than he" (48:19). Discrimination between brothers again, and this for no sound or explained reason. (Fathers dividing their grandsons, too.)

49. Jacob Blesses (and Curses) His Sons
Jacob/Israel blesses his 12 sons/tribes before he dies, "giving each the blessing appropriate to him" (49:28). This proves not even a distributive justice but outright curse on, and discrimination against, some sons, not in all cases accompanied by some sort of explanation or justification (49:3-27).
Leah's sons:

> Reuben: no longer to excel in honor and power, for he went up unto his father's bed.
> Simeon and Levi: their assembly not to be joined by Israel, for they killed men in their anger; to be dispersed in Israel.
> Judah: to be praised and bowed down before by his brothers; a lion and lioness; to be obeyed by nations.
> Zebulun: to live by the seashore.
> Issachar: as a strong donkey, to submit to forced labor in land.

Concubines' sons:

> Dan: to be a serpent by the roadside; to provide justice for his people.
> Gad: to counter-attack his attackers.
> Asher: to provide delicacies fit for a king.
> Naphtali: is to be a doe set free.

Rachel's son:
> Benjamin: as a ravenous wolf, to devour the prey in the morning and to divide the
> plunder in the evening.

Now, Joseph: "as the prince among his brothers, he will be fruitful and powerful" (49:26)

> *because of the hand of the Mighty One of Jacob,*
> *because of the Shepherd, the Rock of Israel,*
> *because of your father's God, who helps you,*
> *because of the Almighty, who blesses you. (49:24-25)*

As can be seen, blessings of power, domination, military prowess, plunder to favorite ones;
curses to those who bedded father's concubines and killed men in anger (rudiments of a
better morality?); and some more neutral prospects for others. (What "Justice" is it that
stands out in this list.)

50. The Death of Joseph
Joseph has his father embalmed in forty days, Egyptians mourn for him seventy days, Israel
is buried in Canaan, Joseph and his brothers return to Egypt. Joseph reassures them about
their safety and well-being, before he, too, dies.

POSTSCRIPT to GENESIS

This is the genesis; this is the origination and codification of monotheistic Western Civilization's basic values (money, power, status), amoral familism and tribalism, possessive individualism, opportunistic pragmatism, inter-national and inter-fraternal hostility,
paternalistic domination and divisive rule, subjection and debasement of women from their
namelessness to their barrenness (unless men's he-God favors them otherwise), private
property in worldly goods as well as in human beings; all propped up by the inegalitarian
ontological-moral hierarchy of God → few chosen men → many unchosen men → all
women → slaves, each echelon with its own internal gradations of worthiness/worthlessness
depending on the degree of chosenness by and proximity to God, which in turn is based
upon a prior faulty creationist epistemology, one which determines our knowledge of material reality, of the nature of society, and of human nature ("only evil," "all the time," "from
childhood").

The emergent political theory, founded on this epistemological-ontological-moral theory, is one which justifies an inegalitarian, oppressive, hierarchical social-political and economic order, conveniently undergirded by the idea of God: fear God → believe God → obey
God and his chosen few who write him and his rule-books—the *Old Testament*, the *New
Testament*, and the *Koran*. And, as a result: prosper! (If of the chosen few.) Or endure! (If of
the half-chosen multitude.) Otherwise, repent or perish! Or, submit or perish! (If an unbeliever.) This, as we shall have ample occasion to see, is the basic mechanics of these three
great religions.

Genesis dictates once and for all by superhuman fiat our knowledge and estimate of our selves as human beings, and our knowledge and estimate of other selves, other human beings. Our identities and our interpersonal relations, in short, as members of the species. "Evil" "dust" is to become the internalized self-image of man for generations to come. Degradation to become self-degradation; humiliation, self-humiliation. The other side of the coin is degrading and humiliating (and killing and plundering) others. God and his chosen few shall dominate most men; all men shall dominate all women; the chosen tribe shall "devour" (Cf. infra) other nations. Legitimacy of domination comes from an unquestionable source: Chosenness, (therefore) holiness, (therefore) superiority. And these bestowed on those who "fear" and (therefore) "believe" and (therefore) "obey" God and his Word. (And "prosper.")

Man is humiliated (not the same thing as being humble), but worldly personal gain is exalted. (What spirituality!) Abraham's (whose name should have been "he who fears") descendants Jacob ("he who deceives") and Joseph ("he who becomes rich?") prosper, respectively, by duplicity and robber-baron business practices at the expense of other human beings' impoverishment or reduction to servitude. (Riches as the proof of electedness does not start with Protestantism or Calvinism.) The Jacob example, particularly, is a 2500-year-old evidence of money and power being the security blanket of weak or unhealthy egos. This cultural-psychological-moral malaise has not changed in our present "business civilization." It remains a basic purpose and meaning of life, which is otherwise, and more than necessarily, confused and nervous about identities, relations, general and political morals. These religions which postulate man as "bad" and self-allegedly set out to curb him with their morality and politics, curb not his greed for money and power and his disrespect for himself and therefore for others, but curiously, his natural inclinations, his (especially sexual) desires, his intimacy with and confidence in fellow human beings, crippling him as a schizoid-paranoid. For the Books themselves are that. They are at best ambivalent, but functionally so, constructing an improvable human nature in a dialectial manner from the latter's potentials and antinomies.

Not only does Genesis always, in the final analysis, vindicate the materialistic greed and egotistic self-interest of the patriarchs/prophets as homo economicus (Jacob is the patron saint of instrumental rationality), but it also condones their other morally dubious behavior—or shall we say their unethical morals—in other matters as homo ethicus by manoeuvers of theological rationalization. Cheating becomes the cleverness of the Israelite over the Aramean, treachery or cruelty becomes the birthright of the chosen and pureblooded ones, etc.

Women are systematically represented as non-human agents, as passive vessels unendowed with any capacity for moral choice. When they take initiative for example in the cases of Rebekah and Esau or Lot and his daughters, these are no edifying, exemplary deeds.

The dubious morality of parents concerning their children is a far cry, for example, from my maxim of "honor thy/the children." Discriminating among children more often than not leads to nothing but sibling (and consequently adult) rivalry, injustice, insecurity on the one hand and to nothing but prosperity and "lording it over" on the other. Furthermore, how can children (and adults) of this sort of belief and psychology feel secure, when to the injustice and undependability of their parents (whom they should unconditionally honor) is added the fear and wrath of God, the he-God, the arch-Father who inseminates and begets and can annihilate everything by his words and acts. Honor thy God, honor thy parents! Who is going to honor "the little ones?"

Given this problematic morality concerning filial brothers and sisters, there logically follows a more problematic morality regarding relations between non-filial tribal brothers and, worse, non-tribal other "human brothers." But I don't want to run faster than the specific textual material of coming chapters. (As empiricist quantitative social scientists speak no more than their sample allows, I shall here talk no more than my texts permit.)

I shall conclude this section by answering the following question: There may not be sound epistemology and good political theory in Genesis, but isn't there at least the germs of an emergent good moral theory in it? Well, no; I can find not much of it beyond a few ambivalent good-looking moral precepts that mankind could have developed any way. On the contrary, I find much bad morality, or unethical morality, which, I think, has impeded and delayed man's achieving the latter. Looking carefully into these sacred texts and basing myself firmly on those texts themselves, I wish to contest, in fact reverse, the staple argument that religions bring good morality to correct and curb an evil man, and that if they are not so good at times this is merely a realistic reflection of the very nature of man. No, it's the other way around. Religions attributed, not always non-functionally or unwittingly, basic evilness to human nature, reified it for millenia, took advantage of it, and, as we noted above, instead of curbing his *cultural* malaises, constricted his natural inclinations and potentials. What for? For money, power, and fame. For domination, oppression, and exploitation.

Genesis, the source-book of all the great Three Books, does not offer good morality but, more gravely, preempts and prevents the construction of one. For example, don't murder your filial or tribal brother does not contain the potential of evolving and unfolding into don't murder human beings in general. Just the reverse is the case: Destroy other nations, break their skull, drink their blood, shall say the following books. (In the *Old Testament*, otherness is predicated on ethnicity etc.; in the *New Testament* and the *Koran*, the two supposedly more universalistically humanistic books, otherness will be judged by disbelief or difference of belief—again mortally sanctioned.)

Let me try to make very, very clear that I am not passing harsh judgments only on the episodic, contextual cultures and moralities of historic peoples. Basic morals, cultural values, "the doctrine of God and man" of Judaism-Christianity-Islam are still very much with us. I am not taking issue normatively with faded away cultures, I am pointing to the basic morals and the resultant politics of the triumphant, contemporary Western civilization. And the first book of that civilization, Genesis, is responsible for nothing less than an error, if not guilt, of commission in diminishing the value of being a human being. In Genesis, and in its offspring books, history proceeds but man does not. He is arrested at a wicked, crippled, infantile stage. At best, he is capable of only some movement between sinning-repenting-sinning. It is vicious circular; it is cyclical; his essential(istic) station being the more regressive point of departure of "evil dust" following ebbs and tides of religious, inhuman "righteousness," ever returning to that point, really, of no departure. It is precisely for this reason that the history of the Books is no serious history: Because, man himself has no history. He does not unfold. He is always the same thing, that is, nothing. And: fearing and trembling. The Books are an huge insult to man's dignity, beginning with the "beginning." And a mortgage on his future.

Beginning is the end. Or is it the beginning of the end?

Notes

1. As in the *New Testament*, too. In *Koran*, God will speak in the first person plural.

2. Cf. The "Spirit of God" in 1:2. (Cf. also the "Holy Spirit" in the *New Testament*.)

3. In no part of Genesis, or the *Old Testament*, is the universe or nature said to be created in the likeness of God. (Note the difference between monotheism and pantheism or mysticism in this respect.) This is an anti-naturalistic religion. It is anthropomorphic, but also anti-humanistic, as we shall see.

4. Nomadism over agriculture? The previous curse on land?

5. With Cain, son of Adam, who left his father's household, the necessity of incest with a sister, who may have accompanied him afar as his wife, seems to be there, unless we suppose that there was at least one other human family with a daughter in this new abode of his. With Seth, son of Adam, who remained in his father's household, the necessity of incest with another sister seems to be overwhelming, since there are no other maidens around. As long as a line has only one son at a time, which seems to be the case with Cain-Enoch-Irad-Mehujael-Methushael up to Lamech (3 sons: Jabal, Jubal, Tubal-Cain), that necessity persists. So with Adam-Seth; the necessity does not cease for Seth during the additional 800 years of Adam's life, when he had "other sons and daughters," for the latter would still be Seth's sisters. The necessity ceases only with Seth's son Enosh. The probability and practice of incest is, of course, something else, as shall be noted below.

6. Sons may mean descendants, successors, nations. Father may mean ancestor, predecessor, founder. Gender is generalized: e.g., nation is male, nationalism is masculine, etc.

7. Means "exalted father" (p.11, fn. f5).

8. Means "father of many" (p.11, fn. g5).

9. "A mighty prince" (23:6).

10. Some theological interpretations have it that Jacob has reformed. On the other hand, wrestling/struggling with God both shows unique nearness and also has associations of still being "stiff-necked."

EXODUS

1. The Israelites Oppressed

Later generations of Israel become too numerous in Egypt, a new king "who did not know about Joseph" (1:6) sees them as a threat, he ruthlessly oppresses the Israelites with forced labor, he moreover instructs midwives to kill the boys in delivery but let the girls live. (Joseph's reducing Egypt to servitude is not recalled.) (Cf. supra.)

2. The Birth of Moses (From the Levites)

A Levite woman gives a son to a Levite man, the son (Moses) is put into the Nile, Pharaoh's daughter feels sorry for the Hebrew baby and adopts him. Moses grows, kills an Egyptian who is beating a Hebrew, flees to Midian, rescues seven daughters of a priest, marries one of the sisters (Zipporah), has a son (Gershom).

In the meantime, the enslaved Israelites cry out to God. "God heard their groaning and he remembered his covenant with Abraham, with Isaac and with Jacob" (2:25). (God had not been concerned with the enslaved Egyptians during Joseph's administration.)

3. Moses and the Burning Bush: "I AM WHO I AM"

God calls to Moses on the mountain of Horeb, does not let him get any closer, tells him that he will rescue "his people" as the God of their fathers. And God says to Moses: "I AM WHO I AM" (3:14). "This is my name forever, the name by which I am to be remembered from generation of generation" (3:15). An axiomatic self-introduction, self-definition. Unquestionable. Not accountable.

Moses and the elders of Israel are to go to the king of Egypt and say to to him: "The LORD, the God of the Hebrews, has met with us. Let us take a three-day journey into the desert to offer sacrifices to the LORD our God" (3:18). But God knows that the king will not allow them to do so; therefore, he will "strike" the Egyptians, he says. Moreover, when the Israelites eventually leave, "(they) will not go empty-handed" (3:21). "Every woman is to ask her neighbor and and any woman living in her house for articles of silver and gold and for clothing, which you will put on your sons and daughters. And so you will plunder the Egyptians" (3:22). Israelite cleverness and prosperity by any means.

4. Signs for Moses, "Hardened Heart" for Pharaoh

In reply to Moses's question "What if they [Israelites] do not believe me or listen to me and say 'The LORD did not appear to you,' " God teaches him several miraculous signs. Moses further tells God that he is "slow of speech and tongue" (4:10); God tells him that his brother Aaron will be his helper: "You shall speak to him and put words in his mouth; I will help both of you speak and will teach you what to do" (4:15).

He will speak to the people for you, and it will be as if you were God to him. (4:16)

God as God to Moses, Moses as God to Aaron, Aaron as God to people. (Not to mention Moses as God to people.) The authoritative hierarchy is established; the sources of Aaron's and Moses's legitimacy are respectively defined.

The book portrays Moses as a reluctant charismatic leader ("O Lord, please send someone else to do it" [4:13]), but God's anger burns against him (4:14), and he forcefully conscripts Moses for spokesmanship. At some point he is even "about to kill him" or his son (4:24). This ambivalence, and the mundane function, of the unique and not so unique relationship between God and his prophet will be repeated later and become clearer.

Moses returns to Egypt, he is to perform wonders before Pharaoh, God "will harden his [Pharaoh's] heart so that he will not let the people go" (4:21). This is the harbinger of Israel's God's consistent strategy against the specified enemies of his chosen people: His anger and punishment is not ex post facto and proportional to the misdeeds thereof; this God premeditatedly "hardens their heart," does not warn them, provokes them, pushes them into committing even graver sins, and then he punishes them, or so that he can punish them, really severely. (*Koran*'s idiom for "hardening hearts" shall be "sealing hearts.")

5, 6. Covenant Remembered, Deliverance Promised

Moses and Aaron talk with Pharaoh, he says he does not recognize God and will not let the Israelites go, he imposes further burdens and deprivations on them, the latter complain, Pharaoh accuses them of being lazy.

God says to Moses:

I am the LORD. I appeared to Abraham, to Isaac and to Jacob as God Almighty, but by my name the LORD I did not make myself known to them. I also established my covenant with them to give them the land of Canaan, where they lived as aliens. Moreover, I have heard the groaning of the Israelites, whom the Egyptians are enslaving, and I have remembered my covenant.

Therefore, say to the Israelites: 'I am the LORD, and I will bring you out from under the yoke of the Egyptians. I will free you from being slaves to them, and I will redeem you with an outstretched arm and with mighty acts of judgment. I will take

you as my own people, and I will be your God. Then you will know that I am the
LORD your God, who brought you out from under the yoke of the Egyptians. And
I will bring you to the land I swore with uplifted hand to give to Abraham, to Isaac
and to Jacob. I will give it to you as a possession. I am the LORD.' (6:2-8)

This is not the only instance of God's voice and Moses's voice intermingling or flowing into
one another. But the message is clear: Moses *is* Lord by Lord God's delegation of power.

Family record of Moses and Aaron is given; mostly fathers and sons are mentioned by
name, and only a few mothers, wives, sisters, or daughters. From the clan of Levi, "Amram
married his father's sister, Jochebed, who bore him Aaron and Moses" (6:20). "Aaron married Elisheba, daughter of Amminadab and sister of Nahshon" (6:23). She bore 4 sons:
Nadab, Abihu, Eleazar, Ithamar.

7, 8, 9, 10, 11. Many Plagues

God says to Moses: "See, I have made you like God to Pharaoh, and your brother Aaron will
be your prophet" (7:1). God hardens Pharaoh's heart, the latter does not listen to Aaron despite Moses's superior wonders, God brings about the plague of blood: water of the Nile
changes into blood.

The plague of frogs, of gnats, of flies ensue. Each time Pharaoh first gives in then makes
an about face because God persistently hardens his heart. In the case of the plague of flies, as
with all plagues, God deals differently with his own people: "I will make a distinction between my people and your people" (8:23).

Then comes the plague on livestock, of boils, of hail.

...so you may know that there is no one like me in all the earth. For by now I could
have stretched out my hand and struck you and your people with a plague that
would have wiped you off the earth. But I have raised you up for this very purpose,
that I might show you my power and that my name might be proclaimed in all the
earth. (9:14:16)

Pharaoh sins again, against the mono-God, the God of monotheism. The plague of locusts
and of darkness follows. God again tells Moses that articles of silver and gold should be
taken from neighbors and that he shall kill every firstborn son in Egypt "from the firstborn
son of Pharaoh, who sits on the throne, to the firstborn son of the slave girl, who is at her
hand mill" (11:5), and "the firstborn of the prisoner, who was in the dungeon" (12:29).
Here, God does not make one of his "distinctions," lumping the slave girl with Pharaoh
simply because of her being an Egyptian.

12. The Passover and the Exodus

On the fourteenth day of the month, which is going to be the first month of the year for Israelites, the latter are to slaughter lamb and eat it roasted and put some of the blood on the
door frames of their houses. God speaking:

On that same night I will pass through Egypt and strike down every firstborn—both men and animals—and I will bring judgment on all the gods of Egypt. I am the LORD. The blood will be a sign for you on the houses where you are; and when I see the blood, I will pass over you. No destructive plague will touch you when I strike Egypt. (12:12-13)

Monotheism arrives bloodily.

This is a day you are to commemorate; for the generations to come you shall celebrate it as a festival to the LORD—a lasting ordinance. For seven days you are to eat bread made without yeast. On the first day remove the yeast from your houses, for whoever eats anything with yeast in it from the first day through the seventh must be cut off from Israel. On the first day hold a sacred assembly, and another one on the seventh day. Do no work at all on these days, except to prepare food for everyone to eat—that is all you may do.

Celebrate the Feast of Unleavened Bread, because it was on this very day that I brought your divisions out of Egypt. Celebrate this day as a lasting ordinance for the generations to come. In the first month you are to eat bread made without yeast, from the evening of the fourteenth day until the evening of the twenty-first day. For seven days no yeast is to be found in your houses. And whoever eats anything with yeast in it must be cut off from the community of Israel, whether he is an alien or native-born. Eat nothing made with yeast. Wherever you live, you must eat unleavened bread. (12:14-20)

These ceremonies are to be also observed when the Israelites arrive in the land God promised them. To the control of bodies is added the control of diet (hygiene, too?), of daily routine, and of calendar-time in a ritualized manner, violation of which is to be punished severely.

God strikes Egypt at midnight and Israelites "plunder" the Egyptians and start their journey. "There were about six hundred thousand men on foot, besides women and children" (12:37) and many other people as well as many livestock, both flocks and herds. Israelite people lived in Egypt for 430 years (12:40).

Passover restrictions: foreigners, temporary residents, hired workers may not eat of it; bought slaves may eat after being circumcised; it must be eaten inside the house; aliens may eat if circumcised; no uncircumcised male may eat it, alien or native-born. Again: distinctions and rituals as control devices.

13. Consecration of the Firstborn

God says to Moses: "The first offspring of every womb among the Israelites belongs to me, whether man or animal" (13:2). (Animals, too, seem to have a nationality.) Bread without yeast is to be eaten:

On that day tell your son, 'I do this because of what the LORD did for me when I came out of Egypt.' This observance will be for you like a sign on your hand and a reminder on your forehead that the law of the LORD is to be on your lips. For the LORD brought you out of Egypt with his mighty hand. (13:8-9)

And:

In days to come, when your son asks you, What does this mean?' say to him, 'With a mighty hand the LORD brought us out of Egypt, out of the land of slavery. When Pharaoh stubbornly refused to let us go, the LORD killed every firstborn in Egypt, both man and animal. This is why I sacrifice to the LORD the first male offspring of every womb and redeem each of my firstborn sons.' And it will be like a sign on your hand and a symbol on your forehead that the LORD brought us out of Egypt with his mighty hand. (13:14-16)

God does not trust "his people" much; he leads them not through the shorter but through the longer road: "If they face war, they might change their minds and return to Egypt" (13:17). God accompanies them in the form of a pillar of cloud by the day and a pillar of fire by the night.

14. Crossing the Sea and the Warrior God

God again hardens Pharaoh's heart and makes him pursue the Israelites. "But I will gain glory for myself through Pharaoh and all his army, and the Egyptians will know that I am the LORD" (14:4). Israelites are terrified and say to Moses:

Was it because there were no graves in Egypt that you brought us to the desert to die? What have you done to us by bringing us out of Egypt? Didn't we say to you in Egypt, 'Leave us alone; let us serve the Egyptians'? It would have been better for us to serve the Egyptians than to die in the desert! (14:11-12)

To this first instance of a long series of Israelite murmuring and grumbling against Moses (and God), Moses replies:

The LORD will fight for you; you need only to be still. (14:14)

Upon God's instruction Moses drives the sea back, turns it into dry land, the Israelites pass through divided waters, waters flow back over the Egyptians, not one of them surviving.

And when the Israelites saw the great power the LORD displayed against the Egyptians, the people feared the LORD and put their trust in him and in Moses his servant. (14:31)

Basis of belief in God (and Moses) is fear, as it is in Islam. He is a powerful, ruthless, and belligerent God, who makes war for his people, as does the Allah of *Koran*.

15. The Song of Moses and Miriam; Consolidation of Monotheism

The Israelites sing and exalt their God as a savior and warrior, as majestic and powerful, as holy and awesome. In response to the "I am who I am," believers of monotheism bestow, in perfect symmetry, a catalogue of "omni" adjectives on their God.

> Who among the gods is like you, O Lord? Who is like you—majestic in holiness, awesome in glory, working wonders? (15:11)

He has "unfailing love"; other nations will "tremble," "be terrified," "melt away," "be as still as a stone," "until the people you bought [created] pass by"; and he will "reign for ever and ever" (15:13-18).

Miriam the prophetess, Aaron's sister, also sings and dances. And:

> There the LORD made a decree and a law for them, and there he tested them. He said, "If you listen carefully to the voice of the LORD your God and do what is right in his eyes, if you pay attention to his commands and keep all his decrees, I will not bring on you any of the diseases I brought on the Egyptians, for I am the LORD, who heals you." (15:25-26)

16. Manna and Quail; Grumbling Begins

"In the desert the whole community grumbled against Moses and Aaron" (16:2):

> The Israelites said to them, "If only we had died by the LORD's hand in Egypt! There we sat around pots of meat and ate all the food we wanted, but you have brought us out into this desert to starve this entire assembly to death."

> Then the LORD said to Moses, "I will rain down bread from heaven for you. The people are to go out each day and gather enough for that day. In this way I will test them and see whether they will follow my instructions. On the sixth day they are to prepare what they bring in, and that is to be twice as much as they gather on the other days."

> So Moses and Aaron said to all the Israelites, "In the evening you will know that it was the LORD who brought you out of Egypt, and in the morning you will see the glory of the LORD, because he has heard your grumbling against him. Who are we, that you should grumble against us?" Moses also said, "You will know that it was the LORD when he gives you meat to eat in the evening and all the bread you want in the morning, because he has heard your grumbling against him. Who are we? You are not grumbling against us, but against the LORD." (16:3-8)

This time God does not punish the Israelites for their backward-looking attitude, but he will do so in due course of time. Also to be noted is Moses's equating himself and Aaron with God. Despite God's instructions to the contrary some people work on the seventh day as well, and God says to Moses: "How long will you refuse to keep my commands?" (16:28)

17. Water From the Rock; Moses Means God

People quarrel with Moses because there is no water to drink. Moses equates this with people's putting not himself but God to the test. "Why do you quarrel with me? Why do you put the LORD to the test?" (17:2) People say: "Why did you bring us up out of Egypt to make us and our children and livestock die of thirst?" (17:3) Moses cries out to God: "What am I to do with these people?" (17:4) God helps him, and water is found. But, the Israelites are by now on record for having been soft in hardship and ungrateful to and mistrustful of Moses *and* God: "Is the LORD among us or not?" (17:7) People displeased with God and Prophet, God and Prophet displeased with people. Still, a "unique relationship."

God continues to fight the Israelites' wars for them through the agency of Moses. The memory of hostile Amalekites are "blotted out" from under heaven by their warrior God, and this is written on a scroll (17:14) for remembrance by the Israelites — the first mention of a written record in the book.

18. Jethro Visits Moses

Moses's father-in-law praises God: "Now I know that the LORD is greater than all other gods" (18:11). When he sees Moses sitting as judge all the time for his people in their disputes, the following exchange takes place.

> Moses answered him, "Because the people come to me to seek God's will. Whenever they have a dispute, it is brought to me, and I decide between the parties and inform them of God's decrees and laws."
>
> Moses' father-in-law replied, "What you are doing is not good. You and these people who come to you will only wear yourselves out. The work is too heavy for you; you cannot handle it alone. Listen now to me and I will give you some advice, and may God be with you. You must be the people's representative before God and bring their disputes to him. Teach them the decrees and laws, and show them the way to live and the duties they are to perform. But select capable men from all the people – men who fear God, trustworthy men who hate dishonest gain – and appoint them as officials over thousands, hundreds, fifties and tens. Have them serve as judges for the people at all times, but have them bring every difficult case to you; the simple cases they can decide themselves. That will make your load lighter, because they will share it with you. If you do this and God so commands, you will be able to stand the strain, and all these people will go home satisfied."
>
> Moses listened to his father-in-law and did everything he said. He chose capable men from all Israel and made them leaders of the people, officials over thousands, hundreds, fifties and tens. They served as judges for the people at all times. The difficult cases they brought to Moses, but the simple ones they decided themselves. (18:15-26)

Here we have the germs of a political, administrative, and judicial organization. It is also a clever act in the sense that an oligarchical elite is coopted, through a certain measure of dispersal of authority. Moses ceases to look like a monocrat, and seems instead to be the head of a collective leadership.

Jethro strengthens monotheism, but God doesn't like Moses's taking advice from someone other than himself, though he will shortly endorse this idea.

19. At Mount Sinai: Foundations of Theocracy

In the camp on the desert in front of Mount Sinai, God says to Moses:

> Now if you obey me fully and keep my covenant, then out of all nations you will be my treasured possession. Although the whole earth is mine, you will be for me a kingdom of priests and a holy nation. These are the words you are to speak to the Israelites. (19:5-6)

"A holy nation" and "a kingdom of priests." The Mosaic theocracy is being inaugurated.

Moses summons (only) the elders of the people and relates these words. God also tells Moses that the people will hear him speaking with Moses and, therefore, "will always put their trust in (Moses)" (19:9), and that the people shall see him but should not come too close to the mountain for fear of death (19:11-12).

Thunder, lightening, cloud, trumpet blast, smoke, trembling people and trembling mountain...Moses (and Aaron) going up, even priests at a distance, and people at a still greater distance.

Moses and Aaron's legitimacy is established both by the word of God and by their spatial proximity to God, in contradistinction to the physical distance of people from God.

20. The Ten Commandments

God opens his speech by reminding his deliverance of Israel from Egypt, the land of slavery, and lists his ten commands:

> You shall have no other gods before[1] me.
>
> You shall not make for yourself an idol in the form of anything in heaven above or on the earth beneath or in the waters below. You shall not bow down to them or worship them; for I, the LORD your God, am a jealous God, punishing the children for the sin of the fathers to the third and fourth generation of those who hate me, but showing love to a thousand generations of those who love me and keep my commandments.
>
> You shall not misuse the name of the LORD your God, for the LORD will not hold anyone guiltless who misuses his name.
>
> Remember the Sabbath day by keeping it holy. Six days you shall labor and do all your work, but the seventh day is a Sabbath to the LORD your God. On it you shall not do any work, neither you, nor your son or daughter, nor your manservant or

maidservant, nor your animals, nor the alien within your gates. For in six days the
LORD made the heavens and the earth, the sea, and all that is in them, but he rested
on the seventh day. Therefore the LORD blessed the Sabbath day and made it holy.

Honor your father and your mother, so that you may live long in the land the
LORD your God is giving you.

You shall not murder.

You shall not commit adultery.

You shall not steal.

You shall not give false testimony against your neighbor.

You shall not covet your neighbor's house. You shall not covet your neighbor's
wife, or his manservant or maidservant, his ox or donkey, or anything that belongs
to your neighbor." (20:3-17)

Here, in fact, are two clusters of rules. The first cluster pertains to cultic matters, the second
to moral conduct.

- No other gods before (besides) God,
- No idols in the form of anything,
- No misuse of the name of the LORD God,
- No work on the seventh day (Sabbath),

make up the foundation of the new monotheistic cult, whose God

- Is jealous and,
- Punishes the children ("for sins of the fathers to the 3rd and 4th generation," [20:5]).

This is politics of fear based on threat of death, more specifically threat of killing one's children. (Cf. infra, Numbers, Ch. 16 for the elaboration and application of this doctrine.) To
be noted is the circularity of argumentation and also the asymmetry between love and hate:
"...punishing...to the third and fourth generation...those who hate me, but showing love
to a thousand generations of those who love me and keep my commandments" (20:5-6).

Moral commandments are, in fact, six:

- *Honor* your father and mother (even when they mistreat you?).
- Do not *murder* (one of the tribe).
- Do not commit *adultery* (within the tribe).
- Do not *steal* (from the tribe).
- Do not give *false testimony* (against you neighbor in the tribe).
- Do not *covet* the house, wife, servants, animals, belongings (of your neighbor in the
  tribe).

These are all in-tribe moral injunctions (everything has a beginning?); all are permissible,
even encouraged, vis-à-vis other tribes: killing, rape, plunder, lie and deceit, coveting and
expropriating enemies' possessions. In other words, this is tribal morality, not generalizable,
universal, humanistic morality.

21. Other Rules ("Laws")

God prescribes other rules or "laws" to the Israelites through Moses:

- Hebrew servants: to serve for 6 years, to go free in the 7th year...Unless he desires to remain as servant for life. (A daughter sold as a servant cannot go free but cannot be resold either.)
- Personal injuries:

    a. Premeditated murder to be punished by death; unintentional killers may flee

    b. Killing or attacking father or mother to be punished by death

    c. Kidnaping, keeping, selling another to be punished by death

    d. Cursing father or mother to be punished by death

    e. Non-fatal injuries to be compensated for

    f. Killing a slave calls for punishment; no punishment if the slave "gets up after a day or two, since the slave is his property" (21:21)

    g. Compensation for accidentally hitting a pregnant women unseriously is to be determined by the husband, but: ...if there is a serious injury, you are to take life for life, eye for eye, tooth for tooth, hand for hand, burn for burn, wound for wound, bruise for bruise. (21:23-25)

Thus instituted, lex talionis shall be continued by Islam. Christianity, as we shall see, will be ambivalent in this respect.

Plus, some other, relatively less significant, rules.

22. Protection of Property

A third (iii) cluster of rules regulate aspects of (private) property, concerning:

    a. theft and thieves

    b. damage to livestock and fields

    c. illegal possession of goods; borrowed and lost property

A fourth (iv) cluster further regulates interpersonal relations:

    a. "If a man seduces a virgin who is not pledged to be married and sleeps with her, he must pay the bride-price, and she shall be his wife. If her father absolutely refuses to give her to him, he must still pay the bride-price for virgins (22:16-17). (The right to rape is a consumer item that can be bought.)

    b. no sorcery (death)

    c. no sodomy (death)

    d. no other god (death)

    e. no mistreatment of aliens ("for you were aliens in Egypt," [22:21])

    f. no taking advantage of widows or orphans (death)

    g. no interest in lending money to an Israelite

    h. "Do not blaspheme God or curse the ruler of your people" (22:28) (Cf. the *New Testament*, Romans, among others.)

i. Offerings to be given

j. Firstborn to be given

There is, to be sure, a system of morality here; the reader is to judge whether it is always ethical, just, egalitarian, humanistic, and universalistic.

23. Laws of Justice and Mercy

A fifth (v) group of laws:

a. no false testimony

b. no siding with the crowd; no favoritism to the poor (regressive egalitarianism)

c. compassion for donkeys

d. no denial of justice to poor people

e. no bribery

f. no sowing of fields on the seventh year, so that poor people may get food from it (a form of almsgiving)

g. three festivals annually:

- Feast of the Unleavened Bread
- Feast of Harvest
- Feast of Ingathering

God closes his speech by reminding the promised land and says, among other things: "I will send my terror ahead of you and throw into confusion every nation you encounter" (23:27). (Foreshadowing Islam's "jihad," holy war.)

Summary of commandments and laws: monotheism, politics of fear based on threat of death and killing children, slavery reaffirmed, women second-class, restitution in mild personal injuries, retaliation in severe ones, some empathy for aliens, widows and orphans, submission to rulers, a trifle of a measure of alms-giving to the poor, in addition to the six in-tribe moral don'ts: murder, adultery, theft, false testimony, coveting, and dishonoring parents.

24. The Covenant Confirmed

Then he [God] said to Moses, "Come up to the LORD, you and Aaron, Nadab and Abihu, and seventy of the elders of Israel. You are to worship at a distance, but Moses alone is to approach the LORD; the others must not come near. And the people may not come up with him."

When Moses went and told the people all the LORD's words and laws, they responded with one voice, "Everything the LORD has said we will do." Moses then wrote down everything the LORD had said.

He got up early the next morning and built an altar at the foot of the mountain and set up twelve stone pillars representing the twelve tribes of Israel. (24:1-4)

After writing down everything the LORD had said, Moses "took the Book of the Covenant and read it to the people. They responded, 'we will do everything the LORD has said; we will obey' " (24:7).

> The LORD said to Moses, "Come up to me on the mountain and stay here, and I will give you the tablets of stone, with the law and commands I have written for their instruction." (24:12)

God dictates, Moses himself "writes down" the Jewish *Torah*, whereas the Christian *Bible* and the Muslim *Koran* are to be "written down" later. Here, in fact, God himself is also the original author. (See also infra.)

Moses enters the cloud, goes up on the mountain, and stays forty days and forty nights.

25, 26, 27. Tabernacle, Ark, Table, Lampstand, Altar, Courtyard: "Holy 'Places' "

> The LORD said to Moses, "Tell the Israelites to bring me an offering. You are to receive the offering for me from each man whose heart prompts him to give. These are the offerings you are to receive from them: gold, silver and bronze; blue, purple and scarlet yarn and fine linen; goat hair; ram skins dyed red and hides of sea cows; acacia wood; olive oil for the light; spices for the anointing oil and for the fragrant incense; and onyx stones and other gems to be mounted on the ephod and breastpiece.
>
> Then have them make a sanctuary for me, and I will dwell among them. Make this tabernacle and all its furnishings exactly like the pattern I will show you. (25:1-9)

Immensely elaborate details follow, gold and other precious materials are abundantly used, Tabernacle-Ark-Table-Lampstand are described. God determines and controls the spatial environment ("Holy Place," "Most Holy Place"), another instrument of controlling men's behavior and thinking. Designs and precise measurements are given by God.

28. The Priestly Garments, Ephod, Breastpiece

> Have Aaron your brother brought to you from among the Israelites, along with his sons Nadab and Abihu, Eleazar and Ithamar, so they may serve me as priests. Make sacred garments for your brother Aaron, to give him dignity and honor. Tell all the skilled men to whom I have given wisdom in such matters that they are to make garments for Aaron, for his consecration, so he may serve me as priest. These are the garments they are to make: a breastpiece, an ephod, a robe, a woven tunic, a turban and a sash. They are to make these sacred garments for your brother Aaron and his sons, so they may serve me as priests. Have them use gold, and blue, purple and scarlet yarn, and fine linen. (28:1-5)

"Sacred garments" to give "dignity and honor." Control of bodies, of space, of clothing, etc., for control of minds. Legitimacy to priests; legitimacy by distinction and by insignia.

Whenever Aaron enters the Holy Place, he will bear the names of the sons of Israel over his heart on the breastpiece of decision as a continuing memorial before the LORD. Also put the Urim and the Thummim in the breastpiece, so they may be over Aaron's heart whenever he enters the presence of the LORD. Thus Aaron will always bear the means of making decisions for the Israelites over his heart before the LORD. (28:29-30)

And:

Make a plate of pure gold and engrave on it as on a seal: HOLY TO THE LORD. Fasten a blue cord to it to attach it to the turban; it is to be on the front of the turban. It will be on Aaron's forehead, and he will bear the guilt involved in the sacred gifts the Israelites consecrate, whatever their gifts may be. It will be on Aaron's forehead continually so that they will be acceptable to the LORD.

Weave the tunic of fine linen and make the turban of fine linen. The sash is to be the work of an embroiderer. Make tunics, sashes and headbands for Aaron's sons, to give them dignity and honor. After you put these clothes on your brother Aaron and his sons, anoint and ordain them. Consecrate them so they may serve me as priests.

Make linen undergarments as a covering for the body, reaching from the waist to the thigh. Aaron and his sons must wear them whenever they enter the Tent of Meeting or approach the altar to minister in the Holy Place, so that they will not incur guilt and die.

This is to be a lasting ordinance for Aaron and his descendants. (28:36-43)

God resides in details, too—details in which ritual, holiness, and gold intermesh. Gold is "holy to the Lord."

29. Consecration of the Priests

God says: "The priesthood is theirs by a lasting ordinance. In this way you shall ordain Aaron and his sons" (29:9). Thus, a dynastic priesthood is created. Ritual abounds. An entire ram is to be burnt on the altar: "It is a burnt offering to the LORD, a pleasing aroma " (29:18).

Consecrate those parts of the ordination ram that belong to Aaron and his sons: the breast that was waved and the thigh that was presented. This is always to be the regular share from the Israelites for Aaron and his sons. It is the contribution the Israelites are to make to the LORD from their fellowship offerings.

Aaron's sacred garments will belong to his descendants so that they can be anointed and ordained in them. The son who succeeds him as priest and comes to the Tent of Meeting to minister in the Holy Place is to wear them seven days.

Take the ram for the ordination and cook the meat in a sacred place. At the entrance to the Tent of Meeting, Aaron and his sons are to eat the meat of the ram and the bread that is in the basket. They are to eat these offerings by which atonement was made for their ordination and consecration. But no one else may eat them, because they are sacred. And if any of the meat of the ordination ram or any bread is left over till morning, burn it up. It must not be eaten, because it is sacred. (29:27-34)

Also, a daily menu is prescribed for the priests for generations to come. Discrimination, distinction, and elitism in eating as well. Sacred and profane...Chosen and unchosen...

30. Incense, Money, Basin, Oil

Incense is to be burnt continuously, and atonement is to be made. God says to Moses:

Then the LORD said to Moses, "When you take a census of the Israelites to count them, each one must pay the LORD a ransom for his life at the time he is counted. Then no plague will come on them when you number them. Each one who crosses over to those already counted is to give a half shekel, according to the sanctuary shekel, which weighs twenty gerahs. This half shekel is an offering to the LORD. All who cross over, those twenty years old or more, are to give an offering to the LORD. The rich are not to give more than a half shekel and the poor are not to give less when you make the offering to the LORD to atone for your lives. Receive the atonement money from the Israelites and use it for the service of the Tent of Meeting. It will be a memorial for the Israelites before the LORD, making atonement for your lives." (30:11-16)

The ransom that the Israelites pay to God for a guarantee of no-plague goes to the priests. In the form of a regressive indirect tax, the rich and the poor are to give the same "half shekel" (= 6 grams x 600.000 [only men] = 3,600,000 grams = 3.6 tons to start with).

The Tent of Meeting, the Ark of the Testimony, the table and all its articles, the lampstand and its accessories, the altar of incense, the altar of burnt offering and all its utensils, and the basin with its stand, all are to be anointed with a special mixture. "Whoever makes perfume like it and whoever puts it on anyone other than a priest must be cut off from his people" (30:33).

31. Bezalel and Oholiab

God appoints Bezalel and Oholiab as craftsmen "with the skill, ability and knowledge in all kinds of crafts—to make artistic designs for work in gold, silver and bronze... stones...wood" (31:4-5). If God has such a penchant for precious metals, how can his creatures not have it?

Also: "Whoever does any work on the Sabbath day must be put to death" (31:14).

"When the Lord finished speaking to Moses on Mount Sinai, he gave him the two tablets of the Testimony, the tablets of stone inscribed by the finger of God" (31:18). (Cf. the "levh-i mahfuz" in the *Koran*.)

32. The Golden Calf; Death for Idolatry

While Moses is on the mountain the people say to Aaron "Come, make us gods who will go before us" (32:1), Aaron casts their gold into an idol—a calf—they present offerings to the idol-god. God says that Israelites have become "corrupt" renegades and that they are a "stiff-necked people" (32:7 and 9). God is going to burn them, but Moses pleads with him, and God relents.

> Moses turned and went down the mountain with the two tablets of the Testimony in his hands. They were inscribed on both sides, front and back. The tablets were the work of God; the writing was the writing of God, engraved on the tablets. (32:15-16)

But:

> When Moses approached the camp and saw the calf and the dancing, his anger burned and he threw the tablets out of his hands, breaking them to pieces at the foot of the mountain. (32:19)

Aaron implores with the angry Moses: "You know how prone these people are to evil" (32:22). (Cf. "human nature.") Moses says to the Levites who rally to him ("Whoever is for the LORD, come to me," [32:26]):

> Then he said to them, "This is what the LORD, the God of Israel, says: 'Each man strap a sword to his side. Go back and forth through the camp from one end to the other, each killing his brother and friend and neighbor.' " The Levites did as Moses commanded, and that day about three thousand of the people died. Then Moses said, "You have been set apart to the LORD today, for you were against your own sons and brothers, and he has blessed you this day." (32:27-29)

By killing 3000 sons, brothers, friends, and neighbors the Levites prove their being "for God" (and "against people?") and are duly "set apart" to God. An executioner-priesthood. The merriment does not end here: "And the LORD struck the people with a plague because of what they did with the calf Aaron had made" (32:15). (This is one of the favorite, much-repeated didactic stories of the *Koran*.)

33. Moses and the Glory of the LORD

God repeats his instructions for the promised land "flowing with milk and honey." "But I will not go with you, because you are a stiff-necked people and I might destroy you on the way" (33:3). (God protecting his chosen people from himself.)

34. The New Stone Tablets

God says to Moses: "Chisel out two stone tablets like the first ones, and I will write on them the words that were on the first tablets, which you broke" (34:1). Moses complies, and God says:

The LORD, the LORD, the compassionate and gracious God, slow to anger, abounding in love and faithfulness, maintaining love to thousands, and forgiving wickedness, rebellion and sin. Yet he does not leave the guilty unpunished; he punishes the children and their children for the sin of the fathers to the third and fourth generation. (34:6-7)

Nothing to add, except that we have, so far, seen ample proof of the second sentence but only counter-evidence to the first. Anger has always prevailed over compassion, and shall continue to do so. (Please note that *none* of the 600,000 shall reach the promised land.)

Moses persuades God to go with them, but God says:

Then the LORD said: "I am making a covenant with you. Before all your people I will do wonders never before done in any nation in all the world. The people you live among will see how awesome is the work that I, the LORD, will do for you. Obey what I command you today. I will drive out before you the Amorites, Canaanites, Hittites, Perizzites, Hivites and Jebusites. Be careful not to make a treaty with those who live in the land where you are going, or they will be a snare among you. Break down their altars, smash their sacred stones and cut down their Asherah poles. Do not worship any other god, for the LORD, whose name is Jealous, is a jealous God.

Be careful not to make a treaty with those who live in the land; for when they prostitute themselves to their gods and sacrifice to them, they will invite you and you will eat their sacrifices. And when you choose some of their daughters as wives for your sons and those daughters prostitute themselves to their gods, they will lead your sons to do the same. (34:10-16)

Israel's God terrorizes both his chosen people and other peoples. Moreover, he instructs the Israelites not to make peace treaties with them and to "smash" their... (This God's "international relations" are not very pacifist or universalist.)

This god, this "LORD, whose name is Jealous, is a jealous God" (34:14). And the daughters of other peoples are almost by definition "prostitutes."

Some rules and laws are repeated. Moses gives the people all the commands of God. It is also added: "No one is to appear before me empty-handed" (34:20). (The priesthood collects sure tribute.)

35, 36, 37. Sabbath, Tabernacle, Ark, Table...

Sabbath law is repeated. Everybody contributes his and her offering as prescribed.

The Tabernacle is built and decorated as commanded—in almost indescribable detail and ritualistic elaborateness. Everything (ark, table, lampstand, altar of incense,...) is completed, along with the sacred anointing oil. (Those who might underestimate the religious function of ceremonial minutiae and ritualistic detail should fully read Exodus 35, 36, 37.)

38. Altar, Basin, Courtyard, and the Materials Used for the Tabernacle

All parts of the holy place(s) are completed as designed and instructed by God in minute detail and measurement.

(See, for example, 38:18-20, as to the color, cloth, size, posts, bases, hooks, bands, and pegs of the curtain for the entrance to the courtyard; or, better read Exodus 38 in its entirety.)

As for the material that goes into the Tabernacle:

> These are the amounts of the materials used for the tabernacle, the tabernacle of the Testimony, which were recorded at Moses' command by the Levites under the direction of Ithamar son of Aaron, the priest. (Bezalel son of Uri, the son of Hur, of the tribe of Judah, made everything the LORD commanded Moses; with him was Oholiab son of Ahisamach, of the tribe of Dan—a craftsman and designer, and an embroiderer in blue, purple and scarlet yarn and fine linen.) The total amount of the gold from the wave offering used for all the work on the sanctuary was 29 talents and 730 shekels, according to the sanctuary shekel.
>
> The silver obtained from those of the community who were counted in the census was 100 talents and 1,775 shekels, according to the sanctuary shekel—one beka per person, that is, half a shekel, according to the sanctuary shekel, from everyone who had crossed over to those counted, twenty years old or more, a total of 603,550 men. The 100 talents of silver were used to cast the bases for the sanctuary and for the curtain—100 bases from the 100 talents, one talent for each base. They used the 1,775 shekels to make the hooks for the posts, to overlay the tops of the posts, and to make their bands.
>
> The bronze from the wave offering was 70 talents and 2,400 shekels. They used it to make the bases for the entrance to the Tent of Meeting, the bronze altar with its bronze grating and all its utensils, the bases for the surrounding courtyard and those for its entrance and all the tent pegs for the tabernacle and those for the surrounding courtyard. (38:21-31)

Thus, approximately seven tons of precious metals are used solely for these parts of the sanctuary:

GOLD	29 talents 730 shekels = over 1 ton	(p. 71, fn. f 24)
SILVER	100 talents 1775 shekels = 3.4 tons	(p. 71, fn. g 25)
BRONZE	70 talents 2400 shekels = 2.4 tons	(p. 71, fn. k 29)

We have already noted above the 3.5 tons of silver "obtained from those of the community who were counted in the census" (38:25) or "(paid to) the LORD (as) a ransom for his life" (20 years old or more)" (30:12-14) so that "no plague will come on them" (30:12). Paid to

God, received by the priests, 3.5 tons of silver to start with, and more to come as a regular revenue as more men "cross over" to 20 years of age. Neither money, nor—alas—plagues will be lacking.

The scripture legitimizes such tribute not only from God's end but also from the people's end:

> And the people continued to bring freewill offerings[2] morning after morning…the people are bringing more than enough for doing the work the LORD commanded to be done…Then Moses gave an order…And so the people were restrained from bringing more… (36:3-7)

39. The Priestly Garments, The Ephod, The Breastpiece

All garments are made, as designed by God, for Aaron and his sons. Last but not least:

> They made the plate, the sacred diadem, out of pure gold and engraved on it, like an inscription on a seal: HOLY TO THE LORD. Then they fastened a blue cord to it to attach it to the turban, as the LORD commanded Moses. (39: 30-31)

Moses inspects all the work done and blesses the workers.

40. Setting Up the Tabernacle (and the Theocracy)

God instructs Moses to start operations and inaugurate the priesthood, of Aaron & Sons, whose "anointing will be to a priesthood that will continue for all generations to come" (40:15). A veritable dynasty of priests.

POSTSCRIPT TO EXODUS

This is the exodus; this is the consolidation of Western monotheism, foundation of theocracy, rule and lordship of the chosen ones over unchosen people, the covenant between a God-fearing humanity to be plagued with the incessant plagues of this omnipotent, omnipresent God of gods who is "Is," "Jealous," "Awesome," and Murderous (of children, too), infinitely more angry and punitive than loving and compassionate—and all this in a mis-èn-scene of elaborate religio-political ritual.

This is the code-book for controlling minds and hearts by divers means of control of bodies, space, and time.

This is a book that shows the organic relationship between ritual and "distinction" and hierarchy.

Prophets are often equated with the mono-God, who stand in closer physical proximity to God than those also chosen but not so favored believers, for whom closeness means death. What discrimination! What inequality between so-called brothers!

Tribalism, that proto-nationalism, is inaugurated: Destroy and plunder other peoples!

This travelog, is also the locus classicus of Western Civilization's basic morality:

- Honor parents.
- Don't murder.
- Don't commit adultery.
- Don't steal.
- Don't give false testimony.
- Don't covet neighbor's possessions

Isn't this, at least, a beginning? Doesn't everything have a beginning? No, I will say.

First, these are only in-tribe moral don'ts, instrumental and functional for securing the internal order and stability of the tribe. You can do all of these to other nations. There is no potential in these rules that provides for their unfolding into universal moral principles. (They are Hegel's contextual, customary morals and mores, not Kant's rational, universal ethics.)

Second, they are injunctions only for the people, the multitude of fearful believers. All of them can and will be, as we shall see in the *Pentatuech* as well as in the whole *Old Testament*, overridden by prophets, kings, prophet-kings anointed by the God *they* have written into existence. And either no sanction applies to their infringements, or they receive some sort of a quarter of an admonition or penalty, but in net balance remain the blessed and rewarded ones.

Third, money, power, and distinction are posited as the ultimate purposes and values and meanings of human life, which take precedence of the don'ts and abort them as the do's.

Notes
1. Or "besides."
2. "Free will offering" or God-Moses levied "ransom?"

LEVITICUS

1, 2, 3, 4, 5. Offerings: Religious Ritual and Sustenance for Priests

Various offerings are prescribed in great ritualistic detail and somewhat repetitiously, repetition being a powerful instrument of the Books for reinforcing the Godly commands and for so numbing the mind as to debilitate its capacity for reasoning. Catechism and recitation.

- Burnt Offering: a male bull or sheep/goat without defect or dove/pigeon to be entirely burned by Aaron's sons with an "aroma pleasing to God."
- Grain Offering: fine flour; a handful of it to be burned by the priests (memorial portion; the rest belongs to Aaron & Sons as "a most holy part of the offerings made to the LORD" (2:3).
- Fellowship Offering: male or female animal from the herd or flock without defect; all the fat to be burned by Aaron's sons; "(a)ll the fat is the LORD's" (3:16); the rest goes to Aaron & Sons. And: "This is a lasting ordinance for the generations to come, wherever you live: You must not eat any fat or any blood" (3:17).
- Sin Offering: "When anyone sins unintentionally and does what is forbidden in any of the LORD's command," (4:2) "the priest will make atonement for him" (4:35).

If the unintentional sinner is:

- a priest: a young bull without defect
- the whole community: a young bull without defect
- a leader: a male goat without defect
- a member of the community: a female goat or female lamb without defect

"Distinctions" again, and the harbingers of "collective sin" and "solidarity in guilt" (Cf. infra.) are required. All fat to be burned on the altar. In the first two instances all of the bull to be burned outside the camp. (Control of space.)

- Guilt Offering: in case of
    withholding testimony,
    touching anything ceremonially unclean,

touching human uncleanness,

taking thoughtless oath;

and female lamb or goat → two doves or young pigeons → fine flour, in the descending order one can afford.

In case of sinning unintentionally "in regard to any of the LORD's holy things" (5:15) ("state property?"), one is to "bring to the LORD (priests) as penalty a ram from the flock, one without defect and of the proper value in silver...He must make restitution for what he has failed to do in regard to the holy things, add a fifth of the value to that and give it all to the priest" (5:15-16).

"If a person sins and does what is forbidden in any of the LORD's commands, even though he does not know it, he is guilty and will be held responsible. He is to bring to the priest as a guilt offering a ram from the flock, one without defect and of the proper value" (5:17-18).

The divinely legitimated theocratic state is founded complete with its moral theory, legal codes, and public finances.

6, 7. More Offerings and the Priests' Share

The LORD said to Moses: "If anyone sins and is unfaithful to the LORD by deceiving his neighbor about something entrusted to him or left in his care or stolen, of if he cheats him, or if he finds lost property and lies about it, or if he swears falsely, or if he commits any such sin that people may do—when he thus sins and becomes guilty, he must return what he has stolen or taken by extortion, or what was entrusted to him, or the lost property he found. He must make restitution in full, add a fifth of the value to it and give it all to the owner on the day he presents his guilt offering. And as a penalty he must bring to the priest, that is, to the LORD, his guilt offering, a ram from the flock, one without defect and of the proper value. In this way the priest will make atonement for him before the LORD, and he will be forgiven for any of these things he did that made him guilty." (6:1-7)

The principle of restitution to the injured is now being complemented by that of priestly commission. The Burnt Offering will be burned completely; LORD's share (memorial portion) of the Grain Offering will be burned and Aaron & Sons and their male descendants shall eat the rest of the holy food; grain offerings of priests will be burned completely; sin offerings of priests can be eaten by themselves and by any male in their family; the same for the Guilt Offering, the hide of the animal belonging to the priest; the Fellowships Offering (for thankfulness or as a vow) belongs to the priest as "a contribution to the LORD" (7:14).

Fat, blood, ceremonially unclean meat should not be eaten, and unclean persons should not eat meat either; otherwise, one must be cut off from his people.

Every ritual increases the importance and legitimacy of the priests. As for their share of the offerings:

The LORD said to Moses, "Say to the Israelites: 'Anyone who brings a fellowship offering to the LORD is to bring part of it as his sacrifice to the LORD. With his own hands he is to bring the offering made to the LORD by fire; he is to bring the fat, together with the breast, and wave the breast before the LORD as a wave offering. The priest shall burn the fat on the altar, but the breast belongs to Aaron and his sons. You are to give the right thigh of your fellowship offerings to the priest as a contribution. The son of Aaron who offers the blood and the fat of the fellowship offering shall have the right thigh as his share. From the fellowship offerings of the Israelites, I have taken the breast that is waved and the thigh that is presented and have given them to Aaron the priest and his sons as their regular share from the Israelites.' "

This is the portion of the offerings made to the LORD by fire that were allotted to Aaron and his sons on the day they were presented to serve the LORD as priests. On the day they were anointed, the LORD commanded that the Israelites give this to them as their regular share for the generations to come. (7:28-36)

8,9. Priests are Ordained and They Begin Their Ministry

God instructs Moses to ordain Aaron & Sons; Moses himself conducts all ritualistic ceremonies. (There is no substitute for reading the text itself of Leviticus 8 and 9.) Every ritualistic detail increases the importance and legitimacy of the priesthood.

10. The Death of Nadab and Abihu

Two of Aaron's sons offer "unauthorized fire" before God, and he consumes them. God is firm with his priests, too.

Then the LORD said to Aaron, "You and your sons are not to drink wine or other fermented drink whenever you go into the Tent of Meeting, or you will die. This is a lasting ordinance for the generations to come. You must distinguish between the holy and the common, between the unclean and the clean, and you must teach the Israelites all the decrees the LORD has given them through Moses." (10:8-11)

Please emphatically note the pairs of binary opposites: Clean and unclean, holy and *common*.

11. Clean and Unclean Food

"Do not make yourselves unclean by any creature that moves about on the ground. I am the LORD who brought you up out of Egypt to be your God; therefore be holy, because I am holy." (11:45)

Rules of hygiene or/and politics of social status? Clean and unclean, holy and common, sacred and profane, cooked and raw, etc. And, of course, man and woman, boy and girl.

12. Purification After Childbirth: Girls are Dirtier than Boys

If a woman gives birth to a son, she will be ceremonially unclean for seven days, and she must wait thirty-three days to be purified from her bleeding. It is exactly the double if she bears a daughter: unclean for two weeks; must wait sixty-six days. She must, at any rate, bring a burnt and a sin offering to the priest to make atonement for her before God. (Priests are everywhere.)

13, 14, 15. Cleansing from Skin Diseases and Bodily Discharges

Rules are prescribed for protection from infectious skin diseases and bodily discharges causing uncleanness. It is for anthropologists to decide to what extent these are also the beginnings of hygiene and preventive or healing medicine, but certain elements of social control and gender discrimination through control of bodies are also unmistakably there: Isolating the unclean individual, diagnosis by the priest, rituals, offerings, atonements...

The gender asymmetry in the case of bodily discharges by men and women is transparent, e.g.: "When a men lies with a woman and there is an emission of semen, both must bathe with water, and they will be unclean till evening" (15:18). Whereas: "If a man lies with her and her monthly flow touches him, he will be unclean for seven days..." (15:24).

16. The Day of Atonement

God gives rules to Moses concerning Aaron's conduct in the Most Holy Place; Aaron makes "atonement for himself, his household and the whole community of Israel" (16:17); 10th day of the 7th month is the fasting day; as a "lasting ordinance"; "(a)tonement is to be made once a year for all the sins of the Israelites" (16:34). (Cf. "solidarity of guilt" infra.)

17. Eating Blood Forbidden

Blood is not to be eaten, and sacrifices are not to be made in open fields: "They must bring them to the priest, that is, to the LORD, at the entrance to the Tent of Meeting" (17:5). Otherwise, one is to be cut off from his people.

18. Unlawful Sexual Relations

God tells his people not to do as Egyptians and Canaanites do but as he decrees. The general sexual law to be obeyed is: "No one is to approach any close relative to have sexual relations" (18:6). Rules against incest are being formulated. (Shortly after Moses's father's marrying his aunt—that is, his father's sister. Cf. supra.)

> Do not dishonor your father by having sexual relations with your mother. She is your mother; do not have relations with her.
>
> Do not have sexual relations with your father's wife; that would dishonor your father.
>
> Do not have sexual relations with your sister, either your father's daughter or your mother's daughter, whether she was born in the same home or elsewhere.

Do not have sexual relations with your son's daughter or your daughter's daughter; that would dishonor you.

Do not have sexual relations with the daughter of your father's wife, born to your father; she is your sister.

Do not have sexual relations with your father's sister; she is your father's close relative.

Do not have sexual relations with your mother's sister, because she is your mother's close relative.

Do not dishonor your father's brother by approaching his wife to have sexual relations; she is your aunt.

Do not have sexual relations with your daughter-in-law. She is your son's wife; do not have relations with her.

Do not have sexual relations with your brother's wife; that would dishonor your brother.

Do not have sexual relations with both a woman and her daughter. Do not have sexual relations with either her son's daughter or her daughter's daughter; they are her close relatives. That is wickedness.

Do not take your wife's sister as a rival wife and have sexual relations with her while your wife is living.

Do not approach a woman to have sexual relations during the uncleanness of her monthly period.

Do not have sexual relations with your neighbor's wife and defile yourself with her.

Do not give any of your children to be sacrificed to Molech, for you must not profane the name of your God. I am the LORD.

Do not lie with a man as one lies with a woman; that is detestable.

Do not have sexual relations with an animal and defile yourself with it. A woman must not present herself to an animal to have sexual relations with it; that is a perversion.

Do not defile yourselves in any of these ways, because this is how the nations that I am going to drive out before you became defiled. Even the land was defiled; so I punished it for its sin, and the land vomited out its inhabitants. But you must keep my decrees and my laws. The native-born and the aliens living among you must not do any of these detestable things, for all these things were done by the people who lived in the land before you, and the land became defiled. And if you defile the land, it will vomit you out as it vomited out the nations that were before you.

Everyone who does any of these detestable things—such persons must be cut off from their people. Keep my requirements and do not follow any of the detestable customs that were practiced before you came and do not defile yourselves with them. I am the LORD your God. (18:7-30)

A summary list of unlawful ("haram" in *Koran*), incestuous sexual relations.[1]

Unlawful partner

> Mother
> Step-mother
> Sister
> Step-sister
> Son's daughter
> Daughter's daughter
> Daughter of step-mother (born to father)
> Father's sister
> Mother's sister
> Father's brother's wife
> Daughter-in-law (Cf. Tamar)
> Brother's wife
> Both a woman and her daughter
> Wife's sister
> Women with menstruation
> Neighbor's wife
> Man
> Animal

We have come a long way, e.g., from Moses's father's marrying his father's sister (18:12) and an even longer way from Jacob's "taking your wife's sister as a rival wife and (having) sexual relations with her while your wife is living" (18:18), or from Judah and Tamar, not to mention earlier cases.

Incest ("unlawful"), homosexuality ("detestable"), and sodomy ("perverse") are forbidden. Disobedience is punished with "cutting off" from the community and by the "land vomit(ing) out its in- habitants." (Further sanctions below.) However, incest for one, was not committed only by other nations/peoples but also by the Israelites, by Israil/Jacob himself and more recently by Moses's father.

Also to be noted is the fact that these sexual-moral injunctions are addressed to men, not perhaps only because they are more prone to violation, but because women are considered to be passive recipients, mere objects of sex, non-subjects or non-agents, without a will of their own. The only exception in the above list is 18:23: "A woman must not present herself to an animal to have sexual relations with it." Apparently, women have will-power only against forms of life lower than human.

There are some absences in the list of unlawful partners: e.g., daughter of stepmother born to another man than one's own father, or mother's brother's wife. But since, conspicuously, one's own daughter is not on the list either, one can infer that such restrictions are now taken for granted. What is perhaps more interesting is that the ground for prohibition in a good number of cases is that the act would "dishonor one's father" and brother or self. No symmetry obtains in the case of women; there is no linguistic and conceptual category as "dishonoring the woman."

19. Various Other Laws

> When you reap the harvest of your land, do not reap to the very edges of your field or gather the gleanings of your harvest. Do not go over your vineyard a second time or pick up the grapes that have fallen. Leave them for the poor and the alien. I am the LORD your God. (19:9-10)

Rudiments of alms-giving, if not redistributive justice. (Cf. the *Koran*'s 1/40, infra.)

And a selective repetition of the 10 (6) commandments:

> Do not steal.
> Do not lie.
> Do not deceive one another.
> Do not swear falsely by my name and so profane the name of your God. I am the LORD.
> Do not defraud your neighbor or rob him. (19:11-13)

Some more rules, economic and moral:

> Do not hold back the wages of a hired man overnight.
> Do not curse the deaf or put a stumbling block in front of the blind, but fear your God. I am the LORD.
> Do not pervert justice; do not show partiality to the poor or favoritism to the great, but judge your neighbor fairly.
> Do not go about spreading slander among your people.
> Do not do anything that endangers your neighbor's life. I am the LORD.
> Do not hate your brother in your heart. Rebuke your neighbor frankly so you will not share in his guilt.
> Do not seek revenge or bear a grudge against one of your people, but love your neighbor as yourself. I am the LORD.
> Keep my decrees.
> Do not mate different kinds of animals.
> Do not plant your field with two kinds of seed.
> Do not wear clothing woven of two kinds of material. (19:13-19)

Punctuality in paying wages of labor, love for and fairness to the neighbor, compassion for the disabled, honesty, brotherly love (at last), etc. Beginnings of a more humanitarian, Christian morality? But note that it is still "one of your people," and that it is still "justice as impartiality," not as equality.

Some more:

> If a man sleeps with a woman who is a slave girl promised to another man but who has not been ransomed or given her freedom, there must be due punishment. Yet they are not to be put to death, because she had not been freed. The man, however, must bring a ram to the entrance to the Tent of Meeting for a guilt offering to the LORD. With the ram of the guilt offering the priest is to make atonement for him before the LORD for the sin he has committed, and his sin will be forgiven. (19:20-22)

Quite an easy way out for men! More rules, some new, some old:

> When you enter the land and plant any kind of fruit tree, regard its fruit as forbidden. For three years you are to consider it forbidden, it must not be eaten. In the fourth year all its fruit will be holy, an offering of praise to the LORD. But in the fifth year you may eat its fruit. In this way your harvest will be increased. I am the LORD your God.
>
> Do not eat any meat with the blood still in it.
>
> Do not practice divination or sorcery.
>
> Do not cut the hair at the sides of your head or clip off the edges of your beard.
>
> Do not cut your bodies for the dead or put tattoo marks on yourselves. I am the LORD.
>
> Do not degrade your daughter by making her a prostitute, or the land will turn to prostitution and be filled with wickedness.
>
> Observe my Sabbaths and have reverence for my sanctuary. I am the LORD.
>
> Do not turn to mediums or seek out spiritists, for you will be defiled by them. I am the LORD your God.
>
> Rise in the presence of the aged, show respect for the elderly and revere your God. I am the LORD.
>
> When an alien lives with you in your land, do not mistreat him. The alien living with you must be treated as one of your native-born. Love him as yourself, for you were aliens in Egypt. I am the LORD your God.
>
> Do not use dishonest standards when measuring length, weight or quantity.
>
> Use honest scales and honest weights, an honest ephah and an honest hin. I am the LORD your God, who brought you out of Egypt.
>
> Keep all my decrees and all my laws and follow them. I am the LORD. (19:23-37)

Most notably, some emergent empathy and compassion for the alien, in addition to agricultural and hygienic advice, reinforcements of monotheism, and body controls.

20. Punishments for (Sexual) Sin

If anyone curses his father or mother, he must be put to death. He has cursed his father or his mother, and his blood will be on his own head.

If a man commits adultery with another man's wife—with the wife of his neighbor—both the adulterer and the adulteress must be put to death.

If a man sleeps with his father's wife, he has dishonored his father. Both the man and the woman must be put to death; their blood will be on their own heads.

If a man sleeps with his daughter-in-law, both of them must be put to death. What they have done is a perversion; their blood will be on their own heads.

If a man lies with a man as one lies with a woman, both of them have done what is detestable. They must be put to death; their blood will be on their own heads.

If a man marries both a woman and her mother, it is wicked. Both he and they must be burned in the fire, so that no wickedness will be among you.

If a man has sexual relations with an animal, he must be put to death, and you must kill the animal.

If a woman approaches an animal to have sexual relations with it, kill both the woman and the animal. They must be put to death; their blood will be on their own heads.

If a man marries his sister, the daughter of either his father or his mother, and they have sexual relations, it is a disgrace. They must be cut off before the eyes of their people. He has dishonored his sister and will be held responsible.

If a man lies with a woman during her monthly period and has sexual relations with her, he has exposed the source of her flow, and she has also uncovered it. Both of them must be cut off from their people.

Do not have sexual relations with the sister of either your mother or your father, for that would dishonor a close relative; both of you would be held responsible. (20:19)

If a man sleeps with his aunt, he has dishonored his uncle. They will be held responsible; they will die childless.

If a man marries his brother's wife, it is an act of impurity; he has dishonored his brother. They will be childless. (20:9-21)

Punishment by death, cutting off, childlessness. Death mainly for high incest, homosexuality, and sodomy. Brother-sister incest still punished by the milder cutting off. Note that 20:19 would have directly applied to Moses's father, and 20:12 to Judah and Tamar. Please also note that "adultery with another man's wife" is promptly qualified as "with the wife of his neighbor."

The chapter closes with a differentiation between abhorable old customs and new laws for the Israelites whom God "has set...apart from the nations":

Keep all my decrees and laws and follow them, so that the land where I am bringing you to live may not vomit you out.

You must not live according to the customs of the nations I am going to drive out before you. Because they did all these things, I abhorred them. But I said to you, "You will possess their land; I will give it to you as an inheritance, a land flowing with milk and honey." I am the LORD your God, who has set you apart from the nations. (20:22-24)

21, 22. Rules for Priests

Priests should not be unclean, they must not shave their heads or shave off the edges of their beards, they must not marry women defiled by prostitution or divorced from their husbands (same thing?), a priest's daughter who becomes a prostitute must be burned in the fire.

The high priest must not let his hair become unkempt, the woman he marries must be a virgin from his own people. Purity of blood.

The LORD said to Moses, "Say to Aaron: 'For the generations to come none of your descendants who has a defect may come near to offer the food of his God. No man who has any defect may come near: no man who is blind or lame, disfigured or deformed; no man with a crippled foot or hand, or who is hunchbacked or dwarfed, or who has any eye defect, or who has festering or running sores or damaged testicles. No descendant of Aaron the priest who has any defect is to come near to present the offerings made to the LORD by fire. He has a defect; he must not come near to offer the food of his God. He may eat the most holy food of his God, as well as the holy food; yet because of his defect, he must not go near the curtain or approach the altar, and so desecrate my sanctuary. I am the LORD, who makes them holy.' " (21:16-23)

God has not much love or compassion for human beings with defect or disability (unlike Jesus), because they "desecrate (his) sanctuary."

Some more rules are prescribed:

The priests are to keep my requirements so that they do not become guilty and die for treating them with contempt. I am the LORD, who makes them holy.

No one outside a priest's family may eat the sacred offering, nor may the guest of a priest or his hired worker eat it. But if a priest buys a slave with money, or if a slave is born in his household, that slave may eat his food. If a priest's daughter marries anyone other than a priest, she may not eat any of the sacred contributions. But if a priest's daughter becomes a widow or is divorced, yet has no children, and she returns to live in her father's house as in her youth, she may eat of her father's food. No unauthorized person, however, may eat any of it.

If anyone eats a sacred offering by mistake, he must make restitution to the priest for the offering and add a fifth of the value to it. The priests must not desecrate the sacred offerings the Israelites present to the LORD by allowing them to eat the sacred offerings and so bring upon them guilt requiring payment. I am the LORD, who makes them holy. (22:9-16)

Incessant classification and hierarchization of human beings. And this in terms of holy and unholy. (See below for more.)

23. Sabbath, Feasts, Atonement

God reminds Moses and the Israelites his "appointed feasts": Sabbath, The Passover, the Feast of Unleavened Bread, of First Fruits, the Feast of Weeks, Trumpets, The Day of Atonement, the Feast of Tabernacles. These are lasting ordinances for generations to come. Ritual and regulation of detail abound.

24. Oil and Bread; Blasphemer Stoned

This bread is to be set out before the LORD regularly, Sabbath after Sabbath, on behalf of the Israelites, as a lasting covenant. It belongs to Aaron and his sons, who are to eat it in a holy place, because it is a most holy part of their regular share of the offerings made to the LORD by fire." (24:8-9)

And, some moral:

Now the son of an Israelite mother and an Egyptian father went out among the Israelites, and a fight broke out in the camp between him and an Israelite. The son of the Israelite woman blasphemed the Name with a curse; so they brought him to Moses. (His mother's name was Shelomith, the daughter of Dibri the Danite.) They put him in custody until the will of the LORD should be made clear to them.

Then the LORD said to Moses: "Take the blasphemer outside the camp. All those who heard him are to lay their hands on his head, and the entire assembly is to stone him. Say to the Israelites: If anyone curses his God, he will be held responsible; anyone who blasphemes the name of the LORD must be put to death. The entire assembly must stone him. Whether an alien or native-born, when he blasphemes the Name, he must be put to death. (24:10-15)

The institution of communal stoning is ushered in. (Cf. the "recm" (stoning) of Islam and the *Koran.*)

The rule and the sanction are extended and codified:

If anyone takes the life of a human being, he must be put to death. Anyone who takes the life of someone's animal must make restitution—life for life. If anyone injures his neighbor, whatever he has done must be done to him: fracture for fracture, eye for eye, tooth for tooth. As he has injured the other, so he is to be injured.

Whoever kills an animal must make restitution, but whoever kills a man must be put to death. You are to have the same law for the alien and the native-born. I am the LORD your God.

Then Moses spoke to the Israelites, and they took the blasphemer outside the camp and stoned him. The Israelites did as the LORD commanded Moses. (24:17-23)

Very un-Jesus-like, as we shall see later.

25. The Sabbath Year and the Year of Jubilee: Land, Welfare, Charity, Social Economics
God, who is in the beginning, is also present in the middle, in the life of the present world, actively participating in the history of mankind as a landlord, through his decrees and laws and punishments in cases of violation. (A God which shall also be present in the end will have to await Christianity and Islam.)

The LORD said to Moses on Mount Sinai, "Speak to the Israelites and say to them: 'When you enter the land I am going to give you, the land itself must observe a Sabbath to the LORD. For six years sow your fields, and for six years prune your vineyards and gather their crops. But in the seventh year the land is to have a Sabbath of rest, a Sabbath to the LORD. Do not sow your fields or prune your vineyards. Do not reap what grows of itself or harvest the grapes of your untended vines. The land is to have a year of rest. Whatever the land yields during the Sabbath year will be food for you—for yourself, your manservant and maidservant, and the hired worker and temporary resident who live among you, as well as for your livestock and the wild animals in your land. Whatever the land produces may be eaten.

Count off seven Sabbaths of years—seven times seven years—so that the seven Sabbaths of years amount to a period of forty-nine years. Then have the trumpet sounded everywhere on the tenth day of the seventh month; on the Day of Atonement sound the trumpet throughout your land. Consecrate the fiftieth year and proclaim liberty throughout the land to all its inhabitants. It shall be a jubilee for you; each one of you is to return to his family property and each to his own clan. The fiftieth year shall be a jubilee for you; do not sow and do not reap what grows of itself or harvest the untended vines. For it is a jubilee and is to be holy for you; eat only what is taken directly from the fields.

In this Year of Jubilee everyone is to return to his own property.

If you sell land to one of your countrymen or buy any from him, do not take advantage of each other. You are to buy from your countryman on the basis of the number of years since the Jubilee. And he is to sell to you on the basis of the number of years left for harvesting crops. When the years are many, you are to increase the price, and when the years are few, you are to decrease the price, because what he is really selling you is the number of crops.

Do not take advantage of each other, but fear your God. I am the LORD your God.

Follow my decrees and be careful to obey my laws, and you will live safely in the land. Then the land will yield its fruit, and you will eat your fill and live there in safety.

You may ask, "What will we eat in the seventh year if we do not plant or harvest our crops?" I will send you such a blessing in the sixth year that the land will yield enough for three years. While you plant during the eighth year, you will eat from the old crop and will continue to eat from it until the harvest of the ninth year comes in.

The land must not be sold permanently, because the land is mine and you are but aliens and my tenants. Throughout the country that you hold as a possession, you must provide for the redemption of the land.

If one of your countrymen becomes poor and sells some of his property, his nearest relative is to come and redeem what his countryman has sold. If, however, a man has no one to redeem it for him but he himself prospers and acquires sufficient means to redeem it, he is to determine the value for the years since he sold it and refund the balance to the man to whom he sold it; he can then go back to his own property. But if he does not acquire the means to repay him, what he sold will remain in the possession of the buyer until the Year of Jubilee. It will be returned in the Jubilee, and he can then go back to his property. (25:1-28)

On the fiftieth year, "liberty throughout the land to all its inhabitants" and "each one...to return to his family property"; selling and buying indexed to the Year of Jubilee; selling of land not permanently "because the land is mine (God's) and you are but aliens and my (God's) tenants"; rules for poor men's redeeming and recovering their landed property.

It is not so easy to redeem once-sold houses in cities, however, and there are different, privileged, regulations for the Levites:

If a man sells a house in a walled city, he retains the right of redemption a full year after its sale. During that time he may redeem it. If it is not redeemed before a full year has passed, the house in the walled city shall belong permanently to the buyer and his descendants. It is not to be returned in the Jubilee. But houses in villages without walls around them are to be considered as open country. They can be redeemed, and they are to be returned in the Jubilee.

The Levites always have the right to redeem their houses in the Levitical towns, which they possess. So the property of the Levites is redeemable—that is, a house sold in any town they hold—and is to be returned in the Jubilee, because the houses in the towns of the Levites are their property among the Israelites. But the pastureland belonging to their towns must not be sold; it is their permanent possession. (25:29-34)

Some leniency and charity for the poor (countrymen) is prescribed; they are to be treated like an alien or a temporary resident and, even if he sells himself, not as a slave but like a hired worker or temporary resident; on the Year of Jubilee, "he and his children are to be released... (b)ecause the Israelites are my [God's] servants, whom I brought out of Egypt, they must not be sold as slaves." (Slavery is for other nations.)

If one of your countrymen becomes poor and is unable to support himself among you, help him as you would an alien or a temporary resident, so he can continue to live among you. Do not take interest of any kind from him, but fear your God, so that your countryman may continue to live among you. You must not lend him money at interest or sell him food at a profit. I am the LORD your God, who brought you out of Egypt to give you the land of Canaan and to be your God.

If one of your countrymen becomes poor among you and sells himself to you, do not make him work as a slave. He is to be treated as a hired worker or a temporary resident among you; he is to work for you until the Year of Jubilee. Then he and his children are to be released, and he will go back to his own clan and to the property of his forefathers. Because the Israelites are my servants, whom I brought out of Egypt, they must not be sold as slaves. Do not rule over them ruthlessly, but fear your God. (25:35-43)

Slaves *do* come from other nations:

Your male and female slaves are to come from the nations around you; from them you may buy slaves. You may also buy some of the temporary residents living among you and members of their clans born in your country, and they will become your property. You can will them to your children as inherited property and can make them slaves for life, but you must not rule over your fellow Israelites ruthlessly.

If an alien or a temporary resident among you becomes rich and one of your countrymen becomes poor and sells himself to the alien living among you or to a member of the alien's clan, he retains the right of redemption after he has sold himself. One of his relatives may redeem him: An uncle or a cousin or any blood relative in his clan may redeem him. Or if he prospers, he may redeem himself. He and his buyer are to count the time from the year he sold himself up to the Year of Jubilee. The price for his release is to be based on the rate paid to a hired man for that number of years. If many years remain, he must pay for his redemption a larger share of the price paid for him. If only a few years remain until the Year of Jubilee, he is to compute that and pay for his redemption accordingly.

He is to be treated as a man hired from year to year; you must see to it that his owner does not rule over him ruthlessly.

Even if he is not redeemed in any of these ways, he and his children are to be released in the Year of Jubilee, for the Israelites belong to me as servants. They are my servants, whom I brought out of Egypt. I am the LORD your God. (25:44-55)

The population is divided into classes of citizens, quarter-citizens, non-citizens; a sort of national identity for the "fellow Israelites" is being forged.

26. Reward for Obedience, Punishment for Disobedience

If obedience to God's commands, then rain, abundance of food, safety and peace in the land, and population increase.

Plus:

You will pursue your enemies, and they will fall by the sword before you. Five of you will chase a hundred, and a hundred of you will chase ten thousand, and your enemies will fall by the sword before you.

I will look on you with favor and make you fruitful and increase your numbers, and I will keep my covenant with you.

You will still be eating last year's harvest when you will have to move it out to make room for the new. I will put my dwelling place among you, and I will not abhor you.

I will walk among you and be your God, and you will be my people. I am the LORD your God, who brought you out of Egypt so that you would no longer be slaves to the Egyptians; I broke the bars of your yoke and enabled you to walk with heads held high. (26:7-13)

Rewards to chosen people conditional, penalties to enemies automatic. See Deuteronomy, Chapter 28, for a devastating elaboration of this theme.

If disobedience to God's commands, then:

But if you will not listen to me and carry out all these commands, and if you reject my decrees and abhor my laws and fail to carry out all my commands and so violate my covenant, then I will do this to you: I will bring upon you sudden terror, wasting diseases and fever that will destroy your sight and drain away your life. You will plant seed in vain, because your enemies will eat it. I will set my face against you so that you will be defeated by your enemies; those who hate you will rule over you, and you will flee even when no one is pursuing you.

If after all this you will not listen to me, I will punish you for your sins seven times over. I will break down your stubborn pride and make the sky above you like iron and the ground beneath you like bronze. Your strength will be spent in vain, because your soil will not yield its crops, nor will the trees of the land yield their fruit.

If you remain hostile toward me and refuse to listen to me, I will multiply your afflictions seven times over, as your sins deserve. I will send wild animals against you, and they will rob you of your children, destroy your cattle and make you so few in number that your roads will be deserted. (26:14-22)

Terror, wasting diseases and fever, loss of sight, draining away of life, shortage of food, defeat in the hand of enemy, oppression, flight, loss of children, destruction of cattle, population decrease...

And, multiplication of afflictions seven times over.

If in spite of these things you do not accept my correction but continue to be hostile toward me, I myself will be hostile toward you and will afflict you for your sins seven times over. And I will bring the sword upon you to avenge the breaking of the covenant. When you withdraw into your cities, I will send a plague among you, and you will be given into enemy hands.

When I cut off your supply of bread, ten women will be able to bake your bread in one oven, and they will dole out the bread by weight. You will eat, but you will not be satisfied.

If in spite of this you still do not listen to me but continue to be hostile toward me, then in my anger I will be hostile toward you, and I myself will punish you for your sins seven times over. You will eat the flesh of your sons and the flesh of your daughters. I will destroy your high places, cut down your incense altars and pile your dead bodies on the lifeless forms of your idols, and I will abhor you. I will turn your cities into ruins and lay waste your sanctuaries, and I will take no delight in the pleasing aroma of your offerings. I will lay waste the land, so that your enemies who live there will be appalled. I will scatter you among the nations and will draw out my sword and pursue you. Your land will be laid waste, and your cities will lie in ruins. Then the land will enjoy its Sabbath years all the time that it lies desolate and you are in the country of your enemies; then the land will rest and enjoy its Sabbaths. All the time that it lies desolate, the land will have the rest it did not have during the Sabbaths you lived in it. (26:23-35)

Plague, fall in productivity, hunger, destruction of shelters and temples, laying waste of city and country, exile and scattering among other nations, flight from God's sword...

Moreover, not only will God pile up dead bodies of people, but also people will eat:

the flesh of their sons

and

the flesh of their daughters.

Awards few, short, plain; punishments many, long, multiple.

Less persuasion and promise; more arm-twisting and threat.

Not a covenant, but an ultimatum.

Politics—theopolitics, Godly politics—politics of fear and threat of death, including the threat of killing children, and making people eat their own children.[2]

As for those of you who are left, I will make their hearts so fearful in the lands of their enemies that the sound of a windblown leaf will put them to flight. They will run as though fleeing from the sword, and they will fall, even though no one is pursuing them. They will stumble over one another as though fleeing from the sword, even though no one is pursuing them. So you will not be able to stand before your enemies. You will perish among the nations; the land of your enemies will devour you. Those of you who are left will waste away in the lands of their enemies because of their sins; also because of their father's sins they will waste away. (26:36-39)

Constant fear and flight even without pursuit; perishing among nations, enemies "devouring" the Israelites. Children as well—because of their fathers' sins.

Doesn't the following come as an (unconvincing) anti-climax? And, who is abhorring whom? Men, God; or God, men?

But if they will confess their sins and the sins of their fathers—their treachery against me and their hostility toward me, which made me hostile toward them so that I sent them into the land of their enemies—then when their uncircumcised hearts[3] are humbled and they pay for their sin, I will remember my covenant with Jacob and my covenant with Isaac and my covenant with Abraham, and I will remember the land. For the land will be deserted by them and will enjoy its Sabbaths while it lies desolate without them. They will pay for their sins because they rejected my laws and abhorred my decrees. Yet in spite of this, when they are in the land of their enemies, I will not reject them or abhor them so as to destroy them completely, breaking my covenant with them. I am the LORD their God. But for their sake I will remember the covenant with their ancestors whom I brought out of Egypt in the sight of the nations to be their God. I am the LORD.

These are the decrees, the laws and the regulations that the LORD established on Mount Sinai between himself and the Israelites through Moses. (26:40-46)

Exile and return. Cyclical punishment and reward.

27. Redeeming What Is the LORD'S

The LORD said to Moses, "Speak to the Israelites and say to them: 'If anyone makes a special vow to dedicate persons to the LORD by giving equivalent values, set the value of a male between the ages of twenty and sixty at fifty shekels of silver, according to the sanctuary shekel; and if it is a female, set her value at thirty shekels. If it is a person between the ages of five and twenty, set the value of a male at twenty shekels and of a female at ten shekels. If it is a person between one month and five years, set the value of a male at five shekels of silver and that of a female at three shekels of silver. If it is a person sixty years old or more, set the value of a male at fifteen shekels and of a female at ten shekels. If anyone making the vow is too poor to pay the specified amount, he is to present the person to the priest, who will set the value for him according to what the man making the vow can afford.' " (27:1-8)

According to this book, most human beings may not have an intrinsic value, but they certainly do have a redemption value, or rather price. And the woman's price is half that of the man. The very idea of dedicating persons to God at a price, by giving equivalent values (to the priests), or to be determined by the priests, is priceless in itself in terms of what may be called pecuniary humanism.

Similarly with animals (plus one fifth if redeemed), with land (plus one fifth if redeemed; if not, becoming the property of the priests in the Jubilee). The priesthood also operates like a one-way bank, continually receiving hot cash or mortgage money, occasionally acquiring property as well. Finally:

A tithe of everything from the land, whether grain from the soil or fruit from the trees, belongs to the LORD; it is holy to the LORD. If a man redeems any of his tithe, he must add a fifth of the value to it. The entire tithe of the herd and flock—every tenth animal that passes under the shepherd's rod—will be holy to the LORD. He must not pick out the good from the bad or make any substitution. If he does make a substitution, both the animal and its substitute become holy and cannot be redeemed.

These are the commands the LORD gave Moses on Mount Sinai for the Israelites. (27:30-34)

POSTSCRIPT to LEVITICUS

This is Leviticus; this is the first law-book of the kingdom of priests (only of them?), of the theocratic state with its penetrative and extractive ideologies and institutions—from control of bodies to tributary taxation—which is also quite "modern," albeit through religious devices, in aspects of state-building, nation-building, and identity-building.

This is the "Law" with its cultic, public financial, legal and moral rules; this is the "Law" that codifies politics of fear, politics of death-threat, politics of child-killing. (More to come in Numbers, Ch. 16 and Deuteronomy, Ch. 28.)

And what a language, what a vocabulary, what imagery, and what style imprinted on the conceptual and affective dispositions of generations to come.

But, isn't there any morality here, in the sense of good ethics? Well, some: Incest and adultery are seriously restrained (but not rape), theft is prohibited (but not plunder), murder is banned (but not genocide), damage to neighbor is barred (but only if he is a "fellow Israelite"). All these embryonic moral rules are tribe-bound; they do not apply to other tribes/nations. In fact, just the reverse is commanded concerning the latter.

Equally importantly, in the negative sense, there are more in-tribal moral rules that are unethical: Priests are holier than the community, men are holier than women, girls are dirtier than boys. "Neighbor" is not the human being next-door, he is one of the ethnic Israelites; even Israelite human beings have a price tag on them like animals ("indulgence" did not start with the corrupt Catholic church); population is divided into castes, and so forth.

Perhaps, more gravely, belief (let alone morality) is based on fear of and obedience to a certain God and his words (which, as we are seeing, are not always good), and not on love, reason, and healthy natural grounds. At the apex of these religious moral rules is the grund-norm of "he who is," who "abhor"s men, who spares not children, who says men are evil but teaches and wills for them worse things, including at least the thought of eating their own children—if he himself does not annihilate them first.

Man, deprived of all dignity, shall fear him and obey his commands, if he ever fails to do so, he shall exile them from their home into the midst of enemy nations—yet without even then "rejecting and abhorring" (26:45) them! His chosen people will be reptiles at home and reptiles in exile, leading a reptilian existence if they are not outright killed. (Remember: not one of the 600,000 made it home.)

I am not aiming at a straw-God, or a ghost, however holy he may be. This good God of bad man is still with us, through the Christian and Muslim eras, right up to the modern, secular times. Some of his moral and political rules may have changed somewhat over time, but the basic rule, the axiom, he himself, is intact in the individual and public epistemologies, psyches, and in basic morals and politics of mankind, continuing to frighten, threaten, dwarf and cripple human beings and their collective life, legitimating overtly or covertly or in mediated ways inequality, insecurity, cruelty, injustice, and so forth.

It is doubtful whether all his early rules and laws have significantly evolved or are seriously evolvable but, to me, it is beyond doubt that his very first rule, the unquestionable existence and nature of himself is still a colossal presence, which continues to afflict civilized Western (and Westernized Eastern) men and women. (Needless to say, Eastern Gods are also on a similar job in their respective jurisdictions.)

Notes
1. Please compare this list with the similar one in *Koran*.
2. See also Numbers, Ch. 16 and Leviticus, Ch. 28 below.
3. Please note that the "circumcision of the heart" motif, too, of Christianity is to be found in the *Old Testament*.

NUMBERS

1. The Census: The Rulers and the Ruled

God instructs Moses to take a census of the Israelites, "listing every man by name," who are twenty years old and more and are able to serve in the army. Twelve (12-Levites=11, but Joseph's family counted as two) ancestral tribes are counted by their clans and families; the total number is 603,550. (The number of men at the time of exodus from Egypt was "about 600,000." Population increase is checked by God.) Levites are not counted, for God says to Moses: "Instead, appoint the Levites to be in charge of the tabernacle of the Testimony—over all its furnishings and everything belonging to it...Anyone else who goes near it shall be put to death" (1:50-51).

Thus, the tribe of Levi is not only exempted from compulsory military service and its attendant risks, it is also elevated to a high social status and privileged position in the community, with both economic advantages and exclusive political-administrative power. Not for a lifetime but for generations to come.

This is a theocracy, dynastically inherited. God gives the Levites the means of administration in Weberian terms; more than that, they own the means of administration. Theocracy in the full sense of the term: The source of the legitimacy of their political, or religio-political, rule is God and his word/book, and the personnel of this political rule is a priesthood. The division of labor here is occupational, political, and social, all at the same time.

The stratification and hierarchy is reinforced by a horizontal and spatio-geographical or locational differentiation as well. In addition to the sanction of death for non-Levites for approaching, let alone entering, the tabernacle,

The Israelites are to set up their tents by division, each man in his own camp under his own standard. The Levites, however, are to set up their tents around the tabernacle of Testimony so that wrath will not fall on the Israelite community. (1:52-53)

The holier you are spiritually, the nearer to God you are physically, too. And vice versa.

2. The Arrangement of the Tribal Camps: Spatial Hierarchy
"The Israelites are to camp around the Tent of Meeting some distance from it…" (2:2), that is, the camp of the Levites is to be in the middle of the camps of the 12 ancestral families. The rest are to settle in concentric circles around the holy center.

157,600

North

Naphtali **(BILHAH)

Asher *(ZILPAH)

Dan   **(BILHAH)

108,100		
West	*Center*	*East*
Benjamin/Manasseh/Ephraim	T. Of T.	Judah/Issachar/Zebulun
(RACHEL) (Joseph)	T. Of M.	(LEAH) (LEAH) (LEAH)
(RACHEL)	Levites (LEAH)	

186,400 appears above *East* column.

151,450

South

Reuben (LEAH)

Simeon (LEAH)

Gad *(ZILPAH)

How is this connected to or consistent with the blessings and curses in Genesis 49? Which direction is more valuable? Is there a meaning to the East-West axis (wives) versus North-South axis (mostly concubines)? Or West/Rachel versus East/Leah? I am sure that theological literature has problematized and tried to answer such questions.

3. The Levites: The Elite of the People
God says to Moses: "Give the Levites to Aaron and his sons ["the anointed priests," (3:3)]; they are the Israelites who are to be given wholly to him" (3:9). Human beings "are given to" other human beings as their patrimony.

> The LORD also said to Moses, "I have taken the Levites from among the Israelites in place of the first male offspring of every Israelite woman. The Levites are mine, for all the firstborn are mine. When I struck down all the firstborn in Egypt, I set apart for myself every firstborn in Israel, whether man or animal. They are to be mine. I am the LORD." (3:11-13)

And:

> The LORD said to Moses in the Desert of Sinai, "Count the Levites by their families and clans. Count every male a month old or more." So Moses counted them, as he was commanded by the word of the LORD. (3:14-16)

The question "Why the Levites?" is answered above (!). The difference of this Levitic census from the general one is that all the males "a month old or more" are counted: the total number is 22,000. The Levite clans have their own internal division of labor and camps around the Tent of Meeting again clockwise: East (Moses and Aaron & Sons), South (Kohathites), West (Gershonites), North (Merarites).

God also has Moses count all the firstborn Israelite males a month old or more (22,273) and instructs him:

> To redeem the 273 firstborn Israelites who exceed the number of the Levites, collect five shekels for each one, according to the sanctuary shekel, which weighs twenty gerahs. Give the money for the redemption of the additional Israelites to Aaron and his sons.
>
> So Moses collected the redemption money from those who exceeded the number redeemed by the Levites. From the firstborn of the Israelites he collected silver weighing 1,365 shekels, according to the sanctuary shekel. Moses gave the redemption money to Aaron and his sons. (3:46-51)

4. The Levite Clans: The Bureaucratic Elite

Men from thirty to fifty years of age from the three Levite clans are to serve in the work of the Tent of Meeting under the direction of Aaron's two remaining sons, Eleazar and Ithamar. Again specified in minute ritualistic detail, they will do so according to an internal division of labor determined in terms of "most holy" and just "holy."

> So Moses, Aaron and the leaders of Israel counted all the Levites by their clans and families. All the men from thirty to fifty years of age who came to do the work of serving and carrying the Tent of Meeting numbered 8,580. At the LORD's command through Moses, each was assigned his work and told what to carry. (4:46-49)

Quite an administrative bureaucracy.

5, 6. The Purity of the Camp

Those who have infectious skin disease (not necessarily leprosy) or are ceremonially unclean are sent away from the camp. Also:

> The LORD said to Moses, "Say to the Israelites: 'When a man or woman wrongs another in any way and so is unfaithful to the LORD, that person is guilty and must confess the sin he has committed. He must make full restitution for his wrong, add one fifth to it and give it all to the person he has wronged. But if that person has no

close relative to whom restitution can be made for the wrong, the restitution belongs to the LORD and must be given to the priest, along with the ram with which atonement is made for him. All the sacred contributions the Israelites bring to a priest will belong to him. Each man's sacred gifts are his own, but what he gives to the priest will belong to the priest.' " (5:5-10)

And:

Then the LORD said to Moses, "Speak to the Israelites and say to them: 'If a man's wife goes astray and is unfaithful to him by sleeping with another man, and this is hidden from her husband and her impurity is undetected (since there is no witness against her and she has not been caught in the act), and if feelings of jealousy come over her husband and he suspects his wife and she is impure—or if he is jealous and suspects her even though she is not impure—then he is to take his wife to the priest. He must also take an offering of a tenth of an ephah of barley flour on her behalf. He must not pour oil on it or put incense on it, because it is a grain offering for jealousy, a reminder offering to draw attention to guilt. (5:11-15)

Curses are written on a scroll—to be washed off into the bitter water.

If she has defiled herself and been unfaithful to her husband, then when she is made to drink the water that brings a curse, it will go into her and cause bitter suffering; her abdomen will swell and her thigh waste away, and she will become accursed among her people. If, however, the woman has not defiled herself and is free from impurity, she will be cleared of guilt and will be able to have children.

This, then, is the law of jealousy when a woman goes astray and defiles herself while married to her husband, or when feelings of jealousy come over a man because he suspects his wife. The priest is to have her stand before the LORD and is to apply this entire law to her. The husband will be innocent of any wrongdoing, but the woman will bear the consequences of her sin. (5:27-31)

Purity of the camp spoilt by diseases and women.

Commission to the priests on every thinkable pretext.

The vice squad against women to consist of husband and priests.

The episode of the Nazirite furnishes another instance of control of bodies.

7, 8, 9, 10. Offerings, Rituals, Passover, Leaving Sinai

Each of the 12 tribes brings offerings at the dedication of the Tabernacle:

A silver plate weighing 130 shekels = 3 1/4 pounds = 1.5 kg. X 12= 18 kg.

A silver sprinkling bowl weighing 70 shekels = 1 3/4 pounds = 0.5 kg. X 12 = 7.6 kg.

A gold dish weighing 10 shekels = 4 ounces = 110 gr. X 12 = 1.4 kg.

Various animals totaling 21 x 12 = 252.

Levites are purified; they shave their whole bodies, etc. "In this way you are to set the Levites apart from the other Israelites, and the Levites will be mine," says God to Moses (8:14). "Of all the Israelites, I have given the Levites as gifts to Aaron and his sons to do the work at the Tent of Meeting on behalf of the Israelites" (8:19). The tenure of the Levites in the actual work at the sanctuary is between the ages 25-50.

The Israelites camp or set out at God's command. The silver trumpets for calling the community to camp or set out are also to be blown by Aaron's sons, the priests. The Israelites leave the Desert of Sinai for the promised land, Moses asks his father-in-law, the Midianite priest, to accompany them: "Please do not leave us. You know where we should camp in the desert, and you can be our eyes" (10:31). (God is to mark this as another minus on the part of Moses, who divides his trust between God and someone else.)

11. Fire From the Lord, who Burns "His People" Because They Wail

Now the people complained about their hardships in the hearing of the LORD, and when he heard them his anger was aroused. Then fire from the LORD burned among them and consumed some of the outskirts of the camp. When the people cried out to Moses, he prayed to the LORD and the fire died down. So that place was called Taberah, because fire from the LORD had burned among them. (11:1-3)

The murmuring, grumbling, wailing of the people will mount and God's punishments will escalate.

Moses heard the people of every family wailing, each at the entrance to his tent. The LORD became exceedingly angry, and Moses was troubled. He asked the LORD, "Why have you brought this trouble on your servant? What have I done to displease you that you put the burden of all these people on me? Did I conceive all these people? Did I give them birth? Why do you tell me to carry them in my arms, as a nurse carries an infant, to the land you promised on oath to their forefathers? Where can I get meat for all these people? They keep wailing to me, 'Give us meat to eat!' I cannot carry all these people by myself; the burden is too heavy for me. If this is how you are going to treat me, put me to death right now—if I have found favor in your eyes—and do not let me face my own ruin." (11:10-15)

A God and a prophet adopting a people as their own, and of their own accord, and then complaining of the self-imposed burden. Infantilization of man, a great theme of Christianity, too, also makes an early entry.

God instructs Moses to assemble seventy of Israil's elders to distribute the burden and to tell them that he will provide meat. (That, initially, was Jethro's advice.)

You will not eat it for just one day, or two days, or five, ten or twenty days, but for a whole month—until it comes out of your nostrils and you loathe it—because you have rejected the LORD, who is among you, and have wailed before him, saying, 'Why did we ever leave Egypt?' (11:19-20)

Two men, listed among the elders, do not attend but prophesy in the camp, God sends quail and then a severe plague. The Israelites "buried the people who had craved other food" (11:34).

12. Miriam and Aaron vs. Moses: One God, One Prophet

Miriam and Aaron began to talk against Moses because of his Cushite wife, for he had married a Cushite. "Has the LORD spoken only through Moses?" they asked. "Hasn't he also spoken through us?" And the LORD heard this.

(Now Moses was a very humble man, more humble than anyone else on the face of the earth.)

At once the LORD said to Moses, Aaron and Miriam, "Come out to the Tent of Meeting, all three of you." So the three of them came out. Then the LORD came down in a pillar of cloud; he stood at the entrance to the Tent and summoned Aaron and Miriam. When both of them stepped forward, he said, "Listen to my words:

When a prophet of the LORD is among you, I reveal myself to him in visions, I speak to him in dreams. But this is not true of my servant Moses; he is faithful in all my house. With him I speak face to face, clearly and not in riddles; he sees the form of the LORD.

Why then were you not afraid to speak against my servant Moses?" (12:1-8)

Hierarchy reminded: God → Moses → and only then Aaron, etc. Another great theme of the *New Testament* and *Koran* is introduced: Speaking properly to the most chosen one(s) and only in riddles/parables to the less chosen ones/multitudes.

God punishes Miriam (but not Aaron) with leprosy (or a skin disease) but then lightens the penalty upon Aaron's and Moses's implorations.

13. Exploring Canaan

Twelve tribal leaders are sent to explore Canaan.

They gave Moses this account: "We went into the land to which you sent us, and it does flow with milk and honey! Here is its fruit. But the people who live there are powerful, and the cities are fortified and very large. We even saw descendants of Anak there. The Amalekites live in the Negev; the Hittites, Jebusites and Amorites live in the hill country; and the Canaanites live near the sea and along the Jordan."

Then Caleb silenced the people before Moses and said, "We should go up and take possession of the land, for we can certainly do it."

But the men who had gone up with him said, "We can't attack those people; they are stronger than we are." And they spread among the Israelites a bad report about the land they had explored. They said, "The land we explored devours those living in it. All the people we saw there are of great size. We saw the Nephilim there (the descendants of Anak come from the Nephilim). We seemed like grasshoppers in our own eyes, and we looked the same to them." (13:27-33)

God marks this cowardice and ingratitude on the part of his chosen people and shall duly retaliate.

14. The People Rebel

The murmuring and grumbling against Moses and Aaron (and, therefore, against God) in the Israelite community gains momentum.

That night all the people of the community raised their voices and wept aloud. All the Israelites grumbled against Moses and Aaron, and the whole assembly said to them, "If only we had died in Egypt! Or in this desert! Why is the LORD bringing us to this land only to let us fall by the sword? Our wives and children will be taken as plunder. Wouldn't it be better for us to go back to Egypt?" And they said to each other, "We should choose a leader and go back to Egypt."

Then Moses and Aaron fell face down in front of the whole Israelite assembly gathered there. Joshua son of Nun and Caleb son of Jephunneh, who were among those who had explored the land, tore their clothes and said to the entire Israelite assembly, "The land we passed through and explored is exceedingly good. If the LORD is pleased with us, he will lead us into that land, a land flowing with milk and honey, and will give it to us. Only do not rebel against the LORD. And do not be afraid of the people of the land, because we will swallow them up. Their protection is gone, but the LORD is with us. Do not be afraid of them."

But the whole assembly talked about stoning them. Then the glory of the LORD appeared at the Tent of Meeting to all the Israelites. The LORD said to Moses, "How long will these people treat me with contempt? How long will they refuse to believe in me, in spite of all the miraculous signs I have performed among them? I will strike them down with a plague and destroy them but I will make you into a nation greater and stronger than they." (14:1-12)

Don't rebel against the Lord *and* the lords he appoints over you. Prophets and/or kings. "Submit to authorities!" the *New Testament*, too, shall command. All authorities, Godly and earthly, for the latter are chosen by the former. You cannot choose your leaders; they are chosen for you by the Lord. You cannot oppose them, criticize them, let alone question their basic legitimacy. People do not choose their leaders; they submit to God-chosen leaders. (Divine right of kings and sultans.)

If you show "contempt" for God or Moseses, you, too, will be "swallowed up" like other nations, however chosen you may be. Moses(es) are "set apart" while all of you are destroyed. (See especially Chapter 16 below.) It is not only that Israelites are superior to other nations; it is also the case that Moses or Moseses are superior to the Israelites. It is not a holy community of equally valuable believers—brothers and sisters.

And if these rebellious people are not put "to death all at one time" by Moses's God, it is because Moses plays the Machiavelli to the Prince. Moses intervenes and implores God thusly:

> If you put these people to death all at one time, the nations who have heard this report about you will say, 'The LORD was not able to bring these people into the land he promised them on oath; so he slaughtered them in the desert.'
>
> "Now may the Lord's strength be displayed, just as you have declared: The LORD is slow to anger, abounding in love and forgiving sin and rebellion. Yet he does not leave the guilty unpunished; he punishes the children for the sin of the fathers to the third and fourth generation.'
>
> In accordance with your great love, forgive the sin of these people, just as you have pardoned them from the time they left Egypt until now." (14:15-19)

Anger has been abundant; where is the love? In not killing? But he kills anyway, if only by the thousands.

> The LORD replied, "I have forgiven them, as you asked. Nevertheless, as surely as I live and as surely as the glory of the LORD fills the whole earth, not one of the men who saw my glory and the miraculous signs I performed in Egypt and in the desert but who disobeyed me and tested me ten times—not one of them will ever see the land I promised on oath to their forefathers. No one who has treated me with contempt will ever see it. But because my servant Caleb has a different spirit and follows me wholeheartedly, I will bring him into the land he went to, and his descendants will inherit it. (14:20-24)

And:

> The LORD said to Moses and Aaron: "How long will this wicked community grumble against me? I have heard the complaints of these grumbling Israelites. So tell them, 'As surely as I live, declares the LORD, I will do to you the very things I heard you say: In this desert your bodies will fall—every one of you twenty years old or more who was counted in the census and who has grumbled against me. Not one of you will enter the land I swore with uplifted hand to make your home, except Caleb son of Jephunneh and Joshua son of Nun. As for your children that you said would be taken as plunder, I will bring them in to enjoy the land you have rejected. But you—your bodies will fall in this desert. Your children will be shepherds here for forty years, suffering for your unfaithfulness, until the last of your bodies lies in the desert. For forty years—one year for each of the forty days you explored the land—you will suffer for your sins and know what it is like to have me against you.'

I, the LORD, have spoken, and I will surely do these things to this whole wicked community, which has banded together against me. They will meet their end in this desert; here they will die."

So the men Moses had sent to explore the land, who returned and made the whole community grumble against him by spreading a bad report about it—these men responsible for spreading the bad report aboud the land were struck down and died of a plague before the LORD. Of the men who went to explore the land, only Joshua son of Nun and Caleb son of Jephunneh survived. (14:26-38)

Bodies (except two) falling in the desert, children and offspring suffering for fathers' alleged sins, and so forth—all out of "love." For whom? For the "people" ("this whole wicked community") or for the "chosen few?"

When Moses reported this to all the Israelites, they mourned bitterly. Early the next morning they went up toward the high hill country. "We have sinned," they said. "We will go up to the place the LORD promised."

But Moses said, "Why are you disobeying the LORD's command? This will not succeed! Do not go up, because the LORD is not with you. You will be defeated by your enemies, for the Amalekites and Canaanites will face you there. Because you have turned away from the LORD, he will not be with you and you will fall by the sword."

Nevertheless, in their presumption they went up toward the high hill country, though neither Moses nor the ark of the LORD's covenant moved from the camp. Then the Amalekites and Canaanites who lived in that hill country came down and attacked them and beat them down all the way to Hormah. (14:39-45)

God's plague aggravated by enemy beating.

15. Supplementary Offerings, and Sins

The community is to have the same rules for you and for the alien living among you; this is a lasting ordinance for the generations to come. You and the alien shall be the same before the LORD: The same laws and regulations will apply both to you and to the alien living among you. (15:15-16)

Intentional (or defiant) sins are seen as a matter of individual responsibility and punishment (cutting off from people), but unintentional sins bind the whole community(!) and can be atoned for by the priest.

The whole Israelite community and the aliens living among them will be forgiven, because all the people were involved in the unintentional wrong. (15:26)

Thus introduced is the concept of "solidarity in guilt," although God had already actually started his collective punishment policies within the framework of this understanding.

16, 17. The First Revolution in Monotheist History: Korah, Dathan and Abiram
People's rebellion reaches its peak (and its abyss) in the uprising of Korah, Dathan, and
Abiram[1] against Moses and Aaron & Sons. God suppresses the action bloodily.

> Korah, son of Izhar, the son of Kohath, the son of Levi, and certain Reubenites
> —Dathan and Abiram, sons of Eliab, and On son of Peleth—became insolent and
> rose up against Moses. With them were 250 Israelite men, well-known community
> leaders who had been appointed members of the council. They came as a group to
> oppose Moses and Aaron and said to them...

Three political leaders, Korah, Dathan and Abiram, that is, not obscure citizens or nameless
riffraff but pedigreed men from the social register of the sacred book, "rise up against" Moses and Aaron, the theo-political monocrat and the chief priest, respectively. With them are
250 Israelite men, again "well-known community leaders who had been appointed members of the council." They come as a group "to oppose" Moses and Aaron. This is not a mass
movement which mobilizes or consists entirely of sans-culottes; it is a sort of moderate
intra-elite protest, however, of considerable size (253 men).

"Rising up against" and "opposing" the powers-that-be are immediately equated by the
verbiage of the text with "becoming insolent" (or "taking men") against Moses and Aaron.
There is a group, a collective, action here to be sure, but no discernible, tight political organization or any premeditated violent deed. In other words, there is no concrete political act
of consequence here, in the strict sense of the term, e.g., any attempt at or threat of altering
the political status quo, of overthrowing the political regime or the persons who occupy political-administrative offices. There are, of course, certain demands and messages, but we
shall come to those later. To be noted is the fact that the text labels, as a reflex, this action as
a clear and present rebellion, which is in fact no more than a collective statement of opinion,
a sentiment, a voice of public conscience by a group of reputable citizens, in a way exercising
their freedom of thought and expression. The text occludes the difference between thought
and action; it collapses them. The opposition party has come just "to say" something. And
what do they say?

> "You have gone too far! The whole community is holy, every one them, and the
> LORD is with them. Why then do you set yourselves above the LORD's assembly?"

Now it becomes clear why the text finds their "opposition" "rebellious" and "insolent."[2]
The opposition party is questioning outright, but only discursively, the legitimacy of Moses's and Aaron's rule. They say that the rulers have exceeded limits, and they say it ele-
gantly: "You have gone too far." This is a beautiful way of employing the concept of
limitation and/or auto-limitation of power (or lack thereof). In fact these three short sentences archetypally capture the essence of power, legitimacy, authority, participation, equal-
ity/inequality, hierarchy, domination, and theopolitics, and God in politics. The group is

judging Moses's and Aaron's rule illegitimate according to the very source or "ground norm" from which the latter claim to derive their legitimacy: the Word, the Book of God.

The event is not, technically, a revolution; yet the act itself can be regarded as a "revolutionary" one in the adjectival sense, and especially in view of the fact that this is the first, the very first, instance in the whole Pentateuch heretofore of someone questioning the authority of rulers, from the patriarchal times to the now elaborately instituted theocracy of Mosaic Israel. Throughout Genesis, Exodus, Leviticus, and the first half of Numbers, the story is a surrealistically smooth one of total domination and perfect submission, which makes one recall Rousseau's question in the *Second Discourse*. Okay, everything started to go downhill once someone fenced his land, but why and how was it that nobody stood up and objected to it?

Here we do have the objection. And the consequences thereof. And the answer to why it could never happen again for ages to come. You don't question power, especially if it is based on God's word. You don't make democratic, egalitarian demands or contest an inegalitarian and anti-democratic order; you don't resist some men's "setting themselves above you." (Whether you are "the Lord's assembly" or not, is not for you to judge.) If you inquire, with Weber, whether that power is also legitimate, that is, whether it is authority proper, you are annihilated—as we shall shortly see. You don't question the given structure of power, the hierarchical elitocracy of Mosaic theocracy either: in descending order of holiness, God → Moses → Aaron & Sons → Levites → the rest of the tribe → women and children → dependent aliens → other nations → the last to be destroyed and plundered. If you do, *you* "go too far." And what, in that case, does Moses (and *his* God) do?

> When Moses heard this, he fell face down. Then he said to Korah and all his followers: "In the morning the LORD will show who belongs to him and who is holy, and he will have that person come near him. The man he chooses he will cause to come near him. You, Korah, and all your followers are to do this: Take censers and tomorrow put fire and incense in them before the LORD. The man the LORD chooses will be the one who is holy. You Levites have gone too far."
>
> Moses also said to Korah, "Now listen, you Levites! Isn't it enough for you that the God of Israel has separated you from the rest of the Israelite community and brought you near himself to do the work at the LORD's tabernacle and to stand before the community and minister to them? He has brought you and all your fellow Levites near himself, but now you are trying to get the priesthood too. It is against the LORD that you and all your followers have banded together. Who is Aaron that you should grumble against him?"

Of course Moses knows his God's word and His (and his) Book better than the protesters: "...the Lord will show who belongs to him and who is holy..." It is the optimistic illusion of believers, then and now, that "the whole community is holy," that "everyone one of them" is holy, and that "the Lord is with them" all. No, not all and every member of the species is equally holy and equally "near" to God in His eyes, as he will himself shortly declare in the same scripture on which the opposition party hopelessly think that they can base their case. No, once more: some are holier and nearer to the God. The notion and the hierarchy of "chosenness," undergirded by (degrees of) "holiness," is by its very nature exclusionary and inegalitarian. Once the very idea of God itself is posited,[3] you get not a community of equally valuable children, brothers and sisters, but you get pyramidal human organization, at the vortex of which sits the God and at the bases of which crawl the least holy: dependent aliens in the tribe and other nations within the species. The Bonapartist and populist asides, sidelines, charities and consolations of monotheistic religions especially, are not to be mistaken for egalitarian precepts. If that had been the case, or the intention of God and his messengers, these sacred books would not have been written like this—or they would not have been written at all. We shall return to this point.

Setting up the mis-en-scène, both physically and psychologically, with the aid of censers, fire, incense, and "coming near"-talk, Moses escalates his retaliation by isolating Korah the Levite for being a double ingrate: "You Levites have gone too far." And: "Isn't it enough for you that *the God of Israel has separated you from the rest of the Israelite Community* and brought you *near himself* to do the work at the Lord's tabernacle and to stand before the community and minister to them?"[4]

"Being nearer to God" (than other humans), therefore "being before the community," thus "ministering to them" and governing them…Now, does all this evoke and imply any egalitarian city of God, or is it an incontrovertible statement to the contrary—morally, socially, politically. It is just the reverse of Tocqueville's "moral or spiritual equality." And the Levites, crème de la crème, elect of the select, most-favored among the chosen, and so ad infinitum, should be content with

their sufficiently high, privileged position and must not aspire further up, offering a dangerous example to those further down on the spiritual, social, and political ladder, jeopardizing the stability of the theo-hierarchy. This is perfectly in conformity with the time-honored principle of distributive justice, where everybody knows his political, social, and human-spiritual station and value (and lesser value).

Moses scolds Korah and Levites for "trying to get the priesthood, too" (rebellion within rebellion?) despite the fact that this not among the opposition party's, or Korah's, utterings according to the text itself. This imputation is a quantum jump in inference by Moses. True, the critics are challenging the autocratic behavior of Moses and Aaron (& Sons), but they are not putting in an express demand for sharing the offices of priesthood.

Moses proceeds, in like manner, to equate "grumbling against Aaron" with "banding against the Lord," and there is a masterly rhetorical maneuver: "Who is Aaron that you should grumble against him?" Translation: Who are you to grumble against Aaron? And, therefore, against God? I will not go here into the merits and an analysis of the "grumbling tradition" or the "murmuring tradition" in the wilderness period or thereafter, nor into the "stiff-neckedness" of the chosen people in their Lord's eyes, but simply note that this is a very effective technique of statecraft, that is, declaring your greater proximity than others to the source of the highest, shared norm of legitimacy. (God chose us (Israelites) as his tribe, and God chose us (Moses and Aaron & Sons) as his ministers/administrators over you.) Also to be noted is the functionality of religion(s) and the idea of God for domination of few men over men and women.

> Then Moses summoned Dathan and Abiram, the sons of Eliab. But they said, "We will not come! Isn't it enough that you have brought us up out of a land flowing with milk and honey to kill us in the desert? And now you also want to lord it over us? Moreover, you haven't brought us into a land flowing with milk and honey or given us an inheritance of fields and vineyards. Will you gouge out the eyes of these men? No, we will not come!"

Dathan and Abiram, in an act of civil disobedience, refuse to comply with Moses's summons and bring in an economic dimension to the protest (another rebellion within rebellion?). Moses not only "lord(s) it over" them but also fails to deliver the goods—one of Weber's prerequisites for the charismatic leader to maintain his position in the eyes of his followers. And, of course, the text immediately turns this economic critique into its own advantage by implying that the protesters are stiff-necked ingrates, impatient to endure the material hardships of the long journey to the promised land, as well as skeptics who do not have full faith in the words of Moses and the Lord—a favorite, frequent theme of the *Old Testament* and grounds for severe punishment.

They not only fail to wait duly for the promised rewards; they also question the validity of the promise itself. This is tantamount to questioning the authority of Moses, and therefore, that of God. They make a case of being put in double jeopardy: political slavery compounded by economic slavery.[5] This makes them multiple-sinners. They have no "loyalty," they "voice" grievances, they even "exit" from the play. ("No, we will not come.")

> Then Moses became very angry and said to the LORD, "Do not accept their offering. I have not taken so much as a donkey from them, nor have I wronged any of them." Moses said to Korah, "You and all your followers are to appear before the LORD tomorrow—you—and they and Aaron. Each man is to take his censer and put incense in it—250 censers in all—and present it before the LORD. You and Aaron are to present your censers also." So each man took his censer, put fire and incense in it, and stood with Moses and Aaron at the entrance to the Tent of Meeting.

Moses gets very angry, and very unstraightforward, too. Although it was originally his idea, he contacts God beforehand and tells him not to accept the others' offering. This is not fair play; he pre-warns God and conditions him. A shepherd, in a sense, laying ambush for his flock. As for the declaimer of having taken anything from them or of having wronged them, one may refer back to the sacred text heretofore for the long list of tributes to the Tabernacle, the Tent, etc.

When Korah had gathered all his followers in opposition to them at the entrance to the Tent of Meeting, the glory of the LORD appeared to the entire assembly. The LORD said to Moses and Aaron, "Separate yourselves from this assembly so I can put an end to them at once."

But Moses and Aaron fell facedown and cried out, "O God, God of the spirits of all mankind, will you be angry with the entire assembly when only one man sins?"

Then the LORD said to Moses, "Say to the assembly, 'Move away from the tents of Korah, Dathan and Abiram.'"

Moses got up and went to Dathan and Abiram, and the elders of Israel followed him. He warned the assembly, "Move back from the tents of these wicked men! Do not touch anything belonging to them, or you will be swept away because of all their sins." So they moved away from the tents of Korah, Dathan and Abiram. Dathan and Abiram had come out and were standing with their wives, children and little ones at the entrances to their tents.

Then Moses said, "This is how you will know that the LORD has sent me to do all these things and that it was not my idea: If these men die a natural death and experience only what usually happens to men, then the LORD has not sent me. But if the LORD brings about something totally new, and the earth opens its mouth and swallows them, with everything that belongs to them, and they go down alive into the grave, then you will know these men have treated the LORD with contempt."

As soon as he finished saying all this, the ground under them split apart and the earth opened its mouth and swallowed them, with their households and all Korah's men and all their possessions. They went down alive into the grave, with everything they owned; the earth closed over them, and they perished and were gone from the community. At their cries, all the Israelites around them fled, shouting, "The earth is going to swallow us too!"

And fire came out from the LORD and consumed the 250 men who were offering the incense.

Whose God it is, whether of the holy all or of the holy few, becomes crystal clear. The Lord says to Moses and Aaron: "Separate yourselves from this [entire] assembly so I can put an end to them at once." Beware: not only the 253 rebels, but the "entire assembly." Moses and Aaron are so special and are to be obeyed so absolutely that, if necessary, God may dispense with all the rest of his chosen people. (We know what he does to other unchosen tribes and nations, too.) What a threat, what an ideology, what a politics. Obey or die! No questions, or else death. Extinction of the race, if necessary. Politics of fear of death, and then politics of killing, collective punishment, and genocide.

But since *some* people are necessary for practicing the business of government, so Moses and Aaron act less Mosaically than their more Mosaic than Moses God: the powers-that-be satisfy themselves by putting an end first to the 3 ringleaders and then to the 250 rebels. The rest of the community/assembly are not to touch any belongings of the sinners (another instance of control of bodies). "Moving away from the tents" of protesters is also a good example of the practice of isolating, of dividing and ruling.

An end is put to Korah, Dathan, Abiram, and to "their wives, children, and little ones." An end is put to them "with everything that belongs to them," "with their households and all (their) men and all their possessions," "with everything they owned," material and human. Punishment is severe but not individual; it covers dependents, too. (Often for generations to come.)

In Heinrich Böll's nice phrase "children are civilians, too." In this sacred text's wording, the "little ones," too, are apparently among political opponents or warring enemies, who also "treated the Lord with contempt." But of course a more effective dosage of politics of fear based on threat of death is the threat of killing one's children.

Moses "becomes very angry," but the Godly wrath, independently from Moses, is even more terrible, and very swift: it puts an end to them at once "bring(ing) about something totally new," something more than "what usually happens to men" in the form of natural death. "… the earth opens its mouth and swallows them … and they go down alive into the grave." The exceptionality and supernaturalness of the punishment fortifies Moses's "legitimacy": "This is how you will know that the lord has sent me to do all these things…" In other words, Moses cannot "go too far"; he has unlimited power which is also unquestionable authority, that is, legitimate power, sanctioned by God and the mission He has given him. Only people can "go too far."

And all this is not "his idea" but "His idea." Impeccable theistic legitimizing ideology, which is hemmed in by a circular argumentation: If the rebels do not die a supernatural death, "then the lord has not sent me." The lesson of politics of fear and death is not lost on the Israelites, who, at the cries of the perishing ones, "fled, shouting: 'The earth is going to swallow us too'."

The LORD said to Moses, "Tell Eleazar son of Aaron, the priest, to take the censers out of the smoldering remains and scatter the coals some distance away, for the censers are holy–the censers of the men who sinned at the cost of their lives. Hammer the censers into sheets to overlay the altar, for they were presented before the LORD and have become holy. Let them be a sign to the Israelites."

So Eleazar the priest collected the bronze censers brought by those who had been burned up, and he had them hammered out to overlay the altar, as the LORD directed him through Moses. This was to remind the Israelites that no one except a descendant of Aaron should come to burn incense before the LORD or he would become like Korah and his followers.

The mass execution is to be remembered by and reminded to generations to come. Hammered censers will be hammered into the collective memory as a durable "sign to the Israelites" that Aaron's descendants are nearest to the God of the chosen people.

The next day the whole Israelite community grumbled against Moses and Aaron. "You have killed the LORD's people," they said.

But when the assembly gathered in opposition to Moses and Aaron and turned toward the Tent of Meeting, suddenly the cloud covered it and the glory of the LORD appeared. Then Moses and Aaron went to the front of the Tent of Meeting, and the LORD said to Moses, "Get away from this assembly so I can put an end to them at once." And they fell face down.

Then Moses said to Aaron, "Take your censer and put incense in it, along with fire from the altar, and hurry to the assembly to make atonement for them. Wrath has come out from the LORD; the plague has started." So Aaron did as Moses said, and ran into the midst of the assembly. The plague had already started among the people, but Aaron offered the incense and made atonement for them. He stood between the living and the dead, and the plague stopped. But 14,700 people died from the plague, in addition to those who had died because of Korah. Then Aaron returned to Moses at the entrance to the Tent of Meeting, for the plague had stopped.

The next day, however, the lesson seems to be somewhat lost on the Israelites. They again grumble against Moses and Aaron for having killed the Lord's people. They have not yet realized that grumbling against Moses and Aaron is the same thing as grumbling against God, and that the people are the Lord's but the Lord is not the people's but of Moses and Aaron. The Lord had said as much: Moses and Aaron to one side, the rest of the community to the other. And he repeats it: "Get away from this assembly so I can put an end to them at once."

Although Moses and Aaron attempt at forestalling another massacre, "Wrath has [already] come out from the Lord; the plague has started." God is more Mosaic than Moses. By the time Moses and Aaron manage to stop the plague, another 14,700 people die, in addition to the previous 253 times their households (several tens of thousands in toto?).

The message is clear. Not only political activists and their households, but sympathizers, too, shall be killed. A sure way of depoliticizing society. Nor does the text offer any hint of regret on the part of Moses and Aaron that they could not keep the death toll at a lower level.

The devastating message of Chapter 16 has sunk well in Judaic, Christian, and Islamic political theory: Rebellion or revolution against God's "chosen rulers" is a cardinal sin and is punished severely. The divine right of kings and sultans is not to be questioned for millennia, for they are the most holy. As God says in Chapter 17: "The staff belonging to the man I chose will sprout, and I will rid myself of this constant grumbling against you by the Israelites" (and by the Christians and Moslems, we may add).[6]

18. Duties of Priests and Levites (And Their Revenues)

God tells Aaron that he and his sons are solely to bear responsibility for offenses against the sanctuary and the priesthood, which he gives to Aaron & Sons "as a gift" (18:7). God also takes care of Aaron & Sons' livelihood, and capital accumulation.

Then the LORD said to Aaron, "I myself have put you in charge of the offerings presented to me; all the holy offerings the Israelites give me I give to you and your sons as your portion and regular share. You are to have the part of the most holy offerings that is kept from the fire. From all the gifts they bring me as most holy offerings, whether grain or sin or guilt offerings, that part belongs to you and your sons. Eat it as something most holy; every male shall eat it. You must regard it as holy.

"This also is yours: whatever is set aside from the gifts of all the wave offerings of the Israelites. I give this to you and your sons and daughters as your regular share. Everyone in your household who is ceremonially clean may eat it.

I give you all the finest olive oil and all the finest new wine and grain they give the LORD as the firstfruits of their harvest. All the land's firstfruits that they bring to the LORD will be yours. Everyone in your household who is ceremonially clean may eat it.

"Everything in Israel that is devoted to the LORD is yours. The first offspring of every womb, both man and animal, that is offered to the LORD is yours. But you must redeem every firstborn son and every firstborn male of unclean animals. When they are a month old, you must redeem them at the redemption price set at five shekels of silver, according to the sanctuary shekel, which weighs twenty gerahs.

"But you must not redeem the firstborn of an ox, a sheep or a goat; they are holy. Sprinkle their blood on the altar and burn their fat as an offering made by fire, an aroma pleasing to the LORD. Their meat is to be yours, just as the breast of the wave offering and the right thigh are yours. Whatever is set aside from the holy offerings the Israelites present to the LORD I give to you and your sons and daughters as your regular share. It is an everlasting covenant of salt before the LORD for both you and your offspring."

The LORD said to Aaron, "You will have no inheritance in their land, nor will you have any share among them; I am your share and your inheritance among the Israelites.

"I give to the Levites all the tithes in Israel as their inheritance in return for the work they do while serving at the Tent of Meeting. From now on the Israelites must not go near the Tent of Meeting, or they will bear the consequences of their sin and will die. It is the Levites who are to do the work at the Tent of Meeting and bear the responsibility for offenses against it. This is a lasting ordinance for the generations to come. They will receive no inheritance among the Israelites. Instead, I give to the

Levites as their inheritance the tithes that the Israelites present as an offering to the LORD. That is why I said concerning them: 'They will have no inheritance among the Israelites.' " (18:8-24)

In sum: "Everything in Israel that is devoted to the LORD is yours" (18:14). Why? And why not "inheritance in land?" (Plato's guardians? Or an occlusion of the comprehensive taxation and large public revenues?)

At any rate, note the interconnection of "most holy" and "every male shall eat it" (gender differentiation even in "eating"), and the commodification of sons of men like offsprings of animals.

Levites, too, are taxpayers to the Aaronite high priesthood:

The LORD said to Moses, "Speak to the Levites and say to them: 'When you receive from the Israelites the tithe I give you as your inheritance, you must present a tenth of that tithe as the LORD's offering.

Your offering will be reckoned to you as grain from the threshing floor or juice from the winepress. In this way you also will present an offering to the LORD from all the tithes you receive from the Israelites. From these tithes you must give the LORD's portion to Aaron the priest. You must present as the LORD's portion the best and holiest part of everything given to you.'

"Say to the Levites: 'When you present the best part, it will be reckoned to you as the product of the threshing floor or the winepress. You and your households may eat the rest of it anywhere, for it is your wages for your work at the Tent of Meeting.

By presenting the best part of it you will not be guilty in this matter; then you will not defile the holy offerings of the Israelites, and you will not die.' " (18:25-32)

19, 20, 21. Waters, Grumbles, Destructions

People again grumble against Moses and Aaron for lack of water, comparing "this terrible place" (20:5) with Egypt. God instructs, Moses performs and brings water.

But the LORD said to Moses and Aaron, "Because you did not trust in me enough to honor me as holy in the sight of the Israelites, you will not bring this community into the land I give them." (20:12)

The Edomites deny passage to the Israelites, the latter change route, God commands Aaron's death.

When the Canaanite king of Arad, who lived in the Negev, heard that Israel was coming along the road to Atharim, he attacked the Israelites and captured some of them. Then Israel made this vow to the LORD: "If you will deliver these people into our hands, we will totally destroy their cities." The LORD listened to Israel's plea and gave the Canaanites over to them. They completely destroyed them and their towns; so the place was named Hormah. (21:1-3)

People grumble again, God sends venomous snakes, "many Israelites die" (21:6).

The Israelites' itinerary is given, the Amorites deny passage, they are put to the sword, Israel "capture(s) all the cities of the Amorites and occup(ies) them." Quotations from the "Book of the Wars of the Lord" are offered (21:14, 21:25). Cities are burned, people are consumed and destroyed, sons become fugitives, daughters captives. Then comes the turn of the Basharistes:

> The LORD said to Moses, "Do not be afraid of him, for I have handed him over to you, with his whole army and his land. Do to him what you did to Sihon king of the Amorites, who reigned in Heshbon."
>
> So they struck him down, together with his sons and his whole army, leaving them no survivors. And they took possession of his land. (21:34-35)

22, 23, 24, 25. Balak, Balaam, Moabites

Now, the Moabites are apprehensive about the approaching Israelite danger and seek Balaam's assistance and ask Balaam to curse them, but God prevents Balaam from doing so.

Instead, God instructs Balaam to give the following messages to the Moabites. I let the poetic text speak for itself:

> How can I curse those whom God has not cursed?
> How can I denounce those whom the LORD has not denounced?
> From the rocky peaks I see them, from the heights I view them.
> I see a people who live apart and do not consider themselves one of the nations.
> Who can count the dust of Jacob or number the fourth part of Israel?
> Let me die the death of the righteous, and may my end be like theirs! (23:8-10)

And:

> God is not a man, that he should lie, nor a son of man, that he should change his mind. Does he speak and then not act? Does he promise and not fulfill?
> I have received a command to bless; he has blessed, and I cannot change it.
> No misfortune is seen in Jacob, no misery observed in Israel.
> The LORD their God is with them; the shout of the King is among them.
> God brought them out of Egypt; they have the strength of a wild ox.
> There is no sorcery against Jacob, no divination against Israel.
> It will now be said of Jacob and of Israel, 'See what God has done!'
> The people rise like a lioness, they rouse themselves like a lion that does not rest till he devours his prey and drinks the blood of his victims (23:19-24)

And:

> Water will flow from their buckets; their seed will have abundant water.
> Their king will be greater than Agag; their kingdom will be exalted.
> God brought them out of Egypt; they have the strength of a wild ox.

They devour hostile nations and break their bones in pieces; with their arrows they pierce them.

Like a lion they crouch and lie down, like a lioness—who dares to rouse them?

May those who bless you be blessed and those who curse you be cursed! (24:7-9)

Summary: A God who gives "no misfortune" and "no misery" (none really!) and a chosen people of a wild ox "who live apart and do not consider themselves one of the nations" and who, as a result of God's blessing, "do not rest till they devour their prey and drink the blood of their victims" and break hostile nations' "bones in pieces" and crush the foreheads and skulls of enemies.

A star will come out of Jacob; a scepter will rise out of Israel. He will crush the foreheads of Moab, the skulls of all the sons of Sheth.

Edom will be conquered; Seir, his enemy, will be conquered, but Israel will grow strong. A ruler will come out of Jacob and destroy the survivors of the city. (24:17-19)

Even if the Israelites are trying to overcome their own fear by a psychology of pretending to be more frightening than fright itself, can this possibly evolve into a humanistic morality, let alone peaceful relations? And thank the law of statistics, orthodox Judaism is not the official religion of a strong world-state.

Israelite men "indulge in sexual immorality" (25:1) with Moabite women and begin to worship their gods, God tells Moses to "(t)ake all the leaders of these people (and) kill them" (25:4), Moses delegates this to Israel's judges, God sends a plague anyway, "those who died in the plague numbered 24,000" (25:9), it could have been higher had Eleazar not turned God's anger away by killing a man and a Midianite woman.

26. The Second Census

After the plague God commands Moses and Aaron to take a second census on the model of the first one: "The total number of the men of Israel was 601,730" (26:51). (It was 603,550 in the first census.) (Death rate greater than birth rate, due to mass killings along the way.)

The promised land is to be distributed by lot according to this census of tribes.

The LORD said to Moses, "The land is to be allotted to them as an inheritance based on the number of names. To a larger group give a larger inheritance, and to a smaller group a smaller one; each is to receive its inheritance according to the number of those listed. Be sure that the land is distributed by lot. What each group inherits will be according to the names for its ancestral tribe. Each inheritance is to be distributed by lot among the larger and smaller groups." (26:52-56)

Levites are "set apart" again:

All the male Levites a month old or more numbered 23,000. They were not counted along with the other Israelites because they received no inheritance among them.

These are the ones counted by Moses and Eleazar the priest when they counted the Israelites on the plains of Moab by the Jordan across from Jericho. *Not one of them was among those counted by Moses and Aaron the priest when they counted the Israelites in the Desert of Sinai. For the LORD had told those Israelites they would surely die in the desert, and not one of them was left except Caleb son of Jephunneh and Joshua son of Nun.* (26:62-65)

My commentary here is my emphasis.

27. Zelophehad's Daughters; Notice of Death to Moses

"Say to the Israelites, 'If a man dies and leaves no son, turn his inheritance over to his daughter. If he has no daughter, give his inheritance to his brothers. If he has no brothers, give his inheritance to his father's brothers. If his father had no brothers, give his inheritance to the nearest relative in his clan, that he may possess it. This is to be a legal requirement for the Israelites, as the LORD commanded Moses.' " (27:8-11)

God gives Moses, too, notice of death, and Moses says to him:

Moses said to the LORD, "May the LORD, the God of the spirits of all mankind, appoint a man over this community to go out and come in before them, one who will lead them out and bring them in, so the LORD's people will not be like sheep without a shepherd."

So the LORD said to Moses, "Take Joshua son of Nun, a man in whom is the spirit, and lay your hand on him. Have him stand before Eleazar the priest and the entire assembly and commission him in their presence. Give him some of your authority so the whole Israelite community will obey him. He is to stand before Eleazar the priest, who will obtain decisions for him by inquiring of the Urim before the LORD. At his command he and the entire community of the Israelites will go out, and at his command they will come in."

Moses did as the LORD commanded him. He took Joshua and had him stand before Eleazar the priest and the whole assembly. Then he laid his hands on him and commissioned him, as the LORD instructed through Moses. (27:15-23)

Appointment of "a man over this community" so that the Lord's people will "not be like sheep without a sheperd"; giving to this man "some of" Moses's "authority" so that the "whole Israelite community will obey him." In short, domination and legitimation of power. In Weber's terms, authority as legitimate power. And the source of legitimacy is God's Word, the word of, say, John Locke's "infinitely wise Maker." Western political theory, or more specifically liberal natural-rights theory, is not very secular: The political ruler "is to stand before Eleazar the priest, who will obtain decisions for him by inquiring of the Urim before the LORD." Please also note the beginnings of the structural differentiation and functional specialization of shepherdly offices: From Moses the Prophet-Ruler to Eleazar the priest and Joshua the political leader, who nevertheless still gets his legitimacy from a divine source. Theocracy only loosening a bit.

28, 29, 30. Offerings, Feasts, Vows

Daily, Sabbath, Monthly, Passover, Feast of Weeks offerings are specified/repeated.

Moses said to the heads of the tribes of Israel: "This is what the LORD commands: When a man makes a vow to the LORD or takes an oath to obligate himself by a pledge, he must not break his word but must do everything he said.

When a young woman still living in her father's house makes a vow to the LORD or obligates herself by a pledge and her father hears about her vow or pledge but says nothing to her, then all her vows and every pledge by which she obligated herself will stand. But if her father forbids her when he hears about it, none of her vows or the pledges by which she obligated herself will stand; the LORD will release her because her father has forbidden her.

If she marries after she makes a vow or after her lips utter a rash promise by which she obligates herself and her husband hears about it but says nothing to her, then her vows or the pledges by which she obligated herself will stand. But if her husband forbids her when he hears about it, he nullifies the vow that obligates her or the rash promise by which she obligates herself, and the LORD will release her.

Any vow or obligation taken by a widow or divorced woman will be binding on her.

If a woman living with her husband makes a vow or obligates herself by a pledge under oath and her husband hears about it but says nothing to her and does not forbid her, then all her vows or the pledges by which she obligated herself will stand. But if her husband nullifies them when he hears about them, then none of the vows or pledges that came from her lips will stand. Her husband has nullified them, and the LORD will release her. Her husband may confirm or nullify any vow she makes or any sworn pledge to deny herself. But if her husband says nothing to her about it from day to day, then he confirms all her vows or the pledges binding on her. He confirms them by saying nothing to her when he hears about them. If, however, he nullifies them some time after he hears about them, then he is responsible for her guilt."

These are the regulations the LORD gave Moses concerning relationships between a man and his wife, and between a father and his young daughter still living in his house. (30:1-16)

In short, women, daughters and wives, are subjugated to men's will, fathers and husbands, as shall be the case with the *New Testament* and the *Koran*. Please also note the emergence of the principle of pacta sunt servanda in the first sentence of the passage, long after the Simon & Levi affair.

31.Vengeance and Plunder

God instructs Moses "to take vengeance" on the Midianites before he dies; 12,000 men fight the latter and "kill...every man" (31:7). Non-vengeance is an in-tribe moral injunction; it does not extend to other tribes.

> The Israelites captured the Midianite women and children and took all the Midianite herds, flocks and goods as plunder. They burned all the towns where the Midianites had settled, as well as all their camps. They took all the plunder and spoils, including the people and animals, and brought the captives, spoils and plunder to Moses and Eleazar the priest and the Israelite assembly at their camp on the plains of Moab, by the Jordan across from Jericho. (31:9-12)

Booty since Egypt is accumulating, but more virgins are wanted. Moses is angry with the officers:

> "Have you allowed all the women to live?" he asked them. "They were the ones who followed Balaam's advice and were the means of turning the Israelites away from the LORD in what happened at Peor, so that a plague struck the LORD's people. Now kill all the boys. And kill every women who has slept with a men, but save for yourselves every girl who has never slept with a man." (31:15-18)

Moses was one of the boys who had escaped wholesale murder of boys. As for dividing the spoils, people and animals, here are Moses's instructions:

> The LORD said to Moses, "You and Eleazar the priest and the family heads of the community are to count all the people and animals that were captured. Divide the spoils between the soldiers who took part in the battle and the rest of the community. From the soldiers who fought in the battle, set apart as tribute for the LORD one out of every five hundred, whether persons, cattle, donkeys, sheep or goats. Take this tribute from their half share and give it to Eleazar the priest as the LORD's part.
>
> From the Israelites' half, select one out of every fifty, whether persons, cattle, donkeys, sheep, goats or other animals. Give them to the Levites, who are responsible for the care of the LORD's tabernacle. So Moses and Eleazar the priest did as the LORD commanded Moses. (31:25-31)

If 1000 pieces of booty, then:

- 1/500 to Eleazar as the Lord's part = 1 piece
- 1/50 to the Levites for their services = 10 pieces

"Pieces," "whether persons, cattle, donkeys, sheep, goats or other animals."

As for the magnitude of the spoils, here is the inventory in this case, to which the above general formula is to be applied:

The plunder remaining from the spoils that the soldiers took was 675,000 sheep, 72,000 cattle, 61,000 donkeys and 32,000 women who had never slept with a man. The half share of those who fought in the battle was:

337,500 sheep, of which the tribute for the LORD was 675;

36,000 cattle, of which the tribute for the LORD was 72;

30,500 donkeys, of which the tribute for the LORD was 61;

16,000 people, of which the tribute for the LORD was 32.

Moses gave the tribute to Eleazar the priest as the LORD's part, as the LORD commanded Moses.

The half belonging to the Israelites, which Moses set apart from that of the fighting men—the community's half—was 337,500 sheep, 36,000 cattle, 30,500 donkeys and 16,000 people. From the Israelites' half, Moses selected one out of every fifty persons and animals, as the LORD commanded him, and gave them to the Levites, who were responsible for the care of the LORD's tabernacle.

Then the officers who were over the units of the army—the commanders of thousands and commanders of hundreds—went to Moses and said to him, "Your servants have counted the soldiers under our command, and not one is missing. So we have brought as an offering to the LORD the gold articles each of us acquired—armlets, bracelets, signet rings, earrings and necklaces—to make atonement for ourselves before the LORD."

Moses and Eleazar the priest accepted from them the gold—all the crafted articles. All the gold from the commanders of thousands and commanders of hundreds that Moses and Eleazar presented as a gift to the LORD weighed 16,750 shekels.[7] Each soldier had taken plunder for himself. Moses and Eleazar the priest accepted the gold from the commanders of thousands and commanders of hundreds and brought it into the Tent of Meeting as a memorial for the Israelites before the LORD.

Beware the above ordering: sheep, cattle, donkeys, people—and human beings to be divided as spoils just like animals. And note the inflow of gold to the hands of God, prophet, and priests.

32. The Transjordan Tribes

In asking for land from Moses, the tribal chiefs address Moses as: "We, your servants" (32:35).

Tribes of Reuben and Gad are given land in the Transjordan.

33. Stages in Israel's Journey
Israel's journey is given in stages: "They left _____ and camped at _____." Over 40 stops are mentioned by name. God repeats his instructions: driving out all the inhabitants, destroying all their idols, and so forth.

34. Boundaries of Canaan
God draws the map:

North: Hazar

West: Coast of the Great Sea   *East:* Galilee

South: Wadi of Egypt

The promised land is to be given—as inheritance and by lot—to nine and a half tribes:
  12 tribes minus: tribe of Reuben
                tribe of Gad
                half-tribe of Manasseh
One leader from each tribe is appointed to help assign the land.

35. Towns for Levites and Cities of Refuge
The Levites, too, are to have their own towns and pastureland: Six of these towns are to be "cities of refuge, to which a person who has killed someone may flee" (35:6). The total number of towns to be given to the Levites from the inheritance of the Israelites will be forty eight. Six cities of refuge also for the other Israelites,

> ...to which a person who has killed someone accidentally may flee. They will be places of refuge from the avenger, so that a person accused of murder may not die before he stands trial before the assembly.
>
> If a man strikes someone with an iron object so that he dies, he is a murderer; the murderer shall be put to death. Or if anyone has a stone in his hand that could kill, and he strikes someone so that he dies, he is a murderer; the murderer shall be put to death. Or if anyone has a wooden object in his hand that could kill, and he hits someone so that he dies, he is a murderer; the murderer shall be put to death. The avenger of blood shall put the murderer to death; when he meets him, he shall put him to death. If anyone with malice aforethought shoves another or throws something at him intentionally so that he dies or if in hostility he hits him with his fist so that he dies, that person shall be put to death; he is a murderer. The avenger of blood shall put the murderer to death when he meets him.
>
> But if without hostility someone suddenly shoves another or throws something at him unintentionally or, without seeing him, drops a stone on him that could kill him, and he dies, then since he was not his enemy and he did not intend to harm him, the assembly must judge between him and the avenger of blood according to

these regulations. The assembly must protect the one accused of murder from the avenger of blood and send him back to the city of refuge to which he fled. He must stay there until the death of the high priest, who was anointed with the holy oil.

But if the accused ever goes outside the limits of the city of refuge to which he has fled and the avenger of blood finds him outside the city, the avenger of blood may kill the accused without being guilty of murder. The accused must stay in his city of refuge until the death of the high priest; only after the death of the high priest may he return to his own property.

These are to be legal requirements for you throughout the generations to come, wherever you live.

Anyone who kills a person is to be put to death as a murderer only on the testimony of witnesses. But no one is to be put to death on the testimony of only one witness.

Do not accept a ransom for the life of a murderer, who deserves to die. He must surely be put to death.

Do not accept a ransom for anyone who has fled to a city of refuge and so allow him to go back and live on his own land before the death of the high priest.

Do not pollute the land where you are. Bloodshed pollutes the land, and atonement cannot be made for the land on which blood has been shed, except by the blood of the one who shed it. Do no defile the land where you live and where I dwell, for I, the LORD, dwell among the Israelites. (35:11-34)

Well, monopoly of legitimate violence (murder) belongs to the state (God), Weber shall much later say.

36. Inheritance of Daughters

The family heads address Moses thus: "When the LORD commanded my Lord (Moses)..." (36:2), and they demand that sonless father's daughters who are given inheritance should not marry husbands from other tribes so that their ancestral land and property will not be "taken from the tribal inheritance of our forefathers" (36:4).

Then at the LORD's command Moses gave this order to the Israelites: "What the tribe of the descendants of Joseph is saying is right. This is what the LORD commands for Zelophehad's daughters: They may marry anyone they please as long as they marry within the tribal clan of their father. No inheritance in Israel is to pass from tribe to tribe, for every Israelite shall keep the tribal land inherited from his forefathers. Every daughter who inherits land in any Israelite tribe must marry someone in her father's tribal clan, so that every Israelite will possess the inheritance of his fathers. No inheritance may pass from tribe to tribe, for each Israelite tribe is to keep the land it inherits." (36:5-9)

Zelophehad's five daughters marry their cousins on their father's side.

POSTSCRIPT TO NUMBERS

This is Numbers; these are the numbers that do not matter to God as worthy/holy human beings, but who do matter to the chosen rulers as so many soldiers and taxpayers.

These are the numbers who murmur and grumble, who are chronically annihilated together with their "little ones." "Who are they"—those stiff-necked multitude—to question the rule of God's few chosen rulers? Who are they not to endure—mind you: not the hardships of life, but—those rulers' lording it over them?

And this is Numbers, especially Chapter 16, which is the first tract par excellence of the theory of power-politics of fear and death, and of an inegalitarian, hierarchical, anti-democratic form of government.

These are the numbers who are not subjects of a supposedly more modern "stato" with its own mechanical "ragione" or a "Leviathan" with its mechanistic-psychological absolutism, but subjects of a supposedly more traditional theocracy, albeit fully equipped with all the modern devices of domination, power, legitimacy, authority, etc., etc., etc.,—only divine, Godly legitimation being the foundation of domination and oppression.

And: a people (that is, its appointed rulers) killing its own children within and a people "drinking the blood of his victims" without—both with the blessing of its loving and compassionate God. Such is one of the uses of monotheism.

That the whole community is holy is a delusion; the reality is that only the few who are "set apart" are really holy; the rest, all of them, can be forsaken at one stroke. This is not a brotherhood of equals. Nor shall such be in Christianity or Islam. Individual human beings are not an end in themselves; they are means. In fact, commodities. There are only some functional, tribal, customary rules here. No general, generalized, generalizable moral laws.

Notes

1. Please note that Korah is Esau's son; Dathan and Abiram are brothers, "community officials," and "followers" of Korah (Numbers, 26: 8-9).

2. Please note that the original text itself says "insolence," "opposition," "rising up" (uprising?), but not "rebellion," let alone "revolution," as was to be done by later theological interpretation—pejoratively, to be sure.

3. What is in a way overdetermined in monotheistic religions is true for theism in general. Without exempting Eastern religions, remember that the Ancient Greek theology, as exemplified in Plato's *Republic*, had its own hierarchy starting with gods, if not the God: god(s), → demigods, → heroes, → philosopher kings, → guardians, → citizens (male), → women, → children, → non-citizen males, → slaves.

4. Emphases mine. In courts, sometimes the counsel says: "Thank you, I have no further comment" or just "Thank you."

5. "Gouging out eyes of men" also means, according to the *Holy Bible*, deceiving or enslaving. In the textual versions used in the *Interpreter's Bible* "putting out the eyes of men" is said to mean "throwing dust in their eyes." And this source comments: "Moses is rightly angered."

6. Please note that Korah is condemned throughout the Abrahamic triology: in the *Old Testament* (e.g., Deuteronomy 11:6), in the *New Testament* (e.g., 2 Timothy, Hebrews, Jude), in the *Koran*.

7. That is, about 420 pounds (about 190 kilograms).

DEUTERONOMY

1, 2, 3. Leaving Horeb, Wandering in the Desert, Defeating Enemies, Dividing the Land

"East of the Jordan in the territory of Moab, Moses began to expound this law, saying" (1:5):

> At that time I said to you, "You are too heavy a burden for me to carry alone. The LORD your God has increased your numbers so that today you are as many as the stars in the sky. May the LORD, the God of your fathers, increase you a thousand times and bless you as he has promised. But how can I bear your problems and your burdens and your disputes all by myself? Choose some wise, understanding and respected men from each of your tribes, and I will set them over you."
>
> You answered me, "What you propose to do is good."
>
> So I took the leading men of your tribes, wise and respected men, and appointed them to have authority over you—as commanders of thousands, of hundreds, of fifties and of tens and as tribal officials. And I charged your judges at that time: Hear the disputes between your brothers and judge fairly, whether the case is between brother Israelites or between one of them and an alien. Do not show partiality in judging; hear both small and great alike. Do not be afraid of any man, for judgment belongs to God. Bring me any case too hard for you, and I will hear it. And at that time I told you everything you were to do. (1:9-18)

"Wise men" to "have authority over" people; no partiality in judging the small and the great, the poor and the rich (equality before the law?[1]). This is the basic political and legal theory of the *Old Testament*.

Local kings are defeated, for God "fights for his people," as he does in the *Koran*.

> This very day I will begin to put the terror and fear of you on all the nations under heaven. They will hear reports of you and will tremble and be in anguish because of you. (2:25)

And:

When Sihon and all his army came out to meet us in battle at Jahaz, the LORD our God delivered him over to us and we struck him down, together with his sons and his whole army. At that time we took all his towns and completely destroyed them—men, women and children. We left no survivors. But the livestock and the plunder from the towns we had captured we carried off for ourselves. (2:33-35)

Same with other kingdoms and peoples. Not Moses but Joshua to lead the Israelites into the promised land.

4. Obedience Commanded (To the Absolute Text)

Hear now, O Israel, the decrees and laws I am about to teach you. Follow them so that you may live and may go in and take possession of the land that the LORD, the God of your fathers, is giving you. Do not add to what I command you and do not subtract from it, but keep the commands of the LORD your God that I give you. (4:1-2)

Absolute obedience to the absolute text (the Law, the *Torah*) is commanded so that one may live, to start with:

"Do not add to what I command you and do not subtract from it."

Compare with the *New Testament*, Revelation 22: 18-19:

I warn everyone who hears the words of the prophecy of this book: If anyone adds anything to them, God will add to him the plagues described in this book. And if anyone takes words away from this book of prophecy, God will take away from him his share in the tree of life and in the holy city, which are described in this book.

In view of this, really, what is orthodoxy, conservatism, reformism in Judaism? Or, for that matter, in Christianity and Islam? And what is, really, the room for and range of interpretation (and belief) in religious texts, books, laws, which are absolute texts—absolute because religious, or better, because Godly.[2]

You saw with your own eyes what the LORD did at Baal Peor. The LORD your God destroyed from among you everyone who followed the Baal of Peor, but all of you who held fast to the LORD your God are still alive today.

See, I have taught you decrees and laws as the LORD my God commanded me, so that you may follow them in the land you are entering to take possession of it. Observe them carefully, for this will show your wisdom and understanding to the nations, who will hear about all these decrees and say, "Surely this great nation is a wise and understanding people." What other nation is so great as to have their gods near them the way the LORD our God is near us whenever we pray to him. And what other nation is so great as to have such righteous decrees and laws as this body of laws I am setting before you today? (4:3-8)

> You came near and stood at the foot of the mountain while it blazed with fire to the very heavens, with black clouds and deep darkness. Then the LORD spoke to you out of the fire. You heard the sound of words but saw no form; there was only a voice. He declared to you his covenant, the Ten Commandments, which he commanded you to follow and then wrote them on two stone tablets. And the LORD directed me at that time to teach you the decrees and laws you are to follow in the land that you are crossing the Jordan to possess. (4:11-14)

Observing decrees and laws is a proof of "wisdom and understanding," "greatness," and "nearness to God," the last being a mixed blessing: delusion of security and fear *and* trembling.

A sense of righteousness, or self-righteousness, is felt amidst a decor of fire, etc. No form (of God) is seen; a voice and the sound of words are heard—no additions and subtractions are allowed. Threat of imminent death hovers above.

Idolatry is forbidden, the covenant should not be forgotten, if forgotten God will destroy, if obeyed "he will not abandon or destroy...(f)or the LORD your God is a merciful God" (4:31). God reminds the Israelites of his power and affection: "Has any god ever tried to take for himself one nation out of another nation, by testings, by miraculous signs and wonders, by war, by a mighty hand and an outstretched arm, or by great and awesome deeds..." (4:34). This great theme of physical proximity and omnipresence shall be refined to perfection by Christianity ("inside your heart") and Islam ("closer than your own jugular vein").

> You were shown these things so that you might know that the LORD is God; besides him there is no other. From heaven he made you hear his voice to discipline you. On earth he showed you his great fire, and you heard his words from out of the fire. Because he loved your forefathers and chose their descendants after them, he brought you out of Egypt by his Presence and his great strength, to drive out before you nations greater and stronger than you and to bring you into their land to give it to you for your inheritance, as it is today.
>
> Acknowledge and take to heart this day that the LORD is God in heaven above and on the earth below. There is no other. Keep his decrees and commands, which I am giving you today, so that it may go well with you and your children after you and that you may live long in the land the LORD your God gives you for all time. (4:35-40)

A mighty hand stretched out, presumably, to grip the stiff neck. Discipline and punish. By death, if necessary.

5. The Ten Commandments Repeated
Moses summons all Israel and, "standing between" God and people says:

Hear, O Israel, the decrees and laws I declare in your hearing today. Learn them and be sure to follow them. The LORD our God made a covenant with us at Horeb. It was not with our fathers that the LORD made this covenant, but with us, with all of us who are alive here today. The LORD spoke to you face to face out of the fire on the mountain. (At that time I stood between the LORD and you to declare to you the word of the LORD, because you were afraid of the fire and did not go up the mountain.)

And he said:

Exodus 20:2-17

I am the LORD your God, who brought you out of Egypt, out of the land of slavery.

You shall have no other gods before me.

You shall not make for yourself an idol in the form of anything in heaven above or on the earth beneath or in the waters below. You shall not bow down to them or worship them; for I, the LORD your God, am a jealous God, punishing the children for the sin of the fathers to the third and fourth generation of those who hate me, but showing love to a thousand generations of those who love me and keep my commandments.

You shall not misuse the name of the LORD your God, for the LORD will not hold anyone guiltless who misuses his name.

Remember the Sabbath day by keeping it holy. Six days you shall labor and do all your work, but the seventh day is a Sabbath to the LORD your God. On it you shall not do any work, neither you, nor your son or daughter, nor your manservant or maidservant, nor your animals, nor the alien within your gates. For in six days the LORD made the heavens and the earth, the sea, and all that is in them, but he

Deuteronomy 5:6-21

I am the LORD your God, who brought you out of Egypt, out of the land of slavery.

You shall have no other gods before me.

You shall not make for yourself an idol in the form of anything in heaven above or on the earth beneath or in the waters below. You shall not bow down to them or worship them; for I, the LORD your God, am a jealous God, punishing the children for the sin of the fathers to the third and fourth generation of those who hate me, but showing love to a thousand generations of those who love me and keep my commandments.

You shall not misuse the name of the LORD your God, for the LORD will not hold anyone guiltless who misuses his name.

Observe the Sabbath day by keeping it holy, *as the LORD your God has commanded you.* Six days you shall labor and do all your work, but the seventh day is a Sabbath to the LORD your God. On it you shall not do any work, neither you, nor your son or daughter, nor your manservant or maidservant, nor *your ox, your donkey or any of your animals,* nor the alien within your gates, *so that your manservant* rested on the seventh day. Therefore the LORD blessed the Sabbath day and made it holy.

and maidservant may rest, as you do. Remember that you were slaves in Egypt and that the LORD your God brought you out of there with a mighty hand and an outstretched arm. Therefore the LORD your God has commanded you to observe the Sabbath day.

Honor your father and your mother, so that you may live long in the land the LORD your God is giving you.

Honor your father and your mother, *as the LORD your God has commanded you*, so that you may live long *and that it may go well with you* in the land the LORD your God is giving you.

You shall not murder.

You shall not commit adultery.

You shall not steal.

You shall not give false testimony against your neighbor.

You shall not covet your neighbor's house. You shall not covet your neighbor's wife, or his manservant or maidservant, his ox or donkey, or anything that belongs to your neighbor.

You shall not murder.

You shall not commit adultery.

You shall not steal.

You shall not give false testimony against your neighbor.

You shall not covet your neighbor's wife. You shall not set your desire on your neighbor's house or land, his manservant or maidservant, his ox or donkey, or anything that belongs to your neighbor.

Repetition almost verbatim. Are the very slight differences (in italics) to be considered "addition" and "subtraction?" I guess not. They are merely stylistic, except perhaps for the omission of the creation story.

Four (cultic) + six (moral) laws are repeated, including "punishing children for the sin of the fathers" *and* "showing love" at the same time.

The LORD heard you when you spoke to me and the LORD said to me, "I have heard what this people said to you. Everything they said was good. Oh, that their hearts would be inclined to fear me and keep all my commands always, so that it might go well with them and their children forever!

Go, tell them to return to their tents. But you stay here with me so that I may give you all the commands, decrees and laws you are to teach them to follow in the land I am giving them to possess.

So be careful to do what the LORD your God has commanded you; do not turn aside to the right or to the left. Walk in all the way that the LORD your God has commanded you, so that you may live and prosper and prolong your days in the land that you will possess. (5:28-33)

Not turning aside to the right or to the left but walking in the way of God to prosper! Fear, believe, obey, and prosper! Otherwise, die!, perish! (Cf. *New Testament*.)

6. Love the LORD Your God

Moses continues:

These are the commands, decrees and laws the LORD your God directed me to teach you to observe in the land that you are crossing the Jordan to possess, so that you, your children and their children after them may fear the LORD your God as long as you live by keeping all his decrees and commands that I give you, and so that you may enjoy long life. Hear, O Israel, and be careful to obey so that it may go well with you and that you may increase greatly in a land flowing with milk and honey, just as the LORD, the God of your fathers, promised you. (6:1-3)

First fear and obey God. If you want to live. Then love him, repeating his commands:

Hear, O Israel: The LORD our God, the LORD is one. Love the LORD your God with all your heart and with all your soul and with all your strength. These commandments that I give you today are to be upon your hearts. Impress them on your children. Talk about them when you sit at home and when you walk along the road, when you lie down and when you get up. Tie them as symbols on your hands and bind them on your foreheads. Write them on the doorframes of your houses and on your gates. (6:4-9)

Commands as catechism, as symbols on bodies and dwellings, God's words penetrating all the way into the private being and sphere of the God-fearing individual. Omnipresence of God within the daily existence of the believer. Control of bodies and space. Control of mind and memory. Pronounce God's name all the time, as *Koran*, too, says.

Fear the LORD your God, serve him only and take your oaths in his name. Do not follow other gods, the gods of the peoples around you; for the LORD your God, who is among you, is a jealous God and his anger will burn against you, and he will destroy you from the face of the land. Do not test the LORD your God... (6:13-16)

Fear always precedes and prevails over love, threat of death over promise of happy life (with the possible exception of prosperity), curses over blessings.

The LORD commanded us to obey all these decrees and to fear the LORD our God, so that we might always prosper and be kept alive, as is the case today. And if we are careful to obey all this law before the LORD our God, as he has commanded us, that will be our righteousness. (6:24-25)

Kept alive prosperous = proof of righteousness.

7. Driving Out the Nations

Moses continues, concerning other nations, or simply "the nations" as a lower category—lower because not "holy" as are the Israelites. When God delivers them to his chosen people:

> Then you must destroy them totally. Make no treaty with them, and show them no mercy. Do not intermarry with them. Do not give your daughters to their sons or take their daughters for your sons, for they will turn your sons away from following me to serve other gods, and the LORD's anger will burn against you and will quickly destroy you. This is what you are to do to them: Break down their altars, smash their sacred stones, cut down their Asherah poles and burn their idols in the fire. For you are a people holy to the LORD your God. The LORD your God has chosen you out of all the peoples on the face of the earth to be his people, his treasured possession.
>
> The LORD did not set his affection on you and choose you because you were more numerous than other peoples, for you were the fewest of all peoples. But it was because the LORD loved you and kept the oath he swore to your forefathers that he brought you out with a mighty hand and redeemed you from the land of slavery, from the power of Pharaoh king of Egypt. Know therefore that the LORD your God is God; he is the faithful God, keeping his covenant of love to a thousand generations of those who love him and keep his commands. (7:2-9)

Cursing and destroying (other) "nations" (rest of humanity) is unconditional or axiomatic, as can be expected from a jealous and terrible God who doesn't spare even "the little ones" of his own chosen people, killing human beings by thousands and ten thousands frequently. No peace with, no mercy for, and total destruction of other/unholy nations. A crudest form of the modern ideology of "national interest," a kind of amoral nationalism.

Blessing the chosen nation is conditional on fearing (and loving) God and observing his laws to the letter; blessing meaning, first and foremost, prosperity and only then other things, like health, fertility, etc. Why was Israel chosen? Not "because you were numerous." But it was "because the Lord loved you..." Like "he who is," "he loves whom he loves?" No, it is not even that. Let us read the sentence through: "...and kept the oath he swore to your forefathers..." Who were they? The ones who first feared and obeyed the mono-God.

The following command stands as an anomaly in the sacred text, which has been urging and justifying as rightful the act of total plunder of other nations' possessions, material and human. (Cf. the time of exodus from Egypt as well as the period of wandering in the desert and approaching the promised land, expropriating all along the assets of "the nations.")

> Do not covet the silver and gold on them, and do not take it for yourselves, or you will be ensnared by it, for it is detestable to the LORD your God. Do not bring a detestable thing into your house or you, like it, will be set apart for destruction. Utterly abhor and detest it, for it is set apart for destruction. (7:25-26)

8. Do Not Forget the Lord

Moses continues:

> He humbled you, causing you to hunger and then feeding you with manna, which neither you nor your fathers had known, to teach you that man does not live on bread alone but on every word that comes from the mouth of the LORD. Your clothes did not wear out and your feet did not swell during these forty years. Know then in your heart that as a man disciplines his son, so the LORD your God disciplines you.

A hierarchy of disciplinarians and the disciplined: God → men → children.

And life = bread and word (of God). The former conditional, the latter absolute:

> When you have eaten and are satisfied, praise the LORD your God for the good land he has given you. Be careful that you do not forget the LORD your God, failing to observe his commands, his laws and his decrees that I am giving you this day. Otherwise, when you eat and are satisfied, when you build fine houses and settle down, and when your herds and flocks grow large and your silver and gold increase and all you have is multiplied, then your heart will become proud and you will forget the LORD your God, who brought you out of Egypt, out of the land of slavery. He led you through the vast and dreadful desert, that thirsty and waterless land, with its venomous snakes and scorpions. He brought you water out of hard rock. He gave you manna to eat in the desert, something your fathers had never known, to humble and to test you so that in the end it might go well with you. You may say to yourself, "My power and the strength of my hands have produced this wealth for me." But remember the LORD your God, for it is he who gives you the ability to produce wealth, and so confirms his covenant, which he swore to your forefathers, as it is today.
>
> If you ever forget the LORD your God and follow other gods and worship and bow down to them, I testify against you today that you will surely be destroyed. Like the nations the LORD destroyed before you, so you will be destroyed for not obeying the LORD your God. (8:10-20)

Holy and righteous people become wealthy; and because it is God "who gives the ability to produce wealth," wealth becomes holy, too. A masterful dialectic, an invincible legitimation of the "holy *and* wealthy family."

Food, prosperity, satisfaction must not give way to pride and self-confidence. Man must remain humble and grateful to God. However, teaching "humility" to people is one thing but ever "humbling" (and abhorring) them is another. "Testing" is one, premeditatedly and prejudicially ever "tempting and failing" is another. Men can't win in this God's scheme.

The ultimate goal of good life, "wealth"—however conditional or temporary it may be in the *Koran*'s eye—is again in the forefront: acquired not by man's power and strength but by God's blessing in "confirm(ation) (of) his covenant" (8:18) upon fearing and obeying.

And, the patent-right of "discipline and punish" belongs not to Foucault but to the *Old Testament*.

9. Not Because of Israel's Righteousness

Israel is chosen and loved not even because of its fearful righteousness, let alone "integrity."

> After the LORD your God has driven them out before you, do not say to yourself, "The LORD has brought me here to take possession of this land because of my righteousness." No, it is on account of the wickedness of these nations that the LORD is going to drive them out before you. It is not because of your righteousness or your integrity that you are going in to take possession of their land; but on account of the wickedness of these nations, the LORD your God will drive them out before you, to accomplish what he swore to your fathers, to Abraham, Isaac and Jacob. Understand, then, that it is not because of your righteousness that the LORD your God is giving you this good land to possess, for you are a stiff-necked people. (9:4-6)

Like wealth, the land, too, is not the reward of man's own merit or labor; it is again God-given. And God-given because of other nations' demerit. Given not because of Israel's righteousness but because of others' wickedness. Israel is stiff-necked, wicked, sinful, too. Is the logic, then, one of "all are wicked, but Israel is less wicked," if the latter is not righteous (yet?), (ever?)?

The episode of the Golden Calf (one of the *Koran*'s favorite as well) is once more reminded and hammered in by Moses, who again underscores his intervention with God for the benefit of the sinful community: "But again the LORD listened to me" (9:19). Moses builds up his own legitimacy: he is no mere prophet (as Muhammad is fond of saying about himself), a passive intermediary; he does have certain clout with God.

> At the end of the forty days and forty nights, the LORD gave me the two stone tablets, the tablets of the covenant. Then the LORD told me, "Go down from here at once, because your people whom you brought out of Egypt have become corrupt. They have turned away quickly from what I commanded them and have made a cast idol for themselves."
>
> And the LORD said to me, "I have seen this people, and they are a stiff-necked people indeed. Let me alone, so that I may destroy them and blot out their name from under heaven. And I will make you into a nation stronger and more numerous than they."
>
> So I turned and went down from the mountain while it was ablaze with fire. And the two tablets of the covenant were in my hands. When I looked, I saw that you had sinned against the LORD your God; you had made for yourselves an idol cast in the shape of a calf. You had turned aside quickly from the way that the LORD had commanded you. So I took the two tablets and threw them out of my hands, breaking them to pieces before your eyes.

Then once again I fell prostrate before the LORD for forty days and forty nights; I ate no bread and drank no water, because of all the sin you had committed, doing what was evil in the LORD's sight and so rovoking him to anger. I feared the anger and wrath of the LORD, for he was angry enough with you to destroy you. But again the LORD listened to me. And the LORD was angry enough with Aaron to destroy him, but at that time I prayed for Aaron too. Also I took that sinful thing of yours, the calf you had made, and burned it in the fire. Then I crushed it and ground it to powder as fine as dust and threw the dust into a stream that flowed down the mountain.

You also made the LORD angry at Taberah, at Massah and at Kibroth Hattaavah. (9:11-22)

Constant, incessant reminding of previous sins, of God's fury, of death and destruction, putting Moses (and Levites) on one side and the rest of the stiff-necked people on the other (remember also Numbers, Ch. 16).

A vicious circle of an incorrigible people's ever-sinning and never-repenting and an insatiably resentful God's ever-punishing and never correcting his so-called chosen people. He never really forgives previous sins; ever holds them up against the astray believers. He punishes to discipline, cannot discipline, punishes indiscipline, and so on, ad infinitum. The deus ex machina of this vicious circle is, of course, the basic assumption of the Abrahamic monotheism about the badness of human nature. What can even a good-willed, loving, and compassionate God do in the face of such odds?—however omnipotent he may be.

He (and Moses), in fact, harbors no hope, despite all blessing-talk: "You have been rebellious against the LORD ever since I have known you." Please note: rebellious not several times or even frequently but "ever since." Similarly, stubbornness-wickedness-sinfulness not to be forgiven or corrected, but to be "overlooked," that is, not to be overlooked.

10, 11. Tablets Like the First Ones; Fear the Lord, Love and Obey the Lord

And now, O Israel, what does the LORD your God ask of you but to fear the LORD your God, to walk in all his ways, to love him, to serve the LORD your God with all your heart and with all your soul, and to observe the LORD's commands and decrees that I am giving you today for your own good?

To the LORD your God belong the heavens, even the highest heavens, the earth and everything in it. Yet the LORD set his affection on your forefathers and loved them, and he chose you, their descendants, above all the nations, as it is today. Circumcise your hearts, therefore and do not be stiff-necked any longer. For the LORD your God is God of gods and Lord of lords, the great God, mighty and awesome, who shows no partiality and accepts no bribes. He defends the cause of the fatherless and the widow, and loves the alien, giving him food and clothing. And you are to love those who are aliens, for you yourselves were aliens in Egypt. Fear the LORD your God and serve him. Hold fast to him and take your oaths in his name. He is your praise; he is your God, who performed for you those great and awesome wonders you saw with your own eyes. Your forefathers who went down into Egypt were seventy in all, and now the LORD your God has made you as numerous as the stars in the sky. (10:12-22)

To be righteous, first fear the Lord, and only then love, serve, obey him: "What does the LORD your God ask of you but to fear the LORD?," who is a big proprietor, owning everything. He has chosen Israel "above all the nations." Therefore: "circumcise your hearts" and don't be "stiff-necked any longer." Please note that one of the basic ideological planks of Christianity, that of "circumcision of heart," too, is embedded in Judaism.

Some compassion: protection of the fatherless and the widow and the alien.

Much repetition of history and punishments (esp. cf. the reference to Dathan and Abiram, 11:6) and conditional promises.

Necessity of monotheism, "fixing" God's words in hearts and minds, tying them as symbols on bodies. Omnipresence. Control.

Reward: driving out and dispossessing other nations.

And, a terrible and ruthless nation as becomes its terrible and ruthless God:

Love the LORD your God and keep his requirements, his decrees, his laws and his commands always. Remember today that your children were not the ones who saw and experienced the discipline of the LORD your God: his majesty, his mighty hand, his outstretched arm; the signs he performed and the things he did in the heart of Egypt, both to Pharaoh king of Egypt and to his whole country; what he did to the Egyptian army, to its horses and chariots, how he overwhelmed them with the waters of the Red Sea as they were pursuing you, and how the LORD brought lasting ruin on them. It was not your children who saw what he did for you in the desert until you arrived at this place, and what he did to Dathan and Abiram, sons of Eliab the Reubenite, when the earth opened its mouth right in the middle of all Israel and swallowed them up with their households, their tents and every living thing that belonged to them. But it was your own eyes that saw all these great things the LORD has done. (11:1-7)

If you carefully observe all these commands I am giving you to follow—to love the LORD your God, to walk in all his ways and to hold fast to him—then the LORD will drive out all these nations before you, and you will dispossess nations larger and stronger than you. Every place where you set your foot will be yours: Your territory will extend from the desert to Lebanon, and from the Euphrates River to the western sea. No man will be able to stand against you. The LORD your God, as he promised you, will put the terror and fear of you on the whole land, wherever you go. (11:22-25)

Infanticide of Chapter 16 is hammered in, as shall be the case throughout the Jewish and Christian *Bible*, to be reiterated in the *Koran* as well.

12, 13. One God, One Place of Worship, Monotheism Reinforced

Destruction of all other gods and idols, observance of the rituals of monotheism, the privileged position of the Levites ("Be careful not to neglect the Levites," 12:19), and the "national interest":

> The LORD your God will cut off before you the nations you are about to invade and dispossess. But when you have driven them out and settled in their land, and after they have been destroyed before you, be careful not to be ensnared by inquiring about their gods, saying, "How do these nations serve their gods? We will do the same." You must not worship the LORD your God in their way, because in worshiping their gods, they do all kinds of detestable things the LORD hates. They even burn their sons and daughters in the fire as sacrifices to their gods. (12:29-31)

And:

> See that you do all I command you; do not add to it or take away from it. (12: 32)

Non-monotheistic prophets are preempted, forbidden, to be punished:

> If a prophet, or one who foretells by dreams, appears among you and announces to you a miraculous sign or wonder, and if the sign or wonder of which he has spoken takes place, and he says, "Let us follow other gods" (gods you have not known) "and let us worship them," you must not listen to the words of that prophet or dreamer. The LORD your God is testing you to find out whether you love him with all your heart and with all your soul. It is the LORD your God you must follow, and him you must revere. Keep his commands and obey him; serve him and hold fast to him. That prophet or dreamer must be put to death, because he preached rebellion against the LORD your God, who brought you out of Egypt and redeemed you from the land of slavery; he has tried to turn you from the way the LORD your God commanded you to follow. You must purge the evil from among you.
>
> If your very own brother, or your son or daughter, or the wife you love, or your closest friend secretly entices you, saying, "Let us go and worship other gods" (gods that neither you nor your fathers have known, gods of the peoples around you, whether near or far, from one end of the land to the other), do not yield to him or listen to him. Show him no pity. Do not spare him or shield him. You must certainly put him to death. Your hand must be the first in putting him to death, and then the hands of all the people. Stone him to death, because he tried to turn you away from the LORD your God, who brought you out of Egypt out of the land of slavery. Then all Israel will hear and be afraid, and no one among you will do such an evil thing again.

If you hear it said about one of the towns the LORD your God is giving you to live in that wicked men have arisen among you and have led the people of their town astray, saying, "Let us go and worship other gods" (gods you have not known), then you must inquire, probe and investigate it thoroughly. And if it is true and it has been proved that this detestable thing has been done among you, you must certainly put to the sword all who live in that town. Destroy it completely, both its people and its livestock. Gather all the plunder of the town into the middle of the public square and completely burn the town and all its plunder as a whole burnt offering to the LORD your God. It is to remain a ruin forever, never to be rebuilt. None of those condemned things shall be found in your hands, so that the LORD will turn from his fierce anger; he will show you mercy, have compassion on you, and increase your numbers, as he promised on oath to your forefathers, because you obey the LORD your God, keeping all his commands that I am giving you today and doing what is right in his eyes. (13: 1-18)

Killing by stoning (family members and one's own children included) if they are unbelievers, putting to the sword not only false prophets but also the whole people of a town, total destruction thereof, but no lawful plunder in this case. That loyalty to God and his commands come before one's family shall become a great theme of both Christianity and Islam.

The question is "Which God and which prophet? Yahweh, Lord, or Allah? Moses, Jesus, or Muhammad? But that is an in-family quarrel of Abrahamic monotheism. The idea of God, of One God, the Greatest God, Lord of Lords is the basic driving idea.

14, 15, 16. Food, Tithes, Debts, Feasts

You are the children of the LORD your God. Do not cut yourselves or shave the front of your heads for the dead, for you are a people holy to the LORD your God. Out of all the peoples on the face of the earth, the LORD has chosen you to be his treasured possession.

Do not eat any detestable thing. These are the animals you may eat... (14:1-3)

Israelites, "the children of the LORD," his "treasured possession," "the holy people" can eat only clean food. A long list is given. Another list is also given of unclean food, headed by the pig. (Like circumcision, one of the hallmarks of Islam, borrowed from Judaism.)

Yet another discrimination among human beings:

Do not eat anything you find already dead. You may give it to an alien living in any of your towns, and he may eat it, or you may sell it to a foreigner. But you are a people holy to the LORD your God. (14:21)

Cleanness, purity, holiness definitely have a social/class dimension.

Tithe rules are repeated and further elaborated, without "neglecting" the Levites:

Be sure to set aside a tenth of all that your fields produce each year. Eat the tithe of your grain, new wine and oil, and the firstborn of your herds and flocks in the presence of the LORD your God at the place he will choose as a dwelling for his Name, so that you may learn to revere the LORD your God always. But if that place is too distant and you have been blessed by the LORD your God and cannot carry your tithe (because the place where the LORD will choose to put his Name is so far away), then exchange your tithe for silver, and take the silver with you and go to the place the LORD your God will choose. Use the silver to buy whatever you like: cattle, sheep, wine or other fermented drink, or anything you wish. Then you and your household shall eat there in the presence of the LORD your God and rejoice. And do not neglect the Levites living in your towns, for they have no allotment or inheritance of their own. (14:22-27)

Some economic charity and some redistributive practices in the form of canceling debts (only of tribal brothers, not of foreigners) and being not tightfisted toward poor brothers.

At the end of every seven years you must cancel debts. This is how it is to be done: Every creditor shall cancel the loan he has made to his fellow Israelite. He shall not require payment from his fellow Israelite or brother, because the LORD's time for canceling debts has been proclaimed. You may require payment from a foreigner, but you must cancel any debt your brother owes you. However, there should be no poor among you, for in the land the LORD your God is giving you to possess as your inheritance, he will richly bless you, if only you fully obey the LORD your God and are careful to follow all these commands I am giving you today. For the LORD your God will bless you as he has promised, and you will lend to many nations but will borrow from none. You will rule over many nations but none will rule over you.

If there is a poor man among your brothers in any of the towns of the land that the LORD your God is giving you, do not be hardhearted or tightfisted toward your poor brother. Rather be openhanded and freely lend him whatever he needs. Be careful not to harbor this wicked thought: "The seventh year, the year for canceling debts, is near," so that you do not show ill will toward your needy brother and give him nothing. He may then appeal to the LORD against you, and you will be found guilty of sin. Give generously to him and do so without a grudging heart; then because of this the LORD your God will bless you in all your work and in everything you put your hand to. There will always be poor people in the land. Therefore I command you to be openhanded toward your brothers and toward the poor and needy in your land.

Charitable openhandedness toward the poor and needy (of the tribe) will be rewarded in this world ("God will bless you in all your work") as distinct from the *Koran*'s rewards in the other world.

As for other tribes, lend but not borrow, rule but not be ruled.

Please also note the essentialism, the economic and social determinism: "There will always be poor people in the land."

And the following rules for servitude:

If a fellow Hebrew, a man or a woman, sells himself to you and serves you six years, in the seventh year you must let him go free. And when you release him, do not send him away empty-handed. Supply him liberally from your flock, your threshing floor and your winepress. Give to him as the LORD your God has blessed you. Remember that you were slaves in Egypt and the LORD your God redeemed you. That is why I give you this command today.

But if your servant says to you, "I do not want to leave you," because he loves you and your family and is well off with you, then take an awl and push it through his ear lobe into the door, and he will become your servant for life. Do the same for your maidservant.

Do not consider it a hardship to set your servant free, because his service to you these six years has been worth twice as much as that of a hired hand. And the LORD your God will bless you in everything you do.

The institution itself is not questioned; it is made charitable.

Firstborn animals are to be set apart for God; the Passover, the Feast of Weeks, the Feast of Tabernacles are to be observed;

"No man should appear before the LORD empty-handed: Each of you must bring a gift in proportion to the way the LORD your God has blessed you." (16:16)

And:

Be joyful at your Feast—you, your sons and daughters, your menservants and maidservants, and the Levites, the aliens, the fatherless and the widows who live in your towns. (16:14)

This is the social stratification in, and the class-composition of, the Israelite community: Families of citizens, their servants, the Levites, and the aliens, plus the fatherless and the widows.

A note on judges and justice—"justice as fairness":

Appoint judges and officials for each of your tribes in every town the LORD your God is giving you, and they shall judge the people fairly. Do not pervert justice or show partiality. Do not accept a bribe, for a bribe blinds the eyes of the wise and twists the words of the righteous. Follow justice and justice alone, so that you may live and possess the land the LORD your God is giving you. (16:18-20)

17(a). Judges, Justice, Law Courts

The due process of law in case of worshiping other gods is as follows:

> If a man or woman living among you in one of the towns the LORD gives you is found doing evil in the eyes of the LORD your God in violation of his covenant, and contrary to my command has worshiped other gods, bowing down to them or to the sun or the moon or the stars of the sky, and this has been brought to your attention, then you must investigate it thoroughly. If it is true and it has been proved that this detestable thing has been done in Israel, take the man or woman who has done this evil deed to your city gate and stone that person to death. On the testimony of two or three witnesses a man shall be put to death, but no one shall be put to death on the testimony of only one witness. The hands of the witnesses must be the first in putting him to death, and then the hands of all the people. You must purge the evil from among you. (17:2-7)

Two or three witnesses, stoning to death, lynching. (Cf. "recm" in the *Koran*.)

Lower, local courts or the Levitic supreme court are to give final decisions:

> If cases come before your courts that are too difficult for you to judge—whether bloodshed, lawsuits or assaults—take them to the place the LORD your God will choose. Go to the priests, who are Levites, and to the judge who is in office at that time. Inquire of them and they will give you the verdict. You must act according to the decisions they give you at the place the LORD will choose. Be careful to do everything they direct you to do. Act according to the law they teach you and the decisions they give you. Do not turn aside from what they tell you, to the right or to the left. The man who shows contempt for the judge or for the priest who stands ministering there to the LORD your God must be put to death. You must purge the evil from Israel. All the people will hear and be afraid, and will not be contemptuous again. (17:8-13)

Contempt for the judge or for the priest is to be punished by death; there is no appeal; popular fear along with the incontestable validity of God's word (as interpreted by priests and judges) is the basis of legitimacy of the law.

17 (b). From the "Priest-King" to the "King and Priests"

> When you enter the land the LORD your God is giving you and have taken possession of it and settled in it, and you say, "Let us set a king over us like all the nations around us," be sure to appoint over you the king the LORD your God chooses. He must be from among your own brothers. Do not place a foreigner over you, one who is not a brother Israelite. The king, moreover, must not acquire great numbers of horses for himself or make the people return to Egypt to get more of them, for the LORD has told you, "You are not to go back that way again." He must not take

many wives, or his heart will be led astray. He must not accumulate large amounts of silver and gold.

When he takes the throne of his kingdom, he is to write for himself on a scroll a copy of this law, taken from that of the priests, who are Levites. It is to be with him, and he is to read it all the days of his life so that he may learn to revere the LORD his God and follow carefully all the words of this law and these decrees and not consider himself better than his brothers and turn from the law to the right or to the left. Then he and his descendants will reign a long time over his kingdom in Israel. (17:14-20)

During the forty-year period of wandering in the desert, the Israelite form of government has been a theocracy in the strict sense of the term: Moses, the prophet of God and the arch-priest ruled over the people with his priestly bureaucracy of Aaron & Sons and the Levites, the law of the state being God's word, the legitimating principle of domination being divine ordinance. The strictest definition of theocracy: the prophet-priest ruling according to and as representative of God and his law.

Now that the Israelites are about to settle in the promised land, a new theory of government is in the making—one that will last for generations and generations to come. We are passing from a "kingdom of priests" to a "Kingdom" in which the Israelites are to "set a (K)ing over (them) like all the nations around (them)." This King shall be a God-chosen one and a brother Israelite. He shall not,

    acquire great numbers of horses,

    take many wives,

    accumulate large amounts of silver and gold.

That is, amass worldly possessions, bestial, feminine, and pecuniary—in that order.

    And: he shall,

    take a copy of the law from the Levitic priests,

    read it all the days of his life,

so that he may learn to revere the Lord his God and follow carefully all the words of this law and these decrees and not consider himself better than his brothers; and he and his descendants will reign a long time. A dynastic monarchy, one which is still theocratic in that the basic norm of the legitimacy of his rule is still the divine law.

Whatever the merit of the injunctions against amassing wealth and wives (to be violated by many, some the greatest, Jewish kings[3]) and against a condescending attitude toward the populace may be, here is a clear political theory of hereditary monarchy, a relatively more secular one than the previous rule of the priests, but still a basically theocratic one (in a looser sense of the term) in that the basis of law and the "grund-norm" of the legitimacy of rule remains a divine one, the Law, the *Torah*, the Word of God.

It is only that some governmental offices are beginning to be separated, or decoupled: the prophetic-king (Moses) and the priestly bureaucracy (Levites) structure is replaced, or modified, by the God-chosen King (David, Solomon, etc.) and the priestly bureaucracy (Levites). In other words, the first term of the former equation is split and is left to a secular (i.e., non-priestly) King, the other (i.e., religious) arm of the government remaining intact. An embryonic version of the "doctrine of two swords," if you will, coexisting with, balancing or countervailing one another. A "modernizing" trend: social differentiation and functional differentiation in the governmental process. At any rate, the Jewish political, governmental theory is a monarchic-theocratic one.

18. Offerings for Priests and Levites

Monopolistic dynastic position of the Levites is reaffirmed; the Levites are "to stand and minister in the LORD's name always," with "the LORD (as) their inheritance":

> The priests, who are Levites—indeed the whole tribe of Levi—are to have no allotment or inheritance with Israel. They shall live on the offerings made to the LORD by fire, for that is their inheritance. They shall have no inheritance among their brothers; the LORD is their inheritance, as he promised them.
>
> This is the share due the priests from the people who sacrifice a bull or a sheep: the shoulder, the jowls and the inner parts. You are to give them the firstfruits of your grain, new wine and oil, and the first wool from the shearing of your sheep, for the LORD your God has chosen them and their descendants out of all your tribes to stand and minister in the LORD's name always.
>
> If a Levite moves from one of your towns anywhere in Israel where he is living, and comes in all earnestness to the place the LORD will choose, he may minister in the name of the LORD his God like all his fellow Levites who serve there in the presence of the LORD. He is to share equally in their benefits, even though he has received money from the sale of family possessions. (18:1-8)

Some "detestable practices" are listed:

> When you enter the land the LORD your God is giving you, do not learn to imitate the detestable ways of the nations there. Let no one be found among you who sacrifices his son or daughter in the fire, who practices divination or sorcery, interprets omens, engages in witchcraft, or casts spells, or who is a medium or spiritualist or who consults the dead. (18:9-11)

Moses (God) proceeds with the credentials of true-prophets:

> The LORD your God will raise up for you a prophet like me from among your own brothers. You must listen to him. For this is what you asked of the LORD your God at Horeb on the day of the assembly when you said, "Let us not hear the voice of the LORD our God nor see this great fire anymore, or we will die."

The LORD said to me: "What they say is good. I will raise up for them a prophet like you from among their brothers; I will put my words in his mouth, and he will tell them everything I command him. If anyone does not listen to my words that the prophet speaks in my name, I myself will call him to account. But a prophet who presumes to speak in my name anything I have not commanded him to say, or a prophet who speaks in the name of other gods, must be put to death."

You may say to yourselves, "How can we know when a message has not been spoken by the LORD?" If what a prophet proclaims in the name of the LORD does not take place or come true, that is a message the LORD has not spoken. That prophet has spoken presumptuously. Do not be afraid of him. (18:15-22)

19. Cities of Refuge

Unintentional killing, "without malice aforethought," is to be treated differently from intentional killing or premeditated murder. Boundary of the (tribal) neighbor is to be respected.

But if a man hates his neighbor and lies in wait for him, assaults and kills him, and then flees to one of these cities, the elders of his town shall send for him, bring him back from the city, and hand him over to the avenger of blood to die. Show him no pity. You must purge from Israel the guilt of shedding innocent blood, so that it may go well with you.

Do not move your neighbor's boundary stone set up by your predecessors in the inheritance you receive in the land the LORD your God is giving you to possess. (19:11-14)

Rules for witnesses and testimony:

One witness is not enough to convict a man accused of any crime or offense he may have committed. A matter must be established by the testimony of two or three witnesses.

If a malicious witness takes the stand to accuse a man of a crime, the two men involved in the dispute must stand in the presence of the LORD before the priests and the judges who are in office at the time. The judges must make a thorough investigation, and if the witness proves to be a liar, giving false testimony against his brother, then do to him as he intended to do to his brother. You must purge the evil from among you. The rest of the people will hear of this and be afraid, and never again will such an evil thing be done among you. Show no pity: life for life, eye for eye, tooth for tooth, hand for hand, foot for foot. (19:15-20)

Lex talionis, retaliative law, is to be continued by Islam, but not so by Christianity (despite some ambivalence). As we shall see, Islam in many ways is closer to Judaism than Christianity is, in spite of the totality of the Judeo-Christian tradition.

20. Going to War: The Jewish "Jihad"

When you go to war against your enemies and see horses and chariots and an army greater than yours, do not be afraid of them, because the LORD your God, who brought you up out of Egypt, will be with you. When you are about to go into battle, the priest shall come forward and address the army. He shall say: "Hear, O Israel, today you are going into battle against your enemies. Do not be fainthearted or afraid; do not be terrified or give way to panic before them. For the LORD your God is the one who goes with you to fight against your enemies to give you victory."

The officers shall say to the army: "Has anyone built a new house and not dedicated it? Let him go home, or he may die in battle and someone else may dedicate it. Has anyone planted a vineyard and not begun to enjoy it? Let him go home, or he may die in battle and someone else enjoy it. Has anyone become pledged to a woman and not married her? Let him go home, or he may die in battle and someone else marry her." Then the officers shall add, "Is any man afraid or fainthearted? Let him go home so that his brothers will not become disheartened too." When the officers have finished speaking to the army, they shall appoint commanders over it. (20:1-9)

A warrior-God who fights for his people (just like the Allah of Islam who does the same for the faithful); a priest who gives morale to the army; officers who do the same.

When you march up to attack a city, make its people an offer of peace. If they accept and open their gates, all the people in it shall be subject to forced labor and shall work for you. If they refuse to make peace and they engage you in battle, lay siege to that city. When the LORD your God delivers it into your hand, put to the sword all the men in it. As for the women, the children, the livestock and everything else in the city, you may take these as plunder for yourselves. And you may use the plunder the LORD your God gives you from your enemies. This is how you are to treat all the cities that are at a distance from you and do not belong to the nations nearby.

However, in the cities of the nations the LORD your God is giving you as an inheritance, do not leave alive anything that breathes. Completely destroy them—the Hittites, Amorites, Canaanites, Perizzites, Hivites and Jebusites—as the LORD your God has commanded you. Otherwise, they will teach you to follow all the detestable things they do in worshiping their gods, and you will sin against the LORD your God.

When you lay siege to a city for a long time, fighting against it to capture it, do not destroy its trees by putting an ax to them, because you can eat their fruit. Do not cut them down. Are the trees of the field people, that you should besiege them? However, you may cut down trees that you know are not fruit trees and use them to build siege works until the city at war with you falls.

If surrender, forced labor; if defiance, beheading of all men and taking of everything else, human and animal, as rightful booty (plunder). Differential treatment of cities belonging to distant nations as opposed to nations nearby that are to be inherited, in which "do not leave alive anything that breathes." (Remember Plato's distinction, in the *Republic*, between Greek cities and barbarian settlements.) Distinction between people and trees.

21. Some Rules Concerning Women and Children

> When you go to war against your enemies and the LORD your God delivers them into your hands and you take captives, if you notice among the captives a beautiful woman and are attracted to her, you may take her as your wife. Bring her into your home and have her shave her head, trim her nails and put aside the clothes she was wearing when captured. After she has lived in your house and mourned her father and mother for a full month, then you may go to her and be her husband and she shall be your wife. If you are not pleased with her, let her go wherever she wishes. You must not sell her or treat her as a slave, since you have dishonored her. (21:10-14)

The text speaks for itself.

> If a man has two wives, and he loves one but not the other, and both bear him sons but the firstborn is the son of the wife he does not love, when he wills his property to his sons, he must not give the rights of the firstborn to the son of the wife he loves in preference to his actual firstborn, the son of the wife he does not love. He must acknowledge the son of his unloved wife as the firstborn by giving him a double share of all he has. That son is the first sign of his father's strength. The right of the firstborn belongs to him. (21:15-17)

Is the ambivalence of primogeniture in the *Old Testament* (remember "the older shall serve the younger") clarified or further complicated here?

> If a man has a stubborn and rebellious son who does not obey his father and mother and will not listen to them when they discipline him, his father and mother shall take hold of him and bring him to the elders at the gate of his town. They shall say to the elders, "This son of ours is stubborn and rebellious. He will not obey us. He is a profligate and a drunkard." Then all the men of his town shall stone him to death. You must purge the evil from among you. All Israel will hear of it and be afraid. (21:18-21)

Another form of infanticide. By the hand of parents, at the hands of the community.

22. Miscellaneous Rules and Marriage Violations

Miscellaneous rules, not very orderly or systematically codified:

> If you see your brother's ox or sheep straying, do not ignore it but be sure to take it back to him. If the brother does not live near you or if you do not know who he is,

take it home with you and keep it until he comes looking for it. Then give it back to him. Do the same if you find your brother's donkey or his cloak or anything he loses. Do not ignore it.

If you see your brother's donkey or his ox fallen on the road, do not ignore it. Help him get it to its feet.

A woman must not wear men's clothing, nor a man wear women's clothing, for the LORD your God detests anyone who does this.

If you come across a bird's nest beside the road, either in a tree or on the ground, and the mother is sitting on the young or on the eggs, do not take the mother with the young. You may take the young, but be sure to let the mother go, so that it may go well with you and you may have a long life.

When you build a new house, make a parapet around your roof so that you may not bring the guilt of bloodshed on your house if someone falls from the roof.

Do not plant two kinds of seed in your vineyard; if you do, not only the crops you plant but also the fruit of the vineyard will be defiled.

Do not plow with an ox and a donkey yoked together.

Do not wear clothes of wool and linen woven together.

Make tassels on the four corners of the cloak you wear. (22:1-12)

Some equity, solidarity and compassion. Control of and uniformity in daily life, perhaps as a discipline and training for conformity in social, religious life.

Concerning virginity, adultery, rape:

If a man takes a wife and, after lying with her, dislikes her and slanders her and gives her a bad name, saying, "I married this woman, but when I approached her, I did not find proof of her virginity," then the girl's father and mother shall bring proof that she was a virgin to the town elders at the gate. The girl's father will say to the elders, "I gave my daughter in marriage to this man, but he dislikes her. Now he has slandered her and said, 'I did not find your daughter to be a virgin.' But here is the proof of my daughter's virginity." Then her parents shall display the cloth before the elders of the town, and the elders shall take the man and punish him. They shall fine him a hundred shekels of silver and give them to the girl's father, because this man has given an Israelite virgin a bad name. She shall continue to be his wife; he must not divorce her as long as he lives.

If, however, the charge is true and no proof of the girl's virginity can be found, she shall be brought to the door of her father's house and there the men of her town shall stone her to death. She has done a disgraceful thing in Israel by being promiscuous while still in her father's house. You must purge the evil from among you. (22:13-21)

To the trio of fathers-husbands-priests as women's moral guardians and custodians, a fourth virtuous element is added: the "town elders." If not found guilty and not stoned to death, the slandered woman's consolation shall be to continue to be the wife of the man who slandered him. And, in this morass, the father "prospers."

> If a man is found sleeping with another man's wife, both the man who slept with her and the woman must die. You must purge the evil from Israel.
>
> If a man happens to meet in a town a virgin pledged to be married and he sleeps with her, you shall take both of them to the gate of that town and stone them to death—the girl because she was in a town and did not scream for help, and the man because he violated another man's wife. You must purge the evil from among you.
>
> But if out in the country a man happens to meet a girl pledged to be married and rapes her, only the man who has done this shall die. Do nothing to the girl; she has committed no sin deserving death. This case is like that of someone who attacks and murders his neighbor, for the man found the girl out in the country, and though the betrothed girl screamed, there was no one to rescue her.
>
> If a man happens to meet a virgin who is not pledged to be married and rapes her and they are discovered, he shall pay the girl's father fifty shekels of silver. He must marry the girl, for he has violated her. He can never divorce her as long as he lives.
>
> A man is not to marry his father's wife; he must not dishonor his father's bed.
>
> (22:22-30)

Death for adultery between consenting adults, between a man and a married woman. Death for both the raper and the raped town virgin (because she doesn't scream). Death only for the raper but not the raped country virgin (because there is no one to rescue her). If the raped virgin is not betrothed, as is the case in the two incidents above, it is happy ending for all concerned except the girl. The raper pays fifty shekels for the girl he likes and marries her; the father pockets the silver; the girl is made to marry her raper. Not an easy life for unpledged virgins.

Note the two inversions, or perversions, in this excerpt and the one above: (1) Woman is presumed guilty until proven innocent, (2) she is compensated for being raped by being married to the raper. (Don't you think some of this is still around?)

23. Exclusions from the Assembly, Easy and Many

> No one who has been emasculated by crushing or cutting may enter the assembly of the LORD.
>
> No one born of a forbidden marriage nor any of his descendants may enter the assembly of the LORD, even down to the tenth generation.
>
> No Ammonite or Moabite or any of his descendants may enter the assembly of the LORD, even down to the tenth generation. For they did not come to meet you with bread and water on your way when you came out of Egypt, and they hired

Balaam son of Beor from Pethor in Aram Naharaim to pronounce a curse on you. However, the LORD your God would not listen to Balaam but turned the curse into a blessing for you, because the LORD your God loves you. Do not seek a treaty of friendship with them as long as you live.

Do not abhor an Edomite, for he is your brother. Do not abhor an Egyptian, because you lived as an alien in his country. The third generation of children born to them may enter the assembly of the LORD. (23:1-8)

What's the crime of the innocent third-party victims in the first and second paragraphs? What kind of mercy, compassion, grace, all-embracing love is this?

If a slave has taken refuge with you, do not hand him over to his master. Let him live among you wherever he likes and in whatever town he chooses. Do not oppress him.

No Israelite man or woman is to become a shrine prostitute. You must not bring the earnings of a female prostitute or of a male prostitute into the house of the LORD your God to pay any vow, because the LORD your God detests them both.

Do not charge your brother interest, whether on money or food or anything else that may earn interest. You may charge a foreigner interest, but not a brother Israelite, so that the LORD your God may bless you in everything you put your hand to in the land you are entering to possess.

If you make a vow to the LORD your God, do not be slow to pay it, for the LORD your God will certainly demand it of you and you will be guilty of sin. But if you refrain from making a vow, you will not be guilty. Whatever your lips utter you must be sure to do, because you made your vow freely to the LORD your God with your own mouth.

If you enter your neighbor's vineyard, you may eat all the grapes you want, but do not put any in your basket. If you enter your neighbor's grainfield, you may pick kernels with your hands, but you must not put a sickle to his standing grain. (23:15-25)

Repeat: "You may charge a foreigner interest, but not a brother Israelite."

24, 25. Various Rules and Laws

If a man marries a woman who becomes displeasing to him because he finds something indecent about her, and he writes her a certificate of divorce, gives it to her and sends her from his house, and if after she leaves his house she becomes the wife of another man, and her second husband dislikes her and writes her a certificate of divorce, gives it to her and sends her from his house, or if he dies, then her first husband, who divorced her, is not allowed to marry her again after she has been defiled. That would be detestable in the eyes of the LORD. Do not bring sin upon the land the LORD your God is giving you as an inheritance. (24:1-4)

Give her the paper, and the kick. (*Koran* will elaborate on this.)

> If a man has recently married, he must not be sent to war or have any other duty laid on him. For one year he is to be free to stay at home and bring happiness to the wife he has married. (24:5)

Beware the inversion: bringing happiness to the wife.

> Do not take a pair of millstones—not even the upper one—as security for a debt, because that would be taking a man's livelihood as security.
>
> If a man is caught kidnaping one of his brother Israelites and treats him as a slave or sells him, the kidnapper must die. You must purge the evil from among you. (24:6-7)
>
> In cases of leprous diseases be very careful to do exactly as the priests, who are Levites, instruct you. You must follow carefully what I have commanded them. Remember what the LORD your God did to Miriam along the way after you came out of Egypt. (25:8-9)

Levites are doctors, too.

> When you make a loan of any kind to your neighbor, do not go into his house to get what he is offering as a pledge. Stay outside and let the man to whom you are making the loan bring the pledge out to you. If the man is poor, do not go to sleep with his pledge in your possession. Return his cloak to him by sunset so that he may sleep in it. Then he will thank you, and it will be regarded as a righteous act in the sight of the LORD your God.
>
> Do not take advantage of a hired man who is poor and needy, whether he is a brother Israelite or an alien living in one of your towns. Pay him his wages each day before sunset, because he is poor and is counting on it. Otherwise he may cry to the LORD against you, and you will be guilty of sin. (25:10-15)

Good morals.

> Fathers shall not be put to death for their children, nor children put to death for their fathers; each is to die for his own sin. (25:16)

We know that, putting children to death for their fathers' sins is a monopoly of God.

> Do not deprive the alien or the fatherless of justice, or take the cloak of the widow as a pledge. Remember that you were slaves in Egypt and the LORD your God redeemed you from there. That is why I command you to do this.
>
> When you are harvesting in your field and you overlook a sheaf, do not go back to get it. Leave it for the alien, the fatherless and the widow, so that the LORD your God may bless you in all the work of your hands. When you beat the olives from your trees, do not go over the branches a second time. Leave what remains for the alien, the fatherless and the widow. When you harvest the grapes in your vineyard,

to not go over the vines again. Leave what remains for the alien, the fatherless and the widow. Remember that you were slaves in Egypt. That is why I command you to do this. (24:17-22)

Some charity for the alien, the fatherless, and the widow.

When men have a dispute, they are to take it to court and the judges will decide the case, acquitting the innocent and condemning the guilty. If the guilty man deserves to be beaten, the judge shall make him lie down and have him flogged in his presence with the number of lashes his crime deserves, but he must not give him more than forty lashes. If he is flogged more than that, your brother will be degraded in your eyes. (25:1-3)

No degradation until 40!

If brothers are living together and one of them dies without a son, his widow must not marry outside the family. Her husband's brother shall take her and marry her and fulfill the duty of a brother-in-law to her. The first son she bears shall carry on the name of the dead brother so that his name will not be blotted out from Israel.

However, if a man does not want to marry his brother's wife, she shall go to the elders at the town gate and say, "My husband's brother refuses to carry on his brother's name in Israel. He will not fulfill the duty of a brother-in-law to me." Then the elders of his town shall summon him and talk to him. If he persists in saying, "I do not want to marry her," his brother's widow shall go up to him in the presence of the elders, take off one of his sandals, spit in his face and say, "This is what is done to the man who will not build up his brother's family line." That man's line shall be known in Israel as The Family of the Unsandaled. (25:5-10)

The woman is not asked, she has no choice, no will-power. (Only the man does, even if he is going to be called "unsandaled.") On the contrary, she has internalized the status of chattel; she demands and protests in an inverted manner. Really, how far have we come from the Tamar episode?

If two men are fighting and the wife of one of them comes to rescue her husband from his assailant, and she reaches out and seizes him by his private parts, you shall cut off her hand. Show her no pity. (25:11-12)

No comment.

Do not have two differing weights in your bag—one heavy, one light. Do not have two differing measures in your house—one large, one small. You must have accurate and honest weights and measures, so that you may live long in the land the LORD your God is giving you. For the LORD your God detests anyone who does these things, anyone who deals dishonestly. (25:13-16)

Honesty and decency here, not shrewdness and cheating.

26. Firstfruits, Tithes, Lord's Commands

Firstfruits in the promised land are to be presented to God (priests), and,

> When you have finished setting aside a tenth of all your produce in the third year, the year of the tithe, you shall give it to the Levite, the alien, the fatherless and the widow, so that they may eat in your towns and be satisfied. Then say to the LORD your God: "I have removed from my house the sacred portion and have given it to the Levite, the alien, the fatherless and the widow, according to all you commanded. I have not turned aside from your commands nor have I forgotten any of them. I have not eaten any of the sacred portion while I was in mourning, nor have I removed any of it while I was unclean, nor have I offered any of it to the dead. I have obeyed the LORD my God; I have done everything you commanded me. Look down from heaven, your holy dwelling place, and bless your people Israel and the land you have given us as you promised on oath to our forefathers, a land flowing with milk and honey."
>
> The LORD your God commands you this day to follow these decrees and laws; carefully observe them with all your heart and with all your soul. You have declared this day that the LORD is your God and that you will walk in his ways, that you will keep his decrees, commands and laws, and that you will obey him. And the LORD has declared this day that you are his people, his treasured possession as he promised, and that you are to keep all his commands. He has declared that he will set you in praise, fame and honor high above all the nations he has made and that you will be a people holy to the LORD your God, as he promised. (26:12-19)

Prosperity, praise, fame, and honor to the chosen people "high above all the nations."

27. Curses from Mount Ebal

An altar of fieldstones is to be built and the Israelites are to "write very clearly all the words of this law on these stones" (27:8). And 6 tribes are to bless and 6 tribes are to curse the people. (Symmetry in cursing but, as we shall shortly see, asymmetry between curses and blessings.) Godly curses are also transformed into a social, communal ritual, a collective action, a religious orgy. On the same day Moses commanded the people:

> When you have crossed the Jordan, these tribes shall stand on Mount Gerizim to bless the people: Simeon, Levi, Judah, Issachar, Joseph and Benjamin. And these tribes shall stand on Mount Ebal to pronounce curses: Reuben, Gad, Asher, Zebulun, Dan and Naphtali.
>
> The Levites shall recite to all the people of Israel in a loud voice: (27: 11-14)
>
> Cursed is the man who carves an image or casts an idol—a thing detestable to the LORD, the work of the craftsman's hands—and sets it up in secret. Then all the people shall say, "Amen!"

Cursed is the man who dishonors his father or his mother. Then all the people shall say, "Amen!"

Cursed is the man who moves his neighbor's boundary stone. Then all the people shall say, "Amen!"

Cursed is the man who leads the blind astray on the road. Then all the people shall say, "Amen!"

Cursed is the man who withholds justice from the alien, the fatherless or the widow. Then all the people shall say, "Amen!"

Cursed is the man who sleeps with his father's wife, for he dishonors his father's bed. Then all the people shall say, "Amen!"

Cursed is the man who has sexual relations with any animal. Then all the people shall say, "Amen!"

Cursed is the man who sleeps with his sister, the daughter of his father or the daughter of his mother. Then all the people shall say, "Amen!"

Cursed is the man who sleeps with his mother-in-law. Then all the people shall say, "Amen!"

Cursed is the man who kills his neighbor secretly. Then all the people shall say, "Amen!"

Cursed is the man who accepts a bribe to kill an innocent person. Then all the people shall say, "Amen!"

Cursed is the man who does not uphold the words of this law by carrying them out. Then all the people shall say, "Amen!" (27:15-26)

Here, curses do not outnumber blessings; they are all there is to it. (Below, curses will outnumber blessings as usual.)

When we look at the 12 don'ts here, which get curses, from the other side, that is as 12 do's, we get the following: be monotheist, honor parents, respect neighbors, guide the blind, protect the alien/the fatherless/the widow, respect life (x2), obey the law = 8. But how are we going to positivize: don't practice incest (x3) and sodomy?

28. Blessings for Obedience, Curses for Disobedience

In 14 paragraphs of blessings and 54 paragraphs of curses, Deuteronomy, Chapter 28, refines to perfection the work that was begun in Leviticus, Chapter 26, the work of scaring human beings.

I have to yield the page to this Biblical classic (of the order of Numbers, Chapter 16), the locus classicus of Western monotheism's psychological warfare against human beings to get their obedience and submission in fear and trembling.

Blessings for Obedience (28:1-14)

If you fully obey the LORD your God and carefully follow all his commands I give you today, the LORD your God will set you high above all the nations on earth. All these blessings will come upon you and accompany you if you obey the LORD your God:

You will be blessed in the city and blessed in the country.

Your basket and your kneading trough will be blessed.

The fruit of your womb will be blessed, and the crops of your land and the young of your livestock—the calves of your herds and the lambs of your flocks.

You will be blessed when you come in and blessed when you go out.

The LORD will grant that the enemies who rise up against you will be defeated before you. They will come at you from one direction but flee from you in seven.

The LORD will send a blessing on your barns and on everything you put your hand to. The LORD your God will bless you in the land he is giving you.

The LORD will establish you as his holy people, as he promised you on oath, if you keep the commands of the LORD your God and walk in his ways. Then all the peoples on earth will see that you are called by the name of the LORD, and they will fear you. The LORD will grant you abundant prosperity—in the fruit of your

Curses for Disobedience (28:15-68)

However, if you do not obey the LORD your God and do not carefully follow all his commands and decrees I am giving you today, all these curses will come upon you and overtake you:

You will be cursed in the city and cursed in the country.

Your basket and your kneading trough will be cursed.

The fruit of your womb will be cursed, and the crops of your land, and the calves of your herds and the lambs of your flocks.

You will be cursed when you come in and cursed when you go out.

The LORD will send on you curses, confusion and rebuke in everything you put your hand to, until you are destroyed and come to sudden ruin because of the evil you have done in forsaking him. The LORD will plague you with diseases until he has destroyed you from the land you are entering to possess. The LORD will strike you with wasting disease, with fever and inflammation, with scorching heat and drought, with blight and mildew, which will plague you until you perish. The sky over your head will be bronze, the ground beneath you iron. The LORD will turn the rain of your country into dust and powder; it will come down from the skies until you are destroyed.

womb, the young of your livestock and the crops of your ground—in the land he swore to your forefathers to give you.

The LORD will open the heavens, the storehouse of his bounty, to send rain on your land in season and to bless all the work of your hands. You will lend to many nations but will borrow from none. The LORD will make you the head, not the tail. If you pay attention to the commands of the LORD your God that I give you this day and carefully follow them, you will always be at the top, never at the bottom. Do not turn aside from any of the commands I give you today, to the right or to the left, following other gods and serving them. (28:1-14)

(Blessings end here. A long, long column of curses continue piercing through the human psyche.)

The LORD will cause you to be defeated before your enemies. You will come at them from one direction but flee from them in seven, and you will become a thing of horror to all the kingdoms on earth. Your carcasses will be food for all the birds of the air and the beasts of the earth, and there will be no one to frighten them away. The LORD will afflict you with the boils of Egypt and with tumors, festering sores and the itch, from which you cannot be cured. The LORD will afflict you with madness, blindness and confusion of mind. At midday you will grope about like a blind man in the dark. You will be unsuccessful in everything you do; day after day you will be oppressed and robbed, with no one to rescue you.

You will be pledged to be married to a woman, but another will take her and ravish her. You will build a house, but you will not live in it. You will plant a vineyard, but you will not even begin to enjoy its fruit. Your ox will be slaughtered before your eyes, but you will eat none of it. Your donkey will be forcibly taken from you and will not be returned. Your sheep will be given to your enemies, and no one will rescue them.

Your sons and daughters will be given to another nation, and you will wear out your eyes watching for them day after day, powerless to lift a hand.

A people that you do not know will eat what your land and labor produce, and you will have nothing but cruel oppression all your days. The sights you see will drive you mad. The LORD will afflict your knees and legs with painful boils that cannot be cured, spreading from the soles of your feet to the top of your head.

The LORD will drive you and the king you set over you to a nation unknown to you or your fathers. There you will worship other gods, gods of wood and stone. You will become a thing of horror and an object of scorn and ridicule to all the nations where the LORD will drive you.

You will sow much seed in the field but you will harvest little, because locusts will devour it. You will plant vineyards and cultivate them but you will not drink the wine or gather the grapes, because worms will eat them. You will have olive trees throughout your country but you will not use the oil, because the olives will drop off.

You will have sons and daughters but you will not keep them, because they will go into captivity. Swarms of locusts will take over all your trees and the crops of your land.

The alien who lives among you will rise above you higher and higher, but you will sink lower and lower. He will lend to you, but you will not lend to him. He will be the head, but you will be the tail.

All these curses will come upon you. They will pursue you and overtake you until you are destroyed, because you did not obey the LORD your God and observe the commands and decrees he gave you.

They will be a sign and a wonder to you and your descendants forever. Because you did not serve the LORD your God joyfully and gladly in the time of prosperity, therefore in hunger and thirst, in nakedness and dire poverty, you will serve the enemies the LORD sends against you. He will put an iron yoke on your neck until he has destroyed you.

The LORD will bring a nation against you from far away, from the ends of the earth, like an eagle swooping down, a nation whose language you will not understand, a fierce-looking nation without respect for the old or pity for the young. They will devour the young of your livestock and the crops of your land until you are destroyed. They will leave you no grain, new wine or oil, nor any calves of your herds or lambs of your flocks until you are ruined. They will lay siege to all the cities throughout your land until the high fortified walls in which you trust fall down.

They will besiege all the cities throughout the land the LORD your God is giving you.

Because of the suffering that your enemy will inflict on you during the siege, you will eat the fruit of the womb, the flesh of the sons and daughters the LORD your God has given you. Even the most gentle and sensitive man among you will have no compassion on his own brother or the wife he loves or his surviving children, and he will not give to one of them any of the flesh of his children that he is eating. It will be all he has left because of the suffering your enemy will inflict on you during the siege of all your cities. The most gentle and sensitive woman among you—so sensitive and gentle that she would not venture to touch the ground with the sole of her foot—will begrudge the husband she loves and her own son or daughter the afterbirth from her womb and the children she bears. For she intends to eat them secretly during the siege and in the distress that your enemy will inflict on you in your cities.

If you do not carefully follow all the words of this law, which are written in this book, and do not revere this glorious and awesome name—the LORD your God—the LORD will send fearful plagues on you and your descendants, harsh and prolonged disasters, and severe and lingering illnesses. He will bring upon you all the diseases of Egypt that you dreaded, and they will cling to you. The LORD will also bring on you every kind of sickness and disaster not recorded in this Book of the Law, until you are destroyed.

You who were as numerous as the stars in the sky will be left but few in number, because you did not obey the LORD your God. Just as it pleased the LORD to make you prosper and increase in number, so it will please him to ruin and destroy you. You will be uprooted from the land you are entering to possess.

Then the LORD will scatter you among all nations, from one end of the earth to the other. There you will worship other gods—gods of wood and stone, which neither you nor your fathers have known. Among those nations you will find no repose, no resting place for the sole of your foot. There the LORD will give you an anxious mind, eyes weary with longing, and a despairing heart. You will live in constant suspense, filled with dread both night and day, never sure of your life. In the morning you will say, "If only it were evening!" and in the evening, "If only it were morning!"—because of the terror that will fill your hearts and the sights that your eyes will see. The LORD will send you back in ships to Egypt on a journey I said you should never make again. There you will offer yourselves for sale to your enemies as male and female slaves, but no one will buy you. (28:15-68)

Thus, in what is one of the longest chapters of the whole *Pentateuch*, which I have quoted in full, curses surpass and outweigh blessings.

Here, everything boils down to, or is derived from, one foundational rule, the "grund norm" of religious law: Fear and obey (and believe in) God, or its converse, don't disobey (and disbelieve in) God. (There is no converse of "fear"; "don't disfear" would be absurd, for we don't yet have a "parole" for that. Accidental? Or religio-cultural! Reward for the former is blessing; punishment for the latter is curse.

Blessings and, much more spectacularly, curses are enumerated. The structure is parsimonious:

Blessings for obedience:	*Curses for disobedience:*
Becoming a "holy people"; "Abundant prosperity"	Curses Poverty and calamities
"Defeating enemies"	Defeat and flight
"Lending to many nations, borrowing from none"	Object of scorn and ridicule to other nations

Being "the head, not the tail" Being "at the top, never at the bottom," "high above all the nations"

That is:

fear → believe →
obey → prosper and →
dominate and exploit others

(Otherwise, perish.)

As simple and mechanical as that. This is the promise of religion. This is the meaning of life offered by religion. (By Judaism, Christianity, and Islam.)

Borrowing from the alien
Sinking lower than the alien
"Iron yoke" on neck

And, most notably:

Plagues until you perish
Wasting diseases
Incurable tumors and sores
Oppression and being robbed
Suffering and annihilation
Slavery to enemies
Ruin and total destruction

And:

"Your carcasses will be food" for animals
"Your sons and daughters will be given to" other nations
"You will eat...the flesh of (your) sons and daughters"
(In sum: infanticidal cannibalism)

Moreover:

"Madness and blindness"
"Confusion of mind"
"Anxious mind"
"Despairing heart"
"Constant suspense"
"Dread both day and night"
"Never sure of life"

"Hearts filled with terror"
(In sum: psychological warfare)

And:, of course:
The threat, the impending doom, of EXILE.

Last, but not least:
Commodification of human beings:
"There you will offer yourselves for sale to your enemies as male and female slaves, but no one will buy you."

Thus, "Five Commandments":

1. Fear
2. Believe
3. Obey
4. Be holy
5. Prosper

Or else, "Infinite Punishments," even greater degradation, and death. Highlights enumerated, but not exhausted, above.

This is what Western, Abrahamic, monotheistic religion is; this is, more importantly, what the idea and construct of God is, which constitutes the linchpin of, or stands at the vortex of, that religion. Institutional, clerical, ritual, and textual religion is but the handmaiden or instrumental paraphernelia of the very "idea" of God, of the God of Western monotheism. (Slight differences between, and rivalry among, Yahweh, Lord, and Allah notwithstanding, what I am terming as the "Five Commandments" are common to Judaism, Christianity and Islam.)

The paramount word of God in the whole of Western textual religion, and all the three sacred Books, is the Five Commandments, which is a declaration of war against human psyche with a view to frighten it to the point of paralyzed submission in order to secure its loyalty to God, his Word and to the religious-political rulers, who are the authors both of the *idea* of Him and of his *Ideas*—not quite an immaculate conceptualization. "This Book of the Law," (and for that matter, as we shall duly see, the *New Testament* and the *Koran*, too) is first and foremost a cognitive and affective assault on human psychology—playing (cruelly and deviously) on its fear instinct as its main target. (The latter two, adding the idea of "hell" to the worldly sufferings of the former.)

Just go over the imagery, the malicious creative energy, the psychological engineering that goes into the architecture of terrorizing human beings in this world. (Christianity will prepare the transition to, and Islam shall perfect this architecture in the other world, too.)

But we should not misconstrue the cause-effect relationship or the direction of the causal arrow. Kierkegaard's "fear and trembling" is not inherent in "human nature" (beyond a measure of instinctual fear—among other instincts); it is exploited, developed, and reified by the Books, the words of God "put in the mouth" of prophets and priests, who are men. It is not that human beings are by nature the "twin of fear" as Hobbes says, but that religions, by using the idea of a terrible god, have to date systematically frightened them and caused them to tremble with fright. Fear, perhaps, is more cultural and social than instinctual. It is "made" a capstone of human psychology and identity.

The "Five Commandments" and its frightening sanctions have done more to human beings in the, let's say, past 3000 years, than their natural constitution. It's not that their "being" is essentially "fearful"; they have been "becoming" so, thanks to religious books and the idea of God, both created and written by some men and put into the mouth of "God."

Similarly, nor is it the case that human beings are "evil" by nature; it has been religions' artful success to portray them as such and make them so. It is not that man—"male and female"—is evil from childhood so that religion had to come to curb his evilness; it is the other way around: such books have made him evil. (Cf. infra for more on this theme.)

The idea, and words, of God has demoralized and immoralized human beings, starting with the very image and very estimate of themselves and the other members of their species.

To pull together the moral, or rather the immoral and anti-humanistic, message of this Chapter 28 of Deuteronomy, I can say that this is the *locus classicus* of Western Civilization's still prevalent psychological, moral and political theory. (See especially "Revelation" of the *New Testament* and any part of the *Koran*.)

And, it is not true that religion and, above all, the idea of God, answers a basic psychological need for him, especially the alleviation of his fear of nature and death; religion and God frighten him with death-threats and with a satanized nature. Rather than protecting him from fear, they create the problem of fear and then claim to protect him from it. They do so in order to make him submit to the Law(s) of a few chosen and more holy men, aided and abetted by their God. "God" and religion are the greatest calamity that has befallen the greatest majority of men ("man-male") and all women ("man-female"). Chapter 28 is the self-explanatory documentary evidence, par excellence, in itself.

29. Renewal of the Covenant

These are the terms of the covenant the LORD commanded Moses to make with the Israelites in Moab, in addition to the covenant he had made with them at Horeb.

Moses summoned all the Israelites and said to them:

Your eyes have seen all that the LORD did in Egypt to Pharaoh, to all his officials and to all his land. With your own eyes you saw those great trials, those miraculous signs and great wonders. But to this day the LORD has not given you a mind that understands or eyes that see or ears that hear. (29:1-4)

People without "minds to understand or eyes that see or ears that hear." Incapable multitude (to be spoken to in riddles and parables) as opposed to capable elite. (Cf. also the *New Testament* and the *Koran*.)

Repetition of wandering in the desert, of defeating enemies...

Obey and prosper:

Carefully follow the terms of this covenant, so that you may prosper in everything you do. All of you are standing today in the presence of the LORD your God—your leaders and chief men, your elders and officials, and all the other men of Israel, together with your children and your wives, and the aliens living in your camps who chop your wood and carry your water. You are standing here in order to enter into a covenant with the LORD your God, a covenant the LORD is making with you this day and sealing with an oath, to confirm you this day as his people, that he may be your God as he promised you and as he swore to your fathers, Abraham, Isaac and Jacob. I am making this covenant, with its oath, not only with you who are standing here with us today in the presence of the LORD our God but also with those who are not here today. (29:9-15)

Exodus, idolatry, purging of idol-worshipers…

When such a person hears the words of this oath, he invokes a blessing on himself and therefore thinks, "I will be safe, even though I persist in going my own way." This will bring disaster on the watered land as well as the dry. The LORD will never be willing to forgive him; his wrath and zeal will burn against that man. All the curses written in this book will fall upon him, and the LORD will blot out his name from under heaven. The LORD will single him out from all the tribes of Israel for disaster, according to all the curses of the covenant written in this Book of the Law.

Your children who follow you in later generations and foreigners who come from distant lands will see the calamities that have fallen on the land and the diseases with which the LORD has afflicted it. The whole land will be a burning waste of salt and sulfur—nothing planted, nothing sprouting, no vegetation growing on it. It will be like the destruction of Sodom and Gomorrah, Admah and Zeboiim, which the LORD overthrew in fierce anger. All the nations will ask: "Why has the LORD done this to this land? Why this fierce, burning anger?"

And the answer will be: "It is because this people abandoned the covenant of the LORD, the God of their fathers, the covenant he made with them when he brought them out of Egypt. They went off and worshiped other gods and bowed down to them, gods they did not know, gods he had not given them. Therefore the LORD's anger burned against this land, so that he brought on it all the curses written in this book. In furious anger and in great wrath the LORD uprooted them from their land and thrust them into another land, as it is now." (29:19-28)

Safety versus disaster, sulfur, wrath, blotting out, curses, exile. Why? Because of not believing in monotheism.

Many incapable men know little, few capable men know more; but it is God who knows all:

The secret things belong to the LORD our God, but the things revealed belong to us and to our children forever, that we may follow all the words of this law. (29:29)

The *Koran* will adopt most of this discourse.

30. Prosperity After Turning to the Lord

Exile and return are foreshadowed:

> When all these blessings and curses I have set before you come upon you and you
> take them to heart wherever the LORD your God disperses you among the nations,
> and when you and your children return to the LORD your God and obey him with
> all your heart and with all your soul according to everything I command you today,
> then the LORD your God will restore your fortunes and have compassion on you
> and gather you again from all the nations where he scattered you. Even if you have
> been banished to the most distant land under the heavens, from there the LORD
> your God will gather you and bring you back. He will bring you to the land that be-
> longed to your fathers, and you will take possession of it. He will make you more
> prosperous and numerous than your fathers. The LORD your God will circumcise
> your hearts and the hearts of your descendants, so that you may love him with all
> your heart and with all your soul, and live. The LORD your God will put all these
> curses on your enemies who hate and persecute you. You will again obey the LORD
> and follow all his commands I am giving you today. Then the LORD your God will
> make you most prosperous in all the work of your hands and in the fruit of your
> womb, the young of your livestock and the crops of your land. The LORD will
> again delight in you and make you prosperous, just as he delighted in your fathers, if
> you obey the LORD your God and keep his commands and decrees that are written
> in this Book of the Law and turn to the LORD your God with all your heart and
> with all your soul. (30:1-10)

Again, belief in and return to God is rewarded with prosperity. The concept of "circumcision of hearts" (presumably of both men and women) is repeated—whereas circumcision of
penises had to be a privilege of men—a closer, innermost, form of bodily control.

> Now what I am commanding you today is not too difficult for you or beyond your
> reach. It is not up in heaven, so that you have to ask, "Who will ascend into heaven
> to get it and proclaim it to us so we may obey it?" Nor is it beyond the sea, to that
> you have to ask, "Who will cross the sea to get it and proclaim it to us so we may
> obey it?" No, the word is very near you; it is in your mouth and in your heart so you
> may obey it. (30:11-14)

Physical proximity of God and his word—in the mouth and in the heart.

> See, I set before you today life and prosperity, death and destruction. For I com-
> mand you today to love the LORD your God, to walk in his ways, and to keep his
> commands, decrees and laws; then you will live and increase, and the LORD your
> God will bless you in the land you are entering to possess.

But if your heart turns away and you are not obedient, and if you are drawn away
to bow down to other gods and worship them. I declare to you this day that you will
certainly be destroyed. You will not live long in the land you are crossing the Jordan
to enter and possess.

This day I call heaven and earth as witnesses against you that I have set before you
life and death, blessings and curses. Now choose life, so that you and your children
may live and that you may love the LORD your God, listen to his voice, and hold
fast to him. For the LORD is your life, and he will give you many years in the land
he swore to give to your fathers, Abraham, Isaac and Jacob. (30:15-20)

God is life and prosperity, obverse is death and destruction. So choose God if you want to
live and your children to live. Otherwise, threat of death and infanticide. The psychology
and politics of fear of death is again at work. "Lord is your life." Therefore, non-Lord is your
death. And your children's.

31. Joshua To Succeed Moses; Israel's Rebellion Predicted

Moses (now 120 years old) announces Joshua's succession, tells the Israelites to be strong
and courageous, writes down the law and gives it to the priests, the sons of Levi, and says to
them:

Assemble the people—men, women and children, and the aliens living in your
towns—so they can listen and learn to fear the LORD your God and follow carefully all the words of this law. Their children, who do not know this law, must hear
it and learn to fear the LORD your God as long as you live in the land you are crossing the Jordan to possess. (31:12-13)

God says to Moses:

You are going to rest with your fathers, and these people will soon prostitute themselves to the foreign gods of the land they are entering. They will forsake me and
break the covenant I made with them. On that day I will become angry with them
and forsake them; I will hide my face from them, and they will be destroyed. Many
disasters and difficulties will come upon them, and on that day they will ask, 'Have
not these disasters come upon us because our God is not with us?' And I will certainly hide my face on that day because of all their wickedness in turning to other
gods. (31:16-18)

People can't win: they "will soon prostitute themselves." In self-fulfilling prophecy, God
(Moses) does not teach or command humility but humbles, humiliates, insults his so-called
chosen people. A God, a religion, a book, a prophet that "abhor" people essentially and
essentialistically.

Now write down for yourselves this song and teach it to the Israelites and have them
sing it, so that it may be a witness for me against them. When I have brought them

into the land flowing with milk and honey, the land I promised on oath to their forefathers, and when they eat their fill and thrive, they will turn to other gods and worship them, rejecting me and breaking my covenant. And when many disasters and difficulties come upon them, this song will testify against them, because it will not be forgotten by their descendants. I know what they are disposed to do, even before I bring them into the land I promised them on oath. So Moses wrote down this song that day and taught it to the Israelites.

The LORD gave this command to Joshua son of Nun: "Be strong and courageous, for you will bring the Israelites into the land I promised them on oath, and I myself will be with you." (31:19-23)

God is predetermined and people are predestinated, indeed.

After Moses finished writing in a book the words of this law from beginning to end, he gave this command to the Levites who carried the ark of the covenant of the LORD:

Take this Book of the Law and place it beside the ark of the covenant of the LORD your God. There it will remain as a witness against you. For I know how rebellious and stiff-necked you are. If you have been rebellious against the LORD while I am still alive and with you, how much more will you rebel after I die! Assemble before me all the elders of your tribes and all your officials, so that I can speak these words in their hearing and call heaven and earth to testify against them. For I know that after my death you are sure to become utterly corrupt and to turn from the way I have commanded you. In days to come, disaster will fall upon you because you will do evil in the sight of the LORD and provoke him to anger by what your hands have made. (31:24-29)

The "Book of the Law" mainly to be and remain as a "witness against" the people, who are surely known to be and to remain "rebellious and stiff-necked." A prophet who primarily "testifies against" his people. A God whose main business is to destroy his own chosen people. Essentialism confirmed: "I know that...you are sure to become utterly corrupt..."

32. The "Song" of Moses

Selections from the peerless prophet's (Cf. 34:10) farewell "song" to his people (song or the libretto of an ultimatum?):

I will proclaim the name of the LORD. Oh, praise the greatness of our God!
He is the Rock, his works are perfect, and all his ways are just.
A faithful God who does no wrong, upright and just is he.
They have acted corruptly toward him; to their shame they are no longer his
Children, but a warped and crooked generation.
Is this the way you repay the LORD, O foolish and unwise people?

Is he not your Father, your Creator, who made you and formed you?

....

The LORD saw this and rejected them
because he was angered by his sons and daughters.
I will hide my face from them, he said, and see what their end will be;
for they are a perverse generation, children who are unfaithful.
They made me jealous by what is no god
and angered me with their worthless idols.
I will make them envious by those who are not a people;
I will make them angry by a nation that has no understanding.
For a fire has been kindled by my wrath,
one that burns to the realm of death below.
It will devour the earth and its harvests
and set afire the foundations of the mountains.
I will heap calamities upon them and spend my arrows against them.
I will send wasting famine against them,
consuming pestilence and deadly plague;
I will send against them the fangs of wild beasts,
the venom of vipers that glide in the dust.
In the street the sword will make them childless;
in their homes terror will reign.
Young men and young women will perish, infants and gray-haired men.
I said I would scatter them and blot out their memory from mankind,
but I dreaded the taunt of the enemy, lest the adversary misunderstand
and say, 'Our hand has triumphed; the LORD has not done all this.'
They are a nation without sense, there is no discernment in them.
If only they were wise and would understand this
and discern what their end will be!

....

The LORD will judge his people and have compassion on his servants
when he sees their strength is gone and no one is left, slave or free.
He will say: "Now where are their gods, the rock they took refuge in,
the gods who ate the fat of their sacrifices
and drank the wine of their drink offerings?
Let them rise up to help you! Let them give you shelter!
See now that I myself am He! There is no god besides me.
I put to death and I bring to life, I have wounded and I will heal,
and no one can deliver out of my hand.
I lift my hand to heaven and declare: As surely as I live forever,

when I sharpen my flashing sword and my hand grasps it in judgment,

I will take vengeance on my adversaries and repay those who hate me.

I will make my arrows drunk with blood, while my sword devours flesh:

the blood of the slain and the captives, the heads of the enemy leaders.

Rejoice, O nations, with his people,

for he will avenge the blood of his servants;

he will take vengeance on his enemies and make atonement for his land and people.

   (32:3-6, 19-29, 36-43)

No esteem for human beings. A heap of insults hurled upon them—by their "Father-Creator." And, of course, a lot of automatic aggression toward "nations."

   Corrupt

   Warped

   Crooked

   Foolish

   Unwise

   Perverse

   Senseless

   Undiscerning

   (Enumerative, not exhaustive.)

Therefore: curses and threats and calamities—that fill the rest of the historical narrative of the *Old Testament*, after "this Book of the Law," in a vicious circular, or cyclical, or pendulum-like movement (certainly not a spiral-like process) of exile and return, desolation and prosperity; punishment and reward(!).

   Moses concludes:

They are not just idle words for you–they are your life. By them you will live long in the land you are crossing the Jordan to possess.

Take religious texts seriously; they are a matter of life and death.

   Moses is to die on Mount Nebo:

On that same day the LORD told Moses, "Go up into the Abarim Range to Mount Nebo in Moab, across from Jericho, and view Canaan, the land I am giving the Israelites as their own possession. There on the mountain that you have climbed you will die and be gathered to your people, just as your brother Aaron died on Mount Hor and was gathered to his people. This is because both of you broke faith with me in the presence of the Israelites at the waters of Meribah Kadesh in the Desert of Zin and because you did not uphold my holiness among the Israelites. Therefore, you will see the land only from a distance; you will not enter the land I am giving to the people of Israel."

A very judicious God who punishes even his most chosen ones! A clever homage paid to the justness, even-handedness, and non-partisanship of a God who privileges no one, not even his prophet(s).

33. Moses Blesses the Tribes

Just like Jacob at the end of Genesis, Moses ("the man of God," 33:1) blesses his twelve tribes/sons at the end of Deuteronomy, before his death:

> Surely it is you who love the people; all the holy ones are in your hand.
> At your feet they all bow down, and from you receive instruction,
> the law that Moses gave us, the possession of the assembly of
> He was king over Jeshurun... Jacob. (33:3-5)[4]

"Lov(ing) the people"—"all the holy ones"—"in your hand," "bowing down" "at your feet."

Now:

> Reuben—to live and not die; his men to be many
> Judah-to be helped against his enemies
> Benjamin—to be protected by God
> Zebulun—to rejoice
> Issachar—to rejoice
> Gad—to enlarge his domain
> Dan—to be lion's cub
> Naphtali—to abound with God's favor
> Asher—to be the most blessed of sons; to be wealthy

Population increase, expansion, prosperity.

Joseph, his two sons, and Levi receive greater attention. Joseph, "the prince among his brothers" (33:16):

> In majesty he is like a firstborn bull; his horns are the horns of a wild ox.
> With them he will gore the nations, even those at the ends of the earth.
> Such are the ten thousands of Ephraim: such are the thousands of Manasseh. (33:17)

Why all this belligerence and martialism?

As for Levi:

> He said of his father and mother, 'I have no regard for them.'
> He did not recognize his brothers or acknowledge his own children,
> but he watched over your word and guarded your covenant.
> He teaches your precepts to Jacob and your law to Israel.
> He offers incense before you and whole burnt offerings on your altar.
> Bless all his skills, O LORD, and be pleased with the work of his hands.

Smite the loins of those who rise up against him; strike his foes till they rise no more. (33: 9-11)

Rejecting parents, brothers (sisters not mentioned), own children for the sake of God and his Word. (Cf. *Koran*, too.) Striking of foes, external and internal (Cf. Numbers, Ch. 16).

Not so much a funeral march as the previous "song" of Moses or a bundle of curses like Jacob's blessing of his sons, at the end of Genesis, with which the interested reader can compare this list. And, of course, sound, divine legitimation and political theory of oppressive power politics. (Remember Numbers, Chapter 16.) Plus: a general blessing to the Israelites (and a curse to other nations as the inevitable corollary):

The eternal God is your refuge, and underneath are the everlasting arms.

He will drive out your enemy before you, saying, 'Destroy him!'

So Israel will live in safety alone; Jacob's spring is secure

in a land of grain and new wine, where the heavens drop dew.

Blessed are you, O Israel!

Who is like you, a people saved by the LORD?

He is your shield and helper and your glorious sword.

Your enemies will cower before you, and you will trample down their high places. (33:27-29)

34. The Death of Moses

Moses was a hundred and twenty years old when he died, yet his eyes were not weak nor his strength gone. The Israelites grieved for Moses in the plains of Moab thirty days, until the time of weeping and mourning was over.

Now Joshua son of Nun was filled with the spirit of wisdom because Moses had laid his hands on him. So the Israelites listened to him and did what the LORD had commanded Moses.

Since then, no prophet has risen in Israel like Moses, whom the LORD knew face to face, who did all those miraculous signs and wonders the LORD sent him to do in Egypt—to Pharaoh and to all his officials and to his whole land. For no one has ever shown the mighty power or performed the awesome deeds that Moses did in the sight of all Israel. (34:7-12)

Divine legitimacy is smoothly transferred, to more earthly kings. Moses was a "king," too (33:5), as shall Jesus be. (Cf. Infra.)

POSTSCRIPT to DEUTERONOMY

This is Deuteronomy, "this Book of the Law" (28:61), to which you cannot add and from which you cannot subtract. This is the absolute text to be obeyed absolutely, without any (much) room for interpretation. Only God and his prophets may do so.

This is the "Five Commandments" of: 1. Fear, 2. Believe, 3. Obey, 4. Be holy, 5. Prosper. (Be wealthy in your holiness *and* be holy in your wealthiness.) Fear God, believe and obey his book(s) and prophet(s) and priests and kings, be the holy people as opposed to the (unholy) human beings and "nations," and, as the basic reward, as the meaning and purpose of life, prosper! Prosperity is righteousness. (And justice is impartiality and fairness to the rich and the poor alike.)

Xenophobic and belligerent and annihilatory and plunderous "international relations." (Which boomerangs.) A warrior God who fights for his people against enemies, but who also, and frequently, fights against his own chosen people who chronically arouse his anger. A "merciful" and "compassionate" God who curses his people more than he blesses them—curses well-listed in Chapter 28, including, infanticide, homicide, torture and child-eating.

A political theory of theocratic monarchy and of dynastic priesthood. A theory of power politics based on fear and threat of death.

A moral-political theory of elitist oppression. Godly few governing incapable, sinful, self-prostituting multitude, who are unrighteous and stiff-necked. Servitude of slaves and women. Rudiments of charity in the form of almsgiving and giving of leftovers. Spiritual inequality of human beings, most notably in the form of condoning unholy ones' eating unclean food.

A legal theory in the narrow sense of the term which also includes such sanctions as stoning, lynching, burning. A Book of Law in the wider sense of the term, which is a moral theory, a legal theory, and a social-political theory, all at once. And all emanating from the fundamental ontological and epistemological theory of God—which in Western mono-theism is crushingly mightier than any poly-theisms. Religion is the oldest and mightiest of all political ideologies; Western monotheism, thanks to the central idea of one omnipotent God, is the most powerful of all, leaving no room for doubt, plurality, division. Strict, unequivocal unity is the surest guarantee of totalitarianism.

A faithful God who always creates scenes, a saving God who destroys all the time, an exiling God who continues to keep company in the exile, a close God who inspires more fear than security, and so forth. What about the other end of this unique relationship? Except for a few really chosen men, most men and all women of the holy people are always debased and degraded. Why, then, do they believe? Are they masochists? Identification with the powerful? Illusion and delusion? Yes and no. Yes, the above are included. No, they (all combined) cannot account for the situation. The definitive answer is in Chapter 28. They

FEAR; they have been turned into a GOD-FEARING people. The *Old Testament* legacy shall be upheld by the *New Testament* and *Koran*—to date. Chapter 28 of the source-book of all may not be too vivid in contemporary memory, but its offspring, Revelation, is the fount of inspiration for much of Western art and literature.

This Middle Eastern God of Western Civilization does not comfort humanity against the fact or fear of death; he threatens him with early, imminent death in life, on top of all other kinds of torture and suffering in life. He makes, in the *Old Testament*, life itself a "hell." The *New Testament*'s and *Koran*'s God shall add to it the other "hell." (Can this be one of the reasons why there are only 15 million Jews—and not all believers—while Christianity and Islam claim 1.5 billion believers each? The greater the fear, the higher the number of believers, despite the latter two's claim that they put a "lighter burden" on the believers?) In short, fear of death is actually transformed into fear of death *and* life, and of other human beings, members of the species.

The ambiguously death-obsessed Genesis had buried humankind's future, now the unequivocally murderous Deuteronomy (and, later, Revelation) puts the lid on it. No escape from sin and punishment, not even for the chosen believers, who shall surely, cyclically, prostitute themselves.

Humankind, in this account of its nature, is incorrigibly, eternally evil. (Then, what's the use of religion, really?) It *has* no future in the sense of an evolving, correctional process of becoming better, and less unhappy.

Is Christianity (and Islam) any different? We shall see.

As for "the rest" of the *Old Testament*, from Joshua to Malachi, it is a repetitive or cyclical or pendulum-like movement toing and froing between exile and return, despair and hope, punishment and reward, which, however, in net balance, is a process predominated by the first terms of the above pairs.

Exile of the chosen people not only from land and prosperity, but also from God; return of the chosen people not only to land and prosperity, but also to God. (And, of course, return to fear and submission.)

Thus, Malachi 3:7:

Ever since the time of your forefathers you have turned away from my decrees and have not kept them. Return to me, and I will return to you, says the LORD Almighty.

"How are we to return?," the people ask.

God answers:

Will a man rob God? Yet you rob me. But you ask, 'How do we rob you?' In tithes and offerings. You are under a curse—the whole nation of you—because you are robbing me. Bring the whole tithe into the storehouse, that there may be food in my house. (3:8-10)

On the Day of Judgment:

> So I will come near to you for judgment. I will be quick to testify against sorcerers, adulterers and perjurers, against those who defraud laborers of their wages, who oppress the widows and the fatherless, and deprive aliens of justice, but do not fear me, says the LORD Almighty. (3:5)

Some morality alongside tithes.

In Malachi ("my messenger"), the concluding chapter of the *Old Testament*, we are also still at the point of the Lord saying, "I have loved Jacob, but Esau I hated" (1:2-3).

The Lord Almighty, "a great king" (1:14) continues to admonish priests and, more importantly, to frighten and curse the chosen faithful in toto (Cf. "the whole nation of you," supra). And:

> See, I will send my messenger, who will prepare the way before me. Then suddenly the Lord you are seeking will come to his temple; the messenger of the covenant, whom you desire, will come, says the LORD Almighty.
>
> But who can endure the day of his coming? Who can stand when he appears? For he will be like a refiner's fire or a launderer's soap. He will sit as a refiner and purifier of silver; he will purify the Levites and refine them like gold and silver. (3:1-3)

The lot of "other" nations, or simply "the nations," shall of course be worse than that of the sinful faithful. Thus, Zechariah 14:12-15, just before Malachi:

> This is the plague with which the LORD will strike all the nations that fought against Jerusalem: Their flesh will rot while they are still standing on their feet, their eyes will rot in their sockets, and their tongues will rot in their mouths. On that day men will be stricken by the LORD with great panic. Each man will seize the hand of another, and they will attack each other. Judah too will fight at Jerusalem. The wealth of all the surrounding nations will be collected—great quantities of gold and silver and clothing. A similar plague will strike the horses and mules, the camels and donkeys, and all the animals in those camps.

Prosperity and gold and silver.

Notes

1. Our philosophy of justice is still arrested at the stage of "justice as impartiality" or "justice as fairness." We are relentless inegalitarians, who can't go beyond legal equality toward real equality based on full political and economic equality.

2. That is, said to be—and believed to be—Godly.

3. David had great wealth, 700 wives and 300 concubines, but remained one of the most-favored sons, certain ambivalent admonitions not withstanding. He is among the favorite prophet-kings of the *Koran*, too.

4. One cannot tell, from the text's use of subjects and pronouns here, who is ventriloquizing whom.

PART TWO

THE NEW TESTAMENT

MATTHEW[1]

1. The Genealogy of Jesus

"A record of the genealogy of Jesus Christ the son of David, the son of Abraham" (1:1) is given. "Thus there were fourteen generations in all from Abraham to David, fourteen from the exile to the Christ" (1:17). Jesus Christ descends from Jacob's son Judah (1:2,3), from King David's son Solomon (1:6,7), (and from Jacob's son Joseph, the husband of Mary of whom Jesus was born, 1:16). That is, Jesus Christ is a Jewish prophet of royal ancestry. Jesus is the Greek form of Joshua, which means "the Lord saves" (p.717, fn. c21). The Christ (Greek) and the Messiah (Hebrew) both mean "the Anointed One" (p.717, fn. b17).

In the above long genealogy, fathers are listed by name (42) and, in good *Torah*-tradition, only three mothers (Tamar, Rahab, Ruth) are mentioned by name. "This is how the birth of Jesus Christ came about: His mother Mary was pledged to be married to Joseph, but before they came together, she was found to be with child through the Holy Spirit" (1:18). The superhuman prophet was given the name of Jesus "because he will save his people from their sins" (1:21). Please note: saving people not, for example, from their misery but from their sins.

The story is narrated by Matthew, a man, who quotes from "an angel of the Lord" (e.g., 1:20-21). Matthew also quotes from the Lord via His prophet: "All this took place to fulfill what the Lord had said through the prophet: 'The virgin will be with child and will give birth to a son, and they will call him Immanuel'[2]—which means 'God with us' " (1:22). (Cf. Luke 3:37: Jesus was the son of ...."Seth, the son of Adam, the son of God." Thus, unlike the *Torah* and, more importantly, the *Koran*, the prophets are "sons of God.")

2. The Visit of the Magi (Wise Men)

Jesus is not only a Jewish prophet by ancestry; he is the "king of the Jews" (2:2) according to the wise men. Also "the people's chief priests and teachers of the law" (2:4) quote to King Herod the prophet Micah's words from the *Torah*:

> ...out of you will come a ruler who will be the shepherd of my people Israel. (2:6; Micah 5:2)

The magi visit and worship the born-ruler and: "They opened their treasures and presented him with gifts of gold and of incense and of myrrh" (2:11). An angel of the Lord tells Joseph in his dream to take the mother and the child to Egypt away from Herod's murderous intentions, until he calls back his son, as he "had said, through the prophet: 'Out of Egypt I called my son' " (2:15; Hosea 11:1).

3. John the Baptist Prepares the Way

John the Baptist is already preaching and saying; "Repent, for the kingdom of heaven is near" (3:2), as anticipated by the prophet Isaiah (esp. Isaiah 40:3), one of the favorite Hebrew prophets of Christianity.

John, a fastidious man, at first refuses to baptize Pharisees and Sadducees ("You brood of vipers," 3:7), compares them unfavorably with stones as candidates for being Abraham's children (3:9), then baptizes them with water for repentance (3:11), and announces Jesus Christ's coming:

> But after me will come one who is more powerful than I, whose sandals I am not fit to carry. He will baptize you with the Holy Spirit and with fire. (3:11)

John, with all humility, baptizes Jesus "to fulfill all righteousness" (3:15), heaven is opened, the Spirit of God is seen descending like a dove, and "a voice from heaven said" (3:17):

> This is my Son, whom I love; with him I am well pleased. (3:17)

"Sonship" will not be recognized by *Koran*.

4. The Temptation of Jesus

The devil cannot tempt Jesus, who retorts:

> It is written: "Man does not live on bread alone, but on every word that comes from the mouth of God." (4:4; Deut. 8:3)

> It is also written: "Do not put the Lord your God to the test." (4:7; Deut. 6:16)

And:

> Away from me, Satan! For it is written: "Worship the Lord your God, and serve him only." (4:10; Deut. 6:13)

Jesus begins preaching ("Repent, for the kingdom of heaven is near," 4:17) and recruits his first two disciples, the fishermen brothers Simon (called Peter) and Andrew:

> Come, follow me...and I will make you fishers of men. (4:19)

Jesus fishes disciples, the latter fish believers. Like James and John who "immediately" left the boat and their father and followed. (Cf. Luke 5:14: "from now on you will catch men.")

"Jesus (goes) throughout Galilee, teaching in their synagogues, preaching the good news of the kingdom, and healing every disease and sickness among the people" (4:23): pain, demon-possession, seizure, paralysis, leprosy, and blindness...Unlike expulsion from the Israelite camp, the Christian sick are healed in the community.

5. The Beatitudes and Laws

Jesus teaches and blesses. He blesses (5:3-10):

the poor in spirit	(who will have the kingdom of heaven)
the mourner	(who will be comforted)
the meek	(who will inherit the world)
the hungry and thirsty	(for righteousness)
the merciful	(who will be shown mercy)
the pure in heart	(who will see God)
the peacemaker	(who will be called sons of God)
the persecuted	(because of righteousness)

Please note that "the poverty" here concerns spirit, "the hunger and thirst" concern righteousness, and that there is no promise of compensation, as in the *Koran*, even in the other world/kingdom to be inherited, for worldly economic or other inequalities; what is promised are rewards (comfort, mercy, sonship, etc.) in the world hereafter for meekness, endurance, patience, passivity, submissiveness, and so forth in this world vis-à-vis the established order and the powers that be. (Cf. infra: "SUBMIT TO AUTHORITIES!")

(Compare with Luke 6:20-26:

Blessed are you who are poor, for yours is the kingdom of God.

Blessed are you who hunger now, for you will be satisfied.

Blessed are you who weep now, for you will laugh.

Blessed are you when men hate you, when they exclude you and insult you
and reject your name as evil, because of the Son of Man.

Rejoice in that day and leap for joy, because great is your reward in heaven.

For that is how their fathers treated the prophets.

But woe to you who are rich, for you have already received your comfort.

Woe to you who are well fed now, for you will go hungry.

Woe to you who laugh now, for you will mourn and weep.

Woe to you when all men speak well of you,

For that is how their fathers treated the false prophets.)

In one of the most important passages in Matthew Jesus says:

Do not think that I have come to abolish the Law or the Prophets: I have not come to abolish them but to fulfill them. I tell you the truth, until heaven and earth disappear, not the smallest letter, not the least stroke of a pen, will by any means disappear from the Law until everything is accomplished. Anyone who breaks one of the least of these commandments and teaches others to do the same will be called least in the kingdom of heaven, but whoever practices and teaches these commands will be called great in the kingdom of heaven. For I tell you that unless your righteousness surpasses that of the Pharisees and the teachers of the law, you will certainly not enter the kingdom of heaven. (5:17-20)

Not abolishing the Law or the Prophets, but fulfilling them. *Torah* as the absolute text to the single letter. Total continuity between the two books, the *Old* and the *New Testaments*. (An argument which is to be taken to its full extension by the *Koran*.)

Some articles of the Law are expanded:

- Murder: Do not murder (Exod. 20:13), plus: do not even be angry with and contemptuous of your brother (5:21-22). Furthermore, if you call your brother a fool, you will be "in danger of the fire of hell" (5:22).
- Settlement: Settle matters quickly with your adversary before he takes you to court (5:25).
- Adultery: Do not commit adultery (Exod. 20:14), plus: "Anyone who looks at a woman lustfully has already committed adultery with her in his heart" (5:28). And threats of hell if you don't gouge out your sinful right eye or cut off your sinful right hand (5:29-30).
- Divorce: Giving a certificate of divorce (Deut. 24:1) is not enough: "...anyone who divorces his wife, except for marital unfaithfulness, causes her to become an adulteress, and anyone who marries the divorced woman commits adultery" (5:31-32).
- Oaths: Do not break your oath, plus: "Do not swear at all...Simply let your Yes be Yes, and your No, No" (5:33-37).
- Eye for eye:

    You have heard that it was said, 'Eye for eye, and tooth for tooth.' But I tell you, Do not resist an evil person. If someone strikes you on the right cheek, turn to him the other also. And if someone wants to sue you and take your tunic, let him have your cloak as well. If someone forces you to go one mile, go with him two miles. Give to the one who asks you, and do not turn away from the one who wants to borrow from you. (5:38-42; Exod. 21:24, Lev. 24:20, Deut. 19:21)

Now, is this the spirit, let alone the letter, of the Law and the Prophets of lex talionis or is it a radical break from the Jewish *Torah* (and the Muslim *Koran*)? By the way, *Koran* will take the "adultery by eyeing" but leave the "Catholic marriage." And it will leave the "Christian cheek" but take Judaic lex talionis. Love for enemies:

    You have heard that it was said, 'Love your neighbor and hate your enemy.' But I tell you: Love your enemies[3] and pray for those who persecute you, that you may be sons of your Father in heaven. He causes his sun to rise on the evil and the good, and sends rain on the righteous and the unrighteous. If you love those who love you, what reward will you get? Are not even the tax collectors doing that? And if you greet

only your brothers, what are you doing more than others? Do not even pagans do
that? Be perfect, therefore, as your heavenly Father is perfect. (5:43-48; Lev. 19:18)

Another radical break with Judaism, or Pentateuch at least.

(Cf. also Luke 6:27-36: But I tell you who hear me: Love your enemies, do good to
those who hate you, bless those who curse you, pray for those who mistreat you. If
someone strikes you on one cheek, turn to him the other also. If someone takes your
cloak, do not stop him from taking your tunic. Give to everyone who asks you, and
if anyone takes what belongs to you, do not demand it back. Do to others as you
would have them do to you.

If you love those who love you, what credit is that to you? Even 'sinners' love
those who love them. And if you do good to those who are good to you, what credit
is that to you? Even 'sinners' do that. And if you lend to those from whom you expect repayment, what credit is that to you? Even 'sinners' lend to 'sinners,' expecting
to be repaid in full. But love your enemies, do good to them, and lend to them without expecting to get anything back. Then your reward will be great, and you will be
sons of the Most High, because he is kind to the ungrateful and wicked. Be merciful,
just as your Father is merciful.)

6. Giving to the Needy

Be careful not to do your 'acts of righteousness' before men, to be seen by them. If
you do, you will have no reward from your Father in heaven.

So when you give to the needy, do not announce it with trumpets, as the hypocrites do in the synagogues and on the streets, to be honored by men. I tell you the
truth, they have received their reward in full. But when you give to the needy, do not
let your left hand know what your right hand is doing, so that your giving may be in
secret. Then your Father, who sees what is done in secret, will reward you. (6:1-4)

Give alms discreetly, don't self-advertise. Pray secretly, silently, properly, thankfully. Forgive those who sin against you, so that you, too, will be forgiven. Fast secretly and properly.
Matthew, I think, goes beyond almsgiving and intimates a serious critique of wealth.

Do not store up for yourselves treasures on earth, where moth and rust destroy, and
where thieves break in and steal. But store up for yourselves treasures in heaven,
where moth and rust do not destroy, and where thieves do not break in and steal.
For where your treasure is, there your heart will be also. (6:19-21)

He goes even further (and further than Mark):

No one can serve two masters. Either he will hate the one and love the other, or he
will be devoted to the one and despise the other. You cannot serve both God and
Money. (6:24)

This is very different from the *Old Testament*, and for that matter from the *Koran*. (Compare especially with Luke.) Needs, not luxuries:

> ...do not worry about your life, what you will eat or drink; or about your body, what you will wear. (6:25)

> For the pagans run after all these things, and your heavenly Father knows that you need them. But seek first his kingdom and his righteousness, and all these things will be given to you as well. Therefore do not worry about tomorrow, for tomorrow will worry about itself. Each day has enough trouble of its own. (6:32-34)

7. Judging Others; Ask, Seek, Knock

> Do not judge, or you too will be judged. For in the same way you judge others, you will be judged, and with the measure you use, it will be measured to you.

> Why do you look at the speck of sawdust in your brother's eye and pay no attention to the plank in your own eye? How can you say to your brother, 'Let me take the speck out of your eye,' when all the time there is a plank in your own eye? You hypocrite, first take the plank out of your own eye, and then you will see clearly to remove the speck from your brother's eye. (7:1-5)

"For everyone who asks receives; he who seeks finds; and to him who knocks, the door will be opened" (7:8).

> So in everything, do to others what you would have them do to you, for this sums up the Law and the Prophets. (7:12)

"When Jesus had finished saying these things, the crowds were amazed at his teaching, because he taught as one who had authority, and not as their teachers of the law" (7:28-29).

Thus, the Prophets and their Book(s), the Law, are affirmed as being absolutely true (as the Word of God); what is faulty is the teaching and interpretation of religious scholars, the teachers of law. This shall become one of the main arguments of Muhammad in the *Koran*, too.

8, 9. Wondrous Healings

Jesus heals leprosy, skin diseases, paralysis, fever, demon-possessedness; he calms a storm by force of faith; he heals a bleeding woman, gives life to a deadly asleep girl, heals the blind and the mute.

Jesus eats with tax collectors and sinners; he is rebuked for this; he answers: "It is not the healthy who need a doctor, but the sick...I desire mercy, not sacrifice. For I have not come to call the righteous, but sinners" (9:12-13). (So religion is for the sinners and for the unhealthy.)

Jesus is the "Son of Man" (8:20) and the "Son of God" (8.29) both at once. He has "authority on earth to forgive sins" (9:6).

"When he saw the crowds, he had compassion on them, because they were harassed and helpless, like sheep without a shepherd." (9:36)

10. Jesus Sends Out the Twelve

Jesus gives the twelve apostles "authority to drive out evil spirits and heal every disease and sickness" (10:1). The twelve are:

Simon (Peter)	Thomas
Andrew	Matthew (tax-collector)
James	James
John	Thaddeus
Philip	Simon (Zealot)
Bartholomew	Judas

Jesus instructs them:

"Do not take along any gold or silver or copper in your belts; take no bag for the journey, or extra tunic, or sandals or a staff; for the worker is worth his keep." (10:10)

They are to go to the "lost sheep of Israel," not to the Gentiles and Samaritans (10:5-6).

These are compassionate and ascetic workers, but those towns that would not "welcome" them and "listen to their words" shall become worse than Sodom and Gomorrah on the day of judgement (10:14-15). "Sheep sent among wolves" (10:16), but not so lambish in the final analysis.

The apostles should stand firm and not fear men, but "(r)ather, be afraid of the One who can destroy both soul and body in hell" (10:25). The apostles are both strengthened vis-à-vis the outer world and controlled internally:

So do not be afraid of them. There is nothing concealed that will not be disclosed, or hidden that will not be made known. (10:26)

And, the "will of the Father" (10:29) not only shapes the world but also controls the very inner being of the "few workers" (apostles) as well:

And even the very hairs of your head are all numbered. (10:31)

To complete the circuit of power and authority from God to Jesus to apostles to men, Jesus says:

Whoever acknowledges me before man, I will also acknowledge him before my Father in heaven. But whoever disowns me before men, I will disown him before my Father in heaven. (10:32)

Like all prophets, Jesus invokes the supreme authority of a superhuman and partisan power in his relations with other men (sons of God, too?). And the lamb(s) of God is (are) not so lambish or lamb-like, after all. Iron paws in velvet gloves:

> Do not suppose that I have come to bring peace to the earth. I did not come to bring peace, but a sword. For I have come to turn a man against his father, a daughter against her mother, a daughter-in-law against her mother-in-law—a man's enemies will be the members of his own household. (10:34-36)

This prediction of the *Old Testament* prophet (Micah 7:6) is adopted by Jesus; it shall also be adopted by Muhammad in the *Koran*.

> Anyone who loves his father or mother more than me is not worthy of me; anyone who loves his son or daughter more than me is not worthy of me; and anyone who does not take his cross and follow me is not worthy of me. Whoever finds his life will lose it, and whoever loses his life for my sake will find it.
>
> He who receives you receives me, and he who receives me receives the one who sent me. (10:37-40)

11. Jesus and John the Baptist

Jesus speaks to the crowd about John: "...those who wear fine clothes are in kings' palaces" (11:8), as opposed to John the prophet, "more than a prophet" (11:9), the one whose coming was already written in Malachi (3:1), namely Elijah.

Jesus denounces unrepentant cities, whose end will be worse than Tyre and Sidon, than Sodom and Gomorrah, on the day of judgment. (Jesus is no less cursing a prophet than Muhammad.) Jesus praises God for having hidden truths from "the wise and learned" and revealing them to "little children" (11:25).

And he invokes his monopolistic authority as "*the* Son":

> All things have been committed to me by my Father. No one knows the Son except the Father, and no one knows the Father except the Son and those to whom the Son chooses to reveal him. (11:27)

God → Son → (prophet) → chosen ones: We have the classical hierarchy once more. But, here, Jesus is a son-prophet, whereas neither Moses was nor Muhammad will be such; they are "mere" prophets, in the language of the *Koran*.

> Come to me, all you who are weary and burdened, and I will give you rest. Take my yoke upon you and learn from me, for I am gentle and humble in heart, and you will find rest for your souls. For my yoke is easy and my burden is light. (11:28-30)

Gentle and humble or sword-bearing and God-like aside, that this religious teaching is light and unburdensome (compared to Judaism) is an argument to be repetitiously stated by the *Koran*.

12. Lord of the Sabbath and God's Chosen Servant

Pharisees rebuke Jesus's disciples for picking and eating grain on the Sabbath, Jesus reminds them of the example of hungry David to the effect that lawfulness according to the spirit of the Law is greater than lawfulness according to the letter of the Law, invoking at the same time his own superior authority over the Jewish Law: "I tell you that one greater than the temple is here...For the Son of Man is Lord of the Sabbath" (12:8). (Meaning: Sabbath is for men, not men is for Sabbath.) (A radical break.) And: "Therefore it is lawful to do good on the Sabbath" (12:10). (Cf. Luke 6:9: "...which is lawful on the Sabbath: to do good or to do evil, to save life or to destroy it?") (Compare with *Torah*'s death penalty.)

Jesus's superior authority is reinforced by the reference to Isaiah (42:1-4), or rather to God (who "spoke through" him), that Jesus is the "chosen servant," "the one I love, in whom I delight;/ I will put my Spirit on him..." (12:18).

Jesus says to Pharisees: "Every kingdom divided against itself will be ruined, and every city or household divided against itself will not stand" (12:25). Order and unity in religion, in the state, in the family. One God, one state, one folk (Ein volk, ein staat, ein führer.) And one (religious) leader:

He who is not with me is against me. (12:30)

And of course, against God (remember Numbers, Ch. 16):

And so I tell you, every sin and blasphemy will be forgiven men, but the blasphemy against the Spirit will not be forgiven. Anyone who speaks a word against the Son of Man will be forgiven, but anyone who speaks against the Holy Spirit will not be forgiven, either in this age or in the age to come. (12:31-32)

In view of 12:30, we may disregard the first sentence of 12:32; the seemingly initial differentiation dissolves, at second glance, into the expected equation and identification of the Son and the Father.

Plus (intimidation, and insult, continues):

You brood of vipers, how can you who are evil say anything good? For out of the overflow of the heart the mouth speaks. The good man brings good things out of the good stored up in him, and the evil man brings evil things out of the evil stored up in him. But I tell you that men will have to give account on the day of judgment for every careless word they have spoken. For by your words you will be acquitted, and by your words you will be condemned. (12:34-37)

"Wicked and adulterous generations" are warned and threatened; Jesus's wisdom is greater than Solomon's wisdom; Jesus's real mother and brothers are his disciples rather than his own mother and brothers: "For whoever does the will of my Father in heaven is my brother and sister and mother" (12:50). (Unity in the family and unity in the Christian community.)

13. Parables: The Sower, The Weeds, The Seed, The Yeast, The Hidden Treasure
and The Pearl, The Net

Jesus speaks in parables because "The knowledge of the secrets of the kingdom of heaven has
been given to you (disciples), but not to them (people)" (13:11). (Election within election.
How can Christianity be egalitarian?)

> And exclusion of the non-elect.
> Though seeing, they do not see; though hearing, they do not hear or understand.
> In them is fulfilled the prophecy of Isaiah:
> You will be ever hearing but never understanding;
> you will be ever seeing but never perceiving.
> For this people's heart has become calloused;
> they hardly hear with their ears, and they have closed their eyes.
> Otherwise they might see with their eyes, hear with their ears,
> understand with their hearts and turn, and I would heal them.
> (13:13-15; Isaiah 6:9-10)

Knowledge versus ignorance; the first from faith, the second from disbelief; the former righteous, the second wicked; and ad infinitum—with corresponding rewards and punishments.

Jesus "did not say anything to them without using a parable. So was fulfilled what was
spoken through the prophet: "I will open my mouth in parables, /I will utter things hidden
since the/creation of the world' " (13:34-35; Psalm 78:2). So, parables are not merely meta-
phorical; they contain Godly wisdom that can become known to and confer power on only
the chosen elect/select.

Jesus is not honored, and is received skeptically, in his hometown, and "he did not do
many miracles there because of their lack of faith" (13:58). (Miracles are for the faithful,
and logically so.)

14. John is Beheaded; Jesus Walks on Water

The tetrarch Herod gives the head of John the Baptist to Herodias, his brother's wife, with
whom he is having an affair; Jesus feeds 5000 ("men, besides women and children," 14:21)
with only five loaves of bread and two fish. Jesus walks on water by force of faith, but Peter
cannot do so properly because he is "of little faith" and he "doubts" (14:31).

15. Clean and Unclean

> Then some Pharisees and teachers of the law came to Jesus from Jerusalem and
> asked, "Why do your disciples break the tradition of the elders? They don't wash
> their hands before they eat!"
> Jesus replied, "And why do you break the command of God for the sake of your
> tradition? For God said, 'Honor your father and mother' and 'Anyone who curses

his father or mother must be put to death.' But you say that if a man says to his father or mother, 'Whatever help you might otherwise have received from me is a gift devoted to God,' he is not to 'honor his father' with it. Thus you nullify the word of God for the sake of your tradition. You hypocrites! Isaiah was right when he prophesied about you:

These people honor me with their lips, but their hearts are far from me.

They worship me in vain; their teachings are but rules taught by men.

Jesus called the crowd to him and said, "Listen and understand. What goes into a man's mouth does not make him 'unclean,' but what comes out of his mouth, that is what makes him 'unclean.' " (15:1-11; Exod. 20:12, 21:17; Lev. 20:9; Deut. 5:16; Isa. 29:13)

Thus, word of God (spirit of the Law) over tradition (forms and the letter of the Law), and inner belief over external worship. And:

Are you still so dull? Jesus asked them. "Don't you see that whatever enters the mouth goes into the stomach and then out of the body? But the things that come out of the mouth come from the heart, and these make a man 'unclean.' For out of the heart come evil thoughts, murder, adultery, sexual immorality, theft, false testimony, slander. These are what make a man 'unclean'; but eating with unwashed hands does not make him 'unclean.' " (15:16-20)

Jesus heals a girl, feeds 4000 ("besides women and children," 15:38) with seven loaves of bread and a few small fish.

16. The Demand for a Sign

When Jesus came to the region of Caesarea Philippi, he asked his disciples, "Who do people say the Son of Man is?"

They replied, "Some say John the Baptist; others say Elijah; and still others, Jeremiah or one of the prophets."

But what about you? he asked. "Who do you say I am?"

Simon Peter answered, "You are the Christ, the Son of the living God."

Jesus replied, "Blessed are you, Simon son of Jonah, for this was not revealed to you by man, but by my Father in heaven. And I tell you that you are Peter, and on this rock I will build my church, and the gates of Hades will not overcome it. I will give you the keys of the kingdom of heaven; whatever you bind on earth will be bound in heaven, and whatever you loose on earth will be loosed in heaven." Then he warned his disciples not to tell anyone that he was the Christ. (16:13-20)

Jesus is the greatest prophet. Jesus predicts his death and says to Peter, who rebukes him: "...you do not have in mind the things of God, but the things of men" (16:23).

From that time on Jesus began to explain to his disciples that he must go to Jerusalem and suffer many things at the hands of the elders, chief priests and teachers of the law, and that he must be killed and on the third day be raised to life. (16:21)

Then Jesus said to his disciples, "If anyone would come after me, he must deny himself and take up his cross and follow me. For whoever wants to save his life will lose it, but whoever loses his life for me will find it. What good will it be for a man if he gains the whole world, yet forfeits his soul? Or what can a man give in exchange for his soul? For the Son of Man is going to come in his Father's glory with his angels, and then he will reward each person according to what he has done. I tell you the truth, some who are standing here will not taste death before they see the Son of Man coming in his kingdom." (16:24-28)

17. The Transfiguration

Jesus is transfigured, he talks with Moses and Elijah (John the Baptist, who came before Jesus), God's voice is heard: "This is my Son.... Listen to him" (17:5).

Jesus saves a boy but also says: "O unbelieving and perverse generation...How long shall I put up with you?" (17:17), in good old Mosaic style.

Jesus disapproves kings' collecting duty and taxes from people, but nevertheless pays the temple tax. A non-confrontational attitude toward worldly authorities that will assume the form of the command: Submit to authorities!

18. The Greatest in the Kingdom of Heaven; Parables

The most humble will be the greatest in the kingdom of heaven: "...whoever humbles himself like this child is the greatest..." (18:4). Note that, not the innocence, but the humility of little children is emphasized. But: "...if anyone causes one of these little ones who believe in me to sin...(18:6), the adult is to be punished, not the "little ones" as was the case in Numbers, Chapter 16.

Sinful hand, foot, eye to be eliminated, or else "fire of hell." Parables of the lost sheep, the sinful brothers, the unmerciful servant, teaching protection, mercifulness, forgiveness, respectively. (Forgiveness not seven times but seventy-seven times, [18:22].)

19. Divorce, Little Children, Rich Young Man

"Catholic marriage" is predicated on Genesis:

Haven't you read, he replied, "that at the beginning the Creator 'made them male and female,' and said, 'For this reason a man will leave his father and mother and be united to his wife, and the two will become one flesh?' So they are no longer two but one. Therefore what God has joined together, let man not separate."

Why then, they asked, "did Moses command that a man give his wife a certificate of divorce and send her away?"

Jesus replied, "Moses permitted you to divorce your wives because your hearts were hard. But it was not this way from the beginning. I tell you that anyone who divorces his wife, except for marital unfaithfulness, and marries another woman commits adultery."

The disciples said to him, "If this is the situation between a husband and wife, it is better not to marry."

Jesus replied, "Not everyone can accept this word, but only those to whom it has been given. For some are eunuchs because they were born that way; others were made that way by men; and others have renounced marriage because of the kingdom of heaven. The one who can accept this should accept it." (19:4-12)

Jesus on "little ones": "Let the little children come to me, and do not hinder them, for the kingdom of heaven belongs to such as these" (19:14).

Jesus on "wealth and poverty":

Now a man came up to Jesus and asked, "Teacher, what good thing must I do to get eternal life?"

"Why do you ask me about what is good?" Jesus replied. "There is only One who is good. If you want to enter life, obey the commandments."

"Which ones?" the man inquired.

Jesus replied, "Do not murder, do not commit adultery, do not steal, do not give false testimony, honor your father and mother, and love your neighbor as yourself." (19:16-19)

In 19:18-19 above, Jesus repeats the 6 moral commandments of Moses's 10 commandments, those concerning murder, adultery, theft, false testimony, honoring parents, and loving neighbors. The full 10 can be further reduced to the 2 highest commandments: First, love your God; second, love your neighbor.

This is the gist of the Judeo-Christian moral theory, the second already present in the *Old Testament* and only to be further elaborated in the *New Testament*. This moral theory is neither very impressive nor very original. In Mesopotemia, specifically in the Code of Hammurabi, before the advent of Abrahamic monotheism, as much, if not more, had already been accomplished. But we won't digress into that.

What is original and historically important about Judeo-Christianity (and Islam) is its seminal contribution to Western political theory, its moral theory being the handmaiden thereof: Fear and love of One and Partnerless God (which is not spoilt but only further reinforced by Christian Trinity, as we shall see below), and His earthly rulers. Submit to all authorities instituted by this mono-God; submit or perish! Middle Eastern—Western (and later partly Eastern) monotheism achieves what could not have been achieved by the softer theisms of pagan Greece, polytheist Mesopotemia or the Far East. Western monotheism furnishes the ideology of sure domination, based on undivided and unquestionable sover-

eignty—divine and earthly. It secures total submission of multitudes to earthly rulers legitimated as God's ministers; total submission in "fear and trembling." Repeat: Submit to
authorities! Submit or perish! (See especially Romans below.)

Not only the more "secular" Leviathan of Hobbes, the absolute monarchy, has its ancestral roots in the Middle Eastern—Western religious tradition, but so do all systems of
inegalitarian political orders, heretofore, in varying degrees, have their basis of legitimacy in
this moral theory.

"All these I have kept," the young man said. "What do I still lack?"

Jesus answered, "If you want to be perfect, go, sell your possessions and give to
the poor, and you will have treasure in heaven. Then come, follow me."

When the young man heard this, he went away sad, because he had great wealth.

Then Jesus said to his disciples, "I tell you the truth, it is hard for a rich man to
enter the kingdom of heaven. Again I tell you, it is easier for a camel to go through
the eye of a needle than for a rich man to enter the kingdom of God." (19:20-24)

The foregoing is, I think, the great schism, the high internal tension, within the *New Testament*. "Selling all possessions and giving to the poor" is obviously more than almsgiving or
limited charity. It is a frontal devaluation of worldly possessions—more so than the *Koran*
and completely contrary to the *Old Testament*. Worldly riches are even an obstacle to enter
heaven. (In the Acts, as we shall see, it is penalized by death in this world.)

This has been a vexing problem for Christian moralists and theologians themselves. The
Catholic church has been for worldly riches (both for itself and in general), the Franciscan
order, for example, has been against. That the latter's renunciation of worldly riches does
not lead to any activism against social and economic injustices in the world is not the main
question here. That, too, remains within the basic Christian quietism in the face of social
injustice and political domination.

My question here is: Which interpretation of the text of the moral theory is correct?
Which Jesus is the real Jesus, or closer to the real Jesus? Similarly which Matthew (or Luke)
is the true one? Are they for or against individual wealth and private property as a moral
value? Have they broken away from the *Old Testament* in this respect or is it but tantamount
to a hesitant, ambiguous critique of worldly riches at the expense of exploited masses? Or
worse, is it but a convenient, if not hypocritical, technique of appeal and policy of recruitment directed to dispossessed popular masses?

Honest prosperous Christians cannot escape this question. If Jesus is against riches, they
are violating his laws. If Jesus is for riches, there is no problem; but then the talk of Je-
sus/Matthew (and Luke/Acts) being against riches should be dropped. (One can serve two
masters, God and Money, given, to my mind, the basic nature of these religions; but one
cannot and, therefore, *should not* be illogical and dishonest.)

When the disciples heard this, they were greatly astonished and asked, "Who then
can be saved?"

Jesus looked at them and said, "With man this is impossible, but with God all things are possible."

Peter answered him, "We have left everything to follow you! What then will there be for us?"

Jesus said to them, "I tell you the truth, at the renewal of all things, when the Son of Man sits on his glorious throne, you who have followed me will also sit on twelve thrones, judging the twelve tribes of Israel.

And everyone who has left houses or brothers or sisters or father or mother or children or fields for my sake will receive: hundred times as much and will inherit eternal life. But many who are first will be last, and many who are last will be first." (19:25-30)

Why first here to be last there and last here to be first there? And not all equal here? Is Christianity activist or quietist?

20. Parables

A landowner pays the same wage to workers who worked in his vineyard for different lengths of time and says: "Don't I have the right to do what I want with my own money? Or are you envious because I am generous?" (20:15). (Cf. 20:16 and 19:30: "first and last.")

Jesus does not grant higher status to any of his 12 apostles:

Instead, whoever wants to become great among you must be your servant, and whoever wants to be first must be your slave—just as the Son of Man did not come to be served, but to serve, and to give his life as a ransom for many. (20:26-28)

21. The Triumphal Entry, The Authority of Jesus, Parables

Jesus enters Jerusalem on a donkey, but as a "king," "gentle and riding on a donkey" (21:5; Zech. 9:9); he enters the temple area and drives out all who were buying and selling there (21:12): My house will be called a house of prayer, but you are making it a den of robbers (21:13; 0sa 56:7 and Jer. 7:11). Is this a critique of money per se or only of illegitimate money-making?

Jesus has a fig tree wither by saying so. He justifies his superhuman, Godly authority:

Jesus entered the temple courts, and, while he was teaching, the chief priests and the elders of the people came to him. "By what authority are you doing these things?" they asked. "And who gave you this authority?"

Jesus replied, "I will also ask you one question. If you answer me, I will tell you by what authority I am doing these things. John's baptism—where did it come from? Was it from heaven, or from men?"

They discussed it among themselves and said, "If we say, 'From heaven,' he will ask, 'Then why didn't you believe him?' But if we say, 'From men'—we are afraid of the people, for they all hold that John was a prophet."

So they answered Jesus, "We don't know."

Then he said, "Neither will I tell you by what authority I am doing these things." (21:23-27)

Jesus favors among two indolent brothers the one who does not lie.

Jesus compares tax collectors and prostitutes favorably with unbelievers. A parable on the final deprivation that will befall the unbelievers.

22. Parable, Taxes to Caesar, Greatest Commandment, Whose Son?

The kingdom of heaven is likened to a wedding banquet and unbelievers to unattending invitees. Plus: "([M]any are invited, but few are chosen" [22:14]).

Is it right to pay taxes to Caesar or not?:

Give to Caesar what is Caesar's and to God what is God's. (22:21)

Jesus prefers not to question the status quo and the powers that be. The doctrine of "two swords" in embryo.

Jesus rebukes the Sadducees, who do not believe in resurrection:

Jesus replied, "You are in error because you do not know the Scriptures or the power of God. At the resurrection people will neither marry nor be given in marriage; they will be like the angels in heaven. But about the resurrection of the dead—have you not read what God said to you, 'I am the God of Abraham, the God of Isaac, and the God of Jacob'? He is not the God of the dead but of the living."

When the crowds heard this, they were astonished at his teaching. (22:29-33)

Jesus rebukes the Pharisees, concerning the Law:

Jesus replied: " 'Love the Lord your God with all your heart and with all your soul and with all your mind.' This is the first and greatest commandment. And the second is like it: 'Love your neighbor as yourself.' All the Law and the Prophets hang on these two commandments." (22:37-40; Deut. 6:5, Lev. 19:18.)

Jesus proves that he is the son of God:

While the Pharisees were gathered together, Jesus asked them, "What do you think about the Christ? Whose son is he?"

"The son of David," they replied.

He said to them, "How is it then that David, speaking by the Spirit, calls him 'Lord'? For he says, The Lord said to my Lord: Sit at my right hand until I put your enemies under your feet.

If then David calls him 'Lord,' how can he be his son?" No one could say a word in reply, and from that day on no one dared to ask him any more questions. (22:41-46; Psalm 110:1)

23. Seven Woes (to the teachers of law and the Pharisees)

Then Jesus said to the crowds and to his disciples: "The teachers of the law and the Pharisees sit in Moses' seat. So you must obey them and do everything they tell you. But do not do what they do, for they do not practice what they preach. They tie up heavy loads and put them on men's shoulders, but they themselves are not willing to lift a finger to move them.

Everything they do is done for men to see: They make their phylacteries wide and the tassels on their garments long; they love the place of honor at banquets and the most important seats in the synagogues; they love to be greeted in the marketplaces and to have men call them 'Rabbi.'

But you are not to be called 'Rabbi,' for you have only one Master and you are all brothers. And do not call anyone on earth 'father,' for you have one Father, and he is in heaven. Nor are you to be called 'teacher,' for you have one Teacher, the Christ. The greatest among you will be your servant. For whoever exalts himself will be humbled, and whoever humbles himself will be exalted." (23:1-12)

Jesus does not question what the teachers of law preach, that is the Law, but what they do. (Not the book but the clergy—like Luther.) Their practice is not up to their (correct) theory; they are hypocritical, exhibitionistic, after power and status and fame. All the same, "you must obey them." (Submit to authorities, even if you do not emulate them.)

One Master, a multitude of brothers; one Father, a mass of believers; one Teacher, many humble servants (however much to be exalted in the other world). A plescibitary leader with a mass following.

Woe to the teachers and the Pharisees because:

- they shut the kingdom of heaven in men's faces
- they convert men to make him a son of hell
- they prefer gold and gifts to temple and altar
- they neglect the more important matters of the law-justice, mercy, and faithfulness
- the outside of their cups are clean but the inside thereof are full of greed and self-indulgence
- they are righteous on the outside but hypocritical and wicked on the inside
- they murder prophets

Reminiscent of the Protestant critique of the Catholic church? So:

You snakes! You brood of vipers! How will you escape being condemned to hell? (23:33)

24. Signs of the End of the Age

Not one stone over another, wars, nations and kings against nations and kings, famines and earthquakes, persecution and death, betrayal of faith and fraternal hate, false prophets and deceptions, wickedness, loss of love…"but he who stands firm to the end will be saved"

(24:13)…"How dreadful it will be in those days for pregnant women and nursing mothers!" (24:19) "Great distress, unequaled from the beginning of the world until now—and never to be equaled again" (24:21). "If those days had not been cut short, no one would survive, but for the sake of the elect, those days will be shortened" (24:22).

"For the sake of the elect." (As if this could be a consolation for the elect!)

Immediately after the distress of those days the sun will be darkened, and the moon will not give its light; the stars will fall from the sky, and the heavenly bodies will be shaken.

At that time the sign of the Son of Man will appear in the sky, and all the nations of the earth will mourn. They will see the Son of Man coming on the clouds of the sky, with power and great glory. And he will send his angels with a loud trumpet call, and they will gather his elect from the four winds, from one end of the heavens to the other. (24:29-31)

So, Jesus, meek in this world, is furious in the other.

No one knows about that day or hour, not even the angels in heaven, nor the Son, but only the Father. As it was in the days of Noah, so it will be at the coming of the Son of Man. For in the days before the flood, people were eating and drinking, marrying and giving in marriage, up to the day Noah entered the ark; and they knew nothing about what would happen until the flood came and took them all away. That is how it will be at the coming of the Son of Man. Two men will be in the field; one will be taken and the other left. Two women will be grinding with a hand mill; one will be taken and the other left.

Therefore keep watch, because you do not know on what day your Lord will come. But understand this: If the owner of the house had known at what time of night the thief was coming, he would have kept watch and would not have let his house be broken into. So you also must be ready, because the Son of Man will come at an hour when you do not expect him.

So, the coming will be slow but sudden—a surprise attack. A favorite motif of *Koran*, too, as we shall see.

25. Parables: Ten Virgins, Talents, Sheep and Goats

Believers are likened to prudent virgins and to industrious servants. Their master had given the latter different amounts of capital…each according to his ability (25:15). And:

For everyone who has will be given more, and he will have an abundance. Whoever does not have, even what he has will be taken from him. (25:29)

Now, the sheep and the goats on the day of judgment:

When the Son of Man comes in his glory, and all the angels with him, he will sit on his throne in heavenly glory. All the nations will be gathered before him, and he will separate the people one from another as a shepherd separates the sheep from the goats. He will put the sheep on his right and the goats on his left.

Then the King will say to those on his right, 'Come you who are blessed by my Father; take your inheritance, the kingdom prepared for you since the creation of the world. For I was hungry and you gave me something to eat, I was thirsty and you gave me something to drink, I was a stranger and you invited me in, I needed clothes and you clothed me, I was sick and you looked after me, I was in prison and you came to visit me.'

Then the righteous will answer him 'Lord, when did we see you hungry and feed you, or thirsty and give you something to drink? When did we see you a stranger and invite you in, or needing clothes and clothe you? When did we see you sick or in prison and go to visit you?'

The King will reply, 'I tell you the truth, whatever you did for one of the least of these brothers of mine, you did for me.

Then he will say to those on his left, 'Depart from me, you who are cursed, into the eternal fire prepared for the devil and his angels. For I was hungry and you gave me nothing to eat, I was thirsty and you gave me nothing to drink, I was a stranger and you did not invite me in, I needed clothes and you did not clothe me, I was sick and in prison and you did not look after me.'

They also will answer, 'Lord, when did we see you hungry or thirsty or a stranger or needing clothes or sick or in prison, and did not help you?'

He will reply, 'I tell you the truth, whatever you did not do for one of the least of these, you did not do for me.'

Then they will go away to eternal punishment, but the righteous to eternal life. (25:31-46)

Son of Man (Son of God) becomes King (Son of his Father the Omnipotent Ruler of All) and sends the sheepish men (faithful and charitable) to heaven and goatish men to hell and eternal fire.

26. Plot, Anointment, Judas, Supper, Peter's Denial, Arrest

The chief priests and the elders of the people plot against Jesus; a woman anoints him; Judas agrees to betray him for thirty silver coins; Jesus has his last supper (on the Passover) with the apostles and gives bread saying "this is my body" (26:26); he passes the wine cup saying "(t)his is my blood of the[4] covenant" (26:28); Jesus predicts Peter's denial, as prophesied by Zechariah (13:7); he is arrested. When one of Jesus's companions reach for his sword, he says:

Put your sword back in its place...for all who draw the sword will die by the sword. (26:52)

27. Judas Hangs Himself, Jesus is Crucified

Judas hangs himself, the thirty silver coins he threw into the temple ("blood money") is used by the chief priests to buy a burial place for foreigners (Jer. 19:1-3, 32:6-9 and Zech. 11:12, 13).

Jesus affirms to the governor that he is "the king of the Jews" (27:11) but does not reply to any other charge, the governor releases not Jesus but Barabbas and has Jesus flogged and hands him over to be crucified, the soldiers mock and spit on Jesus, they crucify him along with two robbers, who also insult him together with the chief priests and the elders:

He saved others, but he can't save himself. He's the King of Israel. (27:42)

When Jesus gives up his spirit "The earth shook and the rocks split. The tombs broke open and the bodies of many holy people who had died were raised to life." (27:51-52)

28. The Resurrection and The Great Commission

On the third day Jesus, too, rises from the dead following a violent earthquake upon the coming down to his tomb of an angel of the Lord, who tells Mary Magdelene and the other Mary that they can see Jesus again in Galilee. On their way, Jesus appears to and speaks to them and the disciples. "Greetings...," he says. Then:

...the eleven disciples went to Galilee, to the mountain where Jesus had told them to go. When they saw him, they worshiped him; but some doubted. Then Jesus came to them and said, "All authority in heaven and on earth has been given to me. Therefore go and make disciples of all nations, baptizing them in the name of the Father and of the Son and of the Holy Spirit, and teaching them to obey everything I have commanded you. And surely I am with you always, to the very end of the age." (28:16-20)

"All authority in heaven and on earth" given to a prophet by God and delegated to the apostles by the prophet: to "make disciples of all nations" and to "baptize them in the name of" the trinity (triumvirate). What for?

To obey everything he commands.

Notes

1. Matthew bases himself 90 percent on Mark, which is the earliest of the synoptic gospels (Mark, Matthew, Luke).

2. Isaiah 7:14.

3. Some late manuscripts: "...enemies, bless those who curse you, do good to those who hate you" (p.720, fn.: i44).

4. In some manuscripts: the "new" (p. 740, fn. b28).

MARK[1]

1. John the Baptist, Baptism and Temptation of Jesus. First Disciples, Healings
John the Baptist, as written in Isaiah (40:3) and Malachi (3:1) prepares the way for Jesus Christ, "preaching a baptism of repentance for the forgiveness of sins" (1:4) and saying that the more powerful Jesus will baptize people not with water, as he does, but with the Holy Spirit (1:8). (The Christian prophet is greater than all Jewish prophets, because he is the "Son of God," 1:1 and 11, "whom He loves and with whom He is well pleased," 1:11)

Jesus resists temptation by Satan, goes into Galilee, proclaims the good news of God ("The Kingdom of God is near. Repent and believe the good news," 1:15), recruits his first disciples (" I will make you fishers of men" 1:17), begins to teach "as one who had authority, not as the teachers of the law," (1:22) is recognised as "the Holy One of God" (1:24), performs miracles and heals, saying to a man whom he has cured of leprosy:

See that you don't tell this to anyone. But go, show yourself to the priest and offer the sacrifices that Moses commanded for your cleansing, as a testimony to them. (1:44)

Jesus's prudent diplomacy does not work, the man begins to talk freely, and as a result Jesus is restricted in his movements. Important is the implication that up to Jesus leprosy was healed by God through priests and through offerings, whereas Jesus heals directly.

2. Healings, Sinners, Fasting, Lord of the Sabbath
Jesus heals, "the Son of Man has authority on earth to forgive sins" (2:10), it is not the healthy but sick who need a doctor ("I have not come to call the righteous, but sinners," 2:17), he challenges old formal rituals concerning fasting and the Sabbath (new wine not into old wineskins, 2:22; David's "hunger" and "need" above letter of Law, 2:25), and Mark puts the matter more succinctly than Matthew:

The Sabbath was made for man, not man for the Sabbath. (2:27)

So the Son of Man is Lord even of the Sabbath. (2:28)

So, in quite a radical break with the *Old Testament*, Jesus declares, in 2:27, that religion, rules, rituals, books are for man, not vice versa. Human needs are superior to religious worship. (The *Koran* will take this attitude further in its argument that Islam is the least burdensome religion in so far as externalities and formalities are concerned.) Jesus, with another stroke of the word in 2:28, makes his own position and authority supreme over the old Law.

3. The Twelve Apostles

Jesus "appoints" twelve apostles and delegates "authority" to preach and heal. He does this on a mountainside. (Cf. God → Moses on a mountain.) He gives the name of Peter to Simon and Boanarges to James and John. (Cf. God names Abram Abraham and Jacob Israel.)

Jesus is thought to be "out of his mind" (3:21) (Cf. *Koran*'s "mad poet"), he speaks in "parables" which are often but tautologies ("If a kingdom is divided against itself, that kingdom cannot stand," 3:24), he draws the limits of forgiveness:

> But whoever blasphemes against the Holy Spirit will never be forgiven; he is guilty of eternal sin. (3:29)

Forgiveness, and tolerance, is conditional (on belief in a monotheism of certain kind) and can readily turn into its opposite—persecution and division of human beings into the faithful and the infidel, not sparing family members either. "Whoever does God's will is my brother and sister and mother" (3:35). Jesus is the Son-Patriarch, God being the Father-Patriarch. And there is no potential or definitional brotherhood and sisterhood of the whole species here, but only membership in the one and the same religious faith, which by its own internal logic is, as Freud says, exclusionary.

4. Parables: Sower, Lamp, Seeds and Calming the Storm

Elitism, a form of exclusion, surfaces early: "He who has ears to hear, let him hear" (4:9), the implication being that some men do not have ears (for a certain message). A priesthood of the elect (e.g., Aaron & Sons) is introduced in softer garb:

> When he was alone, the Twelve and the others around him asked him about the parables. He told them, "The secret of the kingdom of God has been given to you. But to those on the outside everything is said in parables so that, they may be ever seeing but never perceiving, and ever hearing but never understanding; otherwise they might turn and be forgiven!' " (4:10-12; Isaiah 6:9-10)

There are "insiders" and "outsiders." Secrets are given to the elect few (chosen and appointed by Jesus). Everything is said in parables to *those on the outside* (even if faithful). *Everything* in parables. But, are parables for facilitating understanding or for blocking it? Forever! (Ever and ever; *never and never*.) Is it because those on the outside can really never fully understand and perceive although they believe or because Jesus writes them off from the very beginning to build up his neat hierarchy: God (all-knowing) → Prophet (most-knowing) → Apostles (much-knowing) → mass of ordinary believers (little-knowing:

seeing but not perceiving, hearing but not understanding)—a pyramid getting wider as you go down. (Unbelievers are not admitted even to the lowest echelon.) Insiders and outsiders, at any rate.

And concerning the last line: Do you want to forgive as many as you can or are you out to *not forgive* as many as possible?—by employing parables?

That the parables may be, or are, *for* understanding better, is implicit (however ambivalent) in Jesus's rebuking his own apostles: "Don't you understand this parable? How then will you understand any parable? The farmer sows the word...Some people are like seed along the path, where the word is sown... (4:13-15). "Others, like seed sown on good soil, hear the word, accept it, and produce a crop..." (4:20).

As if there can be no development through teaching and learning, people are categorized a priori: fertile soil, unfertile soil.

Concerning word and wealth:

...but the worries of this life, the deceitfulness of wealth, and the desires for other things come in and shake the word... (4:19)

Yet:

Whoever has will be given more; whoever does not have, even what he has will be taken from him. (4:25)

Back to the word and parables:

With many similar parables Jesus spoke the word to them, as much as they could understand. He did not say anything to them without using a parable. But when he was alone with his own disciples, he explained everything. (4:33-34)

Own disciples *vs.* the non-understanding multitude. The latter only to believe without full understanding.

Jesus calms the storm by saying (to the wind and the waves): "Quiet! Be still" (4:39). The force of the word is reinforced by (Godly) control over nature; people are "terrified." "Who is this? Even the wind and the waves obey him!" (4:41) Thus, it is a short step from fear and awe to belief and obedience.

5. Healings
Jesus continues to heal; a 2000-head pig herd is drowned.

6. Hometown, The Twelve, The Baptist Beheaded, Miracles
Jesus "could not do any miracles" in his hometown because of their "lack of faith" (6:5-6); he sends out the 12 apostles to teach "two by two" (6:7); John the Baptist is beheaded by King Herod to whom he says "It is not lawful for you to have (marry) your brother's wife" (6:18). The King knows that John is a "righteous and holy man" (6:20), but Herodias (the grudging woman) wants him killed.

Jesus has compassion on a hungry crowd, he feeds 5000 men miraculously, who are "like sheep without a shepherd" (6:34), overriding the apostles' initial reluctance.

Jesus walks on water; he continues to heal ("all who touched him were healed," 6:56).

7. Clean and Unclean

So the Pharisees and teachers of the law asked Jesus, "Why don't your disciples live according to the tradition of the elders instead of eating their food with 'unclean' hands?"

He replied, "Isaiah was right when he prophesied about you hypocrites; as it is written: These people honor me with their lips, but their hearts are far from me. They worship me in vain; their teachings are but rules taught by men.

You have let go of the commands of God and are holding on to the traditions of men." (7:5-8; Isaiah 29:13)

"Rules taught by men" *vs.* "commands of God," obsolete "tradition" *vs.* the infallible Book(s), hypocrisy of externalities *vs.* heart-felt belief. But it all boils down to: *Who* is God's real mouthpiece carrying his true word?

And he said to them: "You have a fine way of setting aside the commands of God in order to observe your own traditions! For Moses said, 'Honor your father and your mother,' and, 'Anyone who curses his father or mother must be put to death.' But you say that if a man says to his father or mother: 'Whatever help you might otherwise have received from me is Corban' (that is, a gift devoted to God), then you no longer let him do anything for his father or mother. Thus you nullify the word of God by your tradition that you have handed down. And you do many things like that."

Again Jesus called the crowd to him and said, "Listen to me, everyone, and understand this. Nothing outside a man can make him 'unclean' by going into him. Rather, it is what comes out of a man that makes him 'unclean.' "

After he had left the crowd and entered the house, his disciples asked him about this parable. "Are you so dull?" he asked. "Don't you see that nothing that enters a man from the outside can make him 'unclean'? For it doesn't go into his heart but into his stomach, and then out of his body."(In saying this, Jesus declared all foods "clean.")

He went on: "What comes out of a man is what makes him 'unclean.' For from within, out of men's hearts, come evil thoughts, sexual immorality, theft, murder, adultery, greed, malice, deceit, lewdness, envy, slander, arrogance and folly. All these evils come from inside and make a man 'unclean.' " (7:9-23; Exod. 20:12, 21:17, Deut. 5:16)

8. Feeding 4000, Healing, Predicting Own Death

Jesus heals, feeds 4000, predicts his death.

> He then began to teach them that the Son of Man must suffer many things and be rejected by the elders, chief priests and teachers of the law, and that he must be killed and after three days rise again. He spoke plainly about this, and Peter took him aside and began to rebuke him.

> But when Jesus turned and looked at his disciples, he rebuked Peter. "Get behind me, Satan!" he said. "You do not have in mind the things of God, but the things of men."

> Then he called the crowd to him along with his disciples and said: "If anyone would come after me, he must deny himself and take up his cross and follow me. For whoever wants to save his life will lose it, but whoever loses his life for me and for the gospel will save it. What good is it for a man to gain the whole world, yet forfeit his soul? Or what can a man give in exchange for his soul? If anyone is ashamed of me and my words in this adulterous and sinful generation, the Son of Man will be ashamed of him when he comes in his Father's glory with the holy angels." (8:31-38)

9. Transfiguration, Healing, The Greatest, "Us and Them"

Jesus, with Peter, James and John, goes to a mountain; he is transfigured before them, becoming dazzling white; Elijah and Moses appear, talking to Jesus. God is heard saying "This is my Son, whom I love. Listen to him" (9:7). Thus, a greater authority is conferred on Jesus than Moses.

Jesus heals a boy and says to his father: "Everything is possible for him who believes" (9:23); he tells the Twelve: "If anyone wants to be the first, he must be the very last, and the servant of all" (9:35). Jesus takes a little child in his arms and says: "Whoever welcomes one of these little children in my name welcomes me" (9:37). Inclusion *and* exclusion again:

> ...whoever is not against us is for us. (9:40)

Jesus expounds on sin:

> And if anyone causes one of these little ones who believe in me to sin, it would be better for him to be thrown into the sea with a large millstone tied around his neck. If your hand causes you to sin, cut it off. It is better for you to enter life maimed than with two hands to go into hell, where the fire never goes out. And if your foot causes you to sin, cut it off. It is better for you to enter life crippled than to have two feet and be thrown into hell. And if your eye causes you to sin, pluck it out. It is better for you to enter the kingdom of God with one eye than to have two eyes and be thrown into hell, where 'their worm does not die, and the fire is not quenched.' (9:42-48: Isaiah 66:24)

10. Divorce, Little Children, Rich Young Man

Jesus modifies Moses on divorce:

> Some Pharisees came and tested him by asking, "Is it lawful for a man to divorce his wife?"
>
> "What did Moses command you?" he replied.
>
> They said, "Moses permitted a man to write a certificate of divorce and send her away."
>
> "It was because your hearts were hard that Moses wrote you this law," Jesus replied. "But at the beginning of creation God 'made them male and female.' 'For this reason a man will leave his father and mother and be united to his wife, and the two will become one flesh.' So they are no longer two, but one. Therefore what God has joined together, let man not separate."
>
> When they were in the house again, the disciples asked Jesus about this. He answered, "Anyone who divorces his wife and marries another woman commits adultery against her. And if she divorces her husband and marries another man, she commits adultery." (10:2-12; Gen. 1:27, 2:24)

Christianity gives greater marital security to women than do Judaism and Islam. As women fare better with Jesus than Moses, "little children" fare even better: Kingdom of God belongs to them. Jesus has a propensity to infantilize adults as well: "...anyone who will not receive the kingdom of God like a little child will never enter it" (10:15).

The rich do not fare better with Jesus than Moses; the story of the rich young man is told, and, perhaps, a little more forcefully than Matthew. Jesus predicts his death; the mockery and ill-treatment of the Gentiles; he refuses James and John's request to sit at his right and left in his glory.

> When the ten heard about this, they became indignant with James and John. Jesus called them together and said, "You know that those who are regarded as rulers of the Gentiles lord it over them, and their high officials exercise authority over them. Not so with you. Instead, whoever wants to become great among you must be your servant, and whoever wants to be first must be slave of all. For even the Son of Man did not come to be served, but to serve, and to give his life as a ransom for many." (10:41-45)

Jesus, "Son of David" (10:47), heals a blind man.

11. Jerusalem, Jesus's Authority

Jesus, apostles, disciples approach Jerusalem; everybody shouts:

> Blessed is he who comes in the name of the Lord! Blessed is the coming kingdom of our Father David! (11:9-10)

In the temple area, Jesus drives out the traders and "overturns the tables of the money changers" (11:15). (*Koran* will repeat this story.)

The exchange on the authority of Jesus between himself and the chief priests, the teach-ers of the law, and the elders is repeated. (Mark is authorially prior to Matthew, but editori-ally antecedent.)

12. Parables, Taxes to Caesar, Marriage at Resurrection
Matthew has already repeated Mark.

13. Signs of the End of the Age; The Day and Hour Unknown
Matthew has already repeated Mark.

14. Anointment, Supper, Arrest, Betrayal
Upon his arrest, Jesus says he is but teaching and not leading a rebellion, and that "the Scriptures must be fulfilled" (14:48-49). Christianity is equally averse to "rebellion" as Ju-daism is.(Remember Numbers, Ch. 16.)

Again the high priest asked him, "Are you the Christ, the Son of the Blessed One?"

"I am," said Jesus. "And you will see the Son of Man sitting at the right hand of the Mighty one and coming on the clouds of heaven."

The high priest tore his clothes. "Why do we need any more witnesses?" he asked. "You have heard the blasphemy. What do you think?"

They all condemned him as worthy of death. Then some began to spit at him; they blindfolded him, struck him with their fists, and said, "Prophesy!" And the guards took him and beat him. (14:61-65)

15. Jesus Before Pilate, Mockery, Crucifixion, Death, Burial
Jesus accepts that he is "the king of the Jews" (15:2).

More women in this story than the *Old Testament*:

Some women were watching from a distance. Among them were Mary Magdalene, Mary the mother of James the younger and of Joses, and Salome. In Galilee these women had followed him and cared for his needs. Many other women who had come up with him to Jerusalem were also there. (15:40-41)

16. The Resurrection
The women find out that the stone of Jesus's tomb is already rolled away, a young man dressed in white says to them:

He has risen! He is not here…He is going ahead of you into Galilee. There you will see him just as he told you. (16:6-7)

(There is no encounter as in Matthew.)

[The most reliable early manuscripts and other ancient witnesses do not have Mark 16:9-20, among them being the following, in which Jesus appears to the Eleven and says to them (p. 760):

He said to them, "Go into all the world and preach the good news to all creation. Whoever believes and is baptized will be saved, but whoever does not believe will be condemned. And these signs will accompany those who believe: In my name they will drive out demons; they will speak in new tongues; they will pick up snakes with their hands; and when they drink deadly poison, it will not hurt them at all; they will place their hands on sick people, and they will get well."

After the Lord Jesus had spoken to them, he was taken up into heaven and he sat at the right hand of God. Then the disciples went out and preached everywhere, and the Lord worked with them and confirmed his word by the signs that accompanied it. (16:15-20)

Salvation versus condemnation, blesses *vs.* curses, again.]

Notes

1. Mark is chronologically prior to Matthew, whose text repeats more than 90 percent of the content of Mark's gospel. Hence some of my reductions of repetitious passages.

8

LUKE[1]

1. Introduction, Births of John and Jesus

Luke writes:

> Many have undertaken to draw up an account of the things that have been fulfilled among us, just as they were handed down to us by those who from the first were eyewitnesses and servants of the word. Therefore, since I myself have carefully investigated everything from the beginning, it seemed good also to me to write an orderly account for you, most excellent Theophilus, so that you may know the certainty of the things you have been taught. (1:1-4)

"An orderly account," based on "careful investigation," for the purpose of assuring "the certainty of the things you have been taught." "An account of the things that have been fulfilled among us" "just as they were handed down to us by those who from the first were eyewitnesses and servants of the word."

The angel Gabriel tells Zechariah (the priest) that the Lord will give a son, John, to his old wife, and that John will never take wine or other fermented drink and will bring "(m)any of the people of Israel...back to the Lord their God" (1:16).

Prophets bringing people to their God, instead of, for example, bringing God to people. The angel Gabriel also goes to Mary, "who (has) found favor with God" (1:30) (and: "The Lord is with you," [1:28]). The child "will be great and will be called the Son of the Most High. The Lord God will give him the throne of his father David, and he will reign over the house of Jacob forever; his kingdom will never end" (1:32-33). Luke, too, is a royalist.

> "How will this be, since I am a virgin?" (1:34) "The Holy Spirit will come upon you,
> and the power of the Most High will overshadow you." (1:35)

Mary's song: the Lord God is merciful ("his mercy extends to those who fear him," [1:50]), is mighty ("he has scattered those who are proud in their inmost thought," [1:51]), "he has filled the hungry with good things but has sent the rich away empty" (1:53), among other things.

2. The Birth of Jesus

Jesus is born, circumcised, and consecrated. Joseph and Mary do everything required by the Law of Moses and the Law of the Lord.

3. John Prepares the Way, Jesus in Baptized

John the Baptist preaches: "The man with two tunics should share with him who has none, and the one who has food should do the same" (3:11).

Repetitions.

Genealogy of Jesus, going back to Seth, the son of Adam, the son of God—, "s" in this instance being a small "s" (3:38).

4. Temptation, Rejection, Healings

"Man does not live on bread alone." (4:4; Deut. 8:3)

"Do not put the Lord your God to the test." (4:12; Deut. 6:16)

Jesus teaches; he reads the scroll of the prophet Isaiah: preach good news to the poor, proclaim freedom for the prisoners, release the oppressed (4:17-18).

Repetitions.

5. The First Disciples, Healings, Rituals

Repetitions.

6. Lord of the Sabbath, Twelve Apostles, Love for Enemies, Blessings and Woes, Judging Others

Repetitions.

Jesus says to his disciples:

Blessed are you who are poor, for yours is the kingdom of God.

Blessed are you who hunger now, for you will be satisfied.

Blessed are you who weep now, for you will laugh.

Blessed are you when men hate you, when they exclude you and insult you
and reject your name as evil, because of the Son of Man.

Rejoice in that day and leap for joy, because great is your reward in heaven. For
that is how their fathers treated the prophets.

But woe to you who are rich, for you have already received your comfort.

Woe to you who are well fed now, for you will go hungry.

Woe to you who laugh now, for you will mourn and weep.

Woe to you when all men speak well of you, for that is how their fathers treated
the false prophets. (6:20-26)

Blessed are:	Who will:
• the poor	• have the kingdom of God
• the hungry	• be satisfied
• the weeping	• laugh
• the hated	• be rewarded in heaven
Woe to:	Who will:
• the rich	• have no comfort
• the well-fed	• go hungry
• the laughing	• mourn and weep
• the well-spoken of	• (not be rewarded in heaven)

The above seems a rather non-ambivalent condemnation of the rich, among others things. (Compare with Matthew 5, which is ambivalent.) And, by implication, a clear case for economic equality? (No!) Or just a promise of compensation in the other world? (Yes!) And again: Why the first and the last to change places in the other world, instead of becoming equal in this one?

> But I tell you who hear me: Love your enemies, do good to those who hate you, bless those who curse you, pray for those who mistreat you. If someone strikes you on one cheek, turn to him the other also. If someone takes your cloak, do not stop him from taking your tunic. Give to everyone who asks you, and if anyone takes what belongs to you, do not demand it back. Do to others as you would have them do to you.
>
> If you love those who love you, what credit is that to you? Even 'sinners' love those who love them. And if you do good to those who are good to you, what credit is that to you? Even 'sinners' do that. And if you lend to those from whom you expect repayment, what credit is that to you? Even 'sinners' lend to 'sinners,' expecting to be repaid in full. But love your enemies, do good to them, and lend to them without expecting to get anything back. Then your reward will be great, and you will be sons of the Most High, because he is kind to the ungrateful and wicked. Be merciful, just as your Father is merciful. (6:27-36)

This is a radical break with the competitive, possessive individualism and the retaliative civil legalism of the *Old Testament*. Love not only for neighbors but also for enemies. No striking back, but taking in the second blow as well. Total sharing, and even renouncing one's own share. Giving without reciprocity. This is a new morality. And:

> Do not judge, and you will not be judged. Do not condemn, and you will not be condemned. Forgive, and you will be forgiven. Give, and it will be given to you. A good measure, pressed down, shaken together and running over, will be poured into your lap. For with the measure you use, it will be measured you.

He also told them this parable: Can a blind man lead a blind man? Will they not both fall into a pit? A student is not above his teacher, but everyone who is fully trained will be like his teacher.

Why do you look at the speck of sawdust in your brother's eye and pay no attention to the plank in your own eye? How can you say to your brother, 'Brother, let me take the speck out of your eye,' when you yourself fail to see the plank in your own eye? You hypocrite, first take the plank out of your eye, and then you will see clearly to remove the speck from your brother's eye. (6:37-42)

Some moral rules: Forgiveness, auto-critique, integrity, humility.

7. Healings, Jesus and John, Anointment
John praises Jesus, faith saves a sinful woman.

8. Parables: Sower, Lamp; Calming the Storm; Healings
Jesus and the Twelve traveling apostles and some women (Mary Magdalene, Joanna, Susanna, others) "helping to support them out of their own means" (8:3). Repetitions.

9. Sending Out the Twelve, Feeding 5000, The Transfiguration, The Greatest, Samaritan Opposition, Cost of Following Jesus

"(H)e who is least...he is the greatest." (9:48)

"(W)hoever is not against you is for you." (9:50)

Repetitions.

Jesus does not accept burying a father or saying goodby to the family as excuses for not immediately following him.

10. Jesus Sends Out the Seventy-two
The Lord (Jesus) appoints 72^2 others, to go two by two and "like lambs among wolves" (10:3), to go ahead of him to preach and heal, and to warn and threaten the unrepentant.

He who listens to you listens to me; he who rejects you rejects me; but he who rejects me rejects him who sent me. (10:16)

Identification of 12 and 72 with Jesus, but equation of Jesus with God.

At that time Jesus, full of joy through the Holy Spirit, said, "I praise you, Father, Lord of heaven and earth, because you have hidden these things from the wise and learned, and revealed them to little children. Yes, Father, for this was your good pleasure.

All things have been committed to me by my Father. No one knows who the Son is except the Father, and no one knows who the Father is except the Son and those to whom the Son chooses to reveal him."

Then he turned to his disciples and said privately, "Blessed are the eyes that see what you see. For I tell you that many prophets and kings wanted to see what you see but did not see it, and to hear what you hear but did not hear it." (10:21-24)

To an expert in the law who asks him how to inherit eternal life, Jesus responds:

"What is written in the Law?" he replied. "How do you read it?"

He answered: " 'Love the Lord your God with all your heart and with all your soul and with all your strength and with all your mind' and, 'Love your neighbor as yourself.' "

"You have answered correctly," Jesus replied. "Do this and you will live."

But he wanted to justify himself, so he asked Jesus, "And who is my neighbor?" (10:26-29)

Jesus gives the example of the robbed and beaten man: A priest and a Levite pass him by and remain indifferent. But a Samaritan takes care of him, and Jesus describes this merciful Samaritan as the proper "neighbor" to the man. Jesus visits the sisters Martha and Marry and praises the latter for single-mindedly listening to what he says.

11. Prayer, Beelzebub, Six Woes

"Ask-seek-knock" is repeated. "He who is not with me is against me" is repeated.

Jesus's word is equated with God's word: "Blessed rather are those who hear the word of God and obey it" (11:28).

Jesus's wisdom is greater than that of Solomon and Jonah.

Lamp must be put on its stand; the eye is the lamp of the body.

"Six woes" are repeated.

12. Warnings, The Rich Fool, Do Not Worry, Watchfulness, Not Peace But Division

Jesus says that the hypocrisy of the Pharisees will not do:

There is nothing concealed that will not be disclosed, or hidden that will not be made known. What you have said in the dark will be heard in the daylight, and what you have whispered in the ear in the inner rooms will be proclaimed from the roofs. (12:2-3)

God knows and controls everything—not only in this world but also in the other:

I tell you, my friends, do not be afraid of those who kill the body and after that can do no more. But I will show you whom you should fear: Fear him who, after the killing of the body, has power to throw you into hell. Yes, I tell you, fear him. Are not five sparrows sold for two pennies? Yet not one of them is forgotten by God. Indeed, the very hairs of your head are all numbered. Don't be afraid; you are worth more than many sparrows. (12:4-7)

Fear God, fear hell. Your body is under control.

It is said that one will be forgiven for speaking against Jesus but not against God:

I tell you, whoever acknowledges me before men, the Son of Man will also acknowledge him before the angels of God. But he who disowns me before men will be disowned before the angels of God. And everyone who speaks a word against the Son of Man will be forgiven, but anyone who blasphemes against the Holy Spirit will not be forgiven. (12:8-10)

Does this not contradict 10:16 above?

…but he who rejects me rejects him who sent me?

Concerning riches, possessions, worldly goods, and amassing wealth:

"Watch out! Be on your guard against all kinds of greed; a man's life does not consist in the abundance of his possessions."

And he told them this parable: "The ground of a certain rich man produced a good crop. He thought to himself, 'What shall I do? I have no place to store my crops.'

Then he said, 'This is what I'll do. I will tear down my barns and build bigger ones, and there I will store all my grain and my goods. And I'll say to myself, "You have plenty of good things laid up for many years. Take life easy; eat, drink and be merry."

But God said to him, 'You fool! This very night your life will be demanded from you. Then who will get what you have prepared for yourself?'

This is how it will be with anyone who stores up things for himself but is not rich toward God." (12:15-21)

And a repetition:

Then Jesus said to his disciples: "Therefore I tell you do not worry about your life, what you will eat; or about your body, what you will wear. Life is more than food, and the body more than clothes." (12:22-23)

O you of little faith! And do not set your heart on what you will eat or drink; do not worry about it. For the pagan world runs after all such things, and your Father knows that you need them. But seek his kingdom, and these things will be given to you as well.

Do not be afraid, little flock, for your Father has been pleased to give you the kingdom. Sell your possessions and give to the poor. Provide purses for yourselves that will not wear out, a treasure in heaven that will not be exhausted, where no thief comes near and no moth destroys. For where your treasure is, there your heart will be also. (12:28-34)

All this is quite unlike the *Torah* (increase your possessions, prosper, get wealthy at all costs, etc.) and somewhat anticipatory of the *Koran*'s rhetoric. But with a difference from both:

"Sell your possessions and give to the poor." This is more than the "leftovers" of the *Torah* and the 1/40 of the *Koran*. This seems to be more a categorical critique of possessions than one only of illegitimate wealth. (See also, infra, Acts.)

Master-servant (God/Jesus—faithful man) parable is told, Peter asks "Lord, are you telling this parable to us, or to everyone?" (12:41), The Lord Jesus answers:

> That servant who knows his master's will and does not get ready or does not do what his master wants will be beaten with many blows. But the one who does not know and does things deserving punishment will be beaten with few blows. From everyone who has been given much, much will be demanded; and from the one who has been entrusted with much, much more will be asked. (12:47-48)

Few or many blows, but beating anyway.

Jesus declares his mission and the initial division within the family before the eventual advent of peace based on common faith:

> I have come to bring fire on the earth, and how I wish it were already kindled! But I have a baptism to undergo, and how distressed I am until it is completed! Do you think I came to bring peace on earth? No, I tell you, but division. From now on there will be five in one family divided against each other, three against two and two against three. They will be divided, father against son and son against father, mother against daughter and daughter against mother, mother-in-law against daughter-in-law and daughter-in-law against mother-in-law. (12:49-53)

13. Repent or Perish

Unbelief or disbelief is sanctioned by death:

> ...unless you repent, you too will all perish. (13:5)

Since submission is closely related to belief and repentance, this formula of "repent or perish" is easily transformable to that of "submit or perish." (Cf. infra.)

Jesus heals (works) on the Sabbath. Someone asks him, "Lord, are only a few people going to be saved?" (13:23); Jesus answers:

> Make every effort to enter through the narrow door, because many, I tell you, will try to enter and will not be able to. Once the owner of the house gets up and closes the door, you will stand outside knocking and pleading, 'Sir, open the door for us.' (13:24-25)

The door is narrow; not many but few will be able to enter it and be saved. Elitism and exclusionism of religion could not have been better expressed.

Jesus laments for Jerusalem:

> O Jerusalem, Jerusalem, you who kill the prophets and stone those sent to you, how often I have longed to gather your children together, as a hen gathers her chicks un-

der her wings, but you were not willing! Look, your house is left to you desolate. I
tell you, you will not see me again until you say, 'Blessed is he who comes in the
name of the Lord.' (13:34-35; Psalm 118:26)

Infantilization once again through the metaphor of the hen and her chicks. Also utilization
of the basic *Old Testament*-like motif of exile and return, of punishment and (conditional)
reward.

14. Humility, Generosity, The Cost of Being a Disciple

For everyone who exalts himself will be humbled, and he who humbles himself will
be exalted.

Then Jesus said to his host, "When you give a luncheon or dinner, do not invite
your friends, your brothers or relatives, or your rich neighbors; if you do, they may
invite you back and so you will be repaid.

But when you give a banquet, invite the poor, the crippled, the lame, the blind,
and you will be blessed. Although they cannot repay you, you will be repaid at the
resurrection of the righteous." (14:11-14)

Humility, not humiliation; unilateral hospitality(?), not reciprocity.

The parable of the great banquet is repeated: The invitees do not attend the master's (Jesus's) banquet (teaching) for various reasons (business, family matters), so the master says to
his servant:

Go out to the roads and country lanes and make them come in, so that my house
will be full. I tell you, not one of those men who were invited will get a taste of my
banquet. (14:23-24)

Belief and obedience at all costs are required:

Large crowds were traveling with Jesus, and turning to them he said: "If anyone comes to me and does not hate his father and mother, his wife and children, his brothers and sisters—yes, even his own life—he cannot be my disciple. And anyone who
does not carry his cross and follow me cannot be my disciple." (14:25-27)

Religious faith is greater than familial love and loyalty, even at the cost of hating parents.

15. Parables: Lost Sheep, Lost Coin, Lost Son

One sinner (lost sheep) who repents is reason for rejoicing more than having ninety-nine
righteous persons who do not need to repent. So with the one lost silver coin with regard to
the nine unlost silver coins. Similarly with the lost son and the unlost son:

My son, the father said, 'you are always with me, and everything I have is yours. But
we had to celebrate and be glad, because this brother of yours was dead and is alive
again; he was lost and is found.' (15:31-32)

16. Shrewd Manager, Divorce, Rich Man and Lazarus

"The master commend(s) his dishonest manager because he (acts) shrewdly" (16:8). From a Jacobean anecdote, Luke passes on to a moral:

> The master commended the dishonest manager because he had acted shrewdly. For the people of this world are more shrewd in dealing with their own kind than are the people of the light. I tell you, use worldly wealth to gain friends for yourselves, so that when it is gone, you will be welcomed into eternal dwellings. (16:8-9)

Such is one of the uses of "worldly wealth." It does not logically follow, but Luke proceeds:

> Whoever can be trusted with very little can also be trusted with much, and whoever is dishonest with very little will also be dishonest with much. So if you have not been trustworthy in handling worldly wealth, who will trust you with true riches? And if you have not been trustworthy with someone else's property, who will give you property of your own?
>
> No servant can serve two masters. Either he will hate the one and love the other, or he will be devoted to the one and despise the other. You cannot serve both God and Money.
>
> The Pharisees, who loved money, heard all this and were sneering at Jesus. He said to them, "You are the ones who justify yourselves in the eyes of men, but God knows your hearts. What is highly valued among men is detestable in God's sight." (16:10-15)

What is more important here than the logical sequence and derivation of a series of morals is the repetition of the contradictory devotions to God and Money—a rhetorical break from the *Torah* at the first glance—but then we come back full circle to the merit of "worldly wealth" provided it be holy and be used charitably; perhaps a little more charitably than the *Old Testament*. That's all. In the final analysis, it is not God or Money; it is God and Money, but holy and legitimate money. "Devotion to one and despising the other" bit is rhetorical or ambiguous at best. It all should be read as: Don't love money unless you love God more. You cannot serve God and Money as equal masters; serve God as the higher master, only then serve money as the lesser master. (Either my logic is wrong or all Christians are hypocrites. Cf. Paul on Cretans.)

"Additional teachings":

> The Law and the Prophets were proclaimed until John. Since that time, the good news of the kingdom of God is being preached, and everyone is forcing his way into it. It is easier for heaven and earth to disappear than for the least stroke of a pen to drop out of the Law.
>
> Anyone who divorces his wife and marries another woman commits adultery and the man who marries a divorced woman commits adultery. (16:18-19)

"Absolute text" is reaffirmed(?)—in connection first with the Word and then divorce and adultery.

And an anecdote from hell and heaven (a new literary device in the *Bible*):

There was a rich man who was dressed in purple and fine linen and lived in luxury every day. At his gate was laid a beggar named Lazarus, covered with sores and long-ing to eat what fell from the rich man's table. Even the dogs came and licked his sores.

The time came when the beggar died and the angels carried him to Abraham's side. The rich man also died and was buried. In hell, where he was in torment, he looked up and saw Abraham far away, with Lazarus by his side. So he called to him. 'Father Abraham, have pity on me and send Lazarus to dip the tip of his finger in water and cool my tongue, because I am in agony in this fire.'

But Abraham replied, 'Son, remember that in your lifetime you received your good things, while Lazarus received bad things, but now he is comforted here and you are in agony. And besides all this, between us and you a great chasm has been fixed, so that those who want to go from here to you cannot, nor can anyone cross over from there to us.'

He answered, 'Then I beg you, father, send Lazarus to my father's house, for I have five brothers. Let him warn them, so that they will not also come to this place of torment.'

Abraham replied, 'They have Moses and the Prophets; let them listen to them.'

'No', father Abraham, he said, 'but if someone from the dead goes to them, they will repent.'

He said to him, 'If they do not listen to Moses and the Prophets, they will not be convinced even if someone rises from the dead.'

If they did not listen to Moses and the Prophets, and they would not, therefore, listen to "someone from the dead" (Lazarus or Jesus), how can Jesus possibly have sinners repent at all? "Too late to repent" is the message. And the reward for timely belief/repentance is but a change of places in the other world. The categories of haves and have-nots are never morally abrogated. Such is the "egalitarianism" of Luke.

17. Sin, Faith, Duty; Healings; Kingdom of God

If your brother sins, rebuke him, and if he repents, forgive him. If he sins against you seven times in a day, and seven times comes back to you and says, 'I repent,' forgive him.

The apostles said to the Lord, "Increase our faith!"

He replied, "If you have faith as small as a mustard seed, you can say to this mul-berry tree, 'Be uprooted and planted in the sea,' and it will obey you." (17:3-6)

So much for forgiveness for repentance (of small misdeeds). Now, *some* sanction for (serious) unrepentance:

> For the Son of Man in his day will be like the lightning, which flashes and lights up the sky from one end to the other. But first he must suffer many things and be rejected by this generation.
>
> Just as it was in the days of Noah, so also will it be in the days of the Son of Man. People were eating, drinking, marrying and being given in marriage up to the day Noah entered the ark. Then the flood came and destroyed them all.
>
> It was the same in the days of Lot. People were eating and drinking, buying and selling, planting and building. But the day Lot left Sodom, fire and sulfur rained down from heaven and destroyed them all.
>
> It will be just like this on the day the Son of Man is revealed. On that day no one who is on the roof of his house, with his goods inside, should go down to get them. Likewise, no one in the field should go back for anything. Remember Lot's wife!
>
> Whoever tries to keep his life will lose it, and whoever loses his life will preserve it. I tell you, on that night two people will be in one bed; one will be taken and the other left. Two women will be grinding grain together; one will be taken and the other left.
>
> "Where, Lord?" They asked.
>
> He replied, "Where there is a dead body, there the vultures will gather."

The *Old Testament*'s severe punishments in this world are postponed to the other world. And most of this imagery shall be adopted by the *Koran*. Please also note the ratio of fifty percent for the "to be saved remnant."

18. Parables: Widow, Tax Collector, Little Children, Rich Ruler, Healings

Repetitions. One worth repeating here:

> How hard it is for the rich to enter the kingdom of God! Indeed, it is easier for a camel to go through the eye of a needle than for a rich man to enter the kingdom of God.
>
> Those who heard this asked, "Who then can be saved?"
>
> Jesus replied, "What is impossible with men is possible with God."
>
> Peter said to him, "We have left all we had to follow you!"
>
> "I tell you the truth," Jesus said to them, "no one who has left home or wife or brothers or parents or children for the sake of the kingdom of God will fail to receive many times as much in this age and, in the age to come, eternal life." (18:24-30)

For "rich," please read "uncharitable rich." Charity is the insurance of property and social stability of an inegalitarian order. By the same token, the Three Books are the insurance policy of that sort of an (in)human society.

19. Zacchaeus, Ten Minas, Entry, Temple

The very wealthy chief tax collector Zacchaeus gives half of his possessions to the poor, and Jesus calls him a son of Abraham. Contrast this ½ of wealth with Islam's 1/40 of income, and both with the % 100 of Acts, below.

20. Authority, Tenants, Taxes to Caesar, Marriage, Whose Son?

Jesus replied, "The people of this age marry and are given in marriage. But those who are considered worthy of taking part in that age and in the resurrection from the dead will neither marry nor be given in marriage, and they can no longer die; for they are like the angels. They are God's children, since they are children of the resurrection. But in the account of the bush, even Moses showed that the dead rise, for he calls the Lord 'the God of Abraham, and the God of Isaac, and the God of Jacob.' He is not the God of the dead, but of the living, for to him all are alive."

Some of the teachers of the law responded, "Well said, teacher!" And no one dared to ask him any more questions. (20:34-38)

Paul shall (already has) perfect(ed) the preferability of celibacy.

21. Widow's Offering, End of the Age

Repetitions. One worth repeating, which is reminiscent of the *Old Testament* and also anticipatory of *Koran*. Jesus speaking:

For this is the time of punishment in fulfillment of all that has been written. How dreadful it will be in those days for pregnant women and nursing mothers! There will be great distress in the land and wrath against this people. They will fall by the sword and will be taken as prisoners to all the nations. Jerusalem will be trampled on by the Gentiles until the times of the Gentiles are fulfilled.

There will be signs in the sun, moon and stars. On the earth, nations will be in anguish and perplexity at the roaring and tossing of the sea. Men will faint from terror, apprehensive of what is coming on the world, for the heavenly bodies will be shaken. At that time they will see the Son of Man coming in a cloud with power and great glory. (21:22-27)

And:

I tell you the truth, this generation will certainly not pass away until all these things have happened. Heaven and earth will pass away, but my words will never pass away.

Be careful, or your hearts will be weighed down with dissipation, drunkenness and the anxieties of life, and that day will close on you unexpectedly like a trap.

For it will come upon all those who live on the face of the whole earth. (21:32-35)

The *New Testament*, at times, is no less frightening than the *Old*. (Cf. Deuteronomy, Ch. 28.) "No more curses" and "eternal salvation through Jesus" or exile and devastation again. Which is the real, basic Christianity? And the Christianity of which Jesus?

22. Judas, Last Supper, Arrest, Mockery
Repetitions.

23. Pilate, Crucifixion, Death, Burial
Repetitions.

24. Resurrection, Appearance, Ascension
Jesus rises from the dead:

> When they came back from the tomb, they told all these things to the Eleven and to
> all the others. It was Mary Magdalene, Joanna, Mary the mother of James, and the
> others with them who told this to the apostles. But they did not believe the women,
> because their words seemed to them like nonsense. Peter, however, got up and ran
> to the tomb. Bending over, he saw the strips of linen lying by themselves, and he
> went away, wondering to himself what had happened. (24:9-12)

Jesus appears to the disciples:

> "Why are you troubled, and why do doubts rise in your minds? Look at my hands
> and my feet. It is I myself! Touch me and see; a ghost does not have flesh and bones,
> as you see I have." (24:38-39)
>
> Then he opened their minds so they could understand the Scriptures. He told
> them, "This is what is written: The Christ will suffer and rise from the dead on the
> third day, and repentance and forgiveness of sins will be preached in his name to all
> nations, beginning at Jerusalem. You are witnesses of these things. I am going to
> send you what my Father has promised; but stay in the city until you have been
> clothed with power from on high."
>
> When he had led them out to the vicinity of Bethany, he lifted up his hands and
> blessed them. While he was blessing them, he left them and was taken up into
> heaven. Then they worshiped him and returned to Jerusalem with great joy. And
> they stayed continually at the temple, praising God. (24:45-53)

New Testament invokes the authority of *Old Testament* when it is in its interest to do so. It is
both addition and subtraction. It is both "as it is written" and what was written is "obsolete." Yet, this should not be confused with "anything goes" if you have the power; sacred
religious texts do remain the absolute text, or the near-absolute text.

Notes
1. Luke bases himself more than 50 percent on Mark.
2. Some manuscripts 70 (p. 772).

9

JOHN[1]

1. The Word Became Flesh, John, Jesus, First Disciples

In the beginning was the Word, and the Word was with God, and the Word was God. He was with God in the beginning.

Through him all things were made; without him nothing was made that has been made. In him was life, and that life was the light of men. The light shines in the darkness, but the darkness has not understood it. (1:1-5)

It sounds all too poetic. But what does this poem tell us? Sound yes, but what about sense? What is the meaning of this poetic theology, this arch-idealist father or mother of all idealist (and irrational) philosophies? It says one thing: Human beings and human reason are naught. It doesn't even say "I think, therefore I am"; it says "I believe, therefore I exist." Not even, and erroneously, first thought then life; but, more erroneously, first faith then life, and only then "reason within limits of religion." *And*: condemns as darkness every other possible human reasoning that does not start from the idea of God, his prophet-son, their Word. Pre-"Enlightenment" anti-enlightenment itself—as if God and religion themselves were not the product of human imagination.

Multiple equations: the Word is God, the Word is a "*he*," he = God = Word = Jesus, Word = beginning, Word = creation = life = light = light of men. And a chain of causation: God → Word → creation → life → Jesus → men → men's light. (Cf. Genesis and "naming" and "making by saying" and man's naming everything including the woman.)

John the Baptist comes from God "as a witness to testify concerning that light, so that through him all men might believe" (1:7), and as the harbinger of Jesus:

He himself was not the light; he came only as a witness to the light. The true light that gives light to every man was coming into the world.

He was in the world, and though the world was made through him, the world did not recognize him. He came to that which was his own, but his own did not receive him. Yet to all who received him, to those who believed in his name, he gave the right to become children of God—children born not of natural descent, nor of human decision or a husband's will, but born of God.

The Word became flesh and made his dwelling among us. We have seen his glory, the glory of the of the One and Only, who came from the Father, full of grace and truth.

John testifies concerning him. He cries out, saying, "This was he of whom I said, 'He who comes after me has surpassed me because he was before me.' " From the fullness of his grace we have all received one blessing after another. For the law was given through Moses; grace and truth came through Jesus Christ. No one has ever seen God, but God the One and Only, who is at the Father's side, has made him known. (1:8-18)

Thus, Jesus is not, like Muhammad, a humble, human, "mere" prophet, but a God-like, Godly, superhuman prophet (?), greater than all "sons" of "Man." He is the Word (the He-God) become flesh. To those who receive and believe him, he gives the right to become children of God, "children born not of natural descent, nor of human decision or a husband's will, but born of God." In short, belief in God and his son Jesus makes ordinary men, too, sons of God. BELIEF DEIFIES MAN! While at the same time it dehumanizes him. Plus: impotent men and barren women.

Jesus, the "lamb of God," is greater than John (and all), he recruits his first disciples, he is the "Son of God" and the "King of Israel" (1:49). Royalism again—metaphorically or not.

2. Jesus Changes Water to Wine

The "first of his miraculous signs" is to change water to wine.

He clears the temple area from traders and money changers.

Jesus does not entrust himself even to believers, "for he knew all men. He did not need man's testimony about men, for he knew what was in a man" (2:24-25). Jesus does not respect man as man; he has a low estimate of human nature. (Like the *Old Testament* and the *Koran*.)

3. Teaching, Testimony

Jesus answered, "I tell you the truth, no one can enter the kingdom of God unless he is born of water and the Spirit. Flesh gives birth to flesh, but the Spirit gives birth to spirit. You should not be surprised at my saying, 'You must be born again.' (3:5-7)

Tautologies and Manichean oppositions ensue:

For God so loved the world that he gave his one and only Son, that whoever believes in him shall not perish but have eternal life. For God did not send his Son into the world to condemn the world, but to save the world through him. Whoever believes in him is not condemned, but whoever does not believe stands condemned already because he has not believed in the name of God's one and only Son. This is the verdict: Light has come into the world, but men loved darkness instead of light because their deeds were evil. Everyone who does evil hates the light, and will not come into the light for fear that his deeds will be exposed. But whoever lives by the truth comes into the light, so that it may be seen plainly that what he has done has been done through God. (3:16-21)

Repent (early) or perish! Salvation or condemnation. And the Son will save the "world" (not of course the majority but the minority) on condition.

The believers are likened to a "bride" and Jesus to a "bridegroom. John the Baptist says:

The bride belongs to the bridegroom. The friend who attends the bridegroom waits and listens for him, and is full of joy when he hears the bridegroom's voice. That joy is mine, and it is now complete. He must become greater; I must become less.

The one who comes from above is above all; the one who is from the earth belongs to the earth, and speaks as one from the earth. The one who comes from heaven is above all. He testifies to what he has seen and heard, but no one accepts his testimony. The man who has accepted it has certified that God is truthful. For the one whom God has sent speaks the words of God, for God gives the Spirit without limit. The Father loves the Son and has placed everything in his hands. Whoever believes in the Son has eternal life, but whoever rejects the Son will not see life, for God's wrath remains on him. (3:29-36)

The familiar hierarchy: God → Jesus → believers (man → woman) → non-believers. Curses and blesses again.

4. Samaritans, Healings

Jesus says to the Samaritan woman:

Jesus declared, "Believe me, woman, a time is coming when you will worship the Father neither on this mountain nor in Jerusalem. You Samaritans worship what you do not know; we worship what we do know, for salvation is from the Jews. Yet a time is coming and has now come when the true worshipers will worship the Father in spirit and truth, for they are the kind of worshipers the Father seeks. God is spirit, and his worshipers must worship in spirit and in truth."

The woman said, "I know that Messiah" (called Christ) "is coming. When he comes, he will explain everything to us."

Then Jesus declared, "I who speak to you am he." (4:21-26)

Jesus simulating Yahweh's "I am who I am." Jesus also says to the Samaritans:

Unless you people see miraculous signs and wonders…you will never believe. (4:48)

No, it's the other way around: Unless you believe, you will never see miracles.

5. Healing, Life Through the Son, Testimonies
Jesus heals on the Sabbath:

> So, because Jesus was doing these things on the Sabbath, the Jews persecuted him.
> Jesus said to them. "My Father is always at his work to this very day, and I, too, am
> working." For this reason the Jews tried all the harder to kill him; not only was he
> breaking the Sabbath, but he was even calling God his own Father, making himself
> equal with God.
>
> Jesus gave them this answer: "I tell you the truth, the Son can do nothing by him-
> self; he can do only what he sees his Father doing, because whatever the Father does
> the Son also does. For the Father loves the Son and shows him all he does. Yes, to
> your amazement he will show him even greater things than these. For just as the Fa-
> ther raises the dead and gives them life, even so the Son gives life to whom he is
> pleased to give it. Moreover, the Father judges no one, but has entrusted all judg-
> ment to the Son, that all may honor the Son just as they honor the Father. He who
> does not honor the Son does not honor the Father, who sent him. (5:16-23)

What's the net balance? Father greater than Son? Or Son equal to God?

> I tell you the truth, whoever hears my word and believes him who sent me has eter-
> nal life and will not be condemned; he has crossed over from death to life. I tell you
> the truth, a time is coming and has now come when the dead will hear the voice of
> the Son of God and those who hear will live. For as the Father has life in himself, so
> he has granted the Son to have life in himself. And he has given him authority to
> judge because he is the Son of Man.
>
> Do not be amazed at this, for a time is coming when all who are in their graves
> will hear his voice and come out—those who have done good will rise to live, and
> those who have done evil will rise to be condemned. By myself I can do nothing; I
> judge only as I hear, and my judgment is just, for I seek not to please myself but him
> who sent me. (5:24-30)

Son of God? Or Son of Man?

> You have sent to John and he has testified to the truth. Not that I accept human tes-
> timony; but I mention it that you may be saved. John was a lamp that burned and
> gave light, and you chose for a time to enjoy his light.
>
> I have testimony weightier than that of John. For the very work that the Father
> has given me to finish, and which I am doing, testifies that the Father has sent me.
> And the Father who sent me has himself testified concerning me. You have never
> heard his voice nor seen his form, nor does his word dwell in you, for you do not be-
> lieve the one he sent. You diligently study the Scriptures because you think that by
> them you possess eternal life. These are the Scriptures that testify about me, yet you
> refuse to come to me to have life. (5:33-40)

Human testimony is not acceptable. Jesus knows or decides beforehand that he will not be praised. But why, then, bother to persuade. But that prejudicial foreknowledge is necessary as a ground for will to punish.

6. Feeding 5000, Walking on Water, Bread of Life

Then they asked him, "What must we do to do the works God requires?"

Jesus answered, "The work of God is this: to believe in the one he has sent."

So they asked him, "What miraculous sign then will you give that we may see it and believe you? What will you do? Our forefathers ate the manna in the desert; as it is written: 'He gave them bread from heaven to eat.' "

Jesus said to them, "I tell you the truth, it is not Moses who has given you the bread from heaven, but it is my Father who gives you the true bread from heaven. For the bread of God is he who comes down from heaven and gives life to the world."

"Sir," they said, "from now on give us this bread."

Then Jesus declared, "I am the bread of life. He who comes to me will never go hungry, and he who believes in me will never be thirsty. But as I told you, you have seen me and still you do not believe. All that the Father gives me will come to me, and whoever comes to me I will never drive away. For I have come down from heaven not to do my will but to do the will of him who sent me. And this is the will of him who sent me, that I shall lose none of all that he has given me, but raise them up at the last day. For my Father's will is that everyone who looks to the Son and believes in him shall have eternal life, and I will raise him up at the last day."

At this the Jews began to grumble about him because he said, "I am the bread that came down from heaven." They said, "Is this not Jesus, the son of Joseph, whose father and mother we know? How can he now say, 'I came down from heaven'?" (6:28-42)

Faith over/before works. God-like Jesus is greater than Moses. And grumbling people. No grumbling, says Jesus in a Mosaic style:

Stop grumbling among yourselves, Jesus answered. "No one can come to me unless the Father who sent me draws him, and I will raise him up at the last day. It is written in the Prophets: 'They will all be taught by God.' Everyone who listens to the Father and learns from him comes to me. No one has seen the Father except the one who is from God; only he has seen the Father. I tell you the truth, he who believes has everlasting life. I am the bread of life. Your forefathers ate the manna in the desert, yet they died. But here is the bread that comes down from heaven, which a man may eat and not die. I am the living bread that came down from heaven. If anyone eats of this bread, he will live forever. This bread is my flesh, which I will give for the life of the world."

Then the Jews began to argue sharply among themselves, "How can this man give us his flesh to eat?"

Jesus said to them, "I tell you the truth, unless you eat the flesh of the Son of Man and drink his blood, you have no life in you.

Whoever eats my flesh and drinks my blood has eternal life, and I will raise him up at the last day. For my flesh is real food and my blood is real drink. Whoever eats my flesh and drinks my blood remains in me, and I in him. Just as the living Father sent me and I live because of the Father, so the one who feeds on me will live because of me. This is the bread that came down from heaven. Your forefathers ate manna and died, but he who feeds on this bread will live forever." He said this while teaching in the synagogue in Capernaum. (6:43-59)

Moses's manna was no security against death, but Jesus's bread, that is, he himself as bread, will give everlasting life. The *New Testament*, the later and more truthful word of God in the mouth of Jesus, which claims to do away with *Old Testament*-like rituals and animal offerings, here regresses into even greater, and more cannibalistic ritual:

...you eat the flesh of the Son of Man and drink his blood...whoever eats my flesh and drinks my blood...my flesh is real food and my blood is real drink...

Even as a metaphor as a literary device, this is not very edifying, or superior to the *Old Testament* because it substitutes a man's flesh and blood for animal meat. But more important is the meaning it tries to convey through this device: Father in Son, Son in men, God in men and—it's a two-way street—men in son, Son in God, men in God. (In and of.) This is total and ultimate control of bodies and hearts and minds, incomparably more pervasive, penetrative, invasive than any "control device" to be found in Judaism and Islam. It certainly trivializes the circumsion of the penis. And it is much stronger than the other effective device of Christianity, that of "circumcision of hearts." This is animism, monotheistic animism, or the animism of Christian monotheism.

Many disciples find this "hard teaching" (6:60) and desert Jesus; the Twelve remain:

Simon Peter answered him, "Lord, to whom shall we go? You have the words of eternal life. We believe and know that you are the Holy One of God."

Then Jesus replied, "Have I not chosen you, the Twelve? Yet one of you is a devil!" (He meant Judas, the son of Simon Iscariot, who, though one of the Twelve, was later to betray him.) (6:68-71)

7. Feast, Teaching, Is Jesus the Christ, Unbelief of Jewish Leaders
Jesus teaches at the feast:

The Jews were amazed and asked, "How did this man get such learning without having studied?"

Jesus answered, "My teaching is not my own. It comes from him who sent me. If anyone chooses to do God's will, he will find out whether my teaching comes from God or whether I speak on my own. He who speaks on his own does so to gain honor for himself, but he who works for the honor of the one who sent him is a man of truth; there is nothing false about him. Has not Moses given you the Law? Yet not one of you keeps the law. Why are you trying to kill me?"

"You are demon-possessed," the crowd answered. "Who is trying to kill you?"

Jesus said to them, "I did one miracle, and you are all astonished. Yet, because Moses gave you circumcision (though actually it did not come from Moses, but from the patriarchs), you circumcise a child on the Sabbath. Now if a child can be circumcised on the Sabbath so that the law of Moses may not be broken, why are you angry with me for healing the whole man on the Sabbath? Stop judging by mere appearances, and make a right judgment." (7:15-24)

Both continuity and break with Moses and his Law. Spirit of law greater than letter thereof. Not appearances and formalities but inner sincerity and essence of faith.

Of course, Muhammad shall appropriate the theme of being a man of "learning without having studied." True teaching comes from God, not from human knowledge or wisdom.

And:

Then Jesus, still teaching in the temple courts, cried out, "Yes, you know me, and you know where I am from. I am not here on my own, but he who sent me is true. You do not know him, but I know him because I am from him and he sent me." (7:28-29)

8. First Part

[The earliest and most reliable manuscripts and other ancient witnesses do not have John 7:53-8:11.]

Then each went to his own home. (7:53)

But Jesus went to the Mount of Olives.

At dawn he appeared again in the temple courts, where all the people gathered around him, and he sat down to teach them. The teachers of the law and the Pharisees brought in a woman caught in adultery. They made her stand before the group and said to Jesus, "Teacher, this woman was caught in the act of adultery. In the Law Moses commanded us to stone such women. Now what do you say?" They were using this question as a trap, in order to have a basis for accusing him.

But Jesus bent down and started to write on the ground with his finger. When they kept on questioning him, he straightened up and said to them, "If any one of you is without sin, let him be the first to throw a stone at her." Again he stooped down and wrote on the ground.

At this, those who heard began to go away one at a time, the older ones first, until only Jesus was left, with the woman still standing there. Jesus straightened up and asked her, "Woman, where are they? Has no one condemned you?"

"No one, sir," she said.

"Then neither do I condemn you, Jesus declared. "Go now and leave your life of sin." (8:1-11)

Jesus softer on adultery.

8. (Cont'd) Jesus's Testimony, Children of Abraham, Children of the Devil

The Pharisees challenged him, "Here you are, appearing as your own witness; your testimony is not valid."

Jesus answered, "Even if I testify on my own behalf, my testimony is valid, for I know where I came from and where I am going. But you have no idea where I come from or where I am going. You judge by human standards; I pass judgment on no one. But if I do judge, my decisions are right, because I am not alone. I stand with the Father, who sent me. In your own Law it is written that the testimony of two men is valid. I am one who testifies for myself; my other witness is the Father, who sent me."

Then they asked him, "Where is your father?"

"You do not know me or my Father," Jesus replied. 'If you knew me, you would know my Father also. (8:13-19)

Human standards vs. superhuman standards again. And:

"Who are you?" they asked.

"Just what I have been claiming all along," Jesus replied. "I have much to say in judgment of you. But he who sent me is reliable, and what I have heard from him I tell the world." (8:25-26)

And:

Jesus said to them, "If God were your Father, you would love me, for I came from God and now am here. I have not come on my own; but he sent me. Why is my language not clear to you? Because you are unable to hear what I say. You belong to your father, the devil, and you want to carry out your father's desire. He was a murderer from the beginning, not holding to the truth, for there is no truth in him. When he lies, he speaks his native language, for he is a liar and the father of lies. Yet because I tell the truth, you do not believe me! Can any of you prove me guilty of sin? If I am telling the truth, why don't you believe me? He who belongs to God hears what God says. The reason you do not hear is that you do not belong to God."

The Jews retort that he is a Samaritan and demon-possessed:

The Jews answered him. "Aren't we right in saying that you are a Samaritan and demon-possessed?"

"I am not possessed by a demon," said Jesus, "but I honor my Father and you dishonor me. I am not seeking glory for myself; but there is one who seeks it, and he is the judge. I tell you the truth, if anyone keeps my word, he will never see death."

At this the Jews exclaimed, "Now we know that you are demon-possessed! Abraham died and so did the prophets, yet you say that if anyone keeps your word, he will never taste death. Are you greater than our father Abraham? He died, and so did the prophets. Who do you think you are?"

Jesus replied, "If I glorify myself, my glory means nothing. My Father, whom you claim as your God, is the one who glorifies me. Though you do not know him, I know him. If I said I did not, I would be a liar like you, but I do know him and keep his word. Your father Abraham rejoiced at the thought of seeing my day; he saw it and was glad."

"You are not yet fifty years old," the Jews said to him, "and you have seen Abraham!"

"I tell you the truth," Jesus answered, "before Abraham was born, I am!" At this, they picked up stones to stone him, but Jesus hid himself, slipping away from the temple grounds. (8:48-59)

9. Healings

Then they hurled insults at him and said, "You are this fellow's [Jesus's] disciple! We are disciples of Moses! We know that God spoke to Moses, but as for this fellow, we don't even know where he comes from." (9:28-29)

10. The Shepherd and His Flock
Jesus says:

I am the good shepherd; I know my sheep and my sheep know me—just as the Father knows me and I know the Father—and I lay down my life for the sheep. I have other sheep that are not of this sheep pen. I must bring them also. They too will listen to my voice, and there shall be one flock and one shepherd. The reason my Father loves me is that I lay down my life—only to take it up again. No one takes it from me, but I lay it down of my own accord. I have authority to lay it down and authority to take it up again. This command I received from my Father. (10:14-18)

Not universalism but unitarian religious communalism. Authority from the Father, that is a claim of divinely legitimated power. And:

I and the Father are one. (10:30)

The Jews prepare to stone Jesus, who says:

"Is it not written in your Law, 'I have said you are gods'? If he called them 'gods,' to whom the word of God came—and the Scripture cannot be broken—what about the one whom the Father set apart as his very own and sent into the world? Why then do you accuse me of blasphemy because I said, 'I am God's Son'? Do not believe me unless I do what my Father does. But if I do it, even though you do not believe me, believe the miracles, that you may know and understand that the Father is in me, and I in the Father." Again they tried to seize him, but he escaped their grasp. (10:34-39)

11. Lazarus, Jesus Comforts Sisters, The Plot

Jesus raises Lazarus from the dead—who is Mary's and Martha's brother, which sisters Jesus loves—even before the day of resurrection.

A high priest prophesies that "Jesus would die for the Jewish nation, and not only for that nation but also for the scattered children of God, to bring them together and make them one." (11:51-52) "Universalism" only for and of believers. (But why did you Babelize the children of God in the beginning? Cf. Genesis.)

12. Anointment, Entry, Prediction, Unbelief

Mary pours, while Martha serves, perfume on Jesus's feet and wipes it with her hair. Women serving!

The Jews continue in their unbelief because (as Isaiah says in 6:10):

He has blinded their eyes and deadened their hearts, so they can neither see with their eyes, nor understand with their hearts, nor turn—and I would heal them. (12:40)

Jesus says:

As for the person who hears my words but does not keep them, I do not judge him. For I did not come to judge the world, but to save it. There is a judge for the one who rejects me and does not accept my words; that very word which I spoke will condemn him at the last day. For I did not speak of my own accord, but the Father who sent me commanded me what to say and how to say it. I know that his command leads to eternal life. So whatever I say is just what the Father has told me to say. (12:47-50)

Judgment not in this world but in the other, and more frighteningly so.

13. Disciples' Feet, Betrayal, Denial

Jesus washes his disciples' feet and says:

"Do you understand what I have done for you?" he asked them. "You call me 'Teacher' and 'Lord,' and rightly so, for that is what I am. Now that I, your Lord and Teacher, have washed your feet, you also should wash one another's feet. I have set

you an example that you should do as I have done for you. I tell you the truth, no
servant is greater than his master, nor is a messenger greater than the one who sent
him. Now that you know these things, you will be blessed if you do them."
(13:12-17)

This is not equality but a taming justification of inequality. (Very much like Hegel's han-
dling of the master-bondsman relationship.)

Jesus predicts Judas's betrayal and Peter's denial.

14. Jesus Comforts His Disciples and Promises the Holy Spirit

"Do not let your hearts be troubled. Trust in God; trust also in me." (14:1)

And:

I am the way and the truth and the life. No one comes to the Father except through
me. If you really knew me, you would know my Father as well. From now on, you
do know him and have seen him. (14:6-7)

And:

Anyone who has seen me has seen the Father. How can you say, 'Show us the Father'? Don't you believe that I am in the Father, and that the Father is in me? The
words I say to you are not just my own. Rather, it is the Father, living in me, who is
doing his work. Believe me when I say that I am in the Father and the Father is in
me; or at least believe on the evidence of the miracles themselves. (14:9-11)

And:

If you love me, you will obey what I command. And I will ask the Father, and he will
give you another Counselor to be with you forever—the Spirit of truth. The world
cannot accept him, because it neither sees him nor knows him. But you know him,
for he lives with you and will be in you. I will not leave you as orphans; I will come to
you. Before long, the world will not see me anymore, but you will see me. Because I
live, you also will live. On that day you will realize that I am in my Father, and you
are in me, and I am in you. Whoever has my commands and obeys them, he is the
one who loves me. He who loves me will be loved by my Father, and I too will love
him and show myself to him. (14:15-21)

Obedience and love, not blessings and curses, for a change.

15. Vine, Branches, Disciples

Father is the gardener, Jesus is the vine, and the disciples are the branches:

I am the vine; you are the branches. If a man remains in me and I in him, he will bear
much fruit; apart from me you can do nothing. If anyone does not remain in me, he
is like a branch that is thrown away and withers; such branches are picked up,

thrown into the fire and burned. If you remain in me and my words remain in you, ask whatever you wish, and it will be given you. This is to my Father's glory, that you bear much fruit, showing yourselves to be my disciples.

As the Father has loved me, so have I loved you. Now remain in my love. If you obey my commands, you will remain in my love, just as I have obeyed my Father's commands and remain in his love. I have told you this so that my joy may be in you and that your joy may be complete. My command is this: Love each other as I have loved you. Greater love has no one than this, that he lay down his life for his friends. (15:5-14)

Organic, botanical, anatomical totality. A totalitarian formulation of the part-whole relationship. Productivity as a result of belief in and love for God. (Recall the *Old Testament*.) Conditional bestowal of love; unconditional belief and obedience.

You are my friends if you do what I command. I no longer call you servants, because a servant does not know his master's business. Instead, I have called you friends, for everything that I learned from my Father I have made known to you. You did not choose me, but I chose you and appointed you to go and bear fruit—fruit that will last. Then the Father will give you whatever you ask in my name. This is my command: Love each other. (15:16-17)

Conditional friendship and unilateral choice. Human beings not agencies but chosen instruments. And:

If the world hates you, keep in mind that it hated me first. If you belonged to the world, it would love you as its own. As it is, you do not belong to the world, but I have chosen you out of the world. That is why the world hates you. Remember the words I spoke to you: 'No servant is greater than his master.' If they persecuted me, they will persecute you also. If they obeyed my teaching, they will obey yours also. They will treat you this way because of my name, for they do not know the One who sent me. If I had not come and spoken to them, they would not be guilty of sin. Now, however, they have no excuse for their sin. He who hates me hates my Father as well. If I had not done among them what no one else did, they would not be guilty of sin. But now they have seen these miracles, and yet they have hated both me and my Father. But this is to fulfill what is written in their Law: 'They hated me without reason.' (15:18-25; Psalms 35:19, 69:4)

"No servant is greater than his master?" Is this egalitarianism? And why not the converse?

16. Holy Spirit, Grief and Joy

It is for your good that I am going away. Unless I go away, the Counselor will not come to you; but if I go, I will send him to you. When he comes, he will convict the world of guilt in regard to sin and righteousness and judgment: in regard to sin, because men do not believe in me; in regard to righteousness, because I am going to the Father, where you can see me no longer; and in regard to judgment, because the prince of this world now stands condemned. (16:7-11)

The Prince-Son and the King-Father. Threat and "conviction" again.

"Though I have been speaking figuratively, a time is coming when I will no longer use this kind of language but will tell you plainly about my Father. In that day you will ask in my name. I am not saying that I will ask the Father on your behalf. No, the Father himself loves you because you have loved me and have believed that I came from God. I came from the Father and entered the world; now I am leaving the world and going back to the Father."

Then Jesus' disciples said, "Now you are speaking clearly and without figures of speech. Now we can see that you know all things and that you do not even need to have anyone ask you questions. This makes us believe that you came from God." (16:25-30)

Not speaking figuratively or in parables/riddles but speaking clearly and in straightforward language. When and why? In time and because of full revelation?

17. Jesus Prays for Himself, for His Disciples, for All Believers
Jesus prays for himself:

Father, the time has come. Glorify your Son, that your Son may glorify you. For you granted him authority over all people that he might give eternal life to all those you have given him. Now this is eternal life: that they may know you, the only true God, and Jesus Christ, whom you have sent. I have brought you glory on earth by completing the work you gave me to do. And now, Father, glorify me in your presence with the glory I had with you before the world began. (17:1-5)

Is this strict Genesis or Genesis revised? Jesus existing before the creation of the world?
Jesus prays for his disciples:

I have revealed you to those whom you gave me out of the world. They were yours; you gave them to me and they have obeyed your word...I am not praying for the world, but for those you have given me, for they are yours...

Sanctify them by the truth; your word is truth. As you sent me into the world, I have sent them into the world. For them I sanctify myself, that they too may be truly sanctified. (17:6, 9, 17-19)

Human non-agencies are "given to." And only some at that.
Jesus prays for all believers:

My prayer is not for them alone. I pray also for those who will believe in me through their message, that all of them may be one, Father, just as you are in me and I am in you. May they also be in us so that the world may believe that you have sent me. I have given them the glory that you gave me, that they may be one as we are one: I in them and you in me. May they be brought to complete unity to let the world know that you sent me and have loved them even as you have loved me. (17:20-23)

Corpus Christi and Corpus Dei!

18. Arrest, Denials, Pilate
Repetitions.

19. Crucifixion, Death, Burial

"These things happened so that the scripture would be fulfilled: "Not one of his bones will be broken," and, as another scripture says, "They will look on the one they have pierced." (19:36-37; Exod. 12:46, Num. 9:12, Psalm 34:20; Zech. 12:10)

20. Empty Tomb, Appearances
Repetitions. With variations on the theme. And:

Jesus did many other miraculous signs in the presence of his disciples, which are not recorded in this book. But these are written that you may believe that Jesus is the Christ, the Son of God, and that by believing you may have life in his name. (20:30-31)

Life for believers, death for unbelievers.

21. Miraculous Catch of Fish and Reinstatement of Peter
Jesus appears thrice to his disciples after he is raised from the dead. And:

Jesus did many other things as well. If every one of them were written down, I suppose that even the whole world would not have room for the books that would be written. (21:25)

The world is already full and awash with religious books. "The world is too much with religious books," to adapt Wordsworth.

Notes
1. The latest non-synoptic gospel after the synoptic ones of Mark, Matthew, and Luke.

THE ACTS

1. Jesus Taken Up Into Heaven, Matthias Chosen to Replace Judas

Jesus says to the apostles:

> He said to them: "It is not for you to know the times or dates the Father has set by his own authority. But you will receive power when the Holy Spirit comes on you; and you will be my witnesses in Jerusalem, and in all Judea and Samaria, and to the ends of the earth." (1:7-8)

2. The Holy Spirit Comes at Pentecost, Peter Addresses the Crowd

> Now there were staying in Jerusalem God-fearing Jews from every nation under heaven. When they heard this sound, a crowd came together in bewilderment, because each one heard them speaking in his own language. Utterly amazed, they asked: "Are not all these men who are speaking Galileans? Then how is it that each of us hears them in his own native language? Parthians, Medes and Elamites; residents of Mesopotamia, Judea and Cappadocia, Pontus and Asia, Phrygia and Pamphylia, Egypt and the parts of Libya near Cyrene; visitors from Rome (both Jews and converts to Judaism); Cretans and Arabs—we hear them declaring the wonders of God in our own tongues!" Amazed and perplexed, they asked one another, "What does this mean?"
>
> Some, however, made fun of them and said. "They have had too much wine." (2:5:13)

Peter explains to the crowd:

> Men of Israel, listen to this: Jesus of Nazareth was a man accredited by God to you by miracles, wonders and signs, which God did among you through him, as you yourselves know. This man was handed over to you by God's set purpose and foreknowledge; and you, with the help of wicked men, put him to death by nailing him to the cross. But God raised him from the dead, freeing him from the agony of death, because it was impossible for death to keep its hold on him… (2:22-24)

And reminds the words of David:

> The Lord said to my Lord: Sit at my right hand until I make your enemies a footstool for your feet. (2:34-35, Psalm 110:1)

Peter urges repentance and baptism; "three thousand were added to their number that day" (2:41). The believers "devoted themselves to the apostles' teaching and to the fellowship" (2:42), and the following, that is not comparable to anything in the *Old Testament* or the *Koran*:

> All the believers were together and had everything in common. Selling their possessions and goods, they gave to anyone as he had need. Every day they continued to meet together in the temple courts. They broke bread in their homes and ate together with glad and sincere hearts, praising God and enjoying the favor of all the people. And the Lord added to their number daily those who were being saved. (2:44-47)

"Everything in common," "selling (all) their possessions and goods," "giving each as he needs." Communal, even communistic, living. Please note the resemblance of "giving to anyone as he had need" to the second clause of Marx's "from each according to his ability and to each according to his need."

3. Peter Heals and Teaches

Peter heals a crippled man, saying: "Silver or gold I do not have, but what I have I give you" (3:6). And: "The God of Abraham, Isaac and Jacob the God of our fathers, has glorified his servant Jesus" (3:13). Both son and servant.

> Now, brothers, I know that you acted in ignorance, as did your leaders. But this is how God fulfilled what he had foretold through all the prophets, saying that his Christ would suffer. Repent, then, and turn to God, so that your sins may be wiped out, that times of refreshing may come from the Lord, and that he may send the Christ, who has been appointed for you—even Jesus. He must remain in heaven until the time comes for God to restore everything, as he promised long ago through his holy prophets. For Moses said, 'The Lord your God will raise up for you a prophet like me from among your own people; you must listen to everything he tells you. Anyone who does not listen to him will be completely cut off from among his people.'
> Indeed, all the prophets from Samuel on, as many as have spoken, have foretold these days. And you are heirs of the prophets and of the covenant God made with your fathers. He said to Abraham, 'Through your offspring all peoples on earth will be blessed.' When God raised up his servant, he sent him first to you to bless you by turning each of you from your wicked ways. (3:17-26; Deut. 18:15, 18, 19)

Continuity of Judeo-Christian tradition.

4. Sanhedrin, Believers' Prayer, Sharing of Possessions
Peter and John are jailed and brought before the rulers, elders, teachers of the law, the high priest and his family, but are released. The believers pray to God:

> Sovereign Lord, they said, "you made the heaven and the earth and the sea, and everything in them. You spoke by the Holy Spirit through the mouth of your servant, our father David:
>
> Why do the nations rage and the peoples plot in vain? The kings of the earth take their stand and the rulers gather together against the Lord and against his Anointed One. (4:24-26; Psalm 2:1,2)

In total and essential contradistinction to the *Torah* and the *Koran*, Jesus's followers believe in and practice full commonality of possessions (according to Luke's Acts):

> All the believers were one in heart and mind. No one claimed that any of his possessions was his own, but they shared everything they had. With great power the apostles continued to testify to the resurrection of the Lord Jesus, and much grace was upon them all. There were no needy persons among them. For from time to time those who owned lands or houses sold them, brought the money from the sales and put it at the apostles' feet, and it was distributed to anyone as he had need.
>
> Joseph, a Levite from Cyprus, whom the apostles called Barnabas (which means Son of Encouragement), sold a field he owned and brought the money and put it at the apostles' feet. (4:32-37)

To each according to his need. No private property. Total sharing of worldly goods. No inheritance. Giving any and all amount of possessions to the community. A veritable idea and practice of: FROM EACH ACCORDING TO HIS MEANS, TO EACH ACCORDING TO HIS NEED.

The discursively very Marxian ring of this not withstanding (or, should we say, the Lukean-Christian ring of Marx's motto), there is a serious risk of reading more communism into this passage (the strongest in the whole *New Testament*) than there is in it. And the crucial question is the following:

Is this a categorical imperative of Christian moral theory (or at least that of one or two of its canonical books) concerning the value and morality of private property (or at least excess of it), or is it merely a desirable but temporary practice in the history of the development of the church on its way to consolidate itself? In other words, is it a basic, transcontextual moral (and political) principle, or is it a contextual, contingent practice, morally laudable only for a brief period?

Much would hinge on the answer to this question. If the answer is 'yes' to the first question, 95-99 percent of Christians would be in a very embarrassing position. But if the answer 'yes' is to the second question, they can feel relatively more comfortable!

5. Ananias and Sapphira, Healings and Persecutions

The apostolic (and Lukean) imperative of communal property, even if for a transitory period of the Christian church, is very strict:

> Now a man named Ananias, together with his wife Sapphira, also sold a piece of property. With his wife's full knowledge he kept back part of the money for himself, but brought the rest and put it at the apostles' feet.
>
> Then Peter said, "Ananias, how is it that Satan has so filled your heart that you have lied to the Holy Spirit and have kept for yourself some of the money you received for the land? Didn't it belong to you before it was sold? And after it was sold, wasn't the money at your disposal? What made you think of doing such a thing? You have not lied to men but to God."
>
> When Ananias heard this, he fell down and died. And great fear seized all who heard what had happened. Then the young men came forward, wrapped up his body, and carried him out and buried him.
>
> About three hours later his wife came in, not knowing what had happened. Peter asked her, "Tell me, is this the price you and Ananias got for the land?"
>
> "Yes," she said, "that is the price."
>
> Peter said to her, "How could you agree to test the Spirit of the Lord? Look! The feet of the men who buried your husband are at the door, and they will carry you out also."
>
> At that moment she fell down at his feet and died. Then the young men came in and, finding her dead, carried her out and buried her beside her husband. Great fear seized the whole church and all who heard about these events. (5:1-11)

This is a far, far cry from the *Koran*'s almsgiving and zekât (1/40) and from the *Torah*'s charity (e.g., leaving to the poor the leftovers of fields once in a year or every other seven years). In the Christianity of the Acts (and Luke), not even "part of the money" from the sale of property can be kept back from the community. It is a Satanic deed in the eyes of the church against God.

Please also note that the commanding apostle here is Peter and the narrator is his disciple Luke, and their attitude toward private property is radically different from that of Paul (see infra), with whom Peter fell into disagreement. Also to be noted is the fact that Peter's and Luke's stand in this matter is much stronger than the Jesus of other gospels.

Apostles heal and perform miraculous signs and wonders; they are persecuted but say: "We must obey God rather than men" (5:29); they call Jesus "Prince and Savior" (5:31); a Pharisee named Gamaliel, a teacher of the law, intervenes in their favor:

> "Leave these men alone! Let them go! For if their purpose or activity is of human origin, it will fail. But if it is from God, you will not be able to stop these men; you will only find yourselves fighting against God."

His speech persuaded them. They called the apostles in and had them flogged. Then they ordered them not to speak in the name of Jesus, and let them go.

The apostles left the Sanhedrin, rejoicing because they had been counted worthy of suffering disgrace for the Name. Day after day, in the temple courts and from house to house, they never stopped teaching and proclaiming the good news that Jesus is the Christ. (5:38-42)

6. The Choosing of the Seven

In those days when the number of disciples was increasing, the Grecian Jews among them complained against the Hebraic Jews because their widows were being overlooked in the daily distribution of food. So the Twelve gathered all the disciples together and said, "It would not be right for us to neglect the ministry of the word of God in order to wait on tables. Brothers, choose seven men from among you who are known to be full of the Spirit and wisdom. We will turn this responsibility over to them and will give our attention to prayer and the ministry of the word."

This proposal pleased the whole group. They chose Stephen, a man full of faith and of the Holy Spirit; also Philip, Procorus, Nicanor, Timon, Parmenas, and Nicolas from Antioch, a convert to Judaism. They presented these men to the apostles, who prayed and laid their hands on them.

So the word of God spread. The number of disciples in Jerusalem increased rapidly, and a large number of priests became obedient to the faith. (6:1-7)

Stephen is accused of speaking "words of blasphemy against Moses and against God" (6:11) and of saying that Jesus will "change the customs Moses handed down to us" (6:14).

Stephen is seized and brought before the Sanhedrin.

7. Stephen's Speech

Stephen recounts the story of Abraham, Isaac, Jacob, twelve patriarchs, Joseph, famine, Moses ("powerful in speech (!) and action," 7:22), enslavement, exodus, 40 years in the desert, murmuring and grumbling, the golden calf, Moses's telling the Israelites that "God will send you a prophet like me from your own people..." (7:37; Deut. 18:15)

Stephen, in a Mosaic spirit, continues: "But our fathers refused to obey him. Instead, they rejected him and in their hearts returned to Egypt" (7:39), and he says (recall Ch. 16):

This is the same Moses whom they had rejected with the words: "Who made you ruler and judge?" He was sent to be their ruler and deliverer by God himself; through the angel who appeared to him in the bush. (7:35)

The tabernacle of the Testimony, the exile, David and Solomon, God speaking through the prophet (Isaiah 66:1,2):

Heaven is my throne, and the earth is my footstool. What kind of house will you build for me? says the Lord.

Or where will my resting place be? Has not my hand made all these things?

You stiff-necked people, with uncircumcised hearts and ears! You are just like your fathers: You always resist the Holy Spirit! Was there ever a prophet your fathers did not persecute? They even killed those who predicted the coming of the Righteous One. And now you have betrayed and murdered him—you who have received the law that was put into effect through angels but have not obeyed it. (7:49-53)

Stephen is quite Mosaic indeed, from the "stiff-necked" people to a God and his chosen ones whose "footstool" are the enemies and the earth. Still, he is stoned to death. Saul (Paul) gives approval to his death.

8. The Church Persecuted and Scattered

On that day a great persecution broke out against the church at Jerusalem, and all except the apostles were scattered throughout Judea and Samaria. Godly men buried Stephen and mourned deeply for him. But Saul began to destroy the church. Going from house to house, he dragged off men and women and put them in prison. (8:1-3)

The scattered ones preach the word, heal, perform miracles, Simon the sorcerer is converted, money cannot "buy the gift of God" (8:20), an Ethiopian eunuch-official is converted, etc.

9. Saul's Conversion

Jesus first blinds the murderous Saul and then forgives him: "This man is my chosen instrument..." (9:15). Saul is baptized, begins to preach that Jesus is the Son of God, debates with Grecian Jews, is sent off to Tarsus.

The churches in Judea, Galilee, Samaria enjoy a time of peace and grow in numbers.

10. Cornelius and Peter

An angel of God appears to Cornelius, a "devout and God-fearing" centurion in the Italian regiment giving "generously to those in need" (10:2) and tells him to have Simon Peter brought from Joppa to Caesarea.

On the journey Peter has a vision concerning "clean and unclean" ("Do not call anything impure that God has made clean," 10:15).

As Peter entered the house, Cornelius met him and fell at his feet in reverence. But Peter made him get up. "Stand up," he said, "I am only a man myself."

Talking with him, Peter went inside and found a large gathering of people. He said to them: "You are well aware that it is against our law for a Jew to associate with a Gentile or visit him. But God has shown me that I should not call any man impure or unclean. So when I was sent for, I came without raising any objection. May I ask why you sent for me?" (10:25-29)

Cornelius:

> So I sent for you immediately, and it was good of you to come. Now we are all here in the presence of God to listen to everything the Lord has commanded you to tell us. (10:33)

Peter begins to speak:

> I now realize how true it is that God does not show favoritism but accepts men from every nation who fear him and do what is right. You know the message God sent to the people of Israel, telling the good news of peace through Jesus Christ, who is Lord of all. (10:34-36)

Relaxation of exclusionism and beginnings of "universalism?"

> "While Peter was still speaking these words, the Holy Spirit came on all who heard the message. The circumcised believers who had come with Peter were astonished that the gift of the Holy Spirit had been poured out even on the Gentiles. For they heard them speaking in tongues and praising God." (10:44-46)

11. Peter's Explanations, Church in Antioch
Peter explains his actions to the other apostles to remove their reservations ("So then, God has granted even the Gentiles repentance unto life," 11:18).

> "The disciples were called Christians first at Antioch." (11:26)

And it is also in Antioch that the first part of Marx's motto was first coined to precision:

> The disciples, each according to his ability, decided to provide help for the brothers... (11:29)

12. Peter's Miraculous Escape From Prison
Peter escapes; Herod dies. "An angel of the Lord struck him down, and he was eaten by worms and died" (12:23).

13. Barnabas and Saul in Cyprus and Other Places
"In the church at Antioch there were prophets and teachers: Barnabas, Simon called Niger, Lucius of Cyrene, Manaen...and Saul" (13:1). The Holy Spirit sends Barnabas and Saul ("who was also called Paul," 13:9) to do work in Cyprus (Salamis, Paphos) and Pisidian Antioch, "reading from the Law and the Prophets" (13:15). Saul/Paul gives his first long speech:

> Standing up, Paul motioned with his hand and said: "Men of Israel and you Gentiles who worship God, listen to me! The God of the people of Israel chose our fathers; he made the people prosper during their stay in Egypt, with mighty power he led them out of that country, he endured their conduct for about forty years in the desert, he overthrew seven nations in Canaan and gave their land to his people as their inheritance. All this took about 450 years.

After this, God gave them judges until the time of Samuel the prophet. Then the people asked for a king, and he gave them Saul son of Kish, of the tribe of Benjamin, who ruled forty years. After removing Saul, he made David their king. He testified concerning him: 'I have found David son of Jesse a man after my own heart; he will do everything I want him to do.'

From this man's descendants God has brought to Israel the Savior Jesus, as he promised. Before the coming of Jesus, John preached repentance and baptism to all the people of Israel. As John was completing his work, he said: 'Who do you think I am? I am not that one. No, but he is coming after me, whose sandals I am not worthy to untie.' (13:16-25)

We tell you the good news: What God promised our fathers he has fulfilled for us, their children, by raising up Jesus. As it is written in the second Psalm: You are my Son; today I have become your Father. The fact that God raised him from the dead, never to decay, is stated in these words:

I will give you the holy and sure blessings promised to David. So it is stated elsewhere: You will not let your Holy One see decay.

For when David had served God's purpose in his own generation, he fell asleep; he was buried with his fathers and his body decayed. But the one whom God raised from the dead did not see decay." (13:32-37; Psa. 2:7, Isa. 55:3, Psa. 16:10)

Paul, heretofore, emphasizes the continuity of the Judaic-Christian scriptures and places Jesus smoothly in the tradition. But, in concluding, he delineates the originality and superiority of Christ with regard to Moses:

Therefore, my brothers, I want you to know that through Jesus the forgiveness of sins is proclaimed to you. Through him everyone who believes is justified from everything you could not be justified from by the law of Moses. Take care that what the prophets have said does not happen to you: Look, you scoffers, wonder and perish, for I am going to do something in your days that you would never believe, even if someone told you. (13:38-41)

"Scoffers" react:

On the next Sabbath almost the whole city gathered to hear the word of the Lord. When the Jews saw the crowds, they were filled with jealousy and talked abusively against what Paul was saying. Then Paul and Barnabas answered them boldly: "We had to speak the word of God to you first. Since you reject it and do not consider yourselves worthy of eternal life, we now turn to the Gentiles. For this is what the Lord has commanded us: 'I have made you a light for the Gentiles, that you may bring salvation to the ends of the earth.' "

When the Gentiles heard this, they were glad and honored the word of the Lord; and all who were appointed for eternal life believed.

The word of the Lord spread through the whole region. But the Jews incited the God-fearing women of high standing and the leading men of the city. They stirred up persecution against Paul and Barnabas, and expelled them from their region. So they shook the dust from their feet in protest against them and went to Iconium. And the disciples were filled with joy and with the Holy Spirit. (13:44-52; Isa. 49:6)

"Women of high standing and the leading men of the city" is a phrase we shall encounter frequently, the "establishment" whom the apostles will gradually win over. (Cf. also *Koran*.)

14. In Iconium, Lystra and Derbe, Antioch in Syria

Progressively greater numbers of Jews and Gentiles believe; in Lycaonia Barnabas and Paul are called Zeus and Hermes, respectively, because Paul is the "chief speaker" (14:12); the people shout: "The Gods have come down to us in human form" (14:11). They say:

Men, why are you doing this? We too are only men, human like you. We are bring-ing you good news, telling you to turn from these worthless things to the living God, who made heaven and earth and sea and everything in them. In the past, he let all nations go their own way. Yet he has not left himself without testimony. (14:15-17)

They appoint elders in each church, they preach in Pamphylia (Perge, Attalia), they "open the door of faith to the Gentiles" (14:27).

15. The Council at Jerusalem; Paul vs. Barnabas

Then some of the believers who belonged to the party of the Pharisees stood up and said, "The Gentiles must be circumcised and required to obey the law of Moses."

The apostles and elders met to consider this question. After much discussion, Pe-ter got up and addressed them: "Brothers, you know that some time ago God made a choice among you that the Gentiles might hear from my lips the message of the gospel and believe. God, who knows the heart, showed that he accepted them by giving the Holy Spirit to them, just as he did to us. He made no distinction between us and them, for he purified their hearts by faith. Now then, why do you try to test God by putting on the necks of the disciples a yoke that neither we nor our fathers have been able to bear? No! We believe it is through the grace of our Lord Jesus that we are saved, just as they are." (15:5-11)

So, it is not circumcision and the letter of the Law of Moses that assures salvation, but it is the spirit of the law, the Holy Spirit, the grace of Jesus, and purification (and circumcision) of the heart by faith.

James quotes from Amos (9:11,12) and says:

After this I will return and rebuild David's fallen tent. Its ruins I will rebuild, and I will restore it, that the remnant of men may seek the Lord, and all the Gentiles who bear my name, says the Lord, who does these things that have been known for ages.

It is my judgment, therefore, that we should not make it difficult for the Gentiles who are turning to God. Instead we should write to them, telling them to abstain from food polluted by idols, from sexual immorality, from the meat of strangled animals and from blood. For Moses has been preached in every city from the earliest times and is read in the synagogues on every Sabbath. (15:16-21)

"Remnant of men" are to abstain from foul food and sexual immorality, but what about remnants of Moses's law? The apostles and elders then write to the Gentile believers in Antioch, Syria, and Cilicia:

It seemed good to the Holy Spirit and to us not to burden you with anything beyond the following requirements: You are to abstain from food sacrificed to idols, from blood, from the meat of strangled animals and from sexual immorality. You will do well to avoid these things. (15:28-29)

Thus, the requirement of circumcision is dropped from the Law by the church to rescind the words of some who acted "without authorization" (15:24) from "the Holy Spirit and us" (15:28) and "troubling the minds" of Gentile believers, thus relieving them from a "yoke" and a "burden." Barnabas and Paul disagree and part company:

Some time later Paul said to Barnabas, "Let us go back and visit the brothers in all the towns where we preached the word of the Lord and see how they are doing."

Barnabas wanted to take John, also called Mark, with them, but Paul did not think it wise to take him, because he had deserted them in Pamphylia and had not continued with them in the work. They had such a sharp disagreement that they parted company. Barnabas took Mark and sailed for Cyprus, but Paul chose Silas and left, commended by the brothers to the grace of the Lord. He went through Syria and Cilicia, strengthening the churches. (15:36-41)

16. Macedonia

Paul and Silas take along Timothy (from Jewess mother and Greek father) after circumsizing him, they travel throughout Phyrygia and Galatia, they are "kept back by the Holy Spirit from preaching the word in the province of Asia" (16:6), they pass by Mysia and Bithynia because the spirit of Jesus does not allow them, they stay in Troas. The narrative voice changes to the first person plural: "From Troas we put out to sea and sailed straight for Samothrace" (16:11). Next Neopolis and Philippi, where they convert Lydia:

On the Sabbath we went outside the city gate to the river, where we expected to find a place of prayer. We sat down and began to speak to the women who had gathered there. One of those listening was a woman named Lydia, a dealer in purple cloth from the city of Thyatira, who was a worshiper of God. The Lord opened her heart to respond to Paul's message. When she and the members of her household were baptized, she invited us to her home. "If you consider me a believer in the Lord," she said, "come and stay at my house." And she persuaded us. (16:13-15)

Paul drives out the spirit in a fortune-telling slave girl, her owners bring them before the authorities, Paul and company are flogged and imprisoned, a violent earthquake opens prison doors and loosens all inmates' chains, the jailor and his household is converted, in the morning officers order their release:

> But Paul said to the officers: "They beat us publicly without a trial, even though we are Roman citizens, and threw us into prison. And now do they want to get rid of us quietly? No! Let them come themselves and escort us out."
>
> The officers reported this to the magistrates, and when they heard that Paul and Silas were Roman citizens, they were alarmed. They came to appease them and escorted them from the prison, requesting them to leave the city. After Paul and Silas came out of the prison, they went to Lydia's house, where they met with the brothers and encouraged them. Then they left. (16:37-40)

Preacher of super-human law invokes Roman law. Reconciliation of Christian identity with Roman citizenship.

17. Thessalonica, Berea, Athens

> When they had passed through Amphipolis and Apollonia, they came to Thessalonica, where there was a Jewish synagogue. As his custom was, Paul went into the synagogue, and on three Sabbath days he reasoned with them from the Scriptures, explaining and proving that the Christ had to suffer and rise from the dead. "This Jesus I am proclaiming to you is the Christ," he said. Some of the Jews were persuaded and joined Paul and Silas, as did a large number of God-fearing Greeks and not a few prominent women.
>
> But the Jews were jealous; so they rounded up some bad characters from the marketplace, formed a mob and started a riot in the city. (17:1-5)

> As soon as it was night, the brothers sent Paul and Silas away to Berea. On arriving there, they went to the Jewish synagogue. Now the Bereans were of more noble character than the Thessalonians, for they received the message with great eagerness and examined the Scriptures every day to see if what Paul said was true. Many of the Jews believed, as did also a number of prominent Greek women and many Greek men. (17:10-12)

Paul "reasons with" the Jews "from the Scriptures," "explaining and proving" miracles. Reason emanates from fear of God and belief in sacred words. Faith underlies and activates reason. Not infinite but one regress: fear inspires faith. In other words: Fear → faith → reason; fear of God → faith in his Prophet and Book(s) → human reason (first of Paul, then of believers.) Not even Kant's "religion within limits of reason," but Hegel's "reason within limits of religion." And belief confers nobility and holiness.

In Athens, a crucial (or fatal?) encounter takes place between Judeo-Christianity and pagan Greece, which was not totally unready for monotheism.

While Paul was waiting for them in Athens, he was greatly distressed to see that the city was full of idols. So he reasoned in the synagogue with the Jews and the God-fearing Greeks, as well as in the marketplace day by day with those who happened to be there. A group of Epicurean and Stoic philosophers began to dispute with him. Some of them asked, "What is this babbler trying to say? Others remarked, "He seems to be advocating foreign gods." They said this because Paul was preaching the good news about Jesus and the resurrection. Then they took him and brought him to a meeting of the Areopagus, where they said to him, "May we know what this new teaching is that you are presenting? You are bringing some strange ideas to our ears, and we want to know what they mean." (All the Athenians and the foreigners who lived there spent their time doing nothing but talking about and listening to the latest ideas.)

Paul then stood up in the meeting of the Areopagus and said: "Men of Athens! I see that in every way you are very religious. For as I walked around and looked carefully at your objects of worship, I even found an altar with this inscription: TO AN UNKNOWN GOD. Now what you worship as something unknown I am going to proclaim to you.

The God who made the world and everything in it is the Lord of heaven and earth and does not live in temples built by hands. And he is not served by human hands, as if he needed anything, because he himself gives all men life and breath and everything else. From one man he made every nation of men, that they should inhabit the whole earth; and he determined the times set for them and the exact places where they should live. God did this so that men would seek him and perhaps reach out for him and find him, though he is not far from each one of us. 'For in him we live and move and have our being.' As some of your own poets have said, 'We are his offspring.'

Therefore since we are God's offspring, we should not think that the divine being is like gold or silver or stone—an image made by man's design and skill. In the past God overlooked such ignorance, but now he commands all people everywhere to repent. For he has set a day when he will judge the world with justice by the man he has appointed. He has given proof of this to all men by raising him from the dead.

When they heard about the resurrection of the dead, some of them sneered, but others said, "We want to hear you again on this subject." At that, Paul left the Council. A few men became followers of Paul and believed. Among them was Dionysius, a member of the Areopagus, also a woman named Damaris, and others. (17:16-34)

Christianity, Pauline Christianity, is not only against polytheist and idol-worshiping religion, it is also, and to my mind more importantly, against human reason—free, autonomous human reason:

All the Athenians and the foreigners who lived there spent their time doing nothing but talking about and listening to the latest ideas. (17:21)

It is here the natural, non-superhuman Greek rationality is to be overcome for two thousand years by (Judeo-)Christian faith. Reasoning no more with the ideas of the human mind but "from the Scriptures." Not only concerning human society, politics, and morals, but our knowledge of reality, of the world, starting with Creation: "The God who made" the "world," "men," "nations"... (17:24-26). What for? (meaning and purpose of life?):

> God did this so that men would seek him and perhaps reach out for him and find him... (17:27)

Ontology and epistemology complemented with teleology. (Hegel's objective spirit reaching out for the absolute spirit.)

> ...though he is not far from each one of us. For in him we live and move and have our being. As some of you own poets have said, "we are his offspring." (17:27-28)

The *New Testament* lacks a properly named, crucial, separate book called "Athenians."

18. Corinth

Every Sabbath Paul continues to "reason" in the synagogue, trying to "persuade" Jews and Greeks (18:4).

> But when the Jews opposed Paul and became abusive, he shook out his clothes in protest and said to them, "Your blood be on your own heads! I am clear of my responsibility. From now on I will go to the Gentiles." (18:6)

Worshiping God according to which law?

> While Gallio was proconsul of Achaia, the Jews made a united attack on Paul and brought him into court. "This man," they charged, "is persuading the people to worship God in ways contrary to the law."
>
> Just as Paul was about to speak, Gallio said to the Jews, "If you Jews were making a complaint about some misdemeanor or serious crime, it would be reasonable for me listen to you. But since it involves questions about words and names and your own law—settle the matter yourselves. I will not be a judge of such things." So he had them ejected from the court. Then they all turned on Sosthenes the synagogue ruler and beat him in front of the court. But Gallio showed no concern. (18:12-17)

So it is not enough to believe in one God, even the Abrahamic God; it matters how you worship him and according to which law (of Moses, of Jesus, of Muhammad), and "in ways [not] contrary to the law"—which one? (One God, three books?)

19. Ephesus

> While Apollos was at Corinth, Paul took the road through the interior and arrived at Ephesus. There he found some disciples and asked them, "Did you receive the Holy Spirit when you believed?"
>
> They answered, "No, we have not even heard that there is a Holy Spirit."

So Paul asked, "Then what baptism did you receive?"

"John's baptism," they replied.

Paul said, "John's baptism was a baptism of repentance. He told the people to believe in the one coming after him, that is, in Jesus." On hearing this, they were baptized into the name of the Lord Jesus. When Paul placed his hands on them, the Holy Spirit came on them, and they spoke in tongues and prophesied. There were about twelve men in all.

Paul entered the synagogue and spoke boldly there for three months, arguing persuasively about the kingdom of God. But some of them became obstinate; they refused to believe and publicly maligned the Way. So Paul left them. He took the disciples with him and had discussions daily in the lecture hall of Tyrannus. This went on for two years; so that all the Jews and Greeks who lived in the province of Asia heard the word of the Lord.

God did extraordinary miracles through Paul, so that even handkerchiefs and aprons that had touched him were taken to the sick, and their illnesses were cured and the evil spirits left them. (19:1-12)

Paul both "argues persuasively" and performs extraordinary miracles. The silversmith Demetrius incites a riot in the name of declining business of the goddess Artemis, but the city clerk quiets the crowd by invoking due process of law and saves Paul and his disciples.

20. Macedonia and Greece

Troas, Assos, Mitylene, Kios, Samos, Miletus; Paul's farewell speech:

Therefore, I declare to you today that I am innocent of the blood of all men. For I have not hesitated to proclaim to you the whole will of God. Keep watch over yourselves and all the flock of which the Holy Spirit has made you overseers. Be shepherds of the church of God, which he bought with his own blood. I know that after I leave, savage wolves will come in among you and will not spare the flock. Even from your own number men will arise and distort the truth in order to draw away disciples after them. So be on your guard! Remember that for three years I never stopped warning each of you night and day with tears.

Now I commit you to God and to the word of his grace, which can build you up and give you an inheritance among all those who are sanctified. I have not coveted anyone's silver or gold or clothing. You yourselves know that these hands of mine have supplied my own needs and the needs of my companions. In everything I did, I showed you that by this kind of hard work we must help the weak, remembering the words the Lord Jesus himself said: 'It is more blessed to give than to receive.' (20:26-35)

Paul is not Aaron & Company.

21. Jerusalem, Arrest

Cos, Rhodes, Patara, Tyre, Ptolemais, Caesarea, Philip's house ("four unmarried daughters who prophesied," 21:9), Jerusalem; brothers and elders:

> When the seven days were nearly over, some Jews from the province of Asia saw Paul at the temple. They stirred up the whole crowd and seized him, shouting, "Men of Israel, help us! This is the man who teaches all men everywhere against our people and our law and this place. And besides, he has brought Greeks into the temple area and defiled this holy place." (21:27-28)

Paul is seized, the commander of the Roman troops arrests and chains him.

> As the soldiers were about to take Paul into the barracks, he asked the commander, "May I say something to you?"
>
> "Do you speak Greek?" He replied. "Aren't you the Egyptian who started a revolt and led four thousand terrorists out into the desert some time ago?"
>
> Paul answered, "I am a Jew, from Tarsus in Cilicia, a citizen of no ordinary city. Please let me speak to the people."
>
> Having received the commander's permission, Paul stood on the steps and motioned to the crowd. When they were all silent, he said to them in Aramaic... (21:37-40)

22. Paul's Defense

Paul relates that he was a Jew from Tarsus, that he was "thoroughly trained in the law of our fathers and was just as zealous for God as any of you are today. I persecuted the followers of this Way to their death, arresting both men and women and throwing them into prison..." (22:3-4), that on his way to Damascus Jesus talked to him and a bright light from heaven blinded him, that Ananias gave him back his light, saying:

> Then he said: 'The God of our fathers has chosen you to know his will and to see the Righteous One and to hear words from his mouth. You will be his witness to all men of what you have seen and heard. And now what are you waiting for? Get up, be baptized and wash your sins away, calling on his name.' (22:14-16)

In Jerusalem, God himself talks to Paul:

> When I returned to Jerusalem and was praying at the temple, I fell into a trance and saw the Lord speaking. 'Quick!' he said to me. 'Leave Jerusalem immediately, because they will not accept your testimony about me.'
>
> Lord, I replied, 'these men know that I went from one synagogue to another to imprison and beat those who believe in you. And when the blood of your martyr Stephen was shed, I stood there giving my approval and guarding the clothes of those who were killing him.'
>
> Then the Lord said to me, 'Go; I will send you far away to the Gentiles. (22:17-21)

The crowd becomes riotous again, Paul is put back into the barracks, he invokes his Roman citizenship:

> Those who were about to question him withdrew immediately. The commander himself was alarmed when he realized that he had put Paul, a Roman citizen, in chains. (22:22-29)

23. Sanhedrin, Plot, Caesarea

> Then Paul, knowing that some of them were Sadducees and the others Pharisees, called out in the Sanhedrin, "My brothers, I am a Pharisee, the son of a Pharisee. I stand on trial because of my hope in the resurrection of the dead." When he said this, a dispute broke out between the Pharisees and the Sadducees, and the assembly was divided. (The Sadducees say that there is no resurrection, and that there are neither angels nor spirits, but the Pharisees acknowledge them all.)
>
> There was a great uproar, and some of the teachers of the law who were Pharisees stood up and argued vigorously. "We find nothing wrong with this man," they said. "What if a spirit or an angel has spoken to him?" The dispute became so violent that the commander was afraid Paul would be torn to pieces by them. He ordered the troops to go down and take him away from them by force and bring him into the barracks.
>
> The following night the Lord stood near Paul and said, "Take courage! As you have testified about me in Jerusalem, so you must also testify in Rome." (23:6-11)

The Jews (more than forty men) plot to kill Paul, the commander transfers him to Caesarea, writing to the governor:

> This man was seized by the Jews and they were about to kill him, but I came with my troops and rescued him, for I had learned that he is a Roman citizen. I wanted to know why they were accusing him, so I brought him to their Sanhedrin. I found that the accusation had to do with questions about their law, but there was no charge against him that deserved death or imprisonment. When I was informed of a plot to be carried out against the man, I sent him to you at once. I also ordered his accusers to present to you their case against him. (23:27-30)

Paul is escorted by 200 soldiers, 70 horsemen, and 200 spearmen.

24, 25, 26. Trials and Hearing Before Felix, Festus, and King Agrippa
Ananias and Tertullus:

> We have found this man to be a troublemaker, stirring up riots among the Jews all over the world. He is a ringleader of the Nazarene sect and even tried to desecrate the temple; so we seized him. By examining him yourself you will be able to learn the truth about all these charges we are bringing against him. (24:5-8)

Paul:

> My accusers did not find me arguing with anyone at the temple, or stirring up a
> crowd in the synagogues or anywhere else in the city. And they cannot prove to you
> the charges they are now making against me.
>
> However, I admit that I worship the God of our fathers as a follower of the Way,
> which they call a sect. I believe everything that agrees with the Law and that is writ-
> ten in the Prophets, and I have the same hope in God as these men, that there will be
> a resurrection of both the righteous and the wicked. So I strive always to keep my
> conscience clear before God and man.
>
> After an absence of several years, I came to Jerusalem to bring my people gifts for
> the poor and to present offerings. I was ceremonially clean when they found me in
> the temple courts doing this. There was no crowd with me; nor was I involved in any
> disturbance. But there are some Jews from the province of Asia, who ought to be
> here before you and bring charges if they have anything against me. Or these who
> are here should state what crime they found in me when I stood before the Sanhed-
> rin—unless it was this one thing I shouted as I stood in their presence: 'It is concern-
> ing the resurrection of the dead that I am on trial before you today. (24:12-21)

Paul makes clear that he is no rebel (Cf. Ch. 16); he says that his conscience is clear before
God and man(!).

Felix procrastinates, gives some freedom to Paul in prison, expects a bribe from him,
and wanting to grant a favor to the Jews he keeps him in prison for two years until Festus
succeeds him. Festus convenes the court:

> Then Paul made his defense: "I have done nothing wrong against the law of the Jews
> or against the temple or against Caesar."
>
> Festus, wishing to do the Jews a favor, said to Paul, "Are you willing to go up to
> Jerusalem and stand trial before me there on these charges?"
>
> Paul answered: "I am now standing before Caesar's court, where I ought to be
> tried. I have not done any wrong to the Jews, as you yourself know very well. If,
> however, I am guilty of doing anything deserving death, I do not refuse to die. But if
> the charges brought against me by these Jews are not true, no one has the right to
> hand me over to them. I appeal to Caesar!"
>
> After Festus had conferred with his council, he declared: "You have appealed to
> Caesar. To Caesar you will go!" (25:8-12)

Festus consults the visiting King Agrippa:

> When his accusers got up to speak, they did not charge him with any of the crimes I
> had expected. Instead, they had some points of dispute with him about their own re-
> ligion and about a dead man named Jesus who Paul claimed was alive. I was at a loss

how to investigate such matters; so I asked if he would be willing to go to Jerusalem and stand trial there on these charges. When Paul made his appeal to be held over for the Emperor's decision, I ordered him held until I could send him to Caesar.

Then Agrippa said to Festus, "I would like to hear this man myself."

He replied, "Tomorrow you will hear him." (25:18-22)

Note the nice phrase "some points of dispute about religion."

Paul, repeating what Jesus told him, speaks:

I will rescue you from your own people and from the Gentiles. I am sending you to them to open their eyes and turn them from darkness to light, and from the power of Satan to God, so that they may receive forgiveness of sins and a place among those who are sanctified by faith in me.

So then, King Agrippa, I was not disobedient to the vision from heaven. First to those in Damascus, then to those in Jerusalem and in all Judea, and to the Gentiles also, I preached that they should repent and turn to God and prove their repentance by their deeds. That is why the Jews seized me in the temple courts and tried to kill me. But I have had God's help to this very day, and so I stand here and testify to small and great alike. I am saying nothing beyond what the prophets and Moses said would happen—that the Christ would suffer and, as the first to rise from the dead, would proclaim light to his own people and to the Gentiles. (26:17-23)

Festus:

"You are out of your mind," Paul! "He shouted." Your great learning is driving you insane. (26:24)

Paul:

"I am not insane, most excellent Festus," Paul replied. "What I am saying is true and reasonable. The king is familiar with these things, and I can speak freely to him. I am convinced that none of this has escaped his notice, because it was not done in a corner. King Agrippa, do you believe the prophets? I know you do." (26:25-27)

And:

Then Agrippa said to Paul, "Do you think that in such a short time you can persuade me to be a Christian?"

Paul replied, "Short time or long—I pray God that not only you but all who are listening to me today may become what I am, except for these chains."

The king rose, and with him the governor and Bernice and those sitting with them. They left the room, and while talking with one another, they said, "This man is not doing anything that deserves death or imprisonment."

Agrippa said to Festus, "This man could have been set free if he had not appealed to Caesar." (26:28-32)

27. Paul Sails for Rome, The Storm, The Shipwreck

"We boarded a ship from Adramyttium" (27:2). Sidon, Myria (in Lycia), change of ship, Cynidus, past Crete, Lasea, heading for Phoenix (in Crete).

Paul warns against bad weather, he is not heeded, the ship is caught by the storm, cargo is thrown overboard, all hope of being saved is given up, Paul gives morale:

> I urge you to keep up your courage, because not one of you will be lost; only the ship will be destroyed. Last night an angel of the God whose I am and whom I serve stood beside me and said, 'Do not be afraid, Paul. You must stand trial before Caesar; and God has graciously given you the lives of all who sail with you.' So keep up your courage, men, for I have faith in God that it will happen just as he told me. Nevertheless, we must run aground on some island. (27:22-26)

They are driven across the sea for fourteen days, Paul urges them all (276 men) to eat bread, the ship runs aground and is wrecked, all reach land (Malta).

28. Malta, Rome, Paul Preaching Under Guard

Paul performs a miracle, heals the sick, after three months "we" sail for Rome. Syracuse, Rhegium, Puteoli, and Rome.

Paul calls together the leaders of the Jews:

> From morning till evening he explained and declared to them the kingdom of God and tried to convince them about Jesus from the Law of Moses and from the Prophets. Some were convinced by what he said, but others would not believe. They disagreed among themselves and began to leave after Paul had made this final statement: "The Holy Spirit spoke the truth to your forefathers when he said through Isaiah the prophet:
>
> Go to this people and say, you will be ever hearing but never understanding; you will be ever seeing but never perceiving. For this people's heart has become calloused; they hardly hear with their ears, and they have closed their eyes. Otherwise they might see with their eyes, hear with their ears, understand with their hearts and turn, and I would heal them.
>
> Therefore I want you to know that God's salvation has been sent to the Gentiles, and they will listen!"
>
> For two whole years Paul stayed there in his own rented house and welcomed all who came to see him. Boldly and without hindrance he preached the kingdom of God and taught about the Lord Jesus Christ. (28:23-31)

11

PAULINE EPISTLES

ROMANS

1. God's Wrath Against Mankind

Paul addresses all "who are loved by God" and offers "grace and peace" to them "from God our Father and from the Lord Jesus Christ" (1:7). Paul, a servant of Jesus Christ is "set apart" for the gospel of God—"the gospel he promised beforehand through his prophets in the Holy Scriptures regarding his Son, who as to his human nature was a descendant of David…" (1:1-3). Paul calls Gentiles to the "obedience that comes from faith" (1:5). His authority to do this derives from his apostleship. Continuity with the book(s) and prophets of the *Old Testament* is stated; that the required obedience comes from faith is underlined. (Fear → believe → obey.) Paul is here to "have a harvest" (1:13) among people (Cf. fishing, *supra*) and to save "the righteous," righteousness being equated with believing in the gospel (1:16-17).

Paul's speech, which opens with love, grace, peace, prayer, spiritual gift, encouragement, and so forth, immediately turns into the familiar *Old Testament*-like barrage of accusation and insult:

> The wrath of God is being revealed from heaven against all the godlessness and wickedness of men who suppress the truth by their wickedness, since what may be known about God is plain to them, because God has made it plain to them. For since the creation of the world God's invisible qualities—his eternal power and divine nature—have been clearly seen, being understood from what has been made, so that men are without excuse.
>
> For although they knew God, they neither glorified him as God nor gave thanks to him, but their thinking became futile and their foolish hearts were darkened. Although they claimed to be wise, they became fools and exchanged the glory of the immortal God for images made to look like mortal man and birds and animals and reptiles. (1:18-23)

Given the proofs of creation and the book(s), there is "no excuse" for not having been adequately monotheistic.(Cf. *Koran*'s signs/proofs/*ayats*.)

"Futile thinking" and "darkened foolish hearts." *Therefore*: "God giv(ing) them over in the sinful desires of their hearts" to... What? To "sexual impurity" and "shameful lusts" (1:24 and 26). The chain of reasoning: Men sin (do not believe in One God) → God punishes them ("gives them over to sinful desire"—but why sexuality?) → Men, thus, become more wicked ("they have become filled with *every* kind of wickedness," 1:29) → God further punishes them (with death). In other words, God further "hardens" their hearts (*Old Testament*), or "darkens" their hearts (*New Testament*), or "seals" their hearts (*Koran*)—to punish them more severely.

First sin   : unbelief in Abraham's God

Second sin   : sexual sin(s)

Third sin   : all kinds ("every kind of wickedness, evil, greed and depravity," 1:29)

Therefore God gave them over in the sinful desires of their hearts to sexual impurity for the degrading of their bodies with one another. They exchanged the truth of God for a lie, and worshiped and served created things rather than the Creator—who is forever praised. Amen.

Because of this, God gave them over to shameful lusts. Even their women exchanged natural relations for unnatural ones. In the same way the men also abandoned natural relations with women and were inflamed with lust for one another. Men committed indecent acts with other men, and received in themselves the due penalty for their perversion.

Furthermore, since they did not think it worthwhile to retain the knowledge of God, he gave them over to a depraved mind, to do what ought not to be done. They have become filled with every kind of wickedness, evil, greed and depravity. They are full of envy, murder, strife, deceit and malice. They are gossips, slanderers, Godhaters, insolent, arrogant and boastful; they invent ways of doing evil; they disobey their parents; they are senseless, faithless, heartless, ruthless. Although they know God's righteous decree that those who do such things deserve death, they not only continue to do these very things but also approve of those who practice them. (1:24-32)

This is not an attitude or process of men erring and God correcting; it is a premeditated and predetermined mentality and act of God/prophets/books, automatically defining men's error(s) as crime(s) calling for swift and harsh punishment. This does not sound like a religion of salvation but one of condemnation. (Logic of causalities and sequences of reasoning can often be shown to be faulty, but the intention and gesture are clear: Give no exit to avoid crime and guarantee grounds of punishment. So, is it really: "Repent or perish?" or "Keep on sinning and perish," for there seems to be not much room for repentance.)

And why is there a preoccupation with sex, sexual desire, since the times of Genesis, especially with its immediate, reflex-like, identification with impurity, immorality, and perversity (not only that in Sodom and Gomorrah)? And why is there a jump from idolatry and polytheism to sexual sin? As the second sin, *and* as the punishment for the first sin? Is it a fear of, and as its rationalization, a deprecation of, women?

It is only after these that God "gives them over" to a "depraved mind" (1:28), as well. And a list of sins follows, overlapping with those in the Ten Commandments:

2. God's Righteous Judgment, The Jews and the Law

God-hating	Insolence
Disobeying parents	Strife
Murder	Senselessness
Gossip and slander	Faithlessness
Envy	Heartlessness
Deceit and malice	Ruthlessness
Arrogance and boasting	Evil

Only God can judge (truth); you, "a mere man," cannot and should not judge.

> But because of your stubbornness and your unrepentant heart, you are storing up wrath against yourself for the day of God's wrath, when his righteous judgment will be revealed. God "will give to each person according to what he has done." To those who by persistence in doing good seek glory, honor and immortality, he will give eternal life. But for those who are self-seeking and who reject the truth and follow evil, there will be wrath and anger. There will be trouble and distress for every human being who does evil: first for the Jew, then for the Gentile; but glory, honor and peace for everyone who does good: first for the Jew, then for the Gentile. For God does not show favoritism. (2:5-11)

What is "doing good" (to others?) beyond charity, and what is "love" beyond that for other believers? Yet, we have come a long way from the self-seeking quest for individual "prosperity" of the *Old Testament* to the non-selfseeking morality of the *New Testament*. (Have we, really?) And wrath of God, stiffneckedness are still with us. Rewards for belief are glory, honor, peace, immortality, eternal life.

Paul goes on to expose hypocritical Jews who violate their own law and then emphasizes inward belief over outward practice and the spirit of the law over the letter thereof:

> Circumcision has value if you observe the law, but if you break the law, you have become as though you had not been circumcised. If those who are not circumcised keep the law's requirements, will they not be regarded as though they were circumcised? The one who is not circumcised physically and yet obeys the law will con-

demn you who, even though you have the written code and circumcision, are a lawbreaker.

A man is not a Jew if he is only one outwardly, nor is circumcision merely outward and physical. No, a man is a Jew if he is one inwardly; and circumcision is circumcision of the heart, by the Spirit, not by the written code. Such a man's praise is not from men, but from God. (2:25-29)

Which is better (or worse)?: Circumcision of the heart by the Spirit or circumcision of the penis by the written code?

3. God's Faithfulness; Righteousness Through Faith
Theodicy vs. "human argument":

But if our unrighteousness brings out God's righteousness more clearly, what shall we say? That God is unjust in bringing his wrath on us? (I am using a human argument.) Certainly not! If that were so, how could God judge the world? Someone might argue, "If my falsehood enhances God's truthfulness and so increases his glory, why am I still condemned as a sinner?" Why not say—as we are being slanderously reported as saying and as some claim that we say—"Let us do evil that good may result?" Their condemnation is deserved. (3:5-8)

Paul quotes Psalms 14:1-3, 53:1-3, 5:9, 140:3, 10:7, 36:1; Eccles. 7:20; and Isaiah 59:7-8:

What shall we conclude then? Are we any better? Not at all! We have already made the charge that Jews and Gentiles alike are all under sin. As it is written:

There is no one righteous, not even one; there is no one who understands, no one who seeks God. All have turned away, they have together become worthless; there is no one who does good, not even one. Their throats are open graves; their tongues practice deceit. The poison of vipers is on their lips. Their mouths are full of cursing and bitterness.

Their feet are swift to shed blood; ruin and misery mark their ways, and the way of peace they do not know. There is no fear of God before their eyes.

Now we know that whatever the law says, it says to those who are under the law, so that every mouth may be silenced and the whole world held accountable to God. Therefore no one will be declared righteous in his sight by observing the law; rather, through the law we become conscious of sin. (3:9-20)

All this wickedness and worthlessness because of lack of "fear of God," and "through the law" we become conscious of sin and not, for example, of righteousness. Not that formal, if not hypocritical, observance of the law confers righteousness; the law is not for teaching righteousness, it is a penal code which enumerates the sins/crimes and the penalties. And our Jewish view of human nature hasn't changed much, has it? "No one, not even one," let alone "most."

Fear, believe, obey. God, faith, submission. And violence: e.g., "swift to shed blood."
(Another instance of Jesus vs. Paul:)

The Law (old) does not teach righteousness; a new righteousness is "made known."
Men cannot, and did not, learn it from the old law; it is now "made known" to them by a
new "faith," to which, nevertheless the law and the Prophets testify:

> But now a righteousness from God, apart from law, has been made known, to which
> the Law and the Prophets testify. This righteousness from God comes through faith
> in Jesus Christ to all who believe. There is no difference, for all have sinned and fall
> short of the glory of God, and are justified freely by his grace through the redemp-
> tion that came by Christ Jesus. God presented him as a sacrifice of atonement,
> through faith in his blood. He did this to demonstrate his justice, because in his for-
> bearance he had left the sins committed beforehand unpunished—he did it to dem-
> onstrate his justice at the present time, so as to be just and the one who justifies those
> who have faith in Jesus.
>
> Where, then, is boasting? It is excluded. On what principle? On that of observing
> the law? No, but on that of faith. For we maintain that a man is justified by faith
> apart from observing the law. Is God the God of Jews only? Is he not the God of
> Gentiles too? Yes, of Gentiles too, since there is only one God, who will justify the
> circumcised by faith and the uncircumcised through that same faith. Do we, then,
> nullify the law by this faith? Not at all! Rather, we uphold the law. (3:21-31)

Continuity *and* discontinuity, not the law *but* the Law, not observing the law but having
faith, not reasoned learning but fearful belief, not the ethnic-religious tribalism of the *Old
Testament* but the non-ethnic religious unitarianism of the *New Testament*. Old law is not
refuted; it is rejuvenated. (Addition and subtraction?) Not all human beings are embraced,
only those of the new faith are. (Please note that this is what is called Christian "universalism"; in fact, it is unitarian religious communalism. We shall return to a similar problem
with Islamic "universalism.")

4. Abraham Justified by Faith

Abraham was not justified by "works" but by "faith": "Abraham believed God, and it was
credited to him as righteousness" (4:3; Gen. 15:6). So not only "not reason but faith," but
even "not works but faith." (Human agency is obliterated in full.) Also, this accreditation
was not after but before the circumcision (4:10).

> It was not through law that Abraham and his offspring received the promise that he
> would be heir of the world, but through the righteousness that comes by faith. For if
> those who live by law are heirs, faith has no value and the promise is worthless, be-
> cause law brings wrath. And where there is no law there is no transgression.
>
> Therefore, the promise comes by faith, so that it may be by grace and may be
> guaranteed to all Abraham's offspring—not only to those who are of the law but also

to those who are of the faith of Abraham. He is the father of us all. As it is written: "I have made you a father of many nations." He is our father in the sight of God, in whom he believed—the God who gives life to the dead and calls things that are not as though they were. (4:13-17; Gen. 17:5)

And:

... he did not waver through unbelief regarding the promise of God, but was strengthened in his faith and gave glory to God, being fully persuaded that God had power to do what he had promised. This is why "it was credited to him as righteousness." The words "it was credited to him" were written not for him alone, but also for us, to whom God will credit righteousness—for us who believe in him who raised Jesus our Lord from the dead. He was delivered over to death for our sins and was raised to life for our justification. (4:20-25)

Except for the last sentence and a half, this Abrahamic fearful surrender (teslim of İslam) shall be carried to its logical extreme by *Koran*.

5. Peace, Joy, Death, Life

Faith brings justification, peace, joy, and grace. Suffering produces perseverance; perseverance, character; and character, hope (5:3-4). Death of Jesus for the ungodly brings reconciliation between God and men, his blood justifying the sinfulness of the latter.

Therefore, just as sin entered the world through one man, and death through sin, and in this way death came to all men, because all sinned—for before the law was given, sin was in the world. But sin is not taken into account when there is no law. Nevertheless, death reigned from the time of Adam to the time of Moses, even over those who did not sin by breaking a command, as did Adam, who was a pattern of the one to come. (5:12-14)

Forget about logic and justice; just note the statement: "...before the law was given, sin was in the world." Sin is axiomatic; law is a penal code; the Law does not teach or is not a guide for righteous works or behavior but issues death penalty for crimes predetermined to be committed by the majority of men.

Again, overlook the illogic and injustice, note the purpose and function of law:

Consequently, just as the result of one trespass was condemnation for all men, so also the result of one act of righteousness was justification that brings life for all men. For just as through the disobedience of the one man the many were made sinners, so also through the obedience of the one man the many will be made righteous.

The law was added so that the trespass might increase. But where sin increased, grace increased all the more, so that, just as sin reigned in death, so also grace might reign through righteousness to bring eternal life through Jesus Christ our Lord. (5:18-21)

Note especially: "The law was added so that the trespass might increase." So that a greater majority of men could be punished and destroyed, reducing the chosen, righteous elect to an even nicer minimum. Although Christianity seems to be much more comforting and promising in its heralding of the end of sin and punishment, please note that it does not disown Judaism's "works" on most men heretofore.

6. Dead to Sin, Alive in Christ

Paul asks: "Or, am I wrong?":

> If we have been united with him like this in his death, we will certainly also be united with him in his resurrection. For we know that our old self was crucified with him so that the body of sin might be done away with, that we should no longer be slaves to sin—because anyone who has died has been freed from sin.
>
> Now if we died with Christ, we believe that we will also live with him. For we know that since Christ was raised from the dead, he cannot die again; death no longer has mastery over him. The death he died, he died to sin once for all; but the life he lives, he lives to God.
>
> In the same way, count yourselves dead to sin but alive to God in Christ Jesus. Therefore do not let sin reign in your mortal body so that you obey its evil desires. Do not offer the parts of your body to sin, as instruments of wickedness, but rather offer yourselves to God, as those who have been brought from death to life; and offer the parts of your body to him as instruments of righteousness. For sin shall not be your master, because you are not under law, but under grace. (6:5-14)

Resurrection, eternal life, the other world.

No more sin? It is easier said than done. Since the evil desires of the mortal body will have to continue to sin, there is no real exit. By the way, human beings do not really own their bodies; it is as if they are leased from God to be returned to him as instruments, vessels of righteousness. This is an ultimate form of control of bodies.

Christian grace is greater than Jewish law.

Is religion specially and particularly for the curtailment of sexual desires?

> What then? Shall we sin because we are not under law but under grace? By no means! Don't you know that when you offer yourselves to someone to obey him as slaves, you are slaves to the one whom you obey—whether you are slaves to sin, which leads to death, or to obedience, which leads to righteousness? But thanks be to God that, though you used to be slaves to sin, you wholeheartedly obeyed the form of teaching to which you were entrusted. You have been set free from sin and have become slaves to righteousness. (6:15-18)

Slavery to sin leads to death, slavery to righteousness leads to eternal life. Or, slavery to obedience leads to righteousness. Therefore; OBEY OR PERISH! Or: FEAR → BELIEVE →

OBEY OR PERISH! This is the "Three Commandments" of Christianity, like the "Five Commandments" of Judaism.[1] Holiness can be added; prosperity is to be subtracted.

> I put this in human terms because you are weak in your natural selves. Just as you used to offer the parts of your body in slavery to impurity and to ever-increasing wickedness, so now offer them in slavery to righteousness leading to holiness. When you were slaves to sin, you were free from the control of righteousness. What benefit did you reap at that time from the things you are now ashamed of? Those things result in death! But now that you have been set free from sin and have become slaves to God, the benefit you reap leads to holiness, and the result is eternal life. For the wages of sin is death, but the gift of God is eternal life in Christ Jesus our Lord. (6:19-23)

7. Law and Sin

"The law has authority over a man only as long as he lives" (7:1). But Christianity, and Islam too, in fact extend the law to the other world as well.

> So, my brothers, you also died to the law through the body of Christ, that you might belong to another, to him who was raised from the dead, in order that we might bear fruit to God. For when we were controlled by the sinful nature, the sinful passions aroused by the law were at work in our bodies, so that we bore fruit for death. But now, by dying to what once bound us, we have been released from the law so that we serve in the new way of the Spirit, and not in the old way of the written code. (7:4-6)

Christianity supercedes Judaism, Jesus overcomes Jewish Law, the Spirit replaces the "written code," which "*aroused* sinful passions" (!). (Also note "sinful nature" or "the flesh," 7:5.)

> What shall we say, then? Is the law sin? Certainly not! Indeed I would not have known what sin was except through the law. For I would not have known what coveting really was if the law had not said, "Do not covet." But sin, seizing the opportunity afforded by the commandment, produced in me every kind of covetous desire. For apart from law, sin is dead. Once I was alive apart from law; but when the commandment came, sin sprang to life and I died. I found that the very commandment that was intended to bring life actually brought death. For sin, seizing the opportunity afforded by the commandment, deceived me, and through the commandment put me to death. So then, the law is holy, and the commandment is holy, righteous and good. (7:7-12)

"Sin, seizing the opportunity afforded by the commandment"! Still: "the law is holy," etc.! Is this a sort of Pauline dialectic? Or does the following make it any better?

> We know that the law is spiritual; but I am unspiritual, sold as a slave to sin. I do not understand what I do. For what I want to do I do not do, but what I hate I do. And if I do what I do not want to do, I agree that the law is good. As it is, it is no longer I

myself who do it, but it is sin living in me. I know that nothing good lives in me, that is, in my sinful nature. For I have the desire to do what is good, but I cannot carry it out. For what I do is not the good I want to do; no, the evil I do not want to do—this I keep on doing. Now if I do what I do not want to do, it is no longer I who do it, but it is sin living in me that does it.

So I find this law at work: When I want to do good, evil is right there with me. For in my inner being I delight in God's law; but I see another law at work in the members of my body, waging war against the law of my mind and making me a prisoner of the law of sin at work within my members. What a wretched man I am! Who will rescue me from this body of death? Thanks be to God—through Jesus Christ our Lord!

So then, I myself in my mind am a slave to God's law, but in the sinful nature a slave to the law of sin. (7:14-23)

Paul once again divides men and women against and within themselves. Flesh/sex is sinful/unholy. There *was* no escape from it. Now, there is, it seems. Really? Mind vs. body, heart vs. flesh.

"What a wretched man," delighting in God's (Christian) law in his inner being but subject to another law (human nature and Jewish law) which is at work in the members of his body. "Crooked timber of humanity?"

8. Life Through the Spirit and Future Glory

You, however, are controlled not by the sinful nature but by the Spirit, if the Spirit of God lives in you. And if anyone does not have the Spirit of Christ, he does not belong to Christ. But if Christ is in you, your body is dead because of sin, yet your spirit is alive because of righteousness. And if the Spirit of him who raised Jesus from the dead is living in you, he who raised Christ from the dead will also give life to your mortal bodies through his Spirit, who lives in you. (8:9-11)

Life and death. Believe or perish. And many tautologies, as well as Manichean binary oppositions.

In contradistinction to the *Torah*'s cyclical pessimism, the promise of the *New Testament* is eternal goodness.

Therefore, brothers, we have an obligation—but it is not to the sinful nature, to live according to it. For if you live according to the sinful nature, you will die; but if by the Spirit you put to death the misdeeds of the body, you will live, because those who are led by the Spirit of God are sons of God. For you did not receive a spirit that makes you a slave again to fear, but you received the Spirit of sonship. And by him we cry, "Abba, Father." The Spirit himself testifies with our spirit that we are God's children. Now if we are children, then we are heirs—heirs of God and co-heirs with

Christ, if indeed we share in his sufferings in order that we may also share in his glory. (8:12-17)

Desexualization and infantilization of human beings through the promise of immortalization and eternal bliss. Plus: all (believing) men are God's sons(?). (Some favorite, some step-sons.) "Sonship" replaces fear(!) And there is no mention at all of "daughtership."

> For the creation was subjected to frustration, not by its own choice, but by the will of the one who subjected it, in hope that the creation itself will be liberated from its bondage to decay and brought into the glorious freedom of the children of God.
>
> We know that the whole creation has been groaning as in the pains of childbirth right up to the present time. Not only so, but we ourselves, who have the firstfruits of the Spirit, groan inwardly as we wait eagerly for our adoption as sons, the redemption of our bodies. (8:20-23)

Now, Paul is contesting Genesis (or is he vindicating it through his form of dialectic?), its claim that God saw that all he made was good. But he is also stating that God himself made it not so good. What is he driving at? That not Adam but Jesus is his first son? (Christianity is greater than Judaism?)

> And we know that in all things God works for the good of those who love him, who have been called according to his purpose. For those God foreknew he also predestined to be conformed to the likeness of his Son, that he might be the firstborn among many brothers. And those he predestined, he also called; those he called, he also justified; those he justified, he also glorified. (8:28-30)

Here we have, in a nutshell, both predestination and theodicy. Not free will or freedom of choice and action to become righteous, but preselection by God to become a chosen and called one. Goodness to those who love and believe in him, evil to those who do not.

Conditionality and reciprocity, covenant and contract are also there. Causality (or circulatirty?) is also there: Predestined → called → justified → gloried.

And a reinforcement of faith in future glory.

> For I am convinced that neither death nor life, neither angels nor demons, neither the present nor the future, nor any powers, neither height nor depth, nor anything else in all creation, will be able to separate us from the love of God that is in Christ Jesus our Lord. (8:38-39)

And:

> Who shall separate us from the love of Christ? Shall trouble or hardship or persecution or famine or nakedness or danger or sword? (8:35)

9. God's Sovereign Choice

I speak the truth in Christ—I am not lying, my conscience confirms it in the Holy Spirit—I have great sorrow and unceasing anguish in my heart. For I could wish that I myself were cursed and cut off from Christ for the sake of my brothers, those of my own race, the people of Israel. Theirs is the adoption as sons; theirs the divine glory, the covenants, the receiving of the law, the temple worship and the promises. Theirs are the patriarchs, and from them is traced the human ancestry of Christ, who is God over all, forever praised! Amen.

It is not as though God's word had failed. For not all who are descended from Israel are Israel. Nor because they are his descendants are they all Abraham's children. On the contrary, "It is through Isaac that your offspring will be reckoned." In other words, it is not the natural children who are God's children, but it is the children of the promise who are regarded as Abraham's offspring. For this was how the promise was stated: "At the appointed time I will return, and Sarah will have a son."

Not only that, but Rebekah's children had one and the same father, our father Isaac. Yet, before the twins were born or had done anything good or bad—in order that God's purpose in election might stand: not by works but by him who calls—she was told, "The older will serve the younger." Just as it is written: "Jacob I loved, but Esau I hated."

What then shall we say? Is God unjust? Not at all! For he says to Moses, "I will have mercy on whom I have mercy, and I will have compassion on whom I have compassion." (9:1-14; Gen. 25:23, Mal. 1:2-3; Exod. 33:19)

The patriarchs, human ancestors of Christ, who is God over all, are praised. That Paul is not lying but speaking the truth is confirmed by Paul's own conscience (in the Holy Spirit). That is, Paul is his own witness—however much he bases himself on the authority of the Holy Spirit—again according to his own declaration.

Christian Paul firmly places himself in the Judaic tradition (first paragraph, 9:1-5) and finds fault not with the tradition itself but with those Israelites who, according to him, did not observe that tradition (9:6-9). (The *Koran* shall reiterate this argument.)

Also, not "the natural children" but "the children of the promise" are the children of God (9:8). Both "race" and "not race." Not all human beings, at any rate, but the fearing-believing human beings.

It is not "works" or deeds but God's prior choice and "calling" that sets apart the blessed ones. Paul totally, and unquestioningly, adopts Isaac's (and God's) discrimination between the brothers Jacob and Esau and his unjust favoring of the duplicitous Isaac over the deceived and wronged Esau, first by Rebekah, then by Jacob, and finally and decisively by Isaac. The unjust favoritism of the *Torah*, Paul does not even try to rationalize, let alone repudiate it here. The arbitrary and unfair pre-choice is automatically vindicated again:

Yet, before the twins were born or had done anything good or bad—in order that
God's purpose in election might stand: not by works but by him who calls—she was
told, "the older will serve the younger." Just as it is written: "Jacob I loved, but Esau
I hated."

Malacchi (1:2-3) is more Isaacian than Isaac here, but both fail to give grounds for their love
and hate. It is just like that. Why, what for? The answer is simply: "in order that God's purpose in election might stand." (No, it does not stand; it is merely stated.) What is that purpose? To elect and save as many human beings as possible? Or to elect one/few to condemn
many/majority of human beings?

Paul cannot find God (Isaac, Malacchi, the Book) unjust simply because "he says to
Moses." And what does he say?:

I will have mercy on whom I have mercy, and I will have compassion on whom I
have compassion. (9:14; Exod. 33:19)

Arbitrary choice (and discrimination) expressed in the form of a tautology, like "I am who I
am." Judeo-Christianity (its God, its Prophets, its Books, its apostles) does not deign to give
an explanation for setting men apart from men. A religion (religions) of hate and curse and
murder—without explanation, without accountability. And axiomatic Godly sovereignty
without any moral basis of legitimacy.

It does not, therefore, depend on man's desire or effort, but on God's mercy. For the
Scripture says to Pharaoh: "I raised you up for this very purpose, that I might display
my power in you and that my name might be proclaimed in all the earth." Therefore
God has mercy on whom he wants to have mercy, and he hardens whom he wants to
harden.

One of you will say to me: "Then why does God still blame us? For who resists his
will?" But who are you, O man, to talk back to God? "Shall what is formed say to
him who formed it, 'Why did you make me like this?' " Does not the potter have the
right to make out of the same lump of clay some pottery for noble purposes and
some for common use?

What if God, choosing to show his wrath and make his power known, bore with
great patience the objects of his wrath—prepared for destruction? What if he did
this to make the riches of his glory known to the objects of his mercy, whom he prepared in advance for glory—even us, whom he also called, not only from the Jews
but also from the Gentiles? (9:16-24; Exod. 9:16, Isa. 29:16 and 45:19)

The foregoing makes the revered discipline of theodicy redundant. So it does any comment
of mine. But I shall still offer a few.

It does not depend on "man's desire or effort" but "God's mercy" and pre-choice. Not
only Pharaoh "hardened" but also the unchosen majority of men "hardened"—to be
trapped into further sinning for severer punishment. (Cf. Also *Koran*.)

Who are you, O man, to talk back to God?

(Most) men, "the objects of his wrath—prepared for destruction," versus (few) men, "the objects of his mercy, whom he prepared in advance for glory." Freud is right: religions are by nature and by definition exclusionary and segregationist—without and within.

And men are "objects" in any case. They have no free will, no free choice, no freedom of action—even when they wish to please God—in short, they are not human agents. They are formed, handpicked, moved by God. They are not Kant's "ends in themselves"; they are Hegel's peons of history, or the puppets of the artist manipulated by the latter's hand, or, shall we say, the figurines pushed back and forth by the "stretched arm" of God. The *New Testament* does not think any higher of man than the *Old Testament* does. From "evil dust" we have come to the not much more complimentary "clay"—to be put to noble/holy or to common/ignoble uses.

A God who creates to destroy (and glorify), a potter who makes some men objects for common use (and some men for noble purposes), a God who himself elects and leaves no room for human effort and will, a God who displays his power and proclaims his name, etc. Paul gives full approval to the *Old Testament's* view of men, its "doctrine of God and man": "Who are you?," "Who are you, O man, to talk back to God?" (Or to Moses, or to worldly authorities.) Despite a softer God and softer prophets, Christianity is still as Jewish as Judaism. And Isaiah is the bridge between Judaism and Christianity. They both degrade and humiliate human beings even when they call/choose/glorify them. Man, and woman, denuded of self-respect by a bombardment of sayings and writings for 2500 years, can hardly have respect for others. The capricious God of Judaism is adopted by Christianity:

> I will call them 'my people' who are not my people; and I will call her 'my loved one' who is not my loved one, and, it will happen that in the very place where it was said to them, 'You are not my people,' they will be called 'sons of the living God.' (9:25-26; Hosea 2:23,1:10)

Paul further quotes from Isaiah, one of the favorites of Christians:

> Isaiah cries out concerning Israel: Though the number of the Israelites be like the sand by the sea, only the remnant will be saved. For the Lord will carry out his sentence on earth with speed and finality.
>
> It is just as Isaiah said previously: Unless the Lord Almighty had left us descendants, we would have become like Sodom, we would have been like Gomorrah. (9:27-29; Isaiah 10:22-23,1:9)

This God will save "only the remnant" of men, and he is "speedy." (See, the *Koran*, infra, for the fastness of God, the "best trapper.") This God lays "stumbling stones" in the way of human beings, although Paul had just said that that was not the way of the Christian God and his apostles:

See, I lay in Zion a stone that causes men to stumble and a rock that makes them fall,
and the one who trusts in him will never be put to shame. (9:33; Isaiah 8:14,28:16)

Muhammad will perfect this theme and technique in the *Koran*.

"Descendants," the unkilled ones, are always a numerical minority and are flatteringly
called "remnants." (For a ratio of 1/73 saved ones, see *Koran* below.)

10. Israel's Unbelief

Most of the Israelites' fault lies in their putting the letter of the law and the externalities and
works thereof over real faith in and knowledge of God—before Christ and, inexcusably,
even after Jesus, who is "the end of the law" "so that these may be righteousness for everyone
who believes" (10:4)—not only in One God, but our One God. (*Koran* shall appropriate
the "end of the law" argument in its claim that Islam is the last and most developed religion.

Paul goes on to vindicate Jesus by Moses's sayings and concludes with a quote from Isaiah on the disobedience and obstinacy of Israel. Discontinuity and claims of superiority in
times of confident intra-Abrahamic sibling rivalry; continuity, "as it is written," "as it is
said" in times of need for the authority of tradition.

11. The Remnant of Israel

Paul continues to blame the people and uphold the prophets:

I ask then: Did God reject his people? By no means! I am an Israelite myself, a descendant of Abraham, from the tribe of Benjamin. God did not reject his people,
whom he foreknew. Don't you know what the Scripture says in the passage about
Elijah—how he appealed to God against Israel: "Lord, they have killed your prophets and torn down your altars; I am the only one left, and they are trying to kill me?"
And what was God's answer to him? "I have reserved for myself seven thousand who
have not bowed the knee to Baal." So too, at the present time there is a remnant chosen by grace. And if by grace, then it is no longer by works; if it were, grace would no
longer be grace.

What then? What Israel sought so earnestly it did not obtain, but the elect did.
The others were hardened, as it is written.... (11:1-7)

This God, who did not "reject his people," says: I have reserved for myself seven thousand... (1 Kings 19:18). And Paul says: So, too, at the present time, there is a remnant chosen by grace.

Elected remnant lives, non-elected majority perishes. (7000, say, out of 600.000.) Politics, and religio-politics of fear and death. (Cf. Numbers, Ch. 16.) (People) did not obtain,
but the elect did. The others were hardened...

And Paul, on the shoulders of the giants Moses, Isaiah, and David: God gave them a
spirit of stupor, eyes so that they could not see and ears so that they could not hear, to this
very day.

And David says:

> May their table become a snare and a trap, a stumbling block and a retribution for them. May their eyes be darkened so they cannot see, and their backs be bent forever. (11:8-10; Deut. 29:4, Isaiah 29:10, Psalm 69:22-23)

Pauline dialectics again:

> Again I ask: Did they stumble so as to fall beyond recovery? Not at all! Rather, because of their transgression, salvation has come to the Gentiles to make Israel envious. But if their transgression means riches for the world, and their loss means riches for the Gentiles, how much greater riches will their fullness bring! (11:11-12)

And:

> But they were broken off because of unbelief, and you stand by faith. Do not be arrogant, but be afraid. For if God did not spare the natural branches, he will not spare you either.
>
> Consider therefore the kindness and sternness of God: sternness to those who fell, but kindness to you, provided that you continue in his kindness. Otherwise, you also will be cut off. (11:20-22)

BE AFRAID! Fear → believe → obey or perish. Three Commandments. Christianity no less punitive than Judaism. Conditional kindness. Cutting off. Death not only to "natural children" but also to the "children of promise" who fall.

Repent or perish:

> As far as the gospel is concerned, they are enemies on your account; but as far as election is concerned, they are loved on account of the patriarchs, for God's gifts and his call are irrevocable. Just as you who were at one time disobedient to God have now received mercy as a result of their disobedience, so they too have now become disobedient in order that they too may now receive mercy as a result of God's mercy to you. For God has bound all men over to disobedience so that he may have mercy on them all. (11:28-32)

Truth? Logic? Consistency? (Cf. esp. the last sentence—mercy on all!) No, that's not his real purpose. Neither are election and gifts "irrevocable." What happened to 600,000 minus 7,000?

Still, "doxology":

> Oh, the depth of the riches of the wisdom and knowledge of God! How unsearchable his judgments, and his paths beyond tracing out! Who has known the mind of the Lord? Or who has been his counselor? Who has ever given to God, that God should repay him?
>
> For from him and through him and to him are all things. To him be the glory forever! Amen. (11:33-36)

Omniscient, omnipotent, omnipresent. "From him, through him, to him." In the beginning (creation), in the middle (this world, history), at the end (the other world, the future). Praise be to him. He knows, man doesn't know.

12. Living Sacrifices and Love

From burnt offerings with "aroma pleasing to God" to sacrifice of living bodies:

> Therefore, I urge you, brothers, in view of God's mercy, to offer your bodies as living sacrifices, holy and pleasing to God—this is your spiritual act of worship. Do not conform any longer to the pattern of this world, but be transformed by the renewing of your mind. Then you will be able to test and approve what God's will is—his good, pleasing and perfect will. (12:1-2)

From bodies individually sacrificed to Corpus Christi and Corpus Dei, it is a short step to the following:

> For by the grace given me I say to every one of you: Do not think of yourself more highly than you ought but rather think of yourself with sober judgment, in accordance with the measure of faith God has given you. Just as each of us has one body with many members, and these members do not all have the same function, so in Christ we who are many form one body, and each member belongs to all the others. We have different gifts, according to the grace given us. If a man's gift is prophesying, let him use it in proportion to his faith. If it is serving, let him serve; if it is teaching, let him teach; if it is encouraging, let him encourage; if it is contributing to the needs of others, let him give generously; if it is leadership, let him govern diligently; if it is showing mercy, let him do it cheerfully. (12:3-8)

This is not horizontal differentiation; it is vertical ranking. Organicistic unity and functional specialization in human body and in the body social-politic-religious. An anatomical reduction. From human body to social division of labor. "According to the grace given us." From pagan Plato to monotheistic Paul. (To solidaristic Durkheim, we may add.) Each is to specialize in what he is best: serving, teaching, contributing to the needs of others (some, not all, will do this), and leading, among others. Most notably, leading, leadership and governing will be the turf of some, not all. Here is the crux of Christian political theory: governing of men is the domain of some who are given that kind of grace or gift, or gift of grace. No democratic self-government of and by all men, but by few charismatic leaders in the "city of God." This is the underpinning of Christian, and all monotheistic, political theory. (More below.)

No political equality but some moral advice for living in the brotherly city of the "living God."

> Love must be sincere. Hate what is evil; cling to what is good. Be devoted to one another in brotherly love. Honor one another above yourselves. Never be lacking in

zeal, but keep your spiritual fervor, serving the Lord. Be joyful in hope, patient in affliction, faithful in prayer. Share with God's people who are in need. Practice hospitality. Practice hospitality.

Bless those who persecute you; bless and do not curse. Rejoice with those who rejoice; mourn with those who mourn. Live in harmony with one another. Do not be proud, but be willing to associate with people of low position. Do not be conceited.

Do not repay anyone evil for evil. Be careful to do what is right in the eyes of everybody. If it is possible, as far as it depends on you, live at peace with everyone. Do not take revenge, my friends, but leave room for God's wrath, for it is written: "It is mine to avenge; I will repay," says the Lord. On the contrary:

If your enemy is hungry, feed him; if he is thirsty, give him something to drink. In doing this, you will heap burning coals on his head. Do not be overcome by evil, but overcome evil with good. (12:9-21)

Share with the needy (how much?), live in harmony (organically) and at peace with everyone (despite inequalities and injustices?), associate with "people of low position" (a category not abolished but reified, albeit with charitable condescension), do not retaliate (as in the *Old Testament*), do not take revenge (that's God's monopoly).

13. Submission to the Authorities

Everyone must submit himself to the governing authorities, for there is no authority except that which God has established. The authorities that exist have been established by God. Consequently, he who rebels against the authority is rebelling against what God has instituted, and those who do so will bring judgment on themselves. For rulers hold no terror for those who do right, but for those who do wrong. Do you want to be free from fear of the one in authority? Then do what is right and he will commend you. For he is God's servant to do you good. But if you do wrong, be afraid, for he does not bear the sword for nothing. He is God's servant, an agent of wrath to bring punishment on the wrongdoer. Therefore, it is necessary to submit to the authorities, not only because of possible punishment but also because of conscience.

This is also why you pay taxes, for the authorities are God's servants, who give their full time to governing. Give everyone what you owe him: If you owe taxes, pay taxes; if revenue, then revenue; if respect, then respect; if honor, then honor. (13:1-7)

I quote this chapter of the Romans at length because it is the locus classicus of Christian political theory: SUBMIT TO AUTHORITIES! Not only to the authority of God, his Prophet, his Book, but also to the worldly "governing authorities," for: "... there is no authority except that which God has established. The authorities that exist have been established by God" (13:1).

Powers that be, those actually in power, are conferred automatic authority, that is, legitimate power, in Weber's terminology. As different from the faintly ambivalent attitude of the Gospels towards powers that be, Paul concocts a neat theory of might is right. All rulers are, by definition, servants of God and do nothing but good.

Consequently, he who rebels against the authority is rebelling against what God has instituted... (13:2)

This is both very much in the spirit of *Torah*, Numbers, Chapter 16 (Cf. supra) and also much more categorical and oppressive than Chapter 16. There, Moses and Aaron were at least God's specific, chosen deputes; here it is *any* worldly governing authority, or rather power that be, that is being unconditionally legitimated. Politics of fear and death is again employed; might-be rebels are frightened and threatened:

For rulers hold no terror for those who do right, but for those who do wrong. Do you want to be free from fear of the one in authority? (13:3)

Remember Rousseau on Grotius's proceeding from facts, that this may not be the most rational method but that it is one most favorable to tyrants.

... if you do wrong, be afraid, for he does not bear the sword for nothing. He is God's servant, an agent of wrath to bring punishment on the wrongdoer. (13:4)

Submission of the meek to be rewarded or rebellion of the oppressed to be punished? Which is the real message of Christianity? Love of all, by all, for all or persecution of some by some, that is of many by the few.

Therefore, it is necessary to submit to the authorities, not only because of possible punishment but also because of conscience. (13:5)

Coercion mitigated by persuasion; power-politics propped up by legitimating ideology.

That the authorities in question are not only, or at all, spiritual authorities but that they are worldly authorities is very clear.

This is also why you pay taxes, for the authorities are God's servants, who give their full time to governing. (13:6)

Governors are full-time experts. Politics is the business of specialists. Herein lies the basic tenet of Western liberal political theory of elitist democracy, from Mill to Dahl.

Give everyone what you owe him: If you owe taxes, pay taxes; if revenue, then revenue; if respect, then respect; if honor, then honor. (13:7)

GIVE TO CAESAR! All Caesars are vindicated. Respect, honor, reward, all conditional for ordinary man, even if he be a believer; all unconditional, and protected by deadly sanctions, for the rulers of men. Is this a religion of salvation and justice, or is it one immensely convenient for local or imperial powers? No wonder Christianity became the official state religion of imperialistic Rome.

From terror, fear and submission, Paul jumps to brotherly, neighborly (communal) love.

> Let no debt remain outstanding, except the continuing debt to love one another, for he who loves his fellowman has fulfilled the law. The commandments, "Do not commit adultery," "Do not murder," "Do not steal," "Do not covet," and whatever other commandment there may be, are summed up in this one rule: "Love your neighbor as yourself." Love does no harm to its neighbor. Therefore love is the fulfillment of the law.
>
> And do this, understanding the present time. The hour has come for you to wake up from your slumber, because our salvation is nearer now than when we first believed. The night is nearly over; the day is almost here. So let us put aside the deeds of darkness and put on the armor of light. Let us behave decently, as in the daytime, not in orgies and drunkenness, not in sexual immorality and debauchery, not in dissension and jealousy. Rather, clothe yourselves with the Lord Jesus Christ, and do not think about how to gratify the desires of the sinful nature. (13:8-14)

Day and night, light and darkness, Manichean and tautological rhetoric, "desires of the sinful nature," desexualization of man and woman. (More below.) Ten Commandments repeated and subsumed under "love." Communal unity, social stability.

14, 15. The Weak and the Strong

> Who are you to judge someone else's servant? To his own master he stands or falls. And he will stand, for the Lord is able to make him stand. (14:4)

Don't judge others, including rulers. (Cf. supra.) Paul preempts human beings' evaluating and judging any and all acts of other men, primarily those of rulers; justice is not men's domain, even if injustice prevails on earth. Whereas the question is not "to judge or not to judge," but to judge correctly and justly. Justice and injustice in this world are relegated to the other world:

> For this very reason, Christ died and returned to life so that he might be the Lord of both the dead and the living. You, then, why do you judge your brother? Or why do you look down on your brother? For we will all stand before God's judgment seat. It is written: As surely as I live, says the Lord, every knee will bow before me; every tongue will confess to God. (14:9-11; Isaiah 45:23)
>
> So then, each of us will give an account of himself to God. (14:12)

Man is not accountable to man according to rational and moral criteria of the human mind and heart. Man is not an autonomous agent.

The "kingdom of God is not a matter of eating and drinking, but of righteousness..." (14:17). "Whatever you believe about these things keep between yourself and God" (14:22). A personal, individual God; no intermediary between God and the believer (Cf. Luther)—but the Book itself as the supreme authority.

The strong should bear with the failings of the weak. Categories of strong and weak (rich and poor), of master and servant are preserved; merely a divine formula or myth is manufactured for their peaceful coexistence. Religio-communal unity should prevail:

> May the God who gives endurance and encouragement give you a spirit of unity among yourselves as you follow Christ Jesus, so that with one heart and mouth you may glorify the God and Father of our Lord Jesus Christ. (15:5-6)

Unity of thought and of the body religio-politic are balanced with a rhetorical compliment to the competence of individual believers:

> I myself am convinced, my brothers, that you yourselves are full of goodness, complete in knowledge and competent to instruct one another. I have written you quite boldly on some points, as if to remind you of them again, because of the grace God gave me to be a minister of Christ Jesus to the Gentiles with the priestly duty of proclaiming the gospel of God, so that the Gentiles might become an offering acceptable to God, sanctified by the Holy Spirit. (15:14-16)

What happened to the hierarchy of knowing and knowers? Or is there no hierarchy at least among the brotherhood of the elect who know more than men in general?

Paul reaffirms his own authority. Men are seen as an "offering" to God.

16. Personal Greetings

Sisters, too, should be received "in the Lord in a way worthy of the saints" (16:2), apostles are "in Christ" (16:7), Paul loves men "in the Lord" (16:8), "women who work hard in the Lord" (16:12) are mentioned by name, men are "chosen in the Lord" (16:13).

And unity, again:

> I urge you, brothers, to watch out for those who cause divisions and put obstacles in your way that are contrary to the teaching you have learned. Keep away from them. For such people are not serving our Lord Christ, but their own appetites. By smooth talk and flattery they deceive the minds of naïve people. Everyone has heard about your obedience, so I am full of joy over you; but I want you to be wise about what is good, and innocent about what is evil.
> 　　The God of peace will soon crush Satan under your feet. (16:17-20)

Paul concludes on a note of non-tribal "universalism" which is really nothing but a non-pluralistic religious unitarianism and communalism: all nations believing the same God and Book.

> Now to him who is able to establish you by my gospel and the proclamation of Jesus Christ, according to the revelation of the mystery hidden for long ages past, but now revealed and made known through the prophetic writings by the command of the eternal God, so that all nations might believe and obey him—to the only wise God be glory forever through Jesus Christ! Amen. (16:25-27)

1 CORINTHIANS

1,2,3,4. Divisions in the Church and Apostles of Christ

Paul, "called to be an apostle of Christ Jesus by the will of God" (1:1) speaks to the church of God in Corinth: "Grace and peace to you from God our Father and the Lord Jesus Christ" (1:3). He thanks God, "who has called you into fellowship with his Son Jesus Christ our Lord" (1:9).

> I appeal to you, brothers, in the name of our Lord Jesus Christ, that all of you agree with one another so that there may be no divisions among you and that you may be perfectly united in mind and thought. (1:10)

Call to unity in church and to unity of thought and mind. It is not for no reason that religious unity is frequently invoked during calls for "national unity and solidarity." And monotheistic religion is the obvious logical, most efficient instrument.

(To be compared with Romans 15:5-6 and contrasted with Romans 14:5.)

Paul puts human wisdom and religious wisdom as a contradiction in terms:

> For Christ did not send me to baptize, but to preach the gospel—not with words of human wisdom, lest the cross of Christ be emptied of its power.
>
> For the message of the cross is foolishness to those who are perishing, but to us who are being saved it is the power of God. For it is written: I will destroy the wisdom of the wise; the intelligence of the intelligent I will frustrate. (1:17-19; Isaiah 29:14)

Wrong wisdom and intelligence may well be corrected, refuted; why, as a first reflex action, "destroy?"

> Where is the wise man? Where is the scholar? Where is the philosopher of this age? Has not God made foolish the wisdom of the world? For since in the wisdom of God the world through its wisdom did not know him, God was pleased through the foolishness of what was preached to save those who believe. Jews demand miraculous signs and Greeks look for wisdom, but we preach Christ crucified: a stumbling block to Jews and foolishness to Gentiles, but to those whom God has called, both Jews and Greeks, Christ the power of God and the wisdom of God. For the foolishness of God is wiser than man's wisdom, and the weakness of God is stronger than man's strength. (1:20-25)

The Greeks' search for (human) wisdom is treated on par with the Jews' demand for (divine) miracles.

> Brothers, think of what you were when you were called. Not many of you were wise by human standards; not many were influential; not many were of noble birth. But God chose the foolish things of the world to shame the wise; God chose the weak things of the world to shame the strong. He chose the lowly things of this world and

the despised things—and the things that are not—to nullify the things that are, so that no one may boast before him. It is because of him that you are in Christ Jesus, who has become for us wisdom from God—that is, our righteousness, holiness and redemption. Therefore, as it is written: "Let him who boasts boast in the Lord." (1:26-31; Jer. 9:24)

Policy of recruitment. Appeal to popular masses. Righteousness and holiness.

Paul invokes by association the ineloquence of Moses, nullifies "men's wisdom," specifically deprecates Greek wisdom (human rationality) before superhuman Godly wisdom. Plus: "fear and trembling."

When I came to you, brothers, I did not come with eloquence or superior wisdom as I proclaimed to you the testimony about God. For I resolved to know nothing while I was with you except Jesus Christ and him crucified. I came to you in weakness and fear, and with much trembling. My message and my preaching were not with wise and persuasive words, but with a demonstration of the Spirit's power, so that your faith might not rest on men's wisdom, but on God's power. (2:1-5)

Paul, the Hegelian absolute spiritist, continues:

We do, however, speak a message of wisdom among the mature, but not the wisdom of this age or of the rulers of this age, who are coming to nothing. No, we speak of God's secret wisdom, a wisdom that has been hidden and that God destined for our glory before time began. None of the rulers of this age understood it, for if they had, they would not have crucified the Lord of glory. However, as it is written: "No eye has seen, no ear has heard, no mind has conceived what God has prepared for those who love him" but God has revealed it to us by his Spirit.

The Spirit searches all things, even the deep things of God. For who among men knows the thoughts of a man except the man's spirit within him? In the same way no one knows the thoughts of God except the Spirit of God. We have not received the spirit of the world but the Spirit who is from God, that we may understand what God has freely given us. This is what we speak, not in words taught us by human wisdom but in words taught by the Spirit, expressing spiritual truths in spiritual words. The man without the Spirit does not accept the things that come from the Spirit of God, for they are foolishness to him and he cannot understand them, because they are spiritually discerned. The spiritual man makes judgments about all things, but he himself is not subject to any man's judgment: For who has known the mind of the Lord that he may instruct him? But we have the mind of Christ. (2:6-16; Isa. 64:4, 40:13)

The un-Promethean Paul not only dehumanizes man, he also infantilizes him as the paternalistic shepherd speaking Jesus' mind—authoritatively, that is, with legitimate power.

Brothers, I could not address you as spiritual but as worldly—mere infants in Christ. I gave you milk, not solid food, for you were not yet ready for it. Indeed, you are still not ready. You are still worldly. For since there is jealousy and quarreling among you, are you not worldly? Are you not acting like mere men? (3:1-3)

Paul, among other spiritual leaders, is but a servant of God, performing his assigned task:

What, after all, is Apollos? And what is Paul? Only servants through whom you came to believe—as the Lord has assigned to each his task. I planted the seed, Apollos watered it, but God made it grow. So neither he who plants nor he who waters is anything, but only God, who makes things grow. The man who plants and the man who waters have one purpose, and each will be rewarded according to his own labor. For we are God's fellow workers; you are God's field, God's building. (3:5-9)

"Each will be rewarded according to his own labor." Apostles are "God's fellow workers," other men are "God's field." (The *Koran* shall adapt this and make women "men's field." Cf. infra.)

The simile of "builders" is also employed; the building should be sound rather than richly ornamented; Paul offers an ingenious figure of speech:

Don't you know that you yourselves are God's temple and that God's Spirit lives in you? If anyone destroys God's temple, God will destroy him; for God's temple is sacred, and you are that temple. (3:16-17)

At first sight this looks quite complimentary, with implications of the high value of men in general; but it should be noted that men are "built," are "buildings," are used as a space and field (for harvesting and fishing, or even as objects thereof); men are receptors who house God, prophets, priests, and their words, or the Word. They are the temple and not even the congregation there, let alone all being priests. They are mere "parts" because they are "mere men." And:

So then, no more boasting about men! All things are yours, whether Paul or Apollos or Cephas or the world or life or death or the present or the future—all are yours, and you are of Christ, and Christ is of God. (3:21-23)

In Christianity, man is closer to and more a part of God compared to Judaism and Islam. (Is this an unmixed blessing?)

Apostles, and Paul, are above human judgment (like, or even more so than, worldly authorities), but men in general are equal in their condition of being subordinate to the apostles, who have the gift of grace. Rhetorical self-degradation is followed by paternalism, pulling of rank and threat of power:

We are weak, but you are strong! You are honored, we are dishonored! To this very hour we go hungry and thirsty, we are in rags, we are brutally treated, we are homeless. We work hard with our own hands. When we are cursed, we bless; when we are persecuted, we endure it; when we are slandered, we answer kindly. Up to this moment we have become the scum of the earth, the refuse of the world.

I am not writing this to shame you, but to warn you, as my dear children. Even though you have the thousand guardians in Christ, you do not have many fathers, for in Christ Jesus I became your father through the gospel. Therefore I urge you to imitate me.... (4:10-16)

Some of you have become arrogant, as if I were not coming to you. But I will come to you very soon, if the Lord is willing, and then I will find out not only how these arrogant people are talking, but what power they have. For the kingdom of God is not a matter of talk but of power. What do you prefer? Shall I come to you with a whip, or in love and with a gentle spirit? (4:18-21)

Knowledge is power: Paul becomes a father "through" the gospel. Religion, too, is power: "Kingdom of God is not a matter of talk but of power." (Cf. "spiritual words" supra.)

Hierarchy: God → Jesus → Paul → Timothy ("my son whom I love," like God loves Jesus) → believers.

Warning: Paul is coming soon to find out not only how arrogant people are talking but also "what power they have."

Threat: "What do you prefer?" Whip or love and gentle spirit? Sword or persuasion? Coercion or ideology? In reverse order: Submission to authorities or suppression by naked force and power? Repentance or punishment. In imperative case: SUBMIT OR PERISH! If not politics of faith, then power-politics and politics of fear and death. (Quite different from the "reasoned debate" disposition of the Acts. From discursive religio-politics to high-powered Godly power-politics.) Please remember the "5 Commandments" of the *Old Testament*.

The church fathers are trying to consolidate their power.

5, 6, 7. Rules: Sexual Immorality, Lawsuits, Marriage

Paul denounces a kind of sexual immorality "that does not occur even among pagans: A man has his father's wife." (5:1) He says that his concern is not with those who are outside the church but with immoral brothers, who should be expelled, cut off.

Disputes among brothers should be taken before the saints and not before the ungodly and before the law, especially "in front of unbelievers" (6:6). Furthermore:

The very fact that you have lawsuits among you means you have been completely defeated already. Why not rather be wronged? Why not rather be cheated? Instead, you yourselves cheat and do wrong, and you do this to your brothers.

Do you not know that the wicked will not inherit the kingdom of God? Do not be deceived: Neither the sexually immoral nor idolaters nor adulterers nor male prostitutes nor homosexual offenders nor thieves nor the greedy nor drunkards nor slanderers nor swindlers will inherit the kingdom of God. And that is what some of you were. But you were washed, you were sanctified, you were justified in the name of the Lord Jesus Christ and by the Spirit of our God. (6:7-11)

Be wronged or cheated rather than wronging and cheating others! This is a far cry from the *Old Testament*'s Jacobish norm of outsmarting and outcheating others.

A long list of wicked acts ensues, preoccupation with sex being in the forefront. And:

The body is not meant for sexual immorality, but for the Lord, and the Lord for the body. By his power God raised the Lord from the dead, and he will raise us also. Do you not know that your bodies are members of Christ himself? Shall I then take the members of Christ and unite them with a prostitute? Never! Do you not know that he who unites himself with a prostitute is one with her in body? For it is said, "The two will become one flesh." But he who unites himself with the Lord is one with him in spirit.

Flee from sexual immorality. All other sins a man commits are outside his body, but he who sins sexually sins against his own body. Do you not know that your body is a temple of the Holy Spirit, who is in you, whom you have received from God? You are not your own; you were bought at a price. Therefore honor God with your body. (6:13-20)

Human (male) bodies are "for" the Lord; they are "members of" Christ himself; they should not be united with (female) prostitutes; sexual immorality, committed by the body, is the greatest sin.

Human bodies are not only controlled; they are mortgaged. A man does not own his body; it is a temple of the Holy Spirit, "who is in you"; and therefore "honor God with your body."

Now, whose God is closer to man? The Jews' God or the Christians' God? The former dwells in the community but man cannot approach him. He is both proximate and distant at once. Whereas the Christians' Lord is all over the inside of men. Unequivocally proximate. Both omnipotent and omnipresent, including the body and inner being of men. Supposedly, at least here, he is not as burning and terrifying as Yahweh. (Is this one of the reasons why there are more Christians than Jews?)

In short, men are parts, members of Christ and God. Corpus Christi, Corpus Dei. (For more, see below.)

Concerning marriage:

Now for the matters you wrote about: It is good for a man not to marry.[2] But since there is so much immorality, each man should have his own wife, and each woman her own husband. The husband should fulfill his marital duty to his wife, and likewise the wife to her husband. The wife's body does not belong to her alone but also to her husband. In the same way, the husband's body does not belong to him alone but also to his wife. Do not deprive each other except by mutual consent and for a time, so that you may devote yourselves to prayer. Then come together again so that Satan will not tempt you because of your lack of self-control. I say this as a concession, not as a command. I wish that all men were as I am. But each man has his own gift from God; one has this gift, another has that. (7:1-7)

Better not to marry! Christianity is celibate compared to the sexually out-going Judaism and Islam. Monogamy as the lesser evil compared to promiscuity. Prayer and intercourse to be well-balanced. A concession, not a command. Paul's first choice is full celibacy.

Now to the unmarried and the widows I say: It is good for them to stay unmarried, as I am. But if they cannot control themselves, they should marry, for it is better to marry than to burn with passion.

To the married I give this command (not I, but the Lord): A wife must not separate from her husband. But if she does, she must remain unmarried or else be reconciled to her husband. And a husband must not divorce his wife.

To the rest I say this (I, not the Lord): If any brother has a wife who is not a believer and she is willing to live with him, he must not divorce her. And if a woman has a husband who is not a believer and he is willing to live with her, she must not divorce him. For the unbelieving husband has been sanctified through his wife, and the unbelieving wife has been sanctified through her believing husband. Otherwise your children would be unclean, but as it is, they are holy. (7:8-14)

And:

Circumcision is nothing and uncircumcision is nothing. Keeping God's commands is what counts. Each one should remain in the situation which he was in when God called him. (7:19-20)

Muhammad will not listen to Paul. And:

Now about virgins: I have no command from the Lord, but I give a judgment as one who by the Lord's mercy is trustworthy. Because of the present crisis, I think that it is good for you to remain as you are. Are you married? Do not seek a divorce. Are you unmarried? Do not look for a wife. But if you do marry, you have not sinned; and if a virgin marries, she has not sinned. But those who marry will face many troubles in this life, and I want to spare you this.

What I mean, brothers, is that the time is short. From now on those who have wives should live as if they had none; those who mourn, as if they did not; those who are happy, as if they were not; those who buy something, as if it were not theirs to keep; those who use the things of the world, as if not engrossed in them. For this world in its present form is passing away.

I would like you to be free from concern. An unmarried man is concerned about the Lord's affairs—how he can please the Lord. But a married man is concerned about the affairs of this world—how he can please his wife—and his interests are divided. An unmarried woman or virgin is concerned about the Lord's affairs: Her aim is to be devoted to the Lord in both body and spirit. But a married woman is concerned about the affairs of this world—how she can please her husband. I am saying this for your own good, not to restrict you, but that you may live in a right way in undivided devotion to the Lord. (7:25-35)

Paul is in principle against marriage; but once that is the case, he is against divorce; but at the same time he advises the spouses to act almost as if the other did not exist, for there is a conflict of interest between God and the spouse, a zero-sum game between the two concerns. What a dilemma, what anxiety, what a schizophrenic situation! And who is "dividing" whom? Paul is dividing men and women against themselves.

Better to stay virgin or celibate; Paul wants to "spare" believers from the troubles of marriage. Finally:

A woman is bound to her husband as long as he lives. But if her husband dies, she is free to marry anyone she wishes, but he must belong to the Lord. In my judgment, she is happier if she stays as she is—and I think that I too have the Spirit of God. (7:39-40)

In his advices, Paul is either "trustworthy" (7:25) and has "the Spirit of God" (7:40), or fully authorized ("not I, but the Lord").

8. Food Sacrificed to Idols

Now about food sacrificed to idols: We know that we all possess knowledge. Knowledge puffs up, but love builds up. The man who thinks he knows something does not yet know as he ought to know. But the man who loves God is known by God. (8:1-3)

Another instance of deprecating human knowledge.

9. The Rights of an Apostle

Believers are the "result of apostles' work in the Lord." (9:1)

If we have sown spiritual seed among you, is it too much if we reap a material harvest from you? If others have this right of support from you, shouldn't we have it all the more?

But we did not use this right. On the contrary, we put up with anything rather than hinder the gospel of Christ. Don't you know that those who work in the temple get their food from the temple, and those who serve at the altar share in what is offered on the altar? In the same way, the Lord has commanded that those who preach the gospel should receive their living from the gospel. (9:11-14)

Quite reminiscent of the rules for and rights of Jewish priests.

Faith, too, is competitive business, and there are differential rewards.

> Do you not know that in a race all the runners run, but only one gets the prize? Run
> in such a way as to get the prize. Everyone who competes in the games goes into
> strict training. They do it to get a crown that will not last; but we do it to get a crown
> that will last forever. (9:24-25)

10. Warnings from Israel's History

"God was not pleased with most of them (forefathers); their bodies were scattered over the
desert" (10:5). (Please mark the "most.") Paul continues to affirm the *Torah*:

> Now these things occurred as examples to keep us from setting our hearts on evil
> things as they did. Do not be idolaters, as some of them were; as it is written: "The
> people sat down to eat and drink and got up to indulge in pagan revelry." We should
> not commit sexual immorality, as some of them did—and in one day twenty-three
> thousand of them died. We should not test the Lord, as some of them did—and
> were killed by snakes. And do not grumble, as some of them did—and were killed
> by the destroying angel.
>
> These things happened to them as examples and were written down as warnings
> for us, on whom the fulfillment of the ages has come. (10:6-11)

Therefore, no idolatry, no arousing of the "Lord's jealousy" (10:22). And who says Christianity is less genocidal then Judaism, if it vindicates, among many other things, so comfortably the annihilation of 23,000 people?

Then, a little relief:

> Everything is permissible—but not everything is beneficial. "Everything is permissi-
> ble"—but not everything is constructive. Nobody should seek his own good, but
> the good of other.
>
> Eat anything sold in the meat market without raising questions of conscience,
> for, "The earth is the Lord's, and everything in it." (10:23-26)

Some altruism and relaxing of ritual prohibitions.

11, 12. Propriety in Worship, Spiritual Gifts, One Body Many Parts

> Now I want you to realize that the head of every man is Christ, and the head of the
> woman is man, and the head of Christ is God. Every man who prays or prophesies
> with his head covered dishonors his head. And every woman who prays or prophe-
> sies with her head uncovered dishonors her head—it is just as though her head were
> shaved. If a woman does not cover her head, she should have her hair cut off; and if it
> is a disgrace for a woman to have her hair cut or shaved off, she should cover her
> head. A man ought not to cover his head, since he is the image and glory of God; but

the woman is the glory of man. For man did not come from woman, but woman from man; neither was man created for woman, but woman for man. For this reason, and because of the angels, the woman ought to have a sign of authority on her head. (11:3-10)

Hierarchy: God → Christ → man → woman. The head of each being the entity which is one higher up. Man is the "image and glory of God; woman is the "glory of man." As in the creational sequence, man comes before woman. A basic, essential inequality between men and woman, the former being superior. ("One degree superior," in *Koran*'s language. Cf. Infra.) And, of course: Woman is created for man. (Shall we add: Men are created for prophets and rulers; religion and God are also created for prophets and rulers?)

Covering of women's hair does not start with Islam but with Christianity.

There should be no divisions in the church; when brothers come together to eat, they should wait for each other; and when Paul comes he "will give further directions" (11:34).

There are different kinds of gifts, but the same Spirit. There are different kinds of service, but the same Lord. There are different kinds of working, but the same God works all of them in all men.

Now to each one the manifestation of the Spirit is given for the common good. To one there is given through the Spirit the message of wisdom, to another the message of knowledge by means of the same Spirit, to another faith by the same Spirit, to another gifts of healing by that one Spirit, to another miraculous powers, to another prophecy, to another distinguishing between spirits, to another speaking different kinds of tongues, and to still another the interpretation of tongues. All these are the work of one and the same Spirit, and he gives them to each one, just as he determines. (12:4-11)

Different gifts, different functions in the social (-religious) division of labor, each organ serves the common good of the organism, each organ is functionally interdependent and mutually complementary. (It remains for Durkheim, the charitable Christian sociologist, just to somewhat secularize this theological unitarian organicism.) Higher gifts to few, ordinary faith to many—just as God (pre)determines and holds all the parts together, each in its Platonic place, as the Grand Legitimator.

The body is a unit, though it is made up of many parts; and though all its parts are many, they form one body. So it is with Christ. For we were all baptized by one Spirit into one body—whether Jews or Greeks, slave or free—and we were all given the one Spirit to drink. (12:12-13)

And Paul constructs his ladder of religio-social stratification, his organic hierarchy.

Now you are the body of Christ, and each one of you is a part of it. And in the church God has appointed first of all apostles, second prophets, third teachers, then workers of miracles, also those having gifts of healing, those able to help others, those with gifts of administration, and those speaking in different kinds of tongues. Are all apostles? Are all prophets? Are all teachers? Do all work miracles? Do all have gifts of healing? Do all speak in tongues? Do all interpret? But eagerly desire the greater gifts. (12:27-31)

13. Love

Paul eloquently describes "love":

Love is patient, love is kind. It does not envy, it does not boast, it is not proud. It is not rude, it is not self-seeking, it is not easily angered, it keeps no record of wrongs. Love does not delight in evil but rejoices with the truth. It always protects, always trusts, always hopes, always perseveres.

Love never fails. But where there are prophecies, they will cease; where there are tongues, they will be stilled; where there is knowledge, it will pass away. For we know in part and we prophesy in part, but when perfection comes, the imperfect disappears. When I was a child, I talked like a child, I thought like a child, I reasoned like a child. When I became a man, I put childish ways behind me. Now we see but a poor reflection as in a mirror; then we shall see face to face. Now I know in part; then I shall know fully, even as I am fully known. And now these three remain: faith, hope and love. But the greatest of these is love. (13:4-13)

Not knowledge (nor reason) but faith, hope and, above all, love. Not love based on or balanced with reason; not even Rousseau's heart guiding the mind; but "love" that has nothing to do with reason. Like faith, religious love does not allow any space for human reason.

14. Gifts of Prophesy and Tongues; Orderly Worship

Paul says that he who prophesies is greater than one who speaks in tongues (other languages) and continues:

I thank God that I speak in tongues more than all of you. But in the church I would rather speak five intelligible words to instruct others than ten thousand words in a tongue.

Brothers, stop thinking like children. In regard to evil be infants, but in your thinking be adults. In the Law it is written: "Through men of strange tongues and through the lips of foreigners I will speak to this people, but even then they will not listen to me," says the Lord.

Tongues, then, are a sign, not for believers but for unbelievers; prophecy, however, is for believers, not for unbelievers. (14:18-22; Isaiah 28:11,12)

Prophesying, speaking in tongues, everything, "should be done in a fitting and orderly way" (14:40). "For God is not a God of disorder but of peace" (14:33). Accordingly:

As in all the congregations of the saints, women should remain silent in the churches. They are not allowed to speak, but must be in submission, as the Law says.

If they want to inquire about something, they should ask their own husbands at home; for it is disgraceful for a woman to speak in the church. (14:33-35)

Women are the antonyms of order and peace. This is not a religion of brothers and sisters; women are in the church but not of the church.

15. The Resurrection of Christ and the Dead

Promises of immortality and of compensation for earthly oppression:

> For as in Adam all die, so in Christ all will be made alive. But each in his own turn: Christ, the firstfruits; then, when he comes, those who belong to him. Then the end will come, when he hands over the kingdom to God the Father after he has destroyed all dominion, authority and power. For he must reign until he has put all his enemies under his feet. The last enemy to be destroyed is death. For he "has put everything under his feet." (15:22-27)

And Paul, in one of his oratorical best, supposedly restoring some (again non-human) dignity to man, the "evil dust."

> If there is a natural body, there is also a spiritual body. So it is written: "The first man Adam became a living being"; the last Adam, a life-giving spirit. The spiritual did not come first but the natural, and after that the spiritual. The first man was of the dust of the earth, the second man from heaven. As was the earthly man, so are those who are of the earth; and as is the man from heaven, so also are those who are of heaven. And just as we have borne the likeness of the earthly man, so shall we bear the likeness of the man from heaven. (15:44-49)

16. The Collection for God's People

Paul differs from some Gospels' and Acts' total giving of one's possessions to the church but asks of each member "to set aside a sum of money in keeping with his income":

> Now about the collection for God's people: Do what I told the Galatian churches to do. On the first day of every week, each one of you should set aside a sum of money in keeping with his income, saving it up, so that when I come no collections will have to be made. (16:1-2)

Paul writes his final greetings in his "own hand" (16:21).

2 CORINTHIANS

1, 2, 3. Comfort, Forgiveness, the New Covenant

Paul praises "the God and Father of our Lord Jesus Christ, the Father of compassion and the God of all comfort" (1:3). He tells that he has acted "not according to worldly wisdom but according to God's grace" (1:12). He preaches forgiveness for the sinner and describes ministers of the new covenant as the "aroma of Christ" to God (2:15).

Paul tells people that they are "a letter from Christ, the result of our ministry, written not with ink but with the Spirit of the living God, not on tablets of stone but on tablets of human hearts" (3:3). So, Jesus and apostles are authors of mankind, men are texts, and human hearts replace the stone tablets of the *Old Testament*. In net balance: men are texts written by other powers; they are not authors of their own lives.

Apostles, and Paul, speak and write from a position of legitimacy that is ostensibly modest but one which is in fact Godly:

> Such confidence as this is ours through Christ before God. Not that we are competent in ourselves to claim anything for ourselves, but our competence comes from God. He has made us competent as ministers of a new covenant—not of the letter but of the Spirit; for the letter kills, but the Spirit gives life. (3:4-6)

A more distinct claim of superiority over the *Old Testament* follows:

> Now if the ministry that brought death, which was engraved in letters on stone, came with glory, so that the Israelites could not look steadily at the face of Moses because of its glory, fading though it was, will not the ministry of the Spirit be even more glorious? If the ministry that condemns men is glorious, how much more glorious is the ministry that brings righteousness! (3:7-9)

Deadly glory not negated but preserved and surpassed. Or is there a measure of veiled critique involved?

> Therefore, since we have such a hope, we are very bold. We are not like Moses, who would put a veil over his face to keep the Israelites from gazing at it while the radiance was fading away. But their minds were made dull, for to this day the same veil remains when the old covenant is read. It has not been removed, because only in Christ is it taken away. Even to this day when Moses is read, a veil covers their hearts. But whenever anyone turns to the Lord, the veil is taken away. (3:12-16)

One thing is certain: Jesus is greater than Moses; the new covenant is superior to the old one. Jesus is Spirit; Moses was a "mere" prophet?"

4, 5, 6, 7. Apostles, Their Ministry, Paul's Hardships and Joy

Paul describes the apostles' ministry, honesty, sufferings, perseverance, etc. And:

> If we are out of our mind, it is for the sake of God; if we are in our right mind, it is for you. For Christ's love compels us, because we are convinced that one died for all, and therefore all died. And he died for all, that those who live should no longer live for themselves but for him who died for them and was raised again.
>
> So from now on we regard no one from a worldly point of view. Though we once regarded Christ in this way, we do so no longer. Therefore, if anyone is in Christ, he is a new creation; the old has gone, the new has come! All this is from God, who reconciled us to himself through Christ and gave us the ministry of reconciliation: that

God was reconciling the world to himself in Christ, not counting men's sins against them. And he has committed to us the message of reconciliation. We are therefore Christ's ambassadors, as though God were making his appeal through us. We implore you on Christ's behalf: Be reconciled to God. God made him who had no sin to be sin for us, so that in him we might become the righteousness of God. (5:13-21)

Of course, this is "good news," a much better news, to believers than the message, threats, cyclical ebb and flow of the *Old Testament*. The "new has come"; the old will not recurrently return.

And, unlike the "lording over" of the Pentateuch prophets, Christian apostles are "really" humble:

We put no stumbling block in anyone's path, so that our ministry will not be discredited. Rather, as servants of God we commend ourselves in every way: in great endurance; in troubles, hardships and distresses; in beatings, imprisonments and riots; in hard work, sleepless nights and hunger; in purity, understanding, patience and kindness; in the Holy Spirit and in sincere love; in truthful speech and in the power of God; with weapons of righteousness in the right hand and in the left; through glory and dishonor, bad report and good report; genuine, yet regarded as impostors; known, yet regarded as unknown; dying, and yet we live on; beaten, and yet not killed; sorrowful, yet always rejoicing; poor, yet making many rich; having nothing, and yet possessing everything. (6:3-10)

The eloquent Paul then chides the Corinthians a bit:

We have spoken freely to you, Corinthians, and opened wide our hearts to you. We are not withholding our affection from you, but you are withholding yours from us. As a fair exchange—I speak as to my children—open wide your hearts also. (6:11-13)

He tells them not to be yoked with unbelievers.

Therefore come out from them and be separate, says the Lord. Touch no unclean thing, and I will receive you. I will be a Father to you, and you will be my sons and daughters, says the Lord Almighty. (6:17-18; Isaiah 52:11, Ezek.20:34,41; 2 Sam.7:14,8)

Where is "Christian universalism?"

Paul also praises the Corinthians. He concludes, referring to Titus:

...his affection for you is all the greater when he remembers that you were all obedient, receiving him with fear and trembling. I am glad I can have complete confidence in you. (7:15-16)

Fear and trembling and obedience are what win praise for the people.

8, 9, 10. Generous Giving; Paul's Defense of His Ministry

Paul praises the generosity of the Macedonian churches: "... they gave as much as they were able, and even beyond their ability" (8:3)—to the saints. He does not "command" the Corinthians but wants "to test the sincerity of (their) love" (8:8) and urges them to prepare a generous gift. He invokes Exodus (16:18) and Psalm (112:9) for equality, reciprocity, and solidarity.

> Our desire is not that others might be relieved while you are hard pressed, but that there might be equality. At the present time your plenty will supply what they need, so that in turn their plenty will supply what you need. Then there will be equality, as it is written: "He who gathered much did not have too much, and he who gathered little did not have too little." (8:13-15)

And:

> He has scattered abroad his gifts to the poor; his righteousness endures forever. (9:9-10)

Please emphatically note that the categories of rich and poor are not criticized or abolished; "equality" boils down to charitable giving and rotation of fortunes.

Paul is both meek and bold, both peaceful and punitive, both imploring and threatening.

> By the meekness and gentleness of Christ, I appeal to you—I, Paul, who am "timid" when face to face with you, but "bold" when away! I beg you that when I come I may not have to be as bold as I expect to be toward some people who think that we live by the standards of this world. For though we live in the world, we do not wage war as the world does. The weapons we fight with are not the weapons of the world. On the contrary, they have divine power to demolish strongholds. We demolish arguments and every pretension that sets itself up against the knowledge of God, and we take captive every thought to make it obedient to Christ. And we will be ready to punish every act of disobedience, once your obedience is complete. (10:1-6)

"Taking captive every thought to make it obedient to Christ." This is the logic of religion; this is the relationship of faith to reason, that is, total eclipse of human reason by Godly faith, which in fact is a much more destructive weapon than the worldly ones. And: If disobedience, then punishment.

> I do not want to seem to be trying to frighten you with my letters. For some say, "His letters are weighty and forceful, but in person he is unimpressive and his speaking amounts to nothing." Such people should realize that what we are in our letters when we are absent, we will be in our actions when we are present. (10:9-11)

He is forceful in his actions when present, but not boastful beyond proper limits.

We do not dare to classify or compare ourselves with some who commend themselves. When they measure themselves by themselves and compare themselves with themselves, they are not wise. We, however, will not boast beyond proper limits, but will confine our boasting to the field God has assigned to us, a field that reaches even to you. (10:12-13)

A field that encompasses even your innermost being, your heart and your mind, he might have added.

11. Paul and False Apostles

I hope you will put up with a little of my foolishness; but you are already doing that. I am jealous for you with a godly jealousy. I promised you to one husband, to Christ, so that I might present you as a pure virgin to him. But I am afraid that just as Eve was deceived by the serpent's cunning, your minds may somehow be led astray from your sincere and pure devotion to Christ. For if someone comes to you and preaches a Jesus other than the Jesus we preached, or if you receive a different spirit from the one you received, or a different gospel from the one you accepted, you put up with it easily enough. But I do not think I am in the least inferior to those "superapostles." I may not be a trained speaker, but I do have knowledge. We have made this perfectly clear to you in every way. (11:1-6)

Paul plays Yahweh ("godly jealousy"), Moses ("ineloquent speaker"), the companion to Jesus, all at the same time. He is both modest and authoritative. Above all, he promises people "to one husband, to Christ," so that he may present people to him as a pure virgin." People, after having been described as "fish" and as "field," are now being described as "a pure virgin" to be presented to one husband, Jesus Christ. Now, is this an improvement, from the (obsolete) *Old Testament* to the (better) *New Testament*, in terms of human dignity? That is, elevation from the status of "evil dust" to that of innocent fish or pure virgin—female and male[3]—to be "taken captive" by religious thought and religious men and their God?

Paul preaches the gospel of God "free of charge" (11:7), likens false apostles to Satan, tells people not to take him for a fool, and builds up his own legitimacy starting with divine sources but continuing with the labors of his personal biography:

What anyone else dares to boast about—I am speaking as a fool—I also dare to boast about. Are they Hebrews? So am I. Are they Israelites? So am I. Are they Abraham's descendants? So am I. Are they servants of Christ? (I am out of my mind to talk like this.) I am more. I have worked much harder, been in prison more frequently, been flogged more severely, and been exposed to death again and again. Five times I received from the Jews the forty lashes minus one. Three times I was beaten with rods, once I was stoned, three times I was shipwrecked, I spent a night and a day in the open sea, I have been constantly on the move. I have been in danger... (11:21-26)

12. Paul's Vision and His Thorn

Paul continues to ebb and flow between extremes or rather playing with extremes with great oratorical skill.

> Therefore I will boast all the more gladly about my weaknesses, so that Christ's power may rest on me. That is why, for Christ's sake, I delight in weaknesses, in insults, in hardships, in persecutions, in difficulties. For when I am weak, then I am strong.
>
> I have made a fool of myself, but you drove me to it. I ought to have been commended by you, for I am not in the least inferior to the "super-apostles," even though I am nothing. The things that mark an apostle—signs, wonders and miracles—were done among you with great perseverance. How were you inferior to the other churches, except that I was never a burden to you? Forgive me this wrong!
>
> Now I am ready to visit you for the third time, and I will not be a burden to you, because what I want is not your possessions but you. After all, children should not have to save up for their parents, but parents for their children. So I will very gladly spend for you everything I have and expend myself as well. If I love you more, will you love me less? Be that as it may, I have not been a burden to you. Yet, crafty fellow that I am, I caught you by trickery! (12:9-16)

And the paternalistic Paul intimates yet another visit.

13. Final Warnings

Not final greetings but final warnings.

> This will be my third visit to you. "Every matter must be established by the testimony of two or three witnesses." I already gave you a warning when I was with you the second time. I now repeat it while absent: On my return I will not spare those who sinned earlier or any of the others since you are demanding proof that Christ is speaking through me. He is not weak in dealing with you, but is powerful among you. (13:1-3)

And:

> This is why I write these things when I am absent, that when I come I may not have to be harsh in my use of authority—the authority the Lord gave me for building you up, not for tearing you down. (13:10)

Iron paw in velvet glove. Frightening at any rate, despite oratorical, rhetorical disclaimers to the contrary.

GALATIANS

1. No Other Gospel; Paul Called by God

Paul, "an apostle—sent not from men nor by men, but by Jesus Christ and God the Father, who raised him from the dead" (1:1), addresses the churches in Galatia. He "eternally condemn(s)" preachers of other gospels—other than the one Paul has preached (1:8). Claim of superhuman legitimacy is used to secure the absolute uniqueness of his gospel.

> Am I now trying to win the approval of men, or of God? Or am I trying to please men? If I were still trying to please men, I would not be a servant of Christ.
>
> I want you to know, brothers, that the gospel I preached is not something that man made up. I did not receive it from any man, nor was I taught it; rather, I received it by revelation from Jesus Christ. (1:10-11)

Repetition of some personal history, with particular emphasis on being "set apart" to receive revelation:

> For you have heard of my previous way of life in Judaism, how intensely I persecuted the church of God and tried to destroy it. I was advancing in Judaism beyond many Jews of my own age and was extremely zealous for the traditions of my fathers. But when God, who set me apart from birth and called me by his grace, was pleased to reveal his Son in me so that I might preach him among the Gentiles, I did not consult any man, nor did I go up to Jerusalem to see those who were apostles before I was, but I went immediately into Arabia and later returned to Damascus. (1:13-17)

Moses receives revelation from God; Paul from Jesus and Muhammad from Gabriel. Nevertheless, God, Son/Gabriel, and the prophets are one.

2. Paul Accepted by Apostles; Paul Opposes Peter

Paul opposes Peter because he "live(s) like a Gentile and not like a Jew" (2:14).

> We who are Jews by birth and not 'Gentile sinners' know that a man is not justified by observing the law, but by faith in Jesus Christ. So we, too, have put our faith in Christ Jesus that we may be justified by faith in Christ and not by observing the law, because by observing the law no one will be justified. (2:15-16)

The great theme of the superiority of Christian "faith" over Jewish "law" is introduced. (But which part of the law do you keep and which part of it do you discard, the *Koran* shall duly ask.)

3. Faith or Observance of the Law; The Law and the Promise

> You foolish Galatians! Who has bewitched you? Before your very eyes Jesus Christ was clearly portrayed as crucified. I would like to learn just one thing from you: Did you receive the Spirit by observing the law, or by believing what you heard? Are you

so foolish? After beginning with the Spirit, are you now trying to attain your goal by human effort? Have you suffered so much for nothing—if it really was for nothing? Does God give you his Spirit and work miracles among you because you observe the law, or because you believe what you heard? (3:1-5)

Spirit and belief greater than the law and human effort. Those who miss this point are not only foolish but also accursed.

All who rely on observing the law are under a curse, for it is written: "Cursed is everyone who does not continue to do everything written in the Book of the Law." Clearly no one is justified before God by the law, because, "The righteous will live by faith." The law is not based on faith; on the contrary, "The man who does these things will live by them." Christ redeemed us from the curse of the law by becoming a curse for us... (3:10-13)

Paul, in trying to supersede the *Old Testament*, nevertheless marshals its authority by quoting from Deut. 27:26, Habak. 2:4, Lev. 18:5 with great oratorical maneuvering skill, if not impeccable logic.

As most are accursed, the blessed are few—even one:

Brothers, let me take an example from everyday life. Just as no one can set aside or add to a human covenant that has been duly established, so it is in this case. The promises were spoken to Abraham and to his seed. The Scripture does not say "and to seeds," meaning many people, but "and to your seed" meaning one person, who is Christ. What I mean is this: The law, introduced 430 years later, does not set aside the covenant previously established by God and thus do away with the promise. For if the inheritance depends on the law, then it no longer depends on a promise; but God in his grace gave it to Abraham through a promise.

What, then, was the purpose of the law? It was added because of transgressions until the Seed to whom the promise referred had come. The law was put into effect through angels by a mediator. A mediator, however, does not represent just one party; but God is one. (3:15-20)

The seed (singular) is Jesus. "Seeds" meaning all men is out of the question. Paul quotes from Gen. 12:7, 13:15, 24:7.

Paul continues with his argumentation:

Is the law, therefore, opposed to the promises of God? Absolutely not! For if a law had been given that could impart life, then righteousness would certainly have come by the law. But the Scripture declares that the whole world is a prisoner of sin, so that what was promised, being given through faith in Jesus Christ, might be given to those who believe.

Before this faith came, we were held prisoners by the law, locked up until faith should be revealed. So the law was put in charge to lead us to Christ that we might be justified by faith. Now that faith has come, we are no longer under the supervision of the law. (3:21-25)

Jesus and Christianity, in a sense, here, supercede Moses and Judaism, not by annulment but by sublation—an argument that *Koran* shall refine to perfection.

4. Sons of God; Hagar and Sarah

Here comes a—perhaps the—most vexing ambivalence of the Three Books and the three great religions: Seed or seeds, one/few or all, inequality or (rhetorical) equality? Immediately after having said, in the previous passage, "The Scripture does not says 'and to seeds', meaning many people, but 'and to your seed', meaning one person," who is Christ" ["the (most-) chosen one"], Paul now declares that: "You are all sons of God" and "you are Abraham's seed."

You are all sons of God through faith in Christ Jesus, for all of you who were baptized into Christ have clothed yourselves with Christ. There is neither Jew nor Greek, slave nor free, male nor female, for you are all one in Christ Jesus. If you belong to Christ, then you are Abraham's seed, and heirs according to the promise.

What I am saying is that as long as the heir is a child, he is no different from a slave, although he owns the whole estate. He is subject to guardians and trustees until the time set by his father. So also, when we were children, we were in slavery under the basic principles of the world. But when the time had fully come, God sent his Son, born of a woman, born under law, to redeem those under law, that we might receive the full rights of sons. Because you are sons, God sent the Spirit of his Son into our hearts, the Spirit who calls out, "Abba, Father." So you are no longer a slave, but a son; and since you are a son, God has made you also an heir. (3:26-4:7)

Now, is it only a matter of big S and small s, that is, the Son (one prophet) and sons (many/all people)? And real equality among all human beings (if believers, to be sure) with the understandable exceptionality of the prophet? With the attendant universalism, freedom, and gender non-discrimination?

Or: Is it that this is an isolated, rhetorical, propagandistic passage, falsified and annuled many times over by other parts of the *New Testament* and by its totality, inner logic, its basic spirit?

Or: Is it the case that, discernible, even here, is a profound cynicism about and a hidden disclaimer against equality of human beings? "There is neither Jew nor Greek, slave nor free, male nor female," "for you are" (on condition that you are) "all one in Jesus Christ." That is: If and only if you believe in Jesus and if you belong to Jesus, can you become a son and heir. If you don't, you are excluded—as obvious unequals, unqualifiers.

The above is the easier part of the underlying problem. What is harder is the following. Even if you are among the believers, are you really equals with your other brothers and sisters or does your nominal equality consists in nothing but your being offered certain "promises," too for the other world as your "belief-right" while you continue your existence in this world (and be thankful in all circumstances) as a lowly member/organ of the Corpus Christi (Cf. infra), in which your spiritual and social station and limit is fixed in an organic, hierarchical order of "distributive justice?" You are equal only in that you are admitted to the body, to the whole; but you may be the brain or the loins or the toes. (For more, see below.)

To my mind, such implications are already inherent in the ostensibly more egalitarian second passage.

But which is the real Paul? What is his basic meaning? Of the first or the second excerpt? Is the second passage the counterpoint of a dialectic, or is it sheer recruitment policy, an oratorical appeal to the dispossessed, a potential manpower of believers? Who are to cease being "slaves" and to become "sons"—metaphorically—or rather to become *slave-sons* with thankful Christian identities and expectations. (Cf. below for Paul's affirmatory views on slavery.) (I shall treat the themes of paternalism and, its corollary, infantilization later.)

Paul implores the Galatians not to regress back to "those weak and miserable principles" "now that you know God—or rather are known by God" (4:9). Paul tries to eat his cake and save it: keep the book and rescind it. And, more importantly, his "egalitarianism" makes itself clearer:

Tell me, you who want to be under the law, are you not aware of what the law says? For it is written that Abraham had two sons, one by the slave woman and the other by the free woman. His son by the slave woman was born in the ordinary way; but his son by the free woman was born as the result of a promise.

These things may be taken figuratively, for the women represent two covenants. One covenant is from Mount Sinai and bears children who are to be slaves: This is Hagar. Now Hagar stands for Mount Sinai in Arabia and corresponds to the present city of Jerusalem, because she is in slavery with her children. But the Jerusalem that is above is free, and she is our mother. For it is written: "Be glad, O barren woman, who bears no children; break forth and cry aloud, you who have no labor pains; because more are the children of the desolate woman than of her who has a husband."

Now you, brothers, like Isaac, are children of promise. At that time the son born in the ordinary way persecuted the son born by the power of the Spirit. It is the same now. But what does the Scripture say? "Get rid of the slave woman and her son, for the slave woman's son will never share in the inheritance with the free woman's son." Therefore, brothers, we are not children of the slave woman, but of the free woman. (4:21-31)

Discrimination, exclusion, slavery.

5. Freedom in Christ, Life by the Spirit

> It is for freedom that Christ has set us free. Stand firm, then, and do not let your-
> selves be burdened again by a yoke of slavery.
>
> Mark my words! I, Paul, tell you that if you let yourselves be circumcised, Christ
> will be of no value to you at all. Again I declare to every man who lets himself be cir-
> cumcised that he is obligated to obey the whole law. You who are trying to be justi-
> fied by law have been alienated from Christ; you have fallen away from grace. But by
> faith we eagerly await through the Spirit the righteousness for which we hope. For in
> Christ Jesus neither circumcision nor uncircumcision has any value. The only thing
> that counts is faith expressing itself through love. (5:1-6)

Not law but faith, not externals but internals, not rituals but internalization. Is Christianity
better than Judaism? But one should not forget that an allegedly more spiritual circumcision of the heart can be as fanatical and dangerous, if not more, than the physical circumcision of the penis. Metaphors may not always be so innocent, after all. And:

> You, my brothers, were called to be free. But do not use your freedom to indulge the
> sinful nature,[4] rather, serve one another in love. The entire law is summed up in a
> single command: "Love your neighbor as yourself." If you keep on biting and de-
> vouring each other, watch out or you will be destroyed by each other. (5:13-15)

In the *Old Testament*, it was the tribal brother and neighbor; here it is the ethnicity-free but
religion-bound Christian brother, and neighbor. A relative improvement; yet, faith can also
be as divisive and destructive as blood. What is mean is the internal peace and stability of
Christendom, not more.

So, live by the Spirit, in contradistinction to the (evil) passions and desires of the sinful
human nature (of the flesh, above all):

> So I say, live by the Spirit, and you will not gratify the desires of the sinful nature.
> For the sinful nature desires what is contrary to the Spirit, and the Spirit what is con-
> trary to the sinful nature. They are in conflict with each other, so that you do not do
> what you want. But if you are led by the Spirit, you are not under law.
>
> The acts of the sinful nature are obvious: sexual immorality, impurity and de-
> bauchery; idolatry and witchcraft; hatred, discord, jealousy, fits of rage, selfish am-
> bition, dissensions, factions and envy; drunkenness, orgies, and the like. I warn you,
> as I did before, that those who live like this will not inherit the kingdom of God.
>
> But the fruit of the Spirit is love, joy, peace, patience, kindness, goodness, faith-
> fulness, gentleness and self-control. Against such things there is no law. Those who
> belong to Christ Jesus have crucified the sinful nature with its passions and desires.
> Since we live by the Spirit, let us keep in step with the Spirit. Let us not become con-
> ceited, provoking and envying each other. (5:16-26)

Characteristics of the good person opens with sexual modesty and closes with absten-
tion from passions and desires. A list of moral virtues and rules of behavior is given in between. Among characteristics of the good society, monotheistic religious unity and
conformity, social-political peace and stability (the latter as the product of the former?)
stand out. No envy is old hat from the *Old Testament*, but no selfish ambition seems to be
new. No domination or no exploitation are among the absences.

6. Doing Good to All, Not Circumcision But a New Creation
Doing good to all or some?

> Therefore, as we have opportunity, let us do good to all people, *especially to those who*
> *belong to the family of believers.* (6:10)

My comment is my emphasis.

Circumcision or something else?

> Neither circumcision nor uncircumcision means anything; what counts is a new
> creation. Peace and mercy to all who follow this rule, even to the Israel of God.
> (6:15-16)

Koran shall think that circumcision does mean something.

EPHESIANS

1, 2, 3. Blessings in, Alive in, One in Christ
Paul, an apostle of the Lord Christ Jesus by the will of God our Father, addresses the saints
and the faithful in Ephesus (hierarchy: God → Jesus → Paul → saints → the faithful):

> For he chose us in him before the creation of the world to be holy and blameless in
> his sight. In love he predestined us to be adopted as his sons through Jesus Christ, in
> accordance with his pleasure and will. (1:4-5)

The "holy and blameless" "us," whose holiness trickles down to the ordinary faithful. Teleology. Predestination.

> In him we were also chosen, having been predestined according to the plan of him
> who works out everything in conformity with the purpose of his will, in order that
> we, who were the first to hope in Christ, might be for the praise of his glory. And
> you also were included in Christ when you heard the word of truth... (1:11-13)

Paul says that Christ is

> ... far above all rule and authority, power and dominion, and every title that can be
> given, not only in the present age but also in the one to come. And God placed all
> things under his feet and appointed him to be head over everything for the church,
> which is his body, the fullness of him who fills everything in every way. (1:21-23)

That is, omnipotent, omnipresent—just like God. "(T)he fullness of him who fills everything in every way." (Is this much different from the fascist totalitarian motto, "Everything within the state, nothing outside the state" or "Ein führer, ein staat, ein volk?") As for ordinary human beings who populate the church, the body, and who have no free will, no freedom of choice and action:

> For it is by grace you have been saved, through faith—and this not from yourselves, it is the gift of God—not by works, so that no one can boast. For we are God's workmanship, created in Christ Jesus to do good works, which God prepared in advance for us to do. (2:8-10)

And Paul finally strikes the reconciliation he has been groping for. Christ unites the uncircumcised Gentiles with the circumcised Jews:

> For he himself is our peace, who has made the two one and has destroyed the barrier, the dividing wall of hostility, by abolishing in his flesh the law with its commandments and regulations. His purpose was to create in himself one new man out of the two, thus making peace and in this one body to reconcile both of them to God through the cross by which he put to death their hostility. He came and preached peace to you who were far away and peace to those who were near. For through him we both have access to the Father by one Spirit.
>
> Consequently, you are no longer foreigners and aliens, but fellow citizens with God's people and members of God's household, built on the foundation of the apostles and prophets, with Christ Jesus himself as the chief cornerstone. In him the whole building is joined together and rises to become a holy temple in the Lord. And in him you too are being built together to become a dwelling in which God lives by his Spirit. (2:14-22)

Again, this is not to be mistaken for humanistic universalism, for it is sheer unitarian religious communalism, excluding believers of other creeds and those who do not believe in religion or God. "Repent or perish" is always operative. (*Koran* shall prove no more universalistic.)

Paul also reminds his own special position and his unique relationship with the Spirit:

> ... you will be able to understand my insight into the mystery of Christ, which was not made known to men in other generations as it has now been revealed by the Spirit to God's holy apostles and prophets. (3:4-5)

4. Unity in the Body of Christ; Living As Children of Light

As a "prisoner for the Lord," Paul urges men to be humble, gentle, patient, loving, peaceful.

> There is one body and one Spirit—just as you were called to one hope when you were called—one Lord, one faith, one baptism; one God and Father of all, who is over all and through all and in all. (4:4-6)

One body, but different grace to each:

> But to each one of us grace has been given as Christ apportioned it: This is why it
> says: "When he ascended on high, he led captives in his train and gave gifts to men."
> (4:7-8)

Not only "infants" (4:14), but "captives" (4:8) and "prisoners" (4:1) as well.

Unity in hierarchy and hierarchy in unity:

> Instead, speaking the truth in love, we will in all things grow up into him who is the
> Head, that is, Christ. From him the whole body, joined and held together by every
> supporting ligament, grows and builds itself up in love, as each part does its work.
> (4:15-16)

Christianity will make new men, as opposed to the Gentiles, who had lost all sensitivity,
given over to sensuality, with a continual lust for more.

> You were taught, with regard to your former way of life, to put off your old self,
> which is being corrupted by its deceitful desires; to be made new in the attitude of
> your minds; and to put on the new self, created to be like God in true righteousness
> and holiness. (4:22-24)

The new men shall be "all members of one body" (4:25).

Some moral advice:

> Get rid of all bitterness, rage and anger, brawling and slander, along with every form
> of malice. Be kind and compassionate to one another, forgiving each other, just as in
> Christ God forgave you. (4:31-32)

5. Rules; Wives and Husbands

Some more moral advice:

> Be imitators of God, therefore, as dearly loved children and live a life of love, just as
> Christ loved us and gave himself up for us as a fragrant offering and sacrifice to God.
>   But among you there must not be even a hint of sexual immorality, or of any kind
> of impurity, or of greed, because these are improper for God's holy people. Nor
> should there be obscenity, foolish talk or coarse joking, which are out of place, but
> rather thanksgiving. (5:1-4)

"You were once darkness, but now you are light" (5:8).

> Do not get drunk on wine, which leads to debauchery. Instead, be filled with the
> Spirit. Speak to one another with psalms, hymns and spiritual songs. Sing and make
> music in your heart to the Lord, always giving thanks to God the Father for every-
> thing, in the name of our Lord Jesus Christ.
>   Submit to one another out of reverence for Christ. (5:18-21)

Paul repeats the familiar hierarchy of Christ → man → woman:

> Wives, submit to your husbands as to the Lord. For the husband is the head of the wife as Christ is the head of the church, his body, of which he is the Savior. Now as the church submits to Christ, so also wives should submit to their husbands in everything. (5:22-24)

Wives should submit to their husbands *in everything*. This is hard patriarchal political theory. The rest is anticlimax:

> Husbands, love your wives, just as Christ loved the church and gave himself up for her to make her holy, cleansing her by the washing with water through the word, and to present her to himself as a radiant church, without stain or wrinkle or any other blemish, but holy and blameless. In this same way, husbands ought to love their wives as their own bodies. He who loves his wife loves himself. After all, no one ever hated his own body, but he feeds and cares for it, just as Christ does the church—for we are members of his body. For this reason a man will leave his father and mother and be united to his wife, and the two will become one flesh. This is a profound mystery—but I am talking about Christ and the church. However, each one of you also must love his wife as he loves himself, and the wife must respect her husband. (5:25-33)

Husband loves, wife respects.

6. Children and Parents, Slaves and Masters

Children and parents:

> Children, obey your parents in the Lord, for this is right. "Honor your father and mother"—which is the first commandment with a promise—"that it may go well with you and that you may enjoy long life on the earth."
>
> Fathers, do not exasperate your children; instead, bring them up in the training and instruction of the Lord. (6:1-4)

Slaves and masters:

> Slaves, obey your earthly masters with respect and fear, and with sincerity of heart, just as you would obey Christ. Obey them not only to win their favor when their eye is on you, but like slaves of Christ, doing the will of God from your heart. Serve wholeheartedly, as if you were serving the Lord, not men, because you know that the Lord will reward everyone for whatever good he does, whether he is slave or free.
>
> And masters, treat your slaves in the same way. Do not threaten them, since you know that he who is both their Master and yours is in heaven, and there is no favoritism with him. (6:5-9)

Christian egalitarianism? Master and slave equal before God? Just like equality of men, rich or poor, before the law? Western idea of legal equality, without political and economic and real spiritual equality?

The authoritarian (also totalitarian, organicistic?) hierarchy is completed: Husbands over wives, parents over children, masters over slaves—all holy in descending order of degree. The ecclesiastical commonwealth is extended from the church to the family and the household. Family is the cell/molecule of society. The staple articles of Western constitutions, not only fascist but also liberal.

Just as wives are to submit to their husbands as to the Lord, slaves are to obey their "earthly masters" as they would Christ. "Submit to the authorities" across the board. Ordinary men to God's deputies on earth—whether religious or earthly —women to men, children to parents, slaves to masters. Not only pragmatically but also wholeheartedly and religiously. So every echelon in the hierarchy is made into an authority with a submissive constituency: Ordinary men have women to rule, women have children to rule, slaves have their own women and children to rule.

Paul concludes "Ephesians" with a point-counterpoint:

Finally, be strong in the Lord and in his mighty power. Put on the full armor of God so that you can take your stand against the devil's schemes. For our struggle is not against flesh and blood, but against the rulers, against the authorities, against the powers of this dark world and against the spiritual forces of evil in the heavenly realms. (6:10-12)

Which rulers? Which authorities? After all the foregoing? The logical candidates are non-Christian rulers/authorities, against which holy war, with the full armor of God, should be waged. Jews have their "God's holy wars," Christians their "crusades," Muslims their "jihad."

PHILIPPIANS

1. Thanksgiving, Prayer, Paul's Chains
Belief saves, unbelief destroys:

Whatever happens, conduct yourselves in a manner worthy of the gospel of Christ. Then, whether I come and see you or only hear about you in my absence, I will know that you stand firm in one spirit, contending as one man for the faith of the gospel without being frightened in any way by those who oppose you. This is a sign to them that they will be destroyed, but that you will be saved—and that by God. (1:27-28)

Contending "as one man."

2. Imitating Christ's Humility
Christ is both humble and sublime.

Men, too, should be humble like Christ and be one in mind, spirit, and purpose. Not only self-interest (which is there) but also concern for others' interests as well(?).

If you have any encouragement from being united with Christ, if any comfort from his love, if any fellowship with the Spirit, if any tenderness and compassion, then make my joy complete by being like-minded, having the same love, being one in spirit and purpose. Do nothing out of selfish ambition or vain conceit, but in humility consider others better than yourselves. Each of you should look not only to your own interests, but also to the interests of others. (2:1-4)

And:

Therefore, my dear friends, as you have always obeyed—not only in my presence, but now much more in my absence—continue to work out your salvation with fear and trembling, for it is God who works in you to will and to act according to his good purpose.

Do everything without complaining or arguing, so that you may become blameless and pure, children of God without fault in a crooked and depraved generation in which you shine like stars in the universe… (2:12-15)

Fear and tremble, believe and obey, don't complain or argue—if you want salvation. And, don't forget that you have no free will, "for it is God who works in you to will and to act according to his good purpose" (2:13).

3. Not Flesh But the Goal

"Watch out for those dogs, those men who do evil, those mutilators of the flesh" (3:2).

Paul scorns "legalistic righteousness" (3:6), exalts "righteousness that comes from God and is by faith" (3:9), destruction is the destiny of those whose "mind is on earthly things" (3:19), especially on matters of flesh.

4. Thanks for Gifts

Paul thanks the Philippians:

… you sent me aid again and again when I was in need. Not that I am looking for a gift, but I am looking for what may be credited to your account. I have received full payment and even more; I am amply supplied, now that I have received from Epaphroditus the gifts you sent. They are a fragrant offering, an acceptable sacrifice, pleasing to God. And my God will meet all your needs according to his glorious riches in Christ Jesus. (4:16-19)

What is good for Paul is good for God; "my God."

COLOSSIANS

1. The Supremacy of Christ

Paul addresses the "holy and faithful brothers" (1:2). The gospel is the "word of truth" (1:5). Jesus is the "head." He is the son, the God-like son.

He is the image of the invisible God, the firstborn over all creation. For by him all things were created: things in heaven and on earth, visible and invisible, whether thrones or powers or rulers or authorities; all things were created by him and for him. He is before all things, and in him all things hold together. And he is the head of the body, the church; he is the beginning and the firstborn from among the dead, so that in everything he might have the supremacy. For God was pleased to have all his fullness dwell in him... (1:15-19)

2. Freedom from Human Regulations Through Life With Christ

Paul is much more theistic and much less secular than the *Old Testament*. Not human law but faith in God and Christ. Not Jewish teaching and tradition but the new Christian covenant and belief. And the hierarchy and unity of holiness: God in Christ, Christ in Paul, Paul in people. And, of course, God-Christ-Paul, all "in" people. Christianity's God is not the Judaic God, who is frighteningly close to and amidst people; this God is outright within people, within individual human beings, causing constant and immanent fear and trembling—not only when/if they approach him.

See to it that no one takes you captive through hollow and deceptive philosophy, which depends on human tradition and the basic principles of this world rather than on Christ.

For in Christ all the fullness of the Deity lives in bodily form, and you have been given fullness in Christ, who is the head over every power and authority. (2:8-10)

Totalitarian unity. And:

When you were dead in your sins and in the uncircumcision of your sinful nature, God made you alive with Christ. He forgave us all our sins, having canceled the written code, with its regulations, that was against us and that stood opposed to us; he took it away, nailing it to the cross. And having disarmed the powers and authorities, he made a public spectacle of them, triumphing over them by the cross.

Therefore do not let anyone judge you by what you eat or drink, or with regard to a religious festival, a New Moon celebration or a Sabbath day. These are a shadow of the things that were to come; the reality, however, is found in Christ. (2:13-17)

"Cancellation of the written code," "disarming of the powers and authorities," and:

Since you died with Christ to the basic principles of this world, why, as though you still belonged to it, do you submit to its rules: "Do not handle! Do not taste! Do not touch!?" These are all destined to perish with use, because they are based on human commands and teachings. Such regulations indeed have an appearance of wisdom, with their self-imposed worship, their false humility and their harsh treatment of the body, but they lack any value in restraining sensual indulgence. (2:20-23)

In short, the message is that the *Old Testament* is human (Moses') whereas the *New Testament* is superhuman (Jesus Christ's, God's son).

3. Rules for Holy Living and for Christian Households
A list of moral rules:

> Put to death, therefore, whatever belongs to your earthly nature: sexual immorality, impurity, lust, evil desires and greed, which is idolatry. Because of these, the wrath of God is coming. You used to walk in these ways, in the life you once lived. But now you must rid yourselves of all such things as these: anger, rage, malice, slander, and filthy language from your lips. Do not lie to each other, since you have taken off your old self with its practices and have put on the new self, which is being renewed in knowledge in the image of its Creator. Here there is no Greek or Jew, circumcised or uncircumcised, barbarian, Scythian, slave or free, but Christ is all, and is in all.
>
> Therefore, as God's chosen people, holy and dearly loved, clothe yourselves with compassion, kindness, humility, gentleness and patience. Bear with each other and forgive whatever grievances you may have against one another. Forgive as the Lord forgave you. And over all these virtues put on love, which binds them all together in perfect unity. (3:5-14)

And:

> And whatever you do, whether in word or deed, do it all in the name of the Lord Jesus, giving thanks to God the Father through him. (3:17)

Holy living in general and holy living in the household. And, holy family:

> Wives, submit to your husbands, as is fitting in the Lord.
>> Husbands, love your wives and do not be harsh with them.
>> Children, obey your parents in everything, for this pleases the Lord.
>> Fathers, do not embitter your children, or they will become discouraged.
>> Slaves, obey your earthly masters in everything; and do it, not only when their eye is on you and to win their favor, but with sincerity of heart and reverence for the Lord. Whatever you do, work at it with all your heart, as working for the Lord, not for men, since you know that you will receive an inheritance from the Lord as a reward. It is the Lord Christ you are serving. Anyone who does wrong will be repaid for his wrong, and there is no favoritism.
>> Masters, provide your slaves with what is right and fair, because you know that you also have a Master in heaven. (3:18-4:1)

Holy hierarchy: God → Christ → Men → Women, and Masters → Slaves—all to "submit" unequivocally to the one higher up. Family being a microcosm of the polity in the city of God: Paternalism and patriarchy legitimated by theism. Punch line: "Wives, submit to husbands, as is fitting in the Lord."

In the face of this evidence, who can in sound mind and good faith say that Christianity is an egalitarian religion, calling for equality of brothers and equality between men and women?

Paul reminds that he is writing this greeting "in his own hand" (4:18).

1 THESSALONIANS

1, 2, 3. Thanksgiving, Paul's Ministry, Timothy's Report
Paul adds power and spirit to words and offers yet another hierarchy, a hierarchy of imitators:

> For we know, brothers loved by God, that he has chosen you, because our gospel came to you not simply with words, but also with power, with the Holy Spirit and with deep conviction. You know how we lived among you for your sake. You became imitators of us and of the Lord. (1:4-6)

He reaffirms his legitimacy, his self-conferred legitimacy:

> For the appeal we make does not spring from error or impure motives, nor are we trying to trick you. On the contrary, we speak as men approved by God to be entrusted with the gospel. We are not trying to please men but God... (2:3-4)

He repeats his compassionate paternalism, infantilizing believers:

> You are witnesses, and so is God, of how holy, righteous and blameless we were among you who believed. For you know that we dealt with each of you as a father deals with his own children, encouraging, comforting and urging you to live lives worthy of God, who calls you into his kingdom and glory. (2:10-12)

Without, of course, neglecting to remind the unbelievers of the "wrath of God" (2:16).

4. Living to Please God
Why does man live? What is the purpose and meaning of life? To please God, not men:

> Finally, brothers, we instructed you how to live in order to please God, as in fact you are living. Now we ask you and urge you in the Lord Jesus to do this more and more. For you know what instructions we gave you by the authority of the Lord Jesus.
>
> It is God's will that you should be sanctified: that you should avoid sexual immorality; that each of you should learn to control his own body in a way that is holy and honorable, not in passionate lust like the heathen, who do not know God; and that in this matter no one should wrong his brother or take advantage of him. The Lord will punish men for all such sins, as we have already told you and warned you. For God did not call us to be impure, but to live a holy life. Therefore, he who rejects this instruction does not reject man but God, who gives you his Holy Spirit. (4:1-8)

To be sanctified, one should avoid sexual immorality and control one's body in a holy and honorable way. Its opposite, passionate lust, is "not knowing God." The text is ambiguous; is it that excesses and perversions of sex are to be avoided or one is to abstain from sexual desires in a more general way? One thing is clear: there is an essential(istic) antagonism between sex and purity/holiness.

> Now about brotherly love we do not need to write to you, for you yourselves have been taught by God to love each other. And in fact, you do love all the brothers throughout Macedonia. Yet we urge you, brothers, to do so more and more.
>
> Make it your ambition to lead a quiet life, to mind your own business and to work with your hands, just as we told you, so that your daily life may win the respect of outsiders and so that you will not be dependent on anybody. (4:9-12)

Brotherly (and sisterly?) love. Leading a quiet life and minding your own business. Isn't this a philosophy and ideology of capitulative obscurantism, usually and erroneously and exclusively attributed to Islam?

5. Light and Darkness

> Now, brothers, about times and dates we do not need to write to you, for you know very well that the day of the Lord will come like a thief in the night. While people are saying, "Peace and safety," destruction will come on them suddenly, as labor pains on a pregnant woman, and they will not escape.
>
> But you, brothers, are not in darkness so that this day should surprise you like a thief. You are all sons of the light and sons of the day. We do not belong to the night or to the darkness. (5:1-5)

God coming like a thief in the night is a much-repeated common motif of all Three Books. In its nocturnality it may be scary, but it should not be overlooked that it also contains a threat to security of property. (Cf. If holy, then prosper.)

And some final instructions, including holding apostles in the highest regard, "who are over you in the Lord" and who are divinely authorized to "admonish" you. (Who says Christianity, and Judaism and Islam, are brotherhoods of equals, equally valuable sons of God? Some/few are always "over," "set apart," "holier," etc.)

> Now we ask you, brothers, to respect those who work hard among you, who are over you in the Lord and who admonish you. Hold them in the highest regard in love because of their work. Live in peace with each other. And we urge you, brothers, warn those who are idle, encourage the timid, help the weak, be patient with everyone. Make sure that nobody pays back wrong for wrong, but always try to be kind to each other and to everyone else.
>
> Be joyful always; pray continually; give thanks in all circumstances, for this is God's will for you in Christ Jesus.

Do not put out the Spirit's fire; do not treat prophecies with contempt. Test everything. Hold on to the good. Avoid every kind of evil. (5:12-22)

Also, some human charity, no lex talionis (here), thankfulness in "all" circumstances, and so forth.

2 THESSALONIANS

1, 2. Thanksgiving and Prayer; The Man of Lawlessness
Unbelievers are to repent or perish. But repentance is more God-willed than humanly chosen:

> For this reason God sends them a powerful delusion so that they will believe the lie and so that all will be condemned who have not believed the truth but have delighted in wickedness. (2:11-12)

Religions do need sinful people (majority), so they create it. God, as in the *Old Testament* and the *Koran*, does not try to correct and convince, but he sends delusions, he hardens and seals hearts.

3. Warning Against Idleness
A work ethic:

> If a man will not work, he shall not eat. (3:10)

Paul writes this greeting in his own hand, "which is the distinguishing mark in all (his) letters" (3:17).

1 TIMOTHY

1. False Teachers of the Law; Lord's Grace to Paul
Other doctrines, religious or not, are false and mythical; they promote controversies and meaningless talk. Whereas Christian faith, or for that matter any religious faith, is the one and absolute truth. Theistic faith vs. questioning, debating human reason, and reasoning.

> As I urged you when I went into Macedonia, stay there in Ephesus so that you may command certain men not to teach false doctrines any longer nor to devote themselves to myths and endless genealogies. These promote controversies rather than God's work—which is by faith. The goal of this command is love, which comes from a pure heart and a good conscience and a sincere faith. Some have wandered away from these and turned to meaningless talk. They want to be teachers of the law, but they do not know what they are talking about or what they so confidently affirm.
>
> We know that the law is good if one uses it properly. We also know that law is made not for the righteous but for law-breakers and rebels, the ungodly and sinful,

the unholy and irreligious; for those who kill their fathers or mothers, for murderers, for adulterers and perverts, for slave traders and liars and perjurers—and for whatever else is contrary to the sound doctrine that conforms to the glorious gospel of the blessed God, which he entrusted to me. (1:3-10)

Christian gospel is greater than Jewish law.

Now to the King eternal, immortal, invisible, the only God, be honor and glory forever and ever. Amen. (1:17)

Christianity is a very royalist religion.

2. Instructions on Worship

Again, "submit to the authorities":

I urge, then, first of all, that requests, prayers, intercession and thanksgiving be made for everyone—for kings and all those in authority, that we may live peaceful and quiet lives in all godliness and holiness. This is good, and pleases God our Savior, who wants all men to be saved and to come to a knowledge of the truth. (2:1-4)

Peaceful and quiet lives, in godliness and holiness, by thanking and praying for "kings and all those in authority," especially. Divine rights of kings and divine obligations of subjects.

I want men everywhere to lift up holy hands in prayer, without anger and disputing. (2:8)

No disputes, total submission.

Paul also wants women to behave:

I also want women to dress modestly, with decency and propriety, not with braided hair or gold or pearls or expensive clothes, but with good deeds, appropriate for women who profess to worship God.

A woman should learn in quietness and full submission. I do not permit a woman to teach or to have authority over a man; she must be silent. For Adam was formed first, then Eve. And Adam was not the one deceived; it was the woman who was deceived and became a sinner. But women will be saved through childbearing—if they continue in faith, love and holiness with propriety. (2:9-15)

My comment is my emphasis.

3, 4. Bishops and Deacons; Instructions to Timothy

Paul defines the characteristics of the shepherds of the flock.

Here is a trustworthy saying: If anyone sets his heart on being an overseer, he desires a noble task. Now the overseer must be above reproach, the husband of but one wife, temperate, self-controlled, respectable, hospitable, able to teach, not given to drunkenness, not violent but gentle, not quarrelsome, not a lover of money. He must manage his own family well and see that his children obey him with proper respect. (If anyone does not know how to manage his own family, how can he take care of God's church?) He must not be a recent convert, or he may become conceited and fall under the same judgment as the devil. He must also have a good reputation with outsiders, so that he will not fall into disgrace and into the devil's trap.

Deacons, likewise, are to be men worthy of respect, sincere, not indulging in much wine, and not pursuing dishonest gain.

They must keep hold of the deep truths of the faith with a clear conscience. They must first be tested; and then if there is nothing against them, let them serve as deacons.

In the same way, their wives are to be women worthy of respect, not malicious talkers but temperate and trustworthy in everything.

A deacon must be the husband of but one wife and must manage his children and his household well. Those who have served well gain an excellent standing and great assurance in their faith in Christ Jesus.

The holy family is the cell or molecule of the city of God, and of modern "secular" societies. Monogamy, a firm pater familias, not a lover of money, not too much of a wine drinker, etc. And their wives are not to be "malicious talkers."

5. Advice About Widows, Elders, and Slaves

Do not rebuke an older man harshly, but exhort him as if he were your father. Treat younger men as brothers, older women as mothers, and younger women as sisters, with absolute purity. (5:1-2)

But:

As for younger widows, do not put them on such a list. For when their sensual desires overcome their dedication to Christ, they want to marry. Thus they bring judgment on themselves, because they have broken their first pledge. Besides, they get into the habit of being idle and going about from house to house. And not only do they become idlers, but also gossips and busybodies, saying things they ought not to. So I counsel younger widows to marry, to have children, to manage their homes and to give the enemy no opportunity for slander. Some have in fact already turned away to follow Satan. (5:11-15)

After a melange of concern for and misogynistic prejudice against widows, some relaxation for the patriarchs:

Stop drinking only water, and use a little wine because of your stomach and your frequent illnesses. (5:23)

A perfect blueprint for servitude:

All who are under the yoke of slavery should consider their masters worthy of full respect, so that God's name and our teaching may not be slandered. Those who have believing masters are not to show less respect for them because they are brothers. Instead, they are to serve them even better, because those who benefit from their service are believers, and dear to them. These are the things you are to teach and urge on them. (6:1-2)

Is this brotherly equality or fraternal inequality?

6. Love of Money

Paul places believing in "godly teaching" over human discourse and discussion. ("Unhealthy interest in controversies and quarrels about words" versus the absolute "Word" of the Christian God.) Exclusion not only of other human beings but of other views, too.

If anyone teaches false doctrines and does not agree to the sound instruction of our Lord Jesus Christ and to godly teaching, he is conceited and understands nothing. He has an unhealthy interest in controversies and quarrels about words that result in envy, strife, malicious talk, evil suspicions and constant friction between men of corrupt mind, who have been robbed of the truth and who think that godliness is a means to financial gain.

But godliness with contentment is great gain. For we brought nothing into the world, and we can take nothing out of it. But if we have food and clothing, we will be content with that. People who want to get rich fall into temptation and a trap and into many foolish and harmful desires that plunge men into ruin and destruction. For the love of money is a root of all kinds of evil. Some people, eager for money, have wandered from the faith and pierced themselves with many griefs. (6:3-10)

Concerning Money, Paul is less greedy than the accumulationist Pentateuch but more lukewarm compared to the concessionless Luke. (Cf. supra.) But maybe this is the place where he comes closest to him.

Paul says that God provides men with everything, that riches is not all; but note that there is no critique of wealth or property per se, as shall be the case in *Koran*, too.

God, the blessed and only Ruler, the King of kings and Lord of lords, who alone is immortal and who lives in unapproachable light, whom no one has seen or can see. To him be honor and might forever. Amen.

Command those who are rich in this present world not to be arrogant nor to put their hope in wealth, which is so uncertain, but to put their hope in God, who richly provides us with everything for our enjoyment. Command them to do good, to be rich in good deeds, and to be generous and willing to share. In this way they will lay up treasure for themselves as a firm foundation for the coming age, so that they may take hold of the life that is truly life.

Timothy, guard what has been entrusted. Turn away from godless chatter and
the opposing ideas of what is falsely called knowledge, which some have professed
and in so doing have wandered from the faith. Grace be with you. (6:15-21)

Non-religious talk, rational discourse are "chatter"; difference and plurality of ideas, freedom of thought are antagonistic to true knowledge.

2 TIMOTHY

1, 2. Paul's Authority; A Workman Approved by God

Keep reminding them of these things. Warn them before God against quarreling
about words; it is of no value, and only ruins those who listen. Do your best to present yourself to God as one approved, a workman who does not need to be ashamed
and who correctly handles the word of truth. Avoid godless chatter, because those
who indulge in it will become more and more ungodly. Their teaching will spread
like gangrene. Among them are Hymenaeus and Philetus, who have wandered away
from the truth. They say that the resurrection has already taken place, and they destroy the faith of some. Nevertheless, God's solid foundation stands firm, sealed
with this inscription: "The Lord knows those who are his," and, "Everyone who
confesses the name of the Lord must turn away from wickedness." (2:14-19)

"The Lord knows those who are his" (2:19; Numbers 16:5) and Paul endures "everything
for the sake of the elect" (2:10). And some tautology: godless chatter makes one ungodly.

As there should be no arguments against Moses (and God) (Cf. Numbers, Ch. 16), no
arguments against apostles (and Paul), even among believers:

Flee the evil desires of youth, and pursue righteousness, faith, love and peace, along
with those who call on the Lord out of a pure heart. Don't have anything to do with
foolish and stupid arguments, because you know they produce quarrels. And the
Lord's servant must not quarrel; instead, he must be kind to everyone, able to teach,
not resentful. Those who oppose him he must gently instruct, in the hope that God
will grant them repentance leading them to a knowledge of the truth, and that they
will come to their senses and escape from the trap of the devil, who has taken them
captive to do his will. (2:22-26)

3, 4. Godlessness in the Last Days

But mark this: There will be terrible times in the last days. People will be lovers of
themselves, lovers of money, boastful, proud, abusive, disobedient to their parents,
ungrateful, unholy, without love, unforgiving, slanderous, without self-control,
brutal, not lovers of the good, treacherous, rash, conceited, lovers of pleasure rather
than lovers of God—having a form of godliness but denying its power. Have nothing to do with them. (3:1-5)

Some moral rules, a lot of labeling, and exclusion.

TITUS

1. Titus's Task on Crete

Paul, a servant of God and an apostle of Jesus Christ for the faith of God's elect and the knowledge of the truth that leads to godliness—a faith and knowledge resting on the hope of eternal life, which God, who does not lie, promised before the beginning of time, and at his appointed season he brought his word to light through the preaching entrusted to me by the command of God our Savior. (1:3)

Paul writes to Titus. He describes the qualifications of elders in towns.

An elder must be blameless, the husband of but one wife, a man whose children believe and are not open to the charge of being wild and disobedient. Since an overseer is entrusted with God's work, he must be blameless—not overbearing, not quick-tempered, not given to drunkenness, not violent, not pursuing dishonest gain. Rather he must be hospitable, one who loves what is good, who is self-controlled, upright, holy and disciplined. He must hold firmly to the trustworthy message as it has been taught, so that he can encourage others by sound doctrine and refute those who oppose it. (1:6-9)

The opposers must be silenced, for whom Paul has an arsenal of negative adjectives.

For there are many rebellious people, mere talkers and deceivers, especially those of the circumcision group. They must be silenced, because they are ruining whole households by teaching things they ought not to teach—and that for the sake of dishonest gain. Even one of their own prophets has said, "Cretans are always liars, evil brutes, lazy gluttons." This testimony is true. Therefore, rebuke them sharply, so that they will be sound in the faith and will pay no attention to Jewish myths or to the commands of those who reject the truth. To the pure, all things are pure, but to those who are corrupted and do not believe, nothing is pure. In fact, both their minds and consciences are corrupted. They claim to know God, but by their actions they deny him. They are detestable, disobedient and unfit. (1:10-16)

Paul has a propensity to generalize about whole populations: Cretans are always liars, evil brutes, lazy gluttons.

2. What Must Be Taught to Various Groups

You must teach what is in accord with sound doctrine. Teach the older men to be temperate, worthy of respect, self-controlled, and sound in faith, in love and in endurance.

Likewise, teach the older women to be reverent in the way they live, not to be slanderers or addicted to much wine, but to teach what is good. Then they can train the younger women to love their husbands and children, to be self-controlled and pure, to be busy at home, to be kind, and to be subject to their husbands, so that no one will malign the word of God.

Similarly, encourage the young men to be self-controlled. In everything set them an example by doing what is good. In your teaching show integrity, seriousness and soundness of speech that cannot be condemned, so that those who oppose you may be ashamed because they have nothing bad to say about us.

Teach slaves to be subject to their masters in everything, to try to please them, not to talk back to them, and not to steal from them, but to show that they can be fully trusted, so that in every way they will make the teaching about God our Savior attractive. (2:1-10)

Women are to be trained "to be subject to their husbands" and slaves to be taught "to be subject to their masters in everything." Holy family, holy society.

3. Doing What is Good

The sequencing of this subheading is such that the first good seems to be submission:

Remind the people to be subject to rulers and authorities, to be obedient, to be ready to do whatever is good, to slander no one, to be peaceable and considerate, and to show true humility toward all men. (3:1-2)

Submit, obey, do good. Show humility toward all men, above all to rulers and authorities. Disobedience is foolishness, pleasures are enslavement.

At one time we too were foolish, disobedient, deceived and enslaved by all kinds of passions and pleasures. (3:3)

Avoid controversy, warn twice, then cut off discourse.

But avoid foolish controversies and genealogies and arguments and quarrels about the law, because these are unprofitable and useless. Warn a divisive person once, and then warn him a second time. After that, have nothing to do with him. You may be sure that such a man is warped and sinful; he is self-condemned. (3:9-11)

Debate is divisive. Paul is a long way from the "debate" and "reasoning" of the Acts.

PHILEMON

To Philemon "our fellow worker," to Apphia "our sister," to Archippus "our fellow soldier" (1:1), Paul appeals on behalf of Onesimus, his "son."

Therefore, although in Christ I could be bold and order you to do what you ought to do, yet I appeal to you on the basis of love. (8)

I, Paul, am writing this with my own hand. I will pay it back—not to mention that you owe me your very self. I do wish, brother, that I may have some benefit from you in the Lord; refresh my heart in Christ. Confident of your obedience, I write to you, knowing that you will do even more than I ask.

And one thing more: Prepare a guest room for me, because I hope to be restored to you in answer to your prayers. (19-22)

Fellowship and paternalism combined; request and imposition combined. Note especially: You owe me your very self.

HEBREWS

1. The Son Superior to Angels

In the past God spoke to our forefathers through the prophets at many times and in various ways, but in these last days he has spoken to us by his Son, whom he appointed heir of all things, and through whom he made the universe. The Son is the radiance of God's glory and the exact representation of his being, sustaining all things by his powerful word. After he had provided purification for sins, he sat down at the right hand of the Majesty in heaven. So he became as much superior to the angels as the name he has inherited is superior to theirs.

For to which of the angels did God ever say, "You are my Son; today I have become your Father?"

Or again, "I will be his Father, and he will be my Son?" (1:1-5; Psa. 2:7, 2 Sam. 7:14) Jesus is superior to angels and prophets.

2. Jesus Made Like His Brothers

Jesus, who is superior even to angels and prophets, is now made to be equal to other men.

Both the one who makes men holy and those who are made holy are of the same family. So Jesus is not ashamed to call them brothers. (2:11)

3. Jesus Greater than Moses

Jesus is "the apostle and high priest" (3:1) and greater than Moses:

Jesus has been found worthy of greater honor than Moses, just as the builder of a house has greater honor than the house itself. For every house is built by someone, but God is the builder of everything. Moses was faithful as a servant in all God's house, testifying to what would be said in the future. But Christ is faithful as a son over God's house. And we are his house, if we hold on to our courage and the hope of which we boast. (3:3-6)

Unbelievers are warned: no testing, no rebellion; unconditional belief: Today, if you hear his voice, do not harden your hearts as you did in the rebellion (3:15; Psalm 95:7,8).

4, 5, 6. Sabbath; Jesus the Great High Priest; God's Promise

For the word of God is living and active. Sharper than any double-edged sword, it penetrates even to dividing soul and spirit, joints and marrow; it judges the thoughts and attitudes of the heart. Nothing in all creation is hidden from God's sight. Everything is uncovered and laid bare before the eyes of him to whom we must give account. (4:12-13)

The word (and the idea and the fear) of God is a sword that penetrates the mind and the body and the heart. *Koran* shall have similar graphic things to say.

Jesus is a Jewish high priest.

No one takes this honor upon himself; he must be called by God, just as Aaron was. So Christ also did not take upon himself the glory of becoming a high priest. But God said to him... (5:4-5)

The scripture continues to infantilize men:

We have much to say about this, but it is hard to explain because you are slow to learn. In fact, though by this time you ought to be teachers, you need someone to teach you the elementary truths of God's word all over again. You need milk, not solid food! Anyone who lives on milk, being still an infant, is not acquainted with the teaching about righteousness. But solid food is for the mature, who by constant use have trained themselves to distinguish good from evil. (5:11-14)

7. Jesus Like Melchizedek the Priest

Hebrews plays down the old covenant and the old priesthood. To this end it exalts Melchizedek over Levites and puts Jesus Christ on a par with the former.

Without father or mother, without genealogy, without beginning of days or end of life, like the Son of God he remains a priest forever.

Just think how great he [Melchizedek] was: Even the patriarch Abraham gave him a tenth of the plunder! Now the law requires the descendants of Levi who become priests to collect a tenth from the people—that is, their brothers—even though their brothers are descended from Abraham. (7:3-5)

Without genealogy, yet with genealogy (not from Levi but from Judah):

If perfection could have been attained through the Levitical priesthood (for on the basis of it the law was given to the people), why was there still need for another priest to come—one in the order of Melchizedek, not in the order of Aaron? For when there is a change of the priesthood, there must also be a change of the law. He of whom these things are said belonged to a different tribe, and no one from that tribe has ever served at the altar. For it is clear that our Lord descended from Judah, and in regard to that tribe Moses said nothing about priests. And what we have said is even more clear if another priest like Melchizedek appears, one who has become a priest not on the basis of a regulation as to his ancestry but on the basis of the power of an indestructible life. For it is declared: "You are a priest forever, in the order of Melchizedek."

The former regulation is set aside because it was weak and useless (for the law made nothing perfect), and a better hope is introduced, by which we draw near to God.

And it was not without an oath! Others became priests without any oath, but he became a priest with an oath when God said to him: "The Lord has sworn and will not change his mind: 'You are a priest forever.' "

Because of this oath, Jesus has become the guarantee of a better covenant. (7:11-22; Psalm 110:4)

8. The High Priest of a New Covenant

Christianity is differentiating itself from Judaism:

But the ministry Jesus has received is as superior to theirs as the covenant of which he is mediator is superior to the old one, and it is founded on better promises.

For if there had been nothing wrong with that first covenant, no place would have been sought for another. But God found fault with the people and said: "The time is coming, declares the Lord, when I will make a new covenant with the house of Israel and with the house of Judah.

It will not be like the covenant I made with their forefathers when I took them by the hand to lead them out of Egypt, because they did not remain faithful to my covenant, and I turned away from them, declares the Lord.

This is the covenant I will make with the house of Israel after that time, declares the Lord. I will put my laws in their minds and write them on their hearts. I will be their God, and they will be my people. No longer will a man teach his neighbor, or a man his brother, saying, 'Know the Lord.' because they will all know me, from the least of them to the greatest. For I will forgive their wickedness and will remember their sins no more.

By calling this covenant "new," he has made the first one obsolete; and what is obsolete and aging will soon disappear. (8:6-13)

Continuity or break; supersession or making obsolete? Both. Christianity is both post-Jewish and very Judaic at once. The *New Testament* fulfills the *Old Testament*.

9. From "External Regulations" and Worship to the Blood of Christ (as if the latter were less ritualistic)

Now the first covenant had regulations for worship and also an earthly sanctuary. A tabernacle was set up. In its first room were the lamp stand, the table and the consecrated bread; this was called the Holy Place. Behind the second curtain was a room called the Most Holy Place, which had the golden altar of incense and the gold-covered ark of the covenant. This ark contained the gold jar of manna, Aaron's staff that had budded, and the stone tablets of the covenant. Above the ark were the cherubim of the Glory, overshadowing the atonement cover. But we cannot discuss these things in detail now.

When everything had been arranged like this, the priests entered regularly into the outer room to carry on their ministry. But only the high priest entered the inner room, and that only once a year, and never without blood, which he offered for himself and for the sins the people had committed in ignorance. The Holy Spirit was showing by this that the way into the Most Holy Place had not yet been disclosed as long as the first tabernacle was still standing. This is an illustration for the present time, indicating that the gifts and sacrifices being offered were not able to clear the conscience of the worshiper. They are only a matter of food and drink and various ceremonial washings—external regulations applying until the time of the new order. (9:1-10)

"External regulations" of the first covenant and inadequacies of the old priesthood are neatly summarized. Now the new covenant and the new high priest.

When Christ came as high priest of the good things that are already here, he went through the greater and more perfect tabernacle that is not man-made, that is to say, not a part of this creation. He did not enter by means of the blood of goats and calves; but he entered the Most Holy Place once for all by his own blood, having obtained eternal redemption...

For this reason Christ is the mediator of a new covenant, that those who are called may receive the promised eternal inheritance—now that he has died as a ransom to set them free from the sins committed under the first covenant. (9:11-12,15)

A monotheistic Book can criticize and supplant its predecessor only this much and can hardly make monotheism even more super-human than this.

10. Christ's Sacrifice Once for All

Instead of useless priestly rituals, sacrifice of Jesus.

First he said, "Sacrifices and offerings, burnt offerings and sin offerings you did not desire, nor were you pleased with them" (although the law required them to be made). Then he said, "Here I am, I have come to do your will." He sets aside the first to establish the second. And by that will, we have been made holy through the sacrifice of the body of Jesus Christ once for all. (10:8-10)

The Holy Spirit also testifies to us about this. First he says:

This is the covenant I will make with them after that time, says the Lord. I will put my laws in their hearts, and I will write them on their minds.

Then he adds:

Their sins and lawless acts I will remember no more. (10:15-17; Jer. 31:33-34)

Putting/writing God's laws in/on hearts/minds of men. Remembering their sins no more, which is a nice promise compared to *Old Testament*'s ever remembering and reminding and trapping and punishing.

All the same, the *New Testament* is as harsh as the *Old Testament*, perhaps even harsher, in punishing sin. Both in this world (like the *Old Testament*) by the "hands of the living God," who is active in men's historical present, and in the other world as well (in addition to the *Old Testament*).

> If we deliberately keep on sinning after we have received the knowledge of the truth, no sacrifice for sins is left, but only a fearful expectation of judgment and of raging fire that will consume the enemies of God. Anyone who rejected the law of Moses died without mercy on the testimony of two or three witnesses. How much more severely do you think a man deserves to be punished who has trampled the Son of God under foot, who has treated as an unholy thing the blood of the covenant that sanctified him, and who has insulted the Spirit of grace? For we know him who said, "It is mine to avenge; I will repay," and again, "The Lord will judge his people." It is a dreadful thing to fall into the hands of the living God. (10:26-31)

After all this: trust, be confident, persevere, get saved, etc., if you can.

11. By Faith

Faith is defined and described:

> Now faith is being sure of what we hope for and certain of what we do not see. This is what the ancients were commended for.
>
> By faith we understand that the universe was formed at God's command, so that what is seen was not made out of what was visible. (11:1-3)

> And without faith it is impossible to please God, because anyone who comes to him must believe that he exists and that he rewards those who earnestly seek him. (11:6)

I have nothing to add to or subtract from the text to elucidate its meaning. This is what religion is. By faith Abel, Enoch, Noah, Abraham, Isaac, Jacob, Joseph, and Moses were favored. (Note: "By faith *Abel* offered God a better sacrifice than Cain did. By faith he was commended as a righteous man, when God spoke well of his offerings. And by faith he still speaks, even though he is dead" [11:4].)

> And what more shall I say? I do not have time to tell about Gideon, Barak, Samson, Jephthah, David, Samuel and the prophets, who through faith conquered kingdoms, administered justice, and gained what was promised; who shut the mouths of lions, quenched the fury of the flames, and escaped the edge of the sword; whose weakness was turned to strength; and who became powerful in battle and routed foreign armies. Women received back their dead, raised to life again. (11:32-35)

Such are the rewards of faith, including overpowering enemies, according to the "peaceful" Christianity.

And please also note, in addition to the Godly arbitrariness in the case of Cain and Abel, the *New Testament*'s vindication, among others, of one of the most unjust stories of the *Old Testament*, that of Jacob and Esau:

> See that no one is sexually immoral, or is godless like Esau, who for a single meal sold his inheritance rights as the oldest son. Afterward, as you know, when he wanted to inherit this blessing, he was rejected. He could bring about no change of mind, though he sought the blessing with tears. (12:16-17)

Esau vs. the intriguing Rebekah/the opportunistic Jacob/the heartless Isaac. And it is the latter triumvirate that the *New Testament*, too, upholds. Why? How?

Blind faith! Arbitrary choice! I am who I am. I choose what I choose. I love whom I love. I hate whom I hate. No reasoning, no concern for justice and equality.

And note that the *New Testament* here is more *Old Testament*-like than the *Old Testament* itself: there *was* no mention of Esau's "godless"ness in the original text. Moreover, note the ruthlessly indifferent and dismissive tone of the last two sentences. In what ways is the *New Testament* a new covenant, a new morality; in what ways is it a repetition, reinforcement of the old?

12. God Disciplines His Sons

> "My son, do not make light of the Lord's discipline, and do not lose heart when he rebukes you, because the Lord disciplines those he loves, and he punishes everyone he accepts as a son."
>
> Endure hardship as discipline; God is treating you as sons. For what son is not disciplined by his father? If you are not disciplined (and everyone undergoes discipline), then you are illegitimate children and not true sons. Moreover, we have all had human fathers who disciplined us and we respected them for it. How much more should we submit to the Father of our spirits and live! Our fathers disciplined us for a little while as they thought best; but God disciplines us for our good, that we may share in his holiness. No discipline seems pleasant at the time, but painful. Later on, however, it produces a harvest of righteousness and peace for those who have been trained by it. (12:5-11; Prov. 3:11-12)

God the Father, godly fathers, disciplined and punished sons. Discipline and punishment come as a reward for being loved and accepted as a son. They also bring holiness and peace. Submit to the authorities and be happy. Christianity is supposedly more cheerful and joyous than Judaism. So is its God.

> You have not come to a mountain that can be touched and that is burning with fire; to darkness, gloom and storm; to a trumpet blast or to such a voice speaking words that those who heard it begged no further word be spoken to them, because they could not bear what was commanded: If even an animal touches the mountain, it must be stoned. The sight was so terrifying Moses said, "I am trembling with fear."

But you have come to Mount Zion, to the heavenly Jerusalem, the city of the living God. You have come to thousands upon thousands of angels in joyful assembly, to the church of the firstborn, whose names are written in heaven. You have come to God, the judge of all men, to the spirits of righteous men made perfect, to Jesus the mediator of a new covenant, and to the sprinkled blood that speaks a better word than the blood of Abel. (12:18-24)

The God of Christianity, nonetheless, proves not much less terrifying than that of Judaism.

See to it that you do not refuse him who speaks. If they did not escape when they refused him who warned them on earth, how much less will we, if we turn away from him who warns us from heaven? At that time his voice shook the earth, but now he has promised. Once more I will shake not only the earth but also the heavens. The words "once more" indicate the removing of what can be shaken—that is, created things—so that what cannot be shaken may remain.

Therefore, since we are receiving a kingdom that cannot be shaken, let us be thankful, and so worship God acceptably with reverence and awe, for our "God is a consuming fire." (12:25-29; Hag. 2:6, Deut. 4:24)

God as consuming fire will become a favorite motif of *Koran*, too.

13. Concluding Exhortations

Love each other as brothers, entertain strangers, remember those in prison, honor marriage, keep the marriage bed pure, be content with what you have, and "keep your lives free from the love of money" (13:5). A list of good morals, but the "money" part does not convince me. Listen to your religious leaders:

Remember your leaders, who spoke the word of God to you. Consider the outcome of their way of life and imitate their faith. Jesus Christ is the same yesterday and today and forever. (13:7-8)

Submit to the authorities:

Obey your leaders and submit to their authority. They keep watch over you as men who must give an account. Obey them so that their work will be a joy, not a burden, for that would be of no advantage to you. (13:17)

A tint of veiled blackmail.

Notes
1. All of which, in the final analysis, including Islam, can be reduced to "One Commandment": FEAR! Be God-fearing peoples!
2. Or "It is good for a man not to have sexual relations with a woman" (fn. b1, p. 851).
3. Remember Genesis: "man, male and female."
4. Or "flesh" (fn. a13, p. 868).

GENERAL EPISTLES

JAMES

1. Trials and Temptations

James addresses "the twelve tribes scattered among nations."

> The brother in humble circumstances ought to take pride in his high position. But the one who is rich should take pride in his low position, because he will pass away like a wild flower. For the sun rises with scorching heat and withers the plant; its blossom falls and its beauty is destroyed. In the same way, the rich man will fade away even while he goes about his business. (1:9-11)

James defines religion: "Religion that God our Father accepts as pure and faultless is this: "to look after orphans and widows in their distress and to keep one self from being polluted by the world" (1:27).

2. Favoritism Forbidden; Faith and Deeds

> If you show special attention to the man wearing fine clothes and say, "Here's a good seat for you," but say to the poor man, "You stand there" or "Sit on the floor by my feet," have you not discriminated among yourselves and become judges with evil thoughts?
>
> Listen, my dear brothers: Has not God chosen those who are poor in the eyes of the world to be rich in faith and to inherit the kingdom he promised those who love him? But you have insulted the poor. Is it not the rich who are exploiting you? Are they not the ones who are dragging you into court? Are they not the ones who are slandering the noble name of him to whom you belong?
>
> If you really keep the royal law found in Scripture, "Love your neighbor as yourself," you are doing right. But if you show favoritism, you sin and are convicted by the law as lawbreakers. For whoever keeps the whole law and yet stumbles at just one point is guilty of breaking all of it. (2:3-10)

"Is it not the rich who are exploiting you?" This is the one and only instance in the *New Testament* where "exploitation" is mentioned. Still, the main ideas of the equality of rich and poor and impartiality toward both are predominant.

On faith and deeds:

You see that a person is justified by what he does and not by faith alone...As the body without the spirit is dead, so faith without deeds is dead. (2:24 and 26)

This, in its emphasis on deeds, stands out in contradistinction to Paul's "faith over works."

3. Taming and Tongue; Two Kinds of Wisdom

Who is wise and understanding among you? Let him show it by his good life, by deeds done in the humility that comes from wisdom. But if you harbor bitter envy and selfish ambition in your hearts, do not boast about it or deny the truth. Such "wisdom" does not come down from heaven but is earthly, unspiritual, of the devil. For where you have envy and selfish ambition, there you find disorder and every evil practice.

But the wisdom that comes from heaven is first of all pure; then peace-loving, considerate, submissive, full of mercy and good fruit, impartial and sincere. Peace-makers who sow in peace raise a harvest of righteousness. (3:13-18)

Again, deeds and works, not only faith.

4. Submit Yourselves to God

What causes fights and quarrels among you? Don't they come from your desires that battle within you? You want something but don't get it. You kill and covet, but you cannot have what you want. You quarrel and fight. You do not have, because you do not ask God. When you ask, you do not receive, because you ask with wrong motives, that you may spend what you get on your pleasures.

You adulterous people, don't you know that friendship with the world is hatred toward God? Anyone who chooses to be a friend of the world becomes an enemy of God. (4:1-4)

James is less this-worldly than Paul.

James admonishes the sinners: "You double-minded." (4:8)

Now listen, you who say, "Today or tomorrow we will go to this or that city, spend a year there, carry on business and make money." Why, you do not even know what will happen tomorrow. What is your life? You are a mist that appears for a little while and then vanishes. Instead, you ought to say. "If it is the Lord's will, we will live and do this or that." As it is, you boast and brag. All such boasting is evil. Anyone, than, who knows the good he ought to do and doesn't do it, sins. (4:13-17)

Some more critique of business and money.

5. Warning to Rich Oppressors; Patience in Suffering

But the critique is less of wealth per se than of "bad" capitalists.

> Now listen, you rich people, weep and wail because of the misery that is coming upon you. Your wealth has rotted, and moths have eaten your clothes. Your gold and silver are corroded. Their corrosion will testify against you and eat your flesh like fire. You have hoarded wealth in the last days. Look! The wages you failed to pay the workmen who moved your fields are crying out against you. The cries of the harvesters have reached the ears of the Lord Almighty. You have lived on earth in luxury and self-indulgence. You have fattened yourselves in the day of slaughter. You have condemned and murdered innocent men, who were not opposing you. (5:1-5)

Immediately after this barrage of criticism hurled at the rich, James urges the poor to be patient and ungrumbling.

> Be patient, then, brothers, until the Lord's coming. See how the farmer waits for the land to yield its valuable crop and how patient he is for the autumn and spring rains. You too, be patient and stand firm, because the Lord's coming is near. Don't grumble against each other, brothers, or you will be judged. The Judge is standing at the door!
>
> Brothers, as an example of patience in the face of suffering, take the prophets who spoke in the name of the Lord. As you know, we consider blessed those who have persevered. You have heard of Job's perseverance and have seen what the Lord finally brought about. The Lord is full of compassion and mercy.
>
> Above all, my brothers, do not swear—not by heaven or by earth or by anything else. Let your "Yes" be yes, and your "No," no, or you will be condemned. (5:7-12)

Apparently, it is the prerogative of apostles to admonish the "bad" filthy rich; the oppressed people should not even grumble, let alone take action. Submission in this world, expectation of riches in the other one. A basic function of religion(s) is fulfilled: Job's perseverance; no class-struggle, no revolution or rebellion. (See *Koran* below, esp. Ta-Ha sura, and remember Numbers, Ch. 16 above.)

1 PETER

1. Praise God; Be Holy
Peter addresses "God's elect":

> As obedient children, do not conform to the evil desires you had when you lived in ignorance. But just as he who called you is holy, so be holy in all you do; for it is written: "Be holy, because I am holy."
>
> Since you call on a Father who judges each man's work impartially, live your lives as strangers here in reverent fear. For you know that it was not with perishable things such as silver or gold that you were redeemed from the empty way of life handed down to you from your forefathers, but with the precious blood of Christ, a lamb without blemish or defect. He was chosen before the creation of the world, but was revealed in these last times for your sake. Through him you believe in God, who raised him from the dead and glorified him, and so your faith and hope are in God. (1:16-21)

Human life to be "live(d) in reverent fear" and "as strangers."

2. A Chosen People; Submission to Rulers and Masters
Infantilization continues:

> Therefore, rid yourselves of all malice and all deceit, hypocrisy, envy, and slander of every kind. Like newborn babies, crave pure spiritual milk, so that by it you may grow up in your salvation, now that you have tasted that the Lord is good. (2:1-3)

> But you are a chosen people, a royal priesthood, a holy nation, a people belonging to God, that you may declare the praises of him who called you out of darkness into his wonderful light. Once you were not a people, but now you are the people of God; once you had not received mercy, but now you have received mercy. (2:9-10)

The ethnic-tribal supremacy of the *Old Testament* is replaced by the religious-communal supremacy of the *New Testament*. Exhortation to submit, too, continues:

> Submit yourselves for the Lord's sake to every authority instituted among men: whether to the king, as the supreme authority, or to governors, who are sent by him to punish those who do wrong and to commend those who do right. For it is God's will that by doing good you should silence the ignorant talk of foolish men. Live as free men, but do not use your freedom as a cover-up for evil; live as servants of God. Show proper respect to everyone: Love the brotherhood of believers, fear God, honor the king.
>
> Slaves, submit yourselves to your masters with all respect, not only to those who are good and considerate, but also to those who are harsh. (2:13-18)

Now, this is total, categorical, and unequivocal: Submit to every authority instituted among men—king, governors. Who are sent by God to punish... Freedom balanced with servitude. Fear God, honor the king. Freedom is living in reverent fear of and in obedience to even harsh masters. And the disarming example of Christ is given:

> When they hurled their insults at him, he did not retaliate; when he suffered, he made no threats. Instead, he entrusted himself to him who judges justly. He himself bore our sins in his body on the tree, so that we might die to sins and live for righteousness; by his wounds you have been healed. For you were like sheep going astray, but now you have returned to the Shepherd and Overseer of your souls. (2:23-25)

3. Wives and Husbands and Suffering for Doing Good

> Wives, in the same way be submissive to your husbands so that, if any of them do not believe the word, they may be won over without words by the behavior of their wives, when they see the purity and reverence of your lives. Your beauty should not come from outward adornment, such as braided hair and the wearing of gold jewelry and fine clothes. Instead, it should be that of your inner self, the unfading beauty of a gentle and quiet spirit, which is of great worth in God's sight. For this is the way the holy women of the past who put their hope in God used to make themselves beautiful. They were submissive to their own husbands, like Sarah, who obeyed Abraham and called him her master. You are her daughters if you do what is right and do not give way to fear.
>
> Husbands, in the same way be considerate as you live with your wives, and treat them with respect as the weaker partner and as heirs with you of the gracious gift of life, so that nothing will hinder your prayers. (3:1-7)

Wives! Submit to husbands as the "weaker" (and inferior) partner. Take as your role model Sarah "who obeyed Abraham and called him her master"—which master had marketed her. *New Testament* does not repudiate *Old Testament*'s even most dubious ethics. (Nor does the *Koran*, which shall also elaborate on veiling the woman, that is in embryo here.)

Also: "Do not repay evil with evil or insult with insult" (3:9).

And: "It is better, if it is God's will, to suffer for doing good than for doing evil" (3:17).

4. Living for God

> For you have spent enough time in the past doing what pagans choose to do—living in debauchery, lust, drunkenness, orgies, carousing and detestable idolatry...
>
> The end of all things is near. Therefore be clear minded and self-controlled so that you can pray. Above all, love each other deeply, because love covers over a multitude of sins. (4:3,7-8)

5. The Elders and Young Men

> To the elders among you, I appeal as a fellow elder, a witness of Christ's sufferings and one who also will share in the glory to be revealed: Be shepherds of God's flock that is under your care, serving as overseers—not because you must, but because you are willing, as God wants you to be; not greedy for money, but eager to serve; not lording it over those entrusted to you, but being examples to the flock. And when the Chief Shepherd appears, you will receive the crown of glory that will never fade.
>
> Young men, in the same way be submissive to those who are older. All of you, clothe yourselves with humility toward one another, because, "God opposes the proud but gives grace to the humble." (5:1-5)

God → Chief Shepherd → shepherds → flock.

Shepherds to have no greed for money? If this is not the rhetorical but essential message of the *New Testament* (or *Koran*), which I do not think it is, then all Christian (and Muslim) capitalists are in violation of their Book(s). (Remember James 2:10.)

2 PETER

1. Making One's Calling and Election Sure
Exchange of this world for the other:

> His divine power has given us everything we need for life and godliness through our knowledge of him who called us by his own glory. Through these he has given us his very great and precious promises, so that through them you may participate in the divine nature and escape the corruption in the world caused by evil desires.
>
> For this very reason, make every effort to add to your faith goodness; and to goodness, knowledge; and to knowledge, self-control; and to self-control, persever-ance; and to perseverance, godliness; and to godliness, brotherly kindness; and to brotherly kindness, love. (1:3-7)

All of the holy sort, to be sure.

Godly legitimacy of prophets is emphasized. Men have no will to, and capacity for, in-terpretation:

> Above all, you must understand that no prophecy of Scripture came about by the prophet's own interpretation. For prophecy never had its origin in the will of man, but men spoke from God as they were carried along by the Holy Spirit. (1:20-21)

2. False Teachers and Their Destruction
Peter warns against false prophets.

> This is especially true of those who follow the corrupt desire of the sinful nature and despise authority...

They are like brute beasts, creatures of instinct, born only to be caught and destroyed, and like beasts they too will perish.

They will be paid back with harm for the harm they have done. Their idea of pleasure is to carouse in broad daylight. They are blots and blemishes, reveling in their pleasures while they feast with you. With eyes full of adultery, they never stop sinning; they seduce the unstable; they are experts in greed—an accursed brood! (2:10,12-14)

These men are springs without water and mists driven by a storm. Blackest darkness is reserved for them. For they mouth empty, boastful words and, by appealing to the lustful desires of sinful human nature, they entice people who are just escaping from those who live in error. They promise them freedom, while they themselves are slaves of depravity—for a man is a slave to whatever has mastered him. (2:17-19)

Such is not a very soft language. The *New Testament* can be as full of invective and vituperation as the *Old Testament*. And: "A dog returns to its vomit" (2:22; Prov.26:11).

3. The Day of the Lord

By the same word the present heavens and earth are reserved for fire, being kept for the day of judgment and destruction of ungodly men. (3:3-7)

But the day of the Lord will come like a thief. The heavens will disappear with a roar; the elements will be destroyed by fire, and the earth and everything in it will be laid bare.

Since everything will be destroyed in this way, what kind of people ought you to be? You ought to live holy and godly lives as you look forward to the day of God and speed its coming. That day will bring about the destruction of the heavens by fire, and the elements will melt in the heat. But in keeping with his promise we are looking forward to a new heaven and a new earth, the home of righteousness. (3:10-13)

Fire, catastrophe, Lord coming like a thief—all of these are to be adopted by *Koran*. And it is certainly not convincing that this God does not want anyone to perish.

Peter acknowledges Paul:

Bear in mind that our Lord's patience means salvation, just as our dear brother Paul also wrote you with the wisdom that God gave him. He writes the same way in all his letters, speaking in them of these matters. His letters contain some things that are hard to understand, which ignorant and unstable people distort, as they do the other Scriptures, to their own destruction. (3:15-16)

1 JOHN

1. The Word of Life; Walking in the Light

We are sinners anyway:

> If we claim to be without sin, we deceive ourselves and the truth is not in us. If we confess our sins, he is faithful and just and will forgive us our sins and purify us from all unrighteousness. If we claim we have not sinned, we make him out to be a liar and his word has no place in our lives. (1:8-10)

Therefore, perish, or live with the continual fear of perishing.

2. Do Not Love the World; Be Warned Against Antichrists

Love is light; hate is darkness.

Do not love the world; love the Father:

> Do not love the world or anything in the world. If anyone loves the world, the love of the Father is not in him. For everything in the world—the cravings of sinful man, the lust of his eyes and the boasting of what he has and does—comes not from the Father but from the world. The world and its desires pass away, but the man who does the will of God lives forever. (2:15-17)

Antichrist is defined:

> Who is the liar? It is the man who denies that Jesus is the Christ. Such a man is the antichrist—he denies the Father and the Son. No one who denies the Son has the Father; whoever acknowledges the Son has the Father also. (2:22-23)

Muslims, for example, are by definition antichrist.

3. Children of God; Love One Another

Tautologies abound:

> Everyone who sins breaks the law; in fact, sin is lawlessness. But you know that he appeared so that he might take away our sins. And in him is no sin. No one who lives in him keeps on sinning. No one who continues to sin has either seen him or known him. (3:4-6)

And:

> This is how we know who the children of God are and who the children of the devil are: Anyone who does not do what is right is not a child of God; nor is anyone who does not love his brother. (3:10)

Love and help:

> This is how we know what love is: Jesus Christ laid down his life for us. And we ought to lay down our lives for our brothers. If anyone has material possessions and

sees his brother in need but has no pity on him, how can the love of God be in him? (3:16-17)

Pity, charity, almsgiving.

God is omniscient and omnipotent:

God is greater then our hearts, and he knows everything. (3:20)

4. God's Love and Ours

Dear friends, let us love one another, for love comes from God. Everyone who loves has been born of God and knows God. Whoever does not love does not know God, because God is love. This is how God showed his love among us: He sent his one and only Son into the world that we might live through him. This is love: not that we loved God, but that he loved us and sent his Son as an atoning sacrifice for our sins. Dear friends, since God so loved us, we also ought to love one another. No one has ever seen God; but if we love one another, God lives in us and his love is made complete in us. (4:7-12)

God is love. Whoever lives in love lives in God, and God in him. (4:16)

And he has given us this command: Whoever loves God must also love his brother. (4:21)

"We" are from God, "they" are not from God; love comes from God not from human beings; love for Godly Christian brothers not for other human beings.

5. Faith in the Son of God

This is love for God: to obey his commands. And his commands are not burdensome, for everyone born of God overcomes the world. This is the victory that has overcome the world, even our faith. Who is it that overcomes the world? Only he who believes that Jesus is the Son of God. (5:3-5)

Muslims do not believe that Jesus is the Son of God; therefore: "clash of civilizations" and, earlier, crusades.

2 JOHN

To the "chosen lady":

And now, dear lady, I am not writing you a new command but one we have had from the beginning. I ask that we love one another. And this is love: that we walk in obedience to his commands. As you have heard from the beginning, his command is that you walk in love. (5-6)

Anyone who runs ahead and does not continue in the teaching of Christ does not have God; whoever continues in the teaching has both the Father and the Son. If anyone comes to you and does not bring this teaching, do not take him into your house or welcome him. Anyone who welcomes him shares in his wicked work. (9-13)

Love is defined as walking in obedience to God's commands, that is, a sharing of belief in God. Otherwise, exclusion.

3 JOHN

Dear friend, do not imitate what is evil but what is good. Anyone who does what is good is from God. Anyone who does what is evil has not seen God. (11)

Doing what is good is from God; it cannot be from human beings.

JUDE

Jude warns against godless men:

I felt I had to write and urge you to contend for the faith that was once for all entrusted to the saints. For certain men whose condemnation was written about long ago have secretly slipped in among you. They are godless men, who change the grace of our God into a license for immorality and deny Jesus Christ our only Sovereign and Lord.

Though you already know all this, I want to remind you that the Lord delivered his people out of Egypt, but later destroyed those who did not believe. And the angels who did not keep their positions of authority but abandoned their own home—these he has kept in darkness, bound with everlasting chains for judgment on the great Day. In a similar way, Sodom and Gomorrah and the surrounding towns gave themselves up to sexual immorality and perversion. They serve as an example of those who suffer the punishment of eternal fire.

In the very same way, these dreamers pollute their own bodies, reject authority and slander celestial beings. But even the archangel Michael, when he was disputing with the devil about the body of Moses, did not dare to bring a slanderous accusation against him, but said, "The Lord rebuke you!" Yet these men speak abusively against whatever they do not understand; and what things they do understand by instinct, like unreasoning animals—these are the very things that destroy them.

Woe to them! They have taken the way of Cain; they have rushed for profit into Balaam's error; they have been destroyed in Korah's rebellion. (3:11)

The softer, more "universalistic" and "compassionate" Christianity thus condones, as the *Koran* shall do, among others, one of the most ruthless and unjust stories of Judaism, Korah's rebellion, Numbers Ch. 16.

Such men "are grumblers and faultfinders; they follow their own evil desires..." (16).

But, dear friends, remember what the apostles of our Lord Jesus Christ foretold. They said to you, "In the last times there will be scoffers who will follow their own ungodly desires." These are the men who divide you, who follow mere natural instincts and do not have the Spirit.

But you, dear friends, build yourselves up in your most holy faith and pray in the Holy Spirit. Keep yourselves in God's love as you wait for the mercy of our Lord Jesus Christ to bring you to eternal life.

Be merciful to those who doubt; snatch others from the fire and save them; to others show mercy, mixed with fear—hating even the clothing stained by corrupted flesh. (17-23)

And doxology:

To him who is able to keep you from falling and to present you before his glorious presence without fault and with great joy—to the only God our Savior be glory, majesty, power and authority, through Jesus Christ our Lord, before all ages, now and forevermore! Amen. (24-25)

REVELATION

1. Son of Man

John, to the seven churches in the province of Asia (Ephesus, Smyrna, Pergamum, Thyatira, Sardis, Philadelphia, Laodicea), writes on a scroll upon the instruction of the Spirit.

Jesus Christ, "who is, and who was, and who is to come" is the "ruler of the kings of the earth" (1:4-5) and "has made us to be a kingdom and priests to serve his God and Father" (1:6).

Every believer to become a priest. What a promise of election and elitism!

2, 3. To the Churches

John writes in a tone which is both cajoling and threatening.

> Ephesus: "To him who overcomes, I will give the right to eat from the tree of life, which is in the paradise of God." (2:7)

What a generous promise compared to Genesis!

> Smyrna: "He who overcomes, will not be hurt at all by the second death." (2:11)

Promise of immortality?

> Pergamum: "Repent therefore! Otherwise, I will soon come to you and will fight against them with the sword of my mouth." (2:16)

REPENT or PERISH! That's the real message.

> Thyatira: "You tolerate that woman Jezebel, who calls herself a prophetess." (2:20)

> I have given her time to repent of her immorality, but she is unwilling. So I will cast her on a bed of suffering, and I will make those who commit adultery with her suffer intensely, unless they repent of her ways. I will strike her children dead. Then all the churches will know that I am he who searches hearts and minds, and I will repay each of you according to your deeds. (2:21-23)

To him who overcomes and does my will to the end, I will give authority over the nations—'He will rule them with an iron scepter; he will dash them to pieces like pottery'—just as I have received authority from my Father. (2:26-27)

The *Old Testament* is everywhere in the *New Testament*: Ruling other nations, dashing them to pieces like pottery; striking children ("little ones") dead for their parents' sins, collective punishment. No lex talionis between men, but still retaliation by God himself.

Sardis: "...obey it, and repent. But if you do not make up, I will come like a thief, and you will not know at what time I will come to you" (3:3). "He who overcomes...I will never blot out his name from the book of life..." (3:5)

REPENT or PERISH!

Philadelphia: "I will make those who are of the synagogue of Satan, who claim to be Jews though they are not, but are liars—I will make them come and fall down at your feet and acknowledge that I have loved you." (3:9)

Laodicea: So, because you are lukewarm—neither hot nor cold—I am about to spit you out of my mouth. You say, 'I am rich; I have acquired wealth and do not need a thing.' But you do not realize that you are wretched, pitiful, poor, blind and naked. I counsel you to buy from me gold refined in the fire, so you can become rich; and white clothes to wear, so you can cover your shameful nakedness; and salve to put on your eyes, so you can see.

Those whom I love I rebuke and discipline. So be earnest, and repent. (3:16-19)

This is less a critique of wealth than faithlessness. In fact, just the reverse is the case: Faith legitimizes wealth, which is basically a good thing in the Judeo-Christian, and all Abrahamic, tradition. Epistemology of Genesis sustained.

4. The Throne in Heaven

"You are worthy, our Lord and God, to receive glory and honor and power, for you created all things, and by your will they were created and have their being." (4:11)

5. The Scroll and the Lamb

Then one of the elders said to me, "Do not weep! See, the Lion of the tribe of Judah, the Root of David, has triumphed. He is able to open the scroll and its seven seals." (5:5)

Jesus: both Lamb and Lion, and of royal roots.

"You are worthy to take the scroll and to open its seals, because you were slain, and with your blood you purchased men for God from every tribe and language and people and nation. You have made them to be a kingdom and priests to serve our God, and they will reign on the earth." (5:9-10)

6. The First Six of the Seven Seals

The Lamb opens the first four seals: white, red, black, pale horses come out; their riders hold a bow, a sword, a pair of scales, and the power to kill, respectively:

> Its rider was named Death, and Hades was following close behind him. They were given power over a fourth of the earth to kill by sword, famine and plague, and by the wild beasts of the earth.
>
> When he opened the fifth seal, I saw under the altar the souls of those who had been slain because of the word of God and the testimony they had maintained. They called out in a loud voice, "How long, Sovereign Lord, holy and true, until you judge the inhabitants of the earth and avenge our blood?" Then each of them was given a white robe, and they were told to wait a little longer, until the number of their fellow servants and brothers who were to be killed as they had been was completed. (6:8-11)

And:

> I watched as he opened the sixth seal. There was a great earthquake. The sun turned black like sackcloth made of goat hair, the whole moon turned blood red, and the stars in the sky fell to earth, as late figs drop from a fig tree when shaken by a strong wind. The sky receded like a scroll, rolling up, and every mountain and island was removed from its place.
>
> Then the kings of the earth, the princes, the generals, the rich, the mighty, and every slave and every free man hid in caves and among the rocks of the mountains. They called to the mountains and the rocks, "Fall on us and hide us from the face of him who sits on the throne and from the wrath of the Lamb! For the great day of their wrath has come, and who can stand?" (6:12-17)

7. (Only) 144,000 Sealed to be Saved

Some vital, and mortal, statistics; and a veritable Christian "passover."

> After this I saw four angels standing at the four corners of the earth, holding back the four winds of the earth to prevent any wind from blowing on the land or on the sea or on any tree. Then I saw another angel coming up from the east, having the seal of the living God. He called out in a loud voice to the four angels who had been given power to harm the land and the sea: "Do not harm the land or the sea or the trees until we put a seal on the foreheads of the servants of our God." Then I heard the number of those who were sealed: 144,000 from all the tribes of Israel.
>
> From the tribe of Judah 12,000 were sealed, from the tribe of Reuben 12,000, from the tribe of Gad 12,000, from the tribe of Asher 12,000, from the tribe of Naphtali 12,000, from the tribe of Manasseh 12,000, from the tribe of Simeon 12,000, from the tribe of Levi 12,000, from the tribe of Issachar 12,000, from the

tribe of Zebulun 12,000, from the tribe of Joseph 12,000, from the tribe of Benjamin 12,000.

After this I looked and there before me was a great multitude that no one could count, from every nation, tribe, people and language, standing before the throne and in front of the Lamb. They were wearing white robes and were holding palm branches in their hands. And they cried out in a loud voice: "Salvation belongs to our God, who sits on the throne, and to the Lamb."

And he said, "These are they who have come out of the great tribulation; they have washed their robes and made them white in the blood of the Lamb. Therefore, "they are before the throne of God and serve him day and night in his temple; and he who sits on the throne will spread his tent over them. Never again will they hunger; never again will they thirst. The sun will not beat upon them, nor any scorching heat.

For the Lamb at the center of the throne will be their shepherd; he will lead them to springs of living water. And God will wipe away every tear from their eyes." (7:9-10, 14-17)

8, 9. The Seventh Seal and the First Six of the Seven Trumpets

The Lamb opens the seventh seal; half an hour's silence, seven angels with trumpets, another angel with a golden censer; thunder, rumblings, flashes of lightening, earthquake.

The first angel sounded his trumpet, and there came hail and fire mixed with blood, and it was hurled down upon the earth. A third of the earth was burned up, a third of the trees were burned up, and all the green grass was burned up.

The second angel sounded his trumpet, and something like a huge mountain, all ablaze, was thrown into the sea. A third of the sea turned into blood, a third of the living creatures in the sea died, and a third of the ships were destroyed.

The third angel sounded his trumpet, and a great star, blazing like a torch, fell from the sky on a third of the rivers and on the springs of water—the name of the star is Wormwood. A third of the waters turned bitter, and many people died from the waters that had become bitter.

The fourth angel sounded his trumpet, and a third of the sun was struck, a third of the moon, and a third of the stars, so that a third of them turned dark. A third of the day was without light, and also a third of the night. (8:7-12)

As God had promised in the *Old Testament*, not total destruction of nature but only 1/3 destruction. Still as terrifying, if not more, as anything in the *New Testament*'s predecessor.

As I watched, I heard an eagle that was flying in midair call out in a loud voice: "Woe! Woe! Woe to the inhabitants of the earth, because of the trumpet blasts about to be sounded by the other three angels!" (8:13)

The fifth angel sounded his trumpet, and I saw a star that had fallen from the sky to the earth. The star was given the key to the shaft of the Abyss. When he opened the Abyss, smoke rose from it like the smoke from a gigantic furnace. The sun and sky were darkened by the smoke from the Abyss. And out of the smoke locusts came down upon the earth and were given power like that of scorpions of the earth. They were told not to harm the grass of the earth or any plant or tree, but only those people who did not have the seal of God on their foreheads. They were not given power to kill them, but only to torture them for five months. And the agony they suffered was like that of the sting of a scorpion when it strikes a man. During those days men will seek death, but will not find it; they will long to die, but death will elude them.

The locusts looked like horses prepared for battle. On their heads they wore something like crowns of gold, and their faces resembled human faces. Their hair was like women's hair, and their teeth were like lions' teeth. They had breastplates like breastplates of iron, and the sound of their wings was like the thundering of many horses and chariots rushing into battle. They had tails and stings like scorpions, and in their tails they had power to torment people for five months. They had as king over them the angel of the Abyss, whose name in Hebrew is Abaddon, and in Greek, Apollyon. (9:1-11)

Torture for 5 months, even death eluding the tortured ones. (Remember Deuteronomy, Ch. 28.)

The first woe is past; two other woes are yet to come.

The sixth angel sounded his trumpet, and I heard a voice coming from the horns of the golden altar that is before God. It said to the sixth angel who had the trumpet, "Release the four angels who are bound at the great river Euphrates." *And the four angels who had been kept ready for this very hour and day and month and year were released to kill a third of mankind.* [Emphasis mine.] The number of the mounted troops was two hundred million. I heard their number.

The horses and riders I saw in my vision looked like this: Their breastplates were fiery red, dark blue, and yellow as sulfur. The heads of the horses resembled the heads of lions, and out of their mouths came fire, smoke and sulfur. A third of mankind was killed by the three plagues of fire, smoke and sulfur that came out of their mouths. The power of the horses was in their mouths and in their tails; for their tails were like snakes, having heads with which they inflict injury.

The rest of mankind that were not killed by these plagues still did not repent of the work of their hands; they did not stop worshiping demons, and idols of gold, silver, bronze, stone and wood—idols that cannot see or hear or walk. Nor did they repent of their murders, their magic arts, their sexual immorality or their thefts. (9:12-21)

First premeditated torture, then premeditated murder, genocide. What kind of a religion of salvation is this? Mortal statistics: As God had promised in Genesis, not all but only 1/3 of mankind is killed by a 200 million strong troop, or death army, that "had been kept ready for this very hour." Premeditation. Malice aforethought. Fire, smoke, sulfur. No repentance yet: Idolatry, magic, murder, theft, sexual immorality continues. Man is incorrigible in his sinful nature, whereas monotheistic worship, Godly miracle, divine murder, and so forth, are righteousness.

10. The Angel and the Little Scroll

The angel gives the little scroll to John:

> "Take it and eat it. It will turn your stomach sour, but in your mouth it will be as sweet as honey." I took the little scroll from the angel's hand and ate it. It tasted as sweet as honey in my mouth, but when I had eaten it, my stomach turned sour. Then I was told, "You must prophesy again about many peoples, nations, languages and kings." (10:9-11)

11. The Seventh Trumpet

Only 7,000 are killed in the interim:

> At that very hour there was a severe earthquake and a tenth of the city collapsed. Seven thousand people were killed in the earthquake, and the survivors were terrified and gave glory to the God of heaven.
>
> The second woe has passed; the third woe is coming soon. (11:13-14)

The seventh angel sounds his trumpet:

> Then God's temple in heaven was opened, and within his temple was seen the ark of his covenant. And there came flashes of lightning, rumblings, peals of thunder, an earthquake and a great hailstorm. (11:19)

12. The Woman and the Dragon

> The dragon stood in front of the woman who was about to give birth, so that he might devour her child the moment it was born. She gave birth to a son, a male child, who will rule all the nations with an iron scepter. And her child was snatched up to God and to his throne. (12:4-5)

There takes place a war in heaven between Michael and his angel, and the dragon and his angels.

> The great dragon was hurled down—that ancient serpent called the devil, or Satan, who leads the whole world astray. He was hurled to the earth, and his angels with him. (12:9)

Etc., etc.

13. The Beasts out of the Sea and the Earth

A beast comes out of the sea. Ten horns, seven heads, ten crowns on his horns. A mixture of leopard, bear, lion. The dragon gives the beast his power, throne, and authority to blaspheme God and to make war against him and his saint. Then another beast comes out of the earth. And then:

> This calls for wisdom. If anyone has insight, let him calculate the number of the beast, for it is man's number. His number is 666. (13:18)

Obviously, this calls for cabalistic and, perhaps, gnostic wisdom. But the association between man and beast, who is to be killed, stands out.

14. The Lamb and the 144,000; Harvest of the Earth

> Then I looked, and there before me was the Lamb, standing on Mount Zion, and with him 144,000 who had his name and his Father's name written on their foreheads. And I heard a sound from heaven like the roar of rushing waters and like a loud peal of thunder. The sound I heard was like that of harpists playing their harps. And they sang a new song before the throne and before the four living creatures and the elders. No one could learn the song except the 144,000 who had been redeemed from the earth. These are those who did not defile themselves with women, for they kept themselves pure. They follow the Lamb wherever he goes. They were purchased from among men and offered as firstfruits to God and the Lamb. No lie was found in their mouths; they are blameless. (14:1-5)

The elect, the "sealed," the "redeemed," the "purchased" 144,000 are "those who did not defile themselves with women" and "kept themselves pure" (14:4). They are the "pure virgins" (Cf. supra), the pure male-virgins who are given to Jesus the Lord. They are as few as 144,000; they are a small "remnant."

Please also note the generic use of "women" here, as distinct from prostitutes. Isn't this unequivocal misogyny?

The few pure holy elect men are both virgins and seeds. They are both the harvested (fished, caught as fish) and the harvesters, who plant themselves as seed. But this is as yet vaguely emergent in the *New Testament*. We shall have to await the *Koran* for a more distinct use of this metaphor. *Koran* will adapt and adopt it: Men as seed and planter of seed and women—female virgins—as the soil and the field to be "cultivated" by men. In this, the Third Book, closer in this respect and in many others to the First Book, is obviously more heterosexual than the Second Book, and less misogynist than macho.

One angel says fear and worship God, another tells that Babylon has fallen, a third says that those who worship the beast "will be tormented with burning sulfur" (14:10). Other angels appear and announce that "the harvest of the earth is ripe" (14:15).

15. Seven Angels With Seven Plagues

They held harps given them by God and sang the song of Moses the servant of God and the song of the Lamb:

"Great and marvelous are your deeds, Lord God Almighty.
Just and true are your ways, King of the ages.
Who will not fear you, O Lord, and bring glory to your name?
For you alone are holy.
All nations will come and worship before you,
    for your righteous acts have been revealed." (15:2-4)

To the song (funeral march) of Moses, is now added the song of the Lamb.

16. Seven Bowls of God's Wrath

Painful sores on people, blood in the sea, blood in the rivers and springs, the sun scorching people with fire, people still unrepenting, drying up of Euphrates to prepare the way for the kings coming from the East.

Then they gathered the kings together to the place that in Hebrew is called Armageddon. (16:16)

The seventh angel poured out his bowl into the air, and out of the temple came a loud voice from the throne, saying. "It is done!" Then there came flashes of lightning, rumblings, peals of thunder and a severe earthquake. No earthquake like it has ever occurred since man has been on earth, so tremendous was the quake. The great city split into three parts, and the cities of the nations collapsed. God remembered Babylon the Great and gave her the cup filled with the wine of the fury of his wrath. Every island fled away and the mountains could not be found. From the sky huge hailstones of about a hundred pounds each fell upon men. And they cursed God on account of the plague of hail, because the plague was so terrible. (16:17-21)

Psychological and political warfare of frightening and threatening with death. Just remember Deuteronomy, Chapter 28.

17. The Women on the Beast

An angel shows John "the great prostitute" with whom the kings of earth commit adultery.

The woman was dressed in purple and scarlet, and was glittering with gold, precious stones and pearls. She held a golden cup in her hand, filled with abominable things and the filth of her adulteries. This title was written on her forehead:

MYSTERY
BABYLON THE GREAT
THE MOTHER OF PROSTITUTES
AND OF THE ABOMINATIONS OF THE EARTH

I saw that the woman was drunk with the blood of the saints, the blood of those
who bore testimony to Jesus. (17:4-6)

The creator father and the hierarchy of his sons are male; the mother of the abominations of
the earth is axiomatically female. Evil is by definition, or essentially, feminine, or
"man-female." (Remember Genesis.) Misogyny has reached its climax in a crescendo.

They will make war against the Lamb, but the Lamb will overcome them because he
is Lord of lords and King of kings—and with him will be his called, chosen and
faithful followers. (17:14)

Called, chosen, faithful. And pathological, I may add, if they believe all this.

18. The Fall of Babylon

"Fallen! Fallen is Babylon the Great!
She has become a home for demons and a haunt for every evil spirit,
a haunt for every unclean and detestable bird.
For all the nations have drunk the maddening wine of her adulteries.
The kings of the earth committed adultery with her,
and the merchants of the earth grew rich from her excessive luxuries." (18:2-3)

And:

"When the kings of the earth who committed adultery with her and shared her luxury see the smoke of her burning, they will weep and mourn over her. Terrified at
her torment, they will stand far off and cry: " 'Woe! Woe, O great city, O Babylon,
city of power! In one hour your doom has come!'

"The merchants of the earth will weep and mourn over her because no one buys
their cargoes any more: cargoes of gold, silver, precious stones and pearls; fine linen,
purple, silk and scarlet cloth; every sort of citron wood, and articles of every kind
made of ivory, costly wood, bronze, iron and marble; cargoes of cinnamon and
spice, of incense, myrrh and frankincense, of wine and olive oil, of fine flour and
wheat; cattle and sheep; horses and carriages; and bodies and souls of men.

"They will say, 'The fruit you longed for is gone from you. All your riches and
splendor have vanished, never to be recovered.' The merchants who sold these
things and gained their wealth from her will stand far off, terrified at her torment.
They will weep and mourn and cry out: " 'Woe! Woe, O great city, dressed in fine
linen, purple and scarlet, and glittering with gold, precious stones and pearls!

In one hour such great wealth has been brought to ruin!' (18:9-17)

"She will be consumed by fire." (18:8)

A vague attack on (illegitimate) worldly power and wealth, but sure recruitment policy and
appeal.

19. Hallelujah!

After this I heard what sounded like the roar of a great multitude in heaven shout-ing:

"Hallelujah! Salvation and glory and power belong to our God, for true and just are his judgments. He has condemned the great prostitute who corrupted the earth by her adulteries. He has avenged on her the blood of his servants."

For the wedding of the Lamb has come, and his bride has made herself ready. Fine linen, bright and clean, was given her to wear." (Fine linen stands for the righteous acts of the saints.) (19:1-2, 7-8)

All this is not merely misogynist; it is murderously lunatic and criminally dangerous for women. It is religio-criminal. On the other hand, it is not macho or patriarchal, but it is aggressively homosexual (or bisexual?): Virgin brides—"male and female"—to be wedded to the Lamb.

Then the angel said to me, "Write: 'Blessed are those who are invited to the wedding supper of the Lamb!' " And he added, "These are the true words of God."

At this I fell at his feet to worship him. But he said to me, "Do not do it! I am a fel-low servant with you and with your brothers who hold to the testimony of Jesus. Worship God! For the testimony of Jesus is the spirit of prophecy."

I saw heaven standing open and there before me was a white horse, whose rider is called Faithful and True. With justice he judges and makes war. His eyes are like blazing fire, and on his head are many crowns. He has a name written on him that no one knows but he himself. He is dressed in a robe dipped in blood, and his name is the Word of God. The armies of heaven were following him, riding on white horses and dressed in fine linen, white and clean. Out of his mouth comes a sharp sword with which to strike down the nations. "He will rule them with an iron scep-ter." He treads the winepress of the fury of the wrath of God Almighty. On his robe and on his thigh he has this name written:

KING OF KINGS AND LORD OF LORDS. (19:9-16)

The Lamb is also a war-lord, a warrior God, putting nations to the sword, etc. Not a far cry from the Pentateuch!

And quite cinematographic. Science fiction and Hollywood Western of those days?

And I saw an angel standing in the sun, who cried in a loud voice to all the birds fly-ing in midair, "Come, gather together for the great supper of God, so that you may eat the flesh of kings, generals, and mighty men, of horses and their riders, and the flesh of all people, free and slave, small and great."

Then I saw the beast and the kings of the earth and their armies gathered together to make war against the rider on the horse and his army. But the beast was captured, and with him the false prophet who had performed the miraculous signs on his behalf. With these signs he had deluded those who had received the mark of the beast and worshiped his image. The two of them were thrown alive into the fiery lake of burning sulfur. The rest of them were killed with the sword that came out of the mouth of the rider on the horse, and all the birds gorged themselves on their flesh. (19:17-21)

Old Testament-like cannibalism (Cf. esp. Deut., Ch 28) revived (minus, perhaps, the eating of "little ones"); consuming fire, lake of sulfur, bloodbath. (Graphic material for *Koran* already supplied.)

20. The Thousand Years

And I saw an angel coming down out of heaven, having the key to the Abyss and holding in his hand a great chain. He seized the dragon, that ancient serpent, who is the devil, or Satan, and bound him for a thousand years. He threw him into the Abyss, and locked and sealed it over him, to keep him from deceiving the nations anymore until the thousand years were ended. After that, he must be set free for a short time.

I saw thrones on which were seated those who had been given authority to judge. And I saw the souls of those who had been beheaded because of their testimony for Jesus and because of the word of God. They had not worshiped the beast or his image and had not received his mark on their foreheads or their hands. They came to life and reigned with Christ a thousand years. (The rest of the dead did not come to life until the thousand years were ended.) This is the first resurrection. Blessed and holy are those who have part in the first resurrection. The second death has no power over them, but they will be priests of God and of Christ and will reign with him for a thousand years. (20:1-6)

Christian monotheism reinforced with a well-balanced mixture of promise and threat. Eternal life and eternal torment. Resurrection and death.

When the thousand years are over, Satan will be released from his prison and will go out to deceive the nations in the four corners of the earth—Gog and Magog—to gather them for battle. In number they are like the sand on the seashore. They marched across the breadth of the earth and surrounded the camp of God's people, the city he loves. But fire came down from heaven and devoured them. And the devil, who deceived them, was thrown into the lake of burning sulfur, where the beast and the false prophet had been thrown. They will be tormented day and night for ever and ever.

Then I saw a great white throne and him who was seated on it. Earth and sky fled from his presence, and there was no place for them. And I saw the dead, great and small, standing before the throne, and books were opened. Another book was opened, which is the book of life. The dead were judged according to what they had done as recorded in the books. The sea gave up the dead that were in it, and death and Hades gave up the dead that were in them, and each person was judged according to what he had done. Then death and Hades were thrown into the lake of fire. The lake of fire is the second death. If anyone's name was not found written in the book of life, he was thrown into the lake of fire. (20:7-15)

The foregoing graphic imagery will supply fuel for *Koran*'s depiction of hell.

21. The New Jerusalem

Then I saw a new heaven and a new earth, for the first heaven and the first earth had passed away, and there was no longer any sea. I saw the Holy City, the new Jerusalem, coming down out of heaven from God, prepared as a bride beautifully dressed for her husband. And I heard a loud voice from the throne saying, "Now the dwelling of God is with men, and he will live with them. They will be his people, and God himself will be with them and be their God. He will wipe every tear from their eyes. There will be no more death or mourning or crying or pain, for the old order of things has passed away."

He who was seated on the throne said, "I am making everything new!" Then he said, "Write this down, for these words are trustworthy and true."

He said to me: "It is done. I am the Alpha and the Omega, the Beginning and the End. To him who is thirsty I will give to drink without cost from the spring of the water of life. He who overcomes will inherit all this, and I will be his God and he will be my son. But the cowardly, the unbelieving, the vile, the murderers, the sexually immoral, those who practice magic arts, the idolaters and all liars—their place will be in the fiery lake of burning sulfur. This is the second death."

One of the seven angels who had the seven bowls full of the seven last plagues came and said to me, "Come, I will show you the bride, the wife of the Lamb." And he carried me away in the Spirit to a mountain great and high, and showed me the Holy City, Jerusalem, coming down out of heaven from God. It shone with the glory of God, and its brilliance was like that of a very precious jewel, like a jasper, clear as crystal. It had a great, high wall with twelve gates, and with twelve angels at the gates. On the gates were written the names of the twelve tribes of Israel. There were three gates on the east, three on the north, three on the south and three on the west. The wall of the city had twelve foundations, and on them were the names of the twelve apostles of the Lamb.

The angel who talked with me had a measuring rod of gold to measure the city, its gates and its walls. The city was laid out like a square, as long as it was wide. He measured the city with the rod and found it to be 12,000 stadia in length, and as wide and high as it is long. He measured its wall and it was 144 cubits thick, by man's measurement, which the angel was using. The wall was made of jasper, and the city of pure gold, as pure as glass. The foundations of the city walls were decorated with every kind of precious stone. The first foundation was jasper, the second sapphire, the third chalcedony, the fourth emerald, the fifth sardonyx, the sixth carnelian, the seventh chrysolite, the eighth beryl, the ninth topaz, the tenth chrysoprase, the eleventh jacinth, and the twelfth amethyst. The twelve gates were twelve pearls, each gate made of a single pearl. The great street of the city was of pure gold, like transparent glass.

I did not see a temple in the city, because the Lord God Almighty and the Lamb are its temple. The city does not need the sun or the moon to shine on it, for the glory of God gives it light, and the Lamb is its lamp. The nations will walk by its light, and the kings of the earth will bring their splendor into it. On no day will its gates ever be shut, for there will be no night there. The glory and honor of the nations will be brought into it. Nothing impure will ever enter it, nor will anyone who does what is shameful or deceitful, but only those whose names are written in the Lamb's book of life. (21:1-27)

The new Jerusalem, the Holy City, the "City of God," is the apocalyptic realization by the *New Testament* of the promise of the *Old Testament*. Christianity is both Judaic and not Judaic. But it is, here at least, no less money-loving than the latter. It describes its heaven, as shall *Koran* too, mainly in terms of precious metals and stones. Its heaven is a huge jewelry shop; holiness and gold go together. Fear → believe → obey → be holy → prosper! (Or perish!) From the ambivalent 3 Commandments we have come back full circle to the prior 5 Commandments.

22. The River of Life; The Coming of Jesus

Then the angel showed me the river of the water of life, as clear as crystal, flowing from the throne of God and of the Lamb down the middle of the great street of the city. On each side of the river stood the tree of life, bearing twelve crops of fruit, yielding its fruit every month. And the leaves of the tree are for the healing of the nations. No longer will there be any curse. The throne of God and of the Lamb will be in the city, and his servants will serve him. They will see his face, and his name will be on their foreheads. There will be no more night. They will not need the light of a lamp or the light of the sun, for the Lord God will give them light. And they will reign for ever and ever.

The angel said to me, "These words are trustworthy and true. The Lord, the God of the spirits of the prophets, sent his angel to show his servants the things that must soon take place."

"Behold, I am coming soon! Blessed is he who keeps the words of the prophecy in this book."

I, John, am the one who heard and saw these things. And when I had heard and seen them, I fell down to worship at the feet of the angel who had been showing them to me. But he said to me, "Do not do it! I am a fellow servant with you and with your brothers the prophets and of all who keep the words of this book. Worship God!"

Then he told me, "Do not seal up the words of the prophecy of this book, because the time is near. Let him who does wrong continue to do wrong; let him who is vile continue to be vile; let him who does right continue to do right; and let him who is holy continue to be holy."

"Behold, I am coming soon! My reward is with me, and I will give to everyone according to what he has done. I am the Alpha and the Omega, the First and the Last, the Beginning and the End.

"Blessed are those who wash their robes, that they may have the right to the tree of life and may go through the gates into the city. Outside are the dogs, those who practice magic arts, the sexually immoral, the murderers, the idolaters and everyone who loves and practices falsehood.

"I, Jesus, have sent my angel to give you this testimony for the churches. I am the Root and the Offspring of David, and the bright Morning Star."

The Spirit and the bride say, "Come!" And let him who hears say, "Come!" Whoever is thirsty, let him come; and whoever wishes, let him take the free gift of the water of life.

I warn everyone who hears the words of the prophecy of this book: If anyone adds anything to them, God will add to him the plagues described in this book. And if anyone takes words away from this book of prophecy, God will take away from him his share in the tree of life and in the holy city, which are described in this book.

He who testifies to these things says, "Yes, I am coming soon."

Amen. Come, Lord Jesus.

The grace of the Lord Jesus be with God's people. Amen. (22:1-21)

God's Word, The Book(s), absolute text. Back to the *Old Testament*, forward to the *Koran*.

"No more curse" and "plagues described in this book." Both at once.

And I say that Revelation is the most perverse and the most murderous chapter of the whole *Bible*, yet a productive source of inspiration for many works of art and literature of Western Civilization.

In a sense, Revelation is not only the final chapter of the Christian *New Testament*, as Zechariah-Malachi are of the Jewish *Old Testament*; it is also the final chapter of the whole Judeo-Christian *Bible* and, as such, very much in the tradition and spirit of Deuteronomy Chapter 28, the last book/chapter of the Pentateuch, with its psychology of terror and fear and its action of horrors with all its violence and perversity and the additional debasing of women in true Hollywood fashion.

Malachi foreshadows; Revelation vindicates. (*Koran* shall reaffirm both.)

"As it is written" in Malachi:

Surely the day is coming; it will burn like a furnace. All the arrogant and every evil-doer will be stubble, and that day that is coming will set them on fire, says the LORD Almighty. "Not a root or a branch will be left to them. But for you who revere my name, the sun of righteousness will rise with healing in its wings. And you will go out and leap like calves released from the stall. Then you will trample down the wicked; they will be ashes under the soles of your feet on the day when I do these things," says the LORD Almighty.

Remember the law of my servant Moses, the decrees and laws I gave him at Horeb for all Israel.

See, I will send you the prophet Elijah before that great and dreadful day of the LORD comes. He will turn the hearts of the fathers to their children, and the hearts of the children to their fathers; or else I will come and strike the land with a curse. (4:1-6)

As it is also written in Malachi:

Then those who feared the LORD talked with each other, and the LORD listened and heard. A scroll of remembrance was written in his presence concerning those who feared the LORD and honored his name.

"They will be mine," says the LORD Almighty, in the day when I make up my treasured possession. I will spare them, just as in compassion a man spares his son who serves him. And you will again see the distinction between the righteous and the wicked, between those who serve God and those who do not. (3:13-18)

As we know, the other name of the "People(s) of the Book" is "God-fearing people." But one should not miss one fact in the Book(s): To fear God is no guarantee for good treatment. To be "chosen," to be "treasured possession" does not encompass even *all* believers, who believe in fear and trembling. It is only "the *remnant*"[1] among even the believers who are not to be maltreated. The Book's, or the Books', list of the "*other*(s)" is far wider-ranging than what good people think or are given to believe. The majority of them are not included in "the remnant," the really chosen ones; they are doctrinally excluded from the beginning. Because: (1) they are predestined, sure sinners, eventually (majority of men), (2) they are not sinners, they are sin itself (entirety of women) in Christianity—and second-rate at any rate in Judaism and Islam.

In general, the other(s), the non-remnant, comprise, at least, the following:

- other nations
- non believers

- believers of other beliefs
- majority of believers (men)
- entirety of believers (women)

To repeat: even to fear, to believe, to obey, etc., is not enough to live here and avoid further punishment there.

Christianity hasn't become a separate religion mainly, let alone merely, for doctrinal reasons. Doctrinally, it is just one great schism in Judaism, then in Judeo-Christianity, Jesus being but a "major prophet" of Judaism—just remember Matthew 5:17-20:

> Do not think that I have come to abolish the Law or the Prophets; I have not come to abolish them but to fulfill them.[2]

It all begins with and returns to Abraham and Moses; "the rest" not only in the *Old Testament* but also in the *New Testament* (and the *Koran*, as we shall see) are but minor modifications or internal critiques, but above all affirmations and confirmations of "the Law" and, first of all, the "law of God" of Genesis.

Jesus, and Paul, are "major prophets" more like Moses, Isaiah, and, say, Daniel; apostles and other epistle-writers of the *New Testament* can be likened to the "minor prophets" of the *Old Testament*. "The Law" of all is the same at the higher level of abstraction, at the level of basic norms. Later differentiation at lower levels, at the level of details, is less a result of any serious doctrinal differences between these Abrahamic religions than a consequence of their schismatic historical-political-ethnic-etc., conflicts among themselves. Details and differences are effect, not cause.

Revelation is mammoth evidence for the foregoing. After, and only at times, the softer, "lambish" Jesus/Gospels/Acts (like, say, Isaiah, etc.) comes the harsh Revelation as the grand finale (like, say, Zechariah and Malachi), Paul being the connecting bridge. Essence is kept intact. (And shall be kept intact.)

Just like "the rest" of the *Old Testament*, "the rest" of the *New Testament* and the seemingly odd parts of the *New Testament* (e.g., Jesus/Gospels) are in the final analysis affirmations, not negations of, the whole.

Notes
1. Be it 144,000 or 1/73.
2. Muhammad, as we shall see, will proclaim the same.

PART THREE

THE KORAN

14

I. SURAS 1-2: FÂTIHA AND BAKARA¹

1. Fâtiha (The Opening)   (Mecca)

The *Koran* opens not with cosmology and history but directly with divine moral legislation, the good and the evil, right and wrong, being defined, as in the other two Abrahamic monotheistic religions, by the one, greatest God. The "Law," if you will, is proclaimed at the very beginning. Historical narrative in *Koran* is even shorter than that in the *New Testament*; it relies on and just paraphrases the narrative of the *Old Testament*.

Praise belongs to God, the All-merciful and the All-compassionate…Guide us in the straight path… (p. 29)	Praise be to God, who is "rahmân and "rahîm,"²…who shows the way of truth. (1:2-4 and 6)
…the path of those whom Thou hast blessed, not of those against whom Thou art wrathful, nor of those who are astray. (p. 29)	…the way of those whom you blessed and rewarded, not that of the deviants and the accursed [Christians and Jews, respectively as some interpretations have it, but not necessarily restricted to these two groups]. (1:6-7)

2. BAKARA (The Cow)   (Medina, exc. 281)

That is the Book, wherein is no doubt, a guidance to the God fearing, who believe in the Unseen, and perform the prayer, and expend of that we have provided them. (p.30)	There is no doubt whatsoever in this Book, which is a guide for those who fear God, who believe in "gayb" (God, angels, books, prophets, day of judgment, fate and destiny, creation of good and evil by God), who spend in the way of God the possessions we (God) have given them ("zekât"-almsgiving), who perform their prayers ("namaz"). (2:2-3)

Fear → believe → obey →…

Fear of God is reaffirmed as the basis of belief and obedience; belief in the books and prophets (of the *Old* and *New Testaments*) is prescribed at the outset; two (namaz and zekât) of the five pillars of Islam are emphasized—the other three being kelime-i şahadet, oruç, hac" (confession of faith, fasting, pilgrimage, respectively).

Who believe in what has been sent down to thee and what has been sent down before thee, and have faith in the Hereafter…*those are the ones who prosper.* (p.30)

They believe in that [book] which is revealed to you [Muhammad] and in that which was revealed before your time (the *Old* and *New Testaments*), and they have definite faith in the day of judgment. They shall be guided and saved. (2:4-5)

The validity of the previous books of the "Peoples of the Book" is thus doubly stated. The *Koran* is not a brand new book that rescinds or abrogates the *Bible* (Hebrew-Christian *Bible*); it is, on its own account, the latest Book which supersedes the former by updating and incorporating it. A veritable Hegelian synthesis or sublation—to repeat, according to its own intention and declaration.[3]

Please note that Arberry's translation renders the fifth of the "5 Commandments" (supra): Prosper!

The *Koran* classifies people into three groups in terms of their stance towards itself: (1) the faithful or the believers (müminûn, Cf. also suras 23 and 40) described above, (2) the infidels or the nonbelievers (kâfirûn, Cf. also *sura* 109) who do not fear God because God has "sealed their hearts and ears" and "put a curtain before their eyes" (2:6-7) and who are to have great torments in this and the other world, (3) the hypocrits (münafikûn, Cf. also *sura* 63) who pretend to believe without believing, thinking that they can deceive God and the faithful. 2:8-20 describes the delusions and the sorry lot of the 3rd group, worse than the 2nd, and depicts them as sick, liars, subversive, satanic, deaf, mute, and blind. Please note the obvious *Old-* and *New Testament*like discourse and vocabulary.

O you men, serve your Lord Who created you…so set not up compeers to God…And if you are in doubt concerning that We have sent down on our servant, then bring a *sura* like it…if you do not—and you will not—then fear the Fire, whose fuel is men and stones, prepared for unbelievers. (p.32)

God speaks to men: Ye, human beings! Serve your Lord who created you…do not bring a partner to him… If you have any doubts about that which we revealed to our servant [Muhammad], then bring a similar sura…Which you will certainly not be able to do…Beware of the infernal fire prepared for unbelievers, whose fuel is people and stones. (2:21-24)

Monotheism affirmed; absolute belief in the *Koran* commanded; its unique superiority stated; fear of hell invoked. Note that, men will not only be consumed by fire (as in the *Bible*) but will in themselves constitute the burning fuel of that fire. Please also note the capitalization in Arberry's "Fire."

Now God addresses Muhammad: "To those who behave well because they believe, give the good news of heaven in which rivers flow," fruits are served, and purest companions are given (2:25). Their tenure in heaven will be eternal.

Now God addresses people (he speaks in the first person plural alternately to Muhammad and people): "They are such deviants that they go back on their definite promises" (2:27). (Meaning the peoples of the book, Jews and Christians, who do not profess faith in the last prophet Muhammed, although his coming had been announced in the *Old* and *New Testaments*.) This is tantamount to denying God himself, who gives life (exc. nihilo), takes life, and resurrects (2:28).

Creation of Adam as God's "successor" (halife) in the world, his naming all things, seduction of Eve by Satan, their eating from the tree of knowledge, expulsion from heaven are related in a Genesis-like manner (2:30-36), but the *Koran* does not curse Adam, like Genesis. Adam repents; God is compassionate and merciful. The *Koran* swiftly proceeds with the business of recruitment to the new (real-old) faith:

As for the unbelievers who cry lies to Our signs, those shall be the inhabitants of the Fire, therein dwelling forever. Children of Israel, remember My blessing wherewith I blessed you, and fulfil My covenant and I shall fulfil your covenant; and have awe of Me. And believe in that I have sent down, confirming that which is with you. (p.34)

Those who deny and reject our verses (ayat)[4] are marked for hell eternally. Ye, sons of Israel, remember the blessings I gave you and fullfil the promise you gave me so that I may give you what I had promised you. Fear only and only me. Have faith in what I (now(reveal to you (*Koran*(in affirmation of what you have in hand (*Old Testament*). (2:39-41)

Allah-monotheism subsumes Yahweh-monotheism and *Koran* subsumes the *Old Testament*. Islam tries to recruit Jews before (and more than?) Christians. And a renewal of covenant is offered. Fear → believe → obey.

Right and righteousness equals believing and obeying the Word of One God, his Book(s), the absolute text. Wrong and sinfulness, the opposite. Manichean tautology is the hallmark of Abrahamic religions.

Strict continuity is declared by the *Koran* in the conditional-covenantial relationship between the God and the people of Abrahamic monotheism, in the transition from the *Old Testament* to the *Koran*. As we shall have ample occasion to observe, it is one of the persistent, and ingenuous, theses of the *Koran* that it is not the previous book(s) that has (have) been in error but that the peoples of the book who have read and applied their own books erroneously. The books themselves were but harbingers or earlier chapters of the *Koran*. And this is not mere conversion-motivated rhetoric, given not only the volume of the references and acknowledgments made by the *Koran* to the Hebrew-Christian *Bible* (and more to the former than the latter) but also given the fact that it is based in essentials on the previous book(s). Hence: Judeo-Christianity-Islam.

The Israelites, sons of Israel, are called to perform prayer (namaz) and almsgiving (zekât), and to fast (oruç) with patience (2:43, 45). "Ye, (religious) scholars! Don't you use your head...although you know the Book (*Old Testament*)?" (2:44). "Ye, Israelites! Remember the blessing I gave you and remember that I once made you superior to the whole world" (2:47). (Yahweh speaking.) Very reminiscent of *New Testament*'s scolding "teachers of the Law."

Exodus is summarized, the Golden Calf episode is reminded, Moses and Aaron are vindicated, people's grumbling is admonished. "We gave Moses the Book in order that you may find the way of truth" (2:53). Signs, wonders, plagues, punishments are narrated. Israelites' incessant misery is attributed to their having unleashed God's wrath because of their sinfulness. They disobeyed God's commands. Killed their prophets, acted rebelliously.

The *Koran* assumes quite a Mosaic attitude in repeating the narrative and the moral of the Pentateuch, but it sometimes adds certain embellishments which are not to be supported by the original text. The episode of God's converting some Israelites into monkeys (2: 65-66) is one such example. As for substance and discursive style, however, "Bakara" *sura* is very *Old Testament*-like: e.g., God's "hardening the heart" of the wicked (2:74).

"There are some illiterates among them (Israelites) who do not know the Book (*Old Testament*). All they know is hearsay. They just guess and conjecture." (2:78)

Evil deeds of Jews are enumerated, their violation of the covenant ("misak") is stated, and the following question is asked with reference to in-tribe fratricide:

They said, 'We believe in what was sent down on us'; and they disbelieve in what is beyond that, yet it is the truth confirming what is with them. (p.39)	Do you, then, believe in some parts of the Book and reject others? (2:85)
Why then were you slaying the Prophets of God in former time? (p.39)	We gave the Book to Moses. We then sent consecutive prophets. We gave wonders to Jesus son of Mary, to...Yet, you contested some and killed others. (2:87)

Koran considers itself and the *Old Testament* as one book, the latter being only one, and the earlier, part of the whole.

Unlike Jews' rejecting Jesus and Christians' rejecting Muhammad, the *Koran* owns both Moses and Jesus and sees a succession of God's prophets and a continuity in their mission (to be completed by Muhammad, the last and the most perfect) prophet.

Rejecting the *Koran* is the same thing as rejecting the *Old Testament*, says 2:89 and 91; perpetrators of this blasphemy are to be accursed. The former is an affirmation of the latter:

...confirming what was before it, and for a guidance and good tidings to the believers. (p.40)	This *Koran* is the true (hak) Book that has come to confirm the *Old Testament* which is in their hands. (2:91)

The Israelites who reject Muhammad had not fully and sincerely believed in Moses, either (2: 92). Reference to the Golden Calf episode is repeated—one of the favorites of the *Koran* from the Pentateuch. Unrepenting and unbelieving Jews are the "lowliest of human beings" (2:96). They did not believe in the *Old Testament* then, and they refuse the *Koran* now.

Tautological prescriptions and sanctions are infinitely repeated, in the manner of the Pentateuch. God is endowed with many superlative adjectives.

Verses of the *Koran* contain unquestionable truths:

And for whatever verse We abrogate or cast into oblivion, We bring a better or the like of it; knowest thou not that God is powerful over everything?...Or do you desire to question your Messenger as Moses was questioned in former time? (p.41)	If we annul an ayat or wish it to be overlooked, we definitely bring a similar or better one. Don't you know that God is omnipotent?...Ye, Muslims! Do you, too, want to ask questions to your prophet, as was done to Moses? (2:106, 108)

Not only Jews and Christians, if they convert, but all who serve God (Islam's God) righteously can go to heaven (2:111-112). Mutual accusations of Jews and Christians as to who is on the way of truth are all wrong (2:113). Disgrace on earth, torment in the other world for all unbelievers (2:114). Blessings and curses.

Koran is prophetic about the expansion of Islam:

To God belong the East and the West; whithersoever you turn, there is the Face of God; God is All-embracing, All-knowing. (p.42)	Both the East and the West belong to God. Wherever you return, there is the face of God. No doubt he is omnipotent and omniscient. (2:115)

Koran repeats the cosmology of Genesis:

...when He decrees a thing, He but says to it 'Be,' and it is. (p.42)	When he wills something, he just says 'Be,' and it becomes. (2:117)

God does not have a Son (2:116). Islam rejects Christianity's sonship; recognizes Jesus only as the second major prophet after Moses. Islam's God is not as close to man as that of Christianity.

Repetition: "Ye, Israelites! Remember the blessing I gave you and that I had once made you superior to the whole world" (2:122).

God had tested Abraham, chosen him (but not his sinful descendants) as a leader for men (2:124). *Koran* has Abraham, who built the Kâbe (?), speak:

...our Lord, make us submissive to Thee, and of our seed a nation submissive to Thee; and show us our holy rites, and turn towards us... (p.44)	O, Lord! Make us to submit to you, create from our descendants a community (ümmet) that obeys you, show us rules of worship, accept our repentance. (2:128)

God had told Abraham to "surrender" (submit to the mono-God), that is to become a Muslim ("he who surrendered"), and he had obeyed (2:131). Both Abraham and Jacob had told their sons that "God has chosen this religion (Islam) for you" (2:132.) *Koran* makes Abraham & Seed to be the first Muslims.

Jews and Christians tell the Muslims to become Jew or Christian; "Tell them (God instructs Muhammad) that we (Muslims) obey only the religion of the righteous Abraham, who brought no partners to God" (2:135).

Muhammad (and God) puts words in the mouth of Muslims:

We believe in God, and in that which has been sent down on us and sent down on Abraham, Ishmael, Isaac and Jacob, and the Tribes, and that which was given to Moses and Jesus and the Prophets, of their Lord; we make no division between any of them, and to Him we surrender. (p.45)	We believe in God, in what has been sent down on us and in what has been revealed to Abraham, Ishmael, Isaac, Jacob, his sons, Moses, and Jesus, and in what has been given by the Lord to all his prophets, without discriminating between them, and we surrendered only to God. (2:136)

A strong claim for the unity and continuity of the Judeo-Christian-Islamic tradition and real ecumenicalism on part of Islam, in contradistinction to the exclusionariness of Judaism, and more comprehensive than the ecumenicalism of Christianity which is restricted to the realm of Christendom. (Universalism, too? No. We shall see.)

Inclusion by incorporation and appropriation: "Do you mean to say that Abraham, Ishmael, Isaac, Jacob, and their descendants were Jews or Christians? Is it you or God who should know better?" (2:140).

An ingenuous reasoning for assimilationist inclusionism. (A form of "universalism" or, in fact, unitarian religious communalism?)

The *Koran* is the Muslim *Old Testament*, and the *Bible* is the Jewish-Christian *Koran*.

Some people are brainless concerning the Kible (2:142). What has been revealed to Muhammad is science (ilim) (2:145). He is a prophet from within (the Arabs) (2:151).

Doubt and obstinacy are reprimanded, patience and gratitude are commanded. Covenantial relationship is made conditional: "You worship me so that I care for you" (2:152). (Same as in the *Old Testament* and the *New Testament*.)

Patience and endurance is to be tested and rewarded: "We test you with a little fear and hunger and decrease in possessions, lives, and produce" (2:155). (Please note the part "a little decrease in lives.")

Disobedience is eternally cursed, repentance (by immediate conversion) is rewarded. (No incessant self-fulfilling prophecy of sin and punishment, however, as in the *Old Testament*.) For a "thinking community" there is ample proof in the acts and results of creation (Genesis-like account) of the existence and unity/oneness of God (2:164).

Dead animals, pigs, blood are not to be eaten (2:173)—unless there is dire necessity. (Islam is an easy and flexible religion—one of its own self-distinguishing claims.)

The *Koran* is an absolute text:

...God has sent down the Book with the truth; and those that are at variance regarding the Book are in wide schism. (p.50)	...God has revealed the Book as the true book. Those who fall into disagreement as regards the book have certainly fallen into profound conflict! (2:176)

Goodness (righteousness) consists not in turning to the east or west but in believing in "God, the hereafter, angels, books, and prophets" (2:177). Good people are those who

give to relatives, the fatherless, the poor, the homeless, beggars, slaves from his cherished possessions,

give alms (zekat),

perform prayer (namaz),

honor commitments,

show patience in times of distress, illness, and war (2:177).

Some rudimentary morality and a lot of charity.

Lex talionis, retaliative law, is borrowed from the *Old Testament*, as distinct from the *New Testament*, one of the instances whereby the Third Book regresses back to the First Book:

O believers, prescribed for you is retaliation, *touching the slain*; freeman for freeman, slave for slave, female for female. But if aught is pardoned a man by his brother, *let the pursuing be honourable*, and let the payment be with kindliness. (p.51)	Ye, the faithful! It is obligatory for you to retaliate, concerning the murdered ones. Freeman for freeman, slave for slave, woman for woman. However, if the murderer's punishment is forgiven to a certain extent by the brother of the murderee, the parties should act equitably and the murdering side must peacefully pay the blood money. (2:178)

Note the ordering above: freeman → slave → woman. And:

In retaliation there is life for you, men possessed of minds; *haply you will be godfearing.* (p.51)	Ye, man of reason! There is life for you in retaliation. Thus you may refrain from committing murder. (2:179)

In the event of approaching death, it is obligatory to make a testament, bequeathing a proper amount to parents and relatives (2:180). (Nisa *sura* will bring clarity to inheritance rules. Cf. infra.)

Unlawful gain and bribery are forbidden. Five pillars of Islam are explicated. The reasonableness, lightness, and flexibility of Islamic rules are expressed (2:185): "God wishes convenience for you, not difficulty." (In exempting the ill and the traveler from fasting.)

Concerning war:

...fight in the way of God with those who fight with you, but aggress not: God loves not the aggressors. (p.53)	To those who declare war to you, you, too, wage war in God's walk. Don't ever go to extremes, for God does not love extremists. (2:190)

In distinction to the *Old Testament*'s war-ideology of total destruction, the *Koran*, in compliance with its general disposition of "measure" and "limit," advises limited war and, then, (in 2: 194), proportionate or commensurate reprisal: "Attack the aggressor in so-far-as to constitute retaliation."

Those who ask God to give them possessions in this world only are contrasted unfavorably with those who request his blessings both in this and the other world (2:200-202).

"This-worldly life has been made attractive for non-believers. They ridicule the believers. Whereas, the believers shall be superior to them on the day of judgment" (2:212). (Remember *New Testament*'s "first and last.")

Human beings were one community. They fell into conflict. Prophets were sent to reconcile them (2:213). Unlike *Torah* (esp. Cf. the Tower of Babel episode in Genesis), the *Koran* does not set people apart and advocate chronic conflict between a chosen tribe/nation and the others.

What one gives away from one's possessions should be intended for parents, relatives, the fatherless, the poor, and travelers (2:215).

God is omniscient; men don't know:

Yet it may happen that you will hate a thing which is better for you; and it may happen that you will love a thing which is worse for you; God knows, and you know not. (p.57)	It is possible for you not to like something which is useful to you. It is also possible for you to like something which is harmful to you. God knows, you don't know. (2:216)

For example, man does not like war, but it has been made obligatory for him. (This is somewhat different from the intrinsic belligerence of the *Old Testament*.)

"Fitne" (sedition, rebellion, disorder, subversion) is a greater sin than murder (2:217). (A companion deed is "fesat" [malice, intrigue, duplicity].)

Wine and gambling are forbidden and unlawful because their sinfulness and harm is greater than their "certain usefulness" (2:219).

What is "more than one needs" should be given away to do good (2:219). (This is stronger than the *Old Testament* and softer than the Acts of *New Testament*.)

Concerning women and marriage: Don't marry women who worship idols. Don't give your daughters in marriage to men who worship idols. A faithful concubine or a slave is better than an idol-worshiping free woman (2:221).

God speaks to Muhammad: "They would ask you about women's period. Say that it is an illness" (2:222). Quite a modern conception; more understanding than the irritable and isolating attitude of the *Old Testament*.

And:

Your women are a tillage for you; so come unto your tillage as you wish. (p.59)	Your women are your fields. Access your field as you wish. (2:223)

Note the hierarchy of man (landowner) and woman (landed property).

Some other rules: Those who do not touch their women (wives) for four months may divorce or come back to them (2:226-227). Divorced women wait for three months; ex-husbands may take them back (2:228). Divorce and its consequences easier and lighter for men.

And this is the punch line of the *Koran*'s esteem for women and the limits thereof:

Women have such honourable rights as obligations, but their men have a degree above them; God is All-mighty, All-wise. (p.60)	Just as men have rights over women, women have certain rights over men. However, men are one degree superior to women. God is all-powerful, all-wise. (2:228)

This is neatly unequivocal. After paying lip-service to the mutual (not equally reciprocal but unequally mutual) rights and obligations of men and women, the *Koran* gives the net balance: Men are "one degree superior to" women or have "a degree above" them. If the Book is the most authoritative source of dogma, all sorts of talk about Islam's egalitarian attitude toward women must fall. Nothing basically has changed from the time of Abraham-Sarah and Isaac-Rebekah, or for that matter from the *New Testament*'s God → son → husband → wife, in that the man is the Lord and woman the subordinate part of the "one-flesh" organism.

And, of course, the best part of all this is that this domination—subordination relationship is legitimized by the all-powerful, all-wise God—who commands that it be so for the god-fearing, good women.

Men's rights unqualified, women's rights "certain." But more importantly, by the phrase "one degree superior," a categorical—and essentialistic—difference is nevertheless stipulated; beyond that any and all differences in interpretation and practice become a matter of dosage. (The standard interpretation to the effect that one-degree superiority means being the head of the family or the household—a patriarchal concept in itself—is less poor rationalization than unwitting concession.)

A man may divorce (the same woman) twice. After that he either kindly keeps the woman or peacefully lets her go. If the man divorces thrice, then it would not be rightful for him to take her back without her having been married to another man in between (2:230). Apparently, three times is a charitable limit, compared to limitless divorcing and taking back of women.

Upon divorce, one should not be unfair to women.

Breast-feeding is two-years. Parents may agree to cut it shorter.

It is not sinful to harbor or to implicitly express intention of marrying a woman who is in the course of completing her four months and ten days of waiting before formal divorce. "However, do not promise a secret appointment beyond saying legitimate words" (2: 235).

If you divorce a woman without touching her after the marriage ceremony or before specifying a marriage money (mehir) for her, you are not obligated to pay the marriage money. "Just give her some sort of a gift" (2:236). If you divorce a woman before having intercourse with her, for whom you had specified a marriage money, half of that amount is her rightful share, not without some qualifications (2:237).

Widows of relatives should be let to stay in their houses for a year (how long?) and to benefit (how much?) from the possessions of the deceased (2:241).

In summary: women are subordinated, subjugated, and bought or paid away—within, however, charitable limits set by God ("Allah's limits," [2:230]).

Of God and men: God creates, gives death, resurrects. "No doubt God is kind to men. But most of men do not thank" (2:243). "Fight in God's walk and know that he hears and knows everything" (2:244). The Judeo-Christian tradition of seeing man as ungrateful is perpetuated.

Of God and the Israelites: The Israelites had contested Moses (and God) to the effect that the rulers should come from among the rich and wealthy(?), whereas God appoints as rulers those who are "superior in science and body" (2:247), meaning superior in talent and expertise.

The Israelites defeated their enemies with their God's support (and actual fighting, we may add); God gave David sovereignty and wisdom (and wealth); some (few) people are good and some (most) bad and God eliminates the evil of the latter by by the righteousness of the former. Otherwise, "the world have been turned upside down" (2:251). Religio-social stability of order.

Bakara *sura*, the longest and most important *sura* of the *Koran*, its cornerstone and linchpin, in fact the Law, the *Torah* of the *Koran*, concludes with a series of significant âyats on basic issues.

God addresses Muhammad:

These are the signs of God. We recite to you in truth, and assuredly thou art of the number of the Envoys. (p.64)	These are God's âyats. We tell them to you as they are (correctly). Undoubtedly, you are one of the prophets sent by God. (2:252)

And:

And those Messengers, some We have preferred above others; some there are to whom God spoke, and some He raised in rank. And We gave Jesus son of Mary the clear signs and confirmed him with the Holy Spirit. (p.64)	We[5] made some of these prophets superior to others. God talked with some of them and elevated some others in differing degrees. We gave open miracles to Jesus son of Mary and fortified him with Gabriel, [Rûhu'l-Kudüs]. (2:253)

How can all men be equal when there is a hierarchy even of prophets? (The question is being addressed to all three Abrahamic religions.)

"Had God willed otherwise, nations would not have made war with one another after those prophets...yet, God does what he wishes" (2:253). Meaning: God wanted them to fight with each other. (Remember "Babelization.")

2: 255[6] enumerates some of the names, adjectives, and the infinite powers of God and exalts him while diminishing man:

He knows what lies before them and what is after them, and they comprehend not anything of His knowledge save such as He wills. (p.65)	He knows what his servants have done and will do. Men cannot fully know anything of his science other than those he chooses to tell them. (2:255)

We are fixated at the point and time of Genesis, the tree of knowledge, the un-Promethean withholding from man his own status and capacity of being a human agency. God is all, man is naught. And, of course, predetermination and predestination.

God leads the righteous to light; Satan leads the wicked to darkness (2:257). Unbelievers are evildoers. (Tautologies based on binary, Manichean opposites.)

Rewarded will be those who spend their possessions in the way of God without condescension and bragging. Good words and forgiveness are better than almsgiving that is followed by hurtful behavior (2:262-264).

Worldly gains (wealth, power) are temporary and subject to vicissitudes (2:266).

One must give to charity (2:267). Almsgiving and charity better be in secret than open
(2:271). All charity returns back in the same or in greater amounts (2.272). Charity should
be given to the faithful poor (2:273).

Wisdom is granted by God, stinginess is given by the Satan. Only reasonable men
(those who believe in the *Koran*) can receive wisdom (2:269). Belief in Allah and the *Koran*
is made the basis of human reason. Faith is the prerequisite of reason. (The opposites are, of
course, Satan-unreason-evil-this-worldly selfishness, etc.)

Concerning economics:

God has permitted trafficking, and forbidden usury. (p.69)	Allah has made commercial transaction "helâl" [lawful] and interest "haram" [unlawful and punishable by eternal tenure in hell]. (2:275)

Capital accumulated without interest is lawful (2:279).

Debts among the faithful should be recorded by an honest scribe in the presence of two
male witnesses or one male and two female witnesses (if one woman errs, the other would
correct [2:282]). One man equals two women. No need for records in case of cash transactions and payment in advance.

Bakara sura ends with the two very important âyets, 285 and 286, revealed to Muhammad on the Mirac (ascension) night. (They are recommended to the faithful for reading at
night before going to bed.)

The Messenger believes in what was sent down to him from his Lord, and the believers; each one believes in God and His angels, and in His Books and His Messengers; we make no division between any one of His Messengers. They say, 'We hear, and obey. Our Lord, grant us Thy forgiveness; unto Thee is the homecoming.' (p.71)	The prophet believed in that which was revealed to him by his Lord. The faithful, too, believed in it. Both believed in God, his angels, his book, his prophets. They said: 'We don't discriminate between God's prophets. We heard, we obeyed. O, Lord! We took refuge in your mercy. To you shall we be returned. (2:285)

Islam embraces and accommodates Moses and Jesus, Judaism and Christianity, unlike the
other two who exclude other major prophets than their own.

This cross-religious ecumenicalism of Islam is accompanied by a flexibility and leniency which is not be found in the *Old Testament*:

God charges no soul save to its capacity; standing to its account is what it has earned, and against its account what it has merited. Our Lord, take us not to task if we forget, or make mistake. Our Lord, charge us not with a load such as Thou didst lay upon those before us. Our Lord, do Thou not burden us beyond what we have the strength to bear. And pardon us, and forgive us, and have mercy on us... (p.71)

God holds responsible each individual in proportion to his capacity...Our Lord! If we forget or err, do not hold us accountable. O Lord! Do not give us a load as heavy as the one you gave to those before us. O, Lord! Do not give us assignments to which our capacity is not up to. Forgive us. Have mercy. (2:286)

This is one of the major claims, superiorities, or claims of superiority, of Islam vis-à-vis the two previous Abrahamic religions: It is easier, less burdensome, less demanding, and, supposedly, more merciful. Hence its great appeal to world populations, although it has come after Judeo-Christianity, of which it is a not too original derivative. It is the last book/religion, but there is not much that is new in it, except for several ingenuous appeals to the human psyche such as this one.

Notes
1. The right column is my translation, the left is Arberry's.
2. "Rahmân" means the giver of this-worldly blessings undiscriminatingly to all, whether good or evil, whether believer or unbeliever. "Rahîm" means the giver of other-worldly blessings only to the faithful on the judgment day, when the good will be given good, the evil evil.
3. To my mind, as I shall duly expound, *Koran* is in fact a later chapter of the *Bible*, especially of the *Torah* part of it.
4. Ayat (verse) also means sign, wonder, miracle, proof.
5. Voices are intermingled. Who is ventriloquizing whom?
6. Ayat 255 is called Âyet-ül Kürsi and is considered the most important âyet of Bakara, just as Bakara is the most important *sura* of the *Koran*.

15

II. SURAS 3-4: İmrân and Nisâ, and 24 (Nûr), 33 (Ahzâb), 58 (Mücâdele), 65 (Talâk), 66 (Tahrim)

3. İmrân (The House of Imran, Mary's father)   (Medina)

The one, timeless, sovereign, all-knowing, all-powerful, creator God addresses Muhammad:

He sent down upon thee the Book with the truth, confirming what was before it, and He sent down the *Torah* and the Gospel aforetime... (p.73)	[My prophet!] He revealed the Book [*Koran*] to you gradually as the truth and as the affirmation of the *Old Testament* (Tevrat) and the *New Testament* (İncil). (3:3-4)

Koran is also called Furkan, meaning rules that separate the true from the null and void, right from wrong, good from evil.

...wherein are verses clear that are the Essence of the Book, and others ambiguous. As for those in whose hearts is swerving, they follow the ambiguous part, desiring dissension, and desiring its interpretation; and none knows its interpretation, save only God. And those firmly rooted in knowledge say, "We believe in it; all is from our Lord"; yet none remembers, but men possessed of minds. (p.73)	Some *âyats* are "muhkem" (definitive)[1] and are the essence of the Book. Some others are "müteşabih (allegorical).[2] Those with crooked hearts go after the latter in order to cause fitne (disorder, dissension) by distorting (tevil)[3] them. Whereas only God knows their (correct) meaning. But those who are high up in "ilim" (religious science) say: "We believe in him. All *âyats* are from him. Only those with discernment can comprehend." (3:7)

Koran is as absolute a text as the *Old Testament* and the *New Testament*. It is no more open to interpretation than the other two, with their "no addition, no subtraction." But Muham-

mad ingenuously hedges in saying that the sacred text has "hard" and "soft" parts, but re-
serves the prerogative of interpreting the softer parts to God *and* his prophet and men of
religious science and wisdom. (God knows best/all, Prophet next to Him, the "ulema" next
to him; blind faith and catechistic recitation for the mindless multitude of believers, whom
are spoken to only in "parables.")

Please also consider the potential in all this for the relationship between elitist "power"
and "knowledge" and interpretation and manipulation of knowledge.

(If Arberry is correct in his translation of "müteşabih" as ambiguous, then the question
of why put ambiguous things in an absolute, sacred text becomes pertinent. But if
müteşabih is rendered as allegorical, the problem softens up from the point of view of the
Judeo-Christian-Islamic tradition of "parable.")

A mixture of *Old Testament*-like and *New Testament*-like elements, plus men themselves
as "fuel of hell," concerning unbelievers:

...their riches will not avail them, neither
their children...they shall be fuel for the
Fire like Pharaoh's folk, and the people before them...God is terrible in *retribution*.
(p.74)

Neither possessions nor sons of unbelievers will do any good to them...they are fuel
of hell...Their path is the path of the Pharaoh dynasty and their like before...God's
punishment is very severe. (3:10, 11)

Now, more Christian than Jewish:

Decked out fair to men is the love of
lusts—women, children, heaped-up heaps
of gold and silver, horses of mark, cattle
and tillage. That is the enjoyment of the
present life; but God—with him is the
fairest resort. (p.74)

Sensual (carnal) desires, especially for
women and sons (young boys?), selfish
(material) propensities for heaps of gold
and silver, for good horses and milkable
animals, and for earthly produce were
made attractive for men. These are the
temporary interests of this-worldly life.
Whereas the beautiful place to arrive at is
in the presence of God. (3:14)

And even better for the god-fearing men is:

...gardens underneath which rivers flow,
therein dwelling forever, and spouses purified, and God's good pleasure. (p.75)

...the heaven in which rivers flow, in
which they (the faithful) will reside to eter-
nity with the purest of companions, and
above all, there is the favor of God. (3:15)

The heavenly blessings are for those who are patient, honest, obedient, charitable, and
God-fearing. Instead of threat of punishment in this world, promise of reward in the other
world. Also note the lumping of human beings with heaps of gold and silver.

Islam, that borrows hell and heaven from Christianity, in contradistinction to their absence in the more this-worldly Judaism, surpasses the second Abrahamic religion in its faith
appeal in positively describing the blessings of heaven (contrast with the horrifying descriptions of hell in Revelation, for example), and above all the promise of "pure companions"
(or "pure spouses" in Arberry) to men. The reference to the unmeritoriousness of a penchant for women is but a fake lip-service to abstinence (just as the one to worldly riches is);
Islam, compared to the misogynist (and ambivalently anti-wealth) Christianity, is basically
and outspokenly sexual and materialistic—both in this and the other world, very much like
its Judaic ancestor insofar as this world is concerned. Add to it the promise of pure companions and other material ornaments (see below for more) in the other world, too, and, its
emergence as a powerful competitor to Christianity and as a sure victor over Judaism becomes clearer.

In the eyes of God, "true religion"[4] is Islam. Peoples of the book succumbed to conflict
because of mutual (ethnic?) jealousy (3:19). God is the real, sole owner of "mülk," sovereignty, dominion, creation (3:26). God penetrates into you and knows what is in you
(3:29). God to Muhammad: "Say (to them) that if you love God obey him, so that God will
love you and forgive your sins (3:31). Familiar theme.

Adam, Noah, Abraham, İmrân, and their descendants are mentioned as a chosen family
(3:33-34). Zachariah, Mary's aunt's husband, is mentioned as the protector of Mary (and
Jesus) (3:37). Zachariah wants a son, his wife is barren, God gives Mary Jesus by immaculate conception, and God will

...teach him the Book, the wisdom, the *Torah*, the Gospel. (p.80)	...teach Jesus writing, wisdom, the *Old Testament* (Tevrat) and the *New Testament* (İncil). (3:48)

Jesus will say to the Israelites:

I have come to you with a sign from your Lord...confirming the truth of the *Torah* before me, and to make lawful to you cer- tain things that before were forbidden unto you...so fear you God, and obey you me. (p.80)	I am bringing you miracles from your Lord...I am being sent to affirm the *Old Testament* that has preceded me and to make lawful some of the things that were unlawful for you...So fear God and obey me, too. (3:49-50)

Muhammad, in a virtuoso-like manner, using Jesus, appropriates the Christian technique
of affirming Judaism by disconfirming "the Law" and its burdens and constrictions; making
Islam a more appealing chapter in the Abrahamic Book.

He also uses, using Jesus, the Three Commandments effectively: Fear → believe →
obey. Or is it Two?: Fear → Obey? Or can it be reduced to One: FEAR? Variations on the
theme: Five Commandments: Fear, believe, obey, be holy/chosen/elect *and* prosper! As we

shall see, *Koran* will do this, too: Prosperity (trimmed by charity) here and now and then and there. (See infra.) Industrial capitalism may be as young as 300 years old but spiritual capitalism is 1400 years old if we take the *Koran* or 2500 years old if we take the *Old Testament*.

Thus, according to the *Koran*, Jesus both affirms the *Old Testament*, and at the same time, modifies it. The *Koran*, simultaneously posits a basic continuity in the *Old* and the *New Testaments*, as it does between itself and the *Bible*, and certain discontinuities—in interpretation, if not in the theoretical core. The *Koran*, in fact, does not sufficiently problematize the relationship between the two biblical testaments and between Moses and Jesus, as it does not problematize the relationship between itself and the *Bible*. It is theoretically, and diplomatically, pragmatic, generous hearted, flexible, and inclusive.

So inclusionary and, indeed, so gregarious that it makes the Apostles to say the following to Jesus when he asks for assistance in the walk of God:

We will be helpers of God; we believe in God; witness thou our submission. (p.81)

(The Apostles:) We are the helpers in the walk of God. We believed in Allah; be our witness that we are Muslims. (3:52)

The logical anachronism aside, the coverage of *Koran*'s intended appeal is remarkable. Yet, ecumenical flexibility has its limits, for the immediately following âyet rejects trinity, or rather has the very Apostles reject it. The Apostles confirm God's prophets and his oneness/unity (3:53). (How can they, non-anachronically, confirm Muhammad?)

Resurrection of Jesus is confirmed (3:55).

Unbelievers are to be punished both in this world and the world hereafter (3:56).

God created Jesus just like Adam, that is from earth (3:59). (Adam did not have a father and mother, but Jesus did have the latter, if not the former.)

God instructs Muhammad to tell to the peoples of the book that the common denominator among them is the worship of Allah, the one God, and to tell them to say that "We are Muslims" (3:64). (One God, one Prophet, one Book.)

People of the Book! Why do you dispute concerning Abraham? The *Torah* was not sent down, neither the Gospel, but after him. What, have you no reason? (pp.82-83)

Ye, peoples of the book! Why are you quarreling about[5] Abraham. Whereas the *Old Testament* and the *New Testament* were both revealed after him. Don't you ever think? (3:65)

No; Abraham in truth was not a Jew, neither a Christian; but he was a Muslim and one pure of faith; certainly he was never of the idolaters. (p.83)

Abraham was neither Jewish nor Christian; he was outright a Muslim, who recognized Allah as one and brought no partners to him. (3:67)

That Abraham was not a Christian or Jew (by faith) is true chronology-wise; but, by the same taken, he cannot be a Muslim. Yet, the *Koran* states otherwise. Monotheism starts with Abraham—a point on which all three Books agree—and the "quarrel" seems to be about "whose monotheism is better" (ethnic, not religious monotheism?).

3:68 holds that the human being "closest to Abraham" is Muhammad—and his followers. This, too, the infallible *Koran* knows best; people don't know:

Ha, you are the ones who dispute on what you know. Why then dispute you touching a matter of which you know not anything? God knows, and you know not. (p.83)	Ye are such people. Granted you may discuss subjects you know about, but why do you discuss those you don't know about. God knows everything, you don't know. (3:66)

People, unbelievers, can't win against the *Koran*; they either don't know (3:66) or they deny the truth although they know it (3:70) or, even worse, they distort and hide the truth purposefully (3:71). Monotheism (of *Koran*) is reaffirmed, trinity and the godliness of Jesus are rejected (3:79-81).

It is said that the promises given to God by prophets bind the whole community (3:81-82); the prophets Abraham, Ishmael, Isaac, Jacob and his descendants, Moses, Jesus are rementioned (3:84)—Muhammad being the last of the succession:

Whoso desires another religion than Islam, it shall not be accepted of him; in the next world he shall be among the losers. (p.85)	Whoever searches for a religion other than Islam should know that he will not be accepted, and he will be among those who are at a loss in the other world. (3:85)

Those believers turned unbelievers are cursed; but if they repent, God will be compassionate and merciful; if they don't, painful torment awaits even if they offer as ransom a world full of gold (3:86-91). It is said that the first temple is Kâbe, first built by Abraham (3:96).

While in the *Old Testament* God's walk was reserved for the Israelites as the chosen nation, the *Koran* calls all people, without regard to ethnicity, to hold on to "God's rope":

O believers, fear God as He should be feared, and see you do not die, save in surrender. And hold you fast to God's bond, together, and do not scatter; remember God's blessing upon you when you were enemies, and He brought your hearts together, so that by His blessing you became brothers. (pp.86-87)	Ye, believers! Fear God as it becomes him and surrender your lives but as Muslims. All of you together, tightly hold on to Allah's rope (Islam); don't get divided...Once you were enemies of each other, but he united your hearts and you became brothers with his blessing. (3:102-103)

Fear → believe → live; no fear → no faith → death. Tradition continues.

But fraternity, not fraternal strife; peaceful coexistence, not war in the "national inter-est." Yet this "universalism" is immediately marred by certain qualifications. Or is it not?

You are the best *nation* ever brought forth to men, bidding to honour, and forbid-ding dishonour, and believing in God. Had the People of the Book believed, it were better for them; some of them are be-lievers, but the most of them are ungodly. (p.87)	You are the best (most blessed) commu-nity brought forth for the good of human-ity; you command good, forbid evil, and believe in God. Had the peoples of the book, too, believed, that would have been best for themselves. Though there are be-lievers among them, most of them are astray. (3:110)

The above favoring of a particular community seems to rest more on a religious criterion than an ethnic, or ethnic-religious, one. Still some anti-Jewish sentiment that can compete with the *Old Testament* follows immediately:

Abasement shall be pitched on them, wherever they are come upon, except they be in a bond of God, and a bond of the people; they will be laden with the burden of God's anger, and *poverty* shall be pitched on them; that, because they disbe-lieved in God's signs, and slew the Prophets without right; that, for that they acted rebelliously and were transgressors. (p.88)	They (Jews), wherever they are found, are stamped with degradation, are subjected to God's fury, are condemned to apathy, un-less they seek refuge in God's covenant and the protection of the faithful. For they have been denying Allah's *ayats* and un-justly killing God's prophets because of their rebelliousness and going too far.[6] (3:112)

"Rebellious," "going too far" ("who are they?"); therefore, degraded and miserable. (Quite familiar…)

Yet:

Yet they are not all alike; some of the Peo-ple of the Book are a nation upstanding, that recite God's signs…believing in God and in the Last Day… (p.88)	Not all are the same…(some) believe in God and the day of judgment…Recite God's *ayats*[7]… (3:113-114)

In other words, a good Jew is a non-Jew, a Jew turned Muslim. Ecumenicalism not univer-salistic and pluralistic, but ethnically comprehensive and religiously assimilationist. Freud says that all religions are by definition, by the necessity of their inner-logic, are/have to be exclusionary.

| O believers, take not for your intimates outside yourselves; such men spare nothing to ruin you… (p.88) | Ye, believers! Don't confide in those who are not one of you. For they won't ever keep back from doing evil to you. (3:118) |

What are the limits of fraternalism? What are the parameters of universalism? What are the boundaries of "oneness" and "otherness?" Believers of one book are good, believers of other books (though they are basically the same) are bad and evil. God fights for his people (3:123, 125); interest is forbidden (3:130); believers are to spend to do good both in prosperity and poverty (shortage), to restrain their anger, to forgive people (3:134).

The *Koran* is somewhat less strict and less ritualistic than the *Torah* concerning sin and repentance: "when (believers) do evil or wrong themselves(!) they immediately repent…and do not wittingly persist in their evil deeds" (3:135). Books and laws and The Book and The Law: "Before you many divine laws have come and gone. Travel over the world and see the end of those who considered them (Allah's *ayats*) false" (3:137).

The *Koran*, again ingenuously retroactive, continues: "This (*Koran*) is an explanation to all mankind; and it is a spiritual guidance and advice for the believers"[8] (3:138). "If you believe, you shall overcome" (3:139). Those who die while walking with God are not dead but alive (3:169-170). And: Ye, believers! Be patient; be persistent (in the face of enemy); be prepared and vigilant for "jihad"; and fear God so that you can succeed (3:200).

Old and *New Testaments* all over.

4. Nisâ (Women)   (Medina)

God created man from one self (flesh) and his companion, too, from that very self (4:1). (Cf. Genesis.) (Arberry has "soul" for "nefis" (100), and incorrectly, I think.) Do not expropriate, God (Muhammad, *Koran*) says, the possessions of the fatherless (4:2). He continues:

| If you fear that you will not act justly towards the orphans, marry such women as seem good to you, two, three, four; but if you fear you will not be equitable, then only one, or what your right hands own. (p.100) | If you fear that you will not be able to observe the rights of the fatherless, take two or three or four wives, from among women you like. If you cannot afford that, take one or be contented with what you have [concubines]. (4:3) |

The fatherless, or the orphans, in question are young girls under the custody of men.

Concubines (unlimited) plus (up to) four wives are made lawful for the ordinary male faithful. (To the lawful quota of the prophet himself we shall come later.) This is not a command; it is a permission. Virgin females are easily appropriated at any rate.

Islam's penchant for patriarchal polygamy is closer to Judaism and is in stark contrast to the Pauline Christianity's celibacy as the first best and monogamy as the second best, the schizophrenic nature of the latter notwithstanding. (Supra.)

Islam does have a robust appetite for women as well as their wealth.

And give the women their dowries as a gift spontaneous; but if they are pleased to offer you any of it, consume it with wholesome appetite. But do not give to fools their property that God has assigned to you to manage... (p.100)

Give women their "mehir" (marriage money) willingly. If they donate (reimburse) part of their "mehir" to you, consume it with a good appetite. But do not give to those who are not discerning (not of age) their property that God has given you to maintain your livelihood. (4:4-5)

Elder men living off the property of fatherless younger girls under the auspices of God and with divine legitimation.

"Until they reach the age of marriage, protect the fatherless (girls); when they mature mentally, give their possessions back to them; do not waste their possessions" (4:6).

Both men and women are to have a share from inheritance of parents and relatives (4:7). This and the following *âyets* clarify, complement, and supersede Bakara 2:180. No need to will an inheritance to lawful heirs any more—since here specified—but shares may still be willed for the poor and for charitable institutions.

Give a share, as well, to relatives who are not regular heirs, to the fatherless, and to the poor if they are present at the distribution of the inheritance (4:8).

"Those who unjustly encroach upon the possessions of the fatherless will surely have their stomachs filled up with fire" (4:10).

The *Koran* regulates the distribution of inheritance, after debts and testaments are deducted (4:11-12):

- Sons get twice as much daughters;
- 2/3 to daughters if they are more than two;
- 1/2 to the daughter if she is the only child;
- 1/6 to each of the parents if the deceased has children;
- 1/3 to the mother, 2/3 to the father if the deceased has no children;
- 1/6 to the mother if the deceased has brothers (and sisters).

The golden rule of 1 to 2 (one male witness vs. 2 female witnesses, Cf. Bakara supra) is basically upheld here as well. The list continues, *Koran* addressing men:

- 1/2 is yours (man's) if your (deceased) wife has no children;
- 1/4 is yours (man's) if your (deceased) wife has children;
- 1/4 belongs to your (deceased man's) wives, if you have no children;
- 1/8 belongs to your (deceased man's) wives, if you have children; and so forth.

If you obey these rules, you go to heaven; if you violate them, you go to hell (4:13-14). Divine legal binary oppositions of not manmade law but God-made law, that is, in John Locke's celebrated phrase, the law of the "infinitely wise Maker."

The rule concerning prostitution: "Bring four witnesses against your women who practice prostitution. Put those women into solitary confinement until death takes them or God opens a way for them" (4:15).

This punishment, milder than that of the Pentateuch, is further mitigated in the case of single women. "Punish both parties to the prostitution. But if they repent and behave properly do not punish and torment them, for God is most forgiving and protective" (4:16).

4:15 is for married women and 4:16 is for unmarried women. (Later *sura* 24, Nûr, will supersede these and bring "recm" [stoning to death] and "sopa" [beating with stick] penalties, respectively.)

What God forgives and accepts are only those repentances made after unintentional sins, as opposed to intentional sins (4:17).

Some rules concerning women:

Treat women well and kindly (4:19).

If you abandon a woman, do not get back the "mehir"[9] (marriage money) from her. (The amount determined according to custom and usage.)

"What happened in the past aside, do not marry women who had formerly been married to your father" (4:22).

To the rule of 2 woman = 1 man and to other unequal and asymmetric relationships between men and women, must be added the fact that rules concerning women are "addressed to" men (women are not valid interlocutors); they are the inferior gender which is being systematically categorized and classified (objects for classification by classifying subjects/male agents appointed by God).

Thus, the following women cannot be lawfully[10] married. They are *Koran*ically-legally ineligible (4:23):

"Your" Mothers,

"Your" Daughters,

"Your" Sisters,

"Your" Aunts (both),

"Your" Nieces (both),

"Your" Milk-mothers,

"Your" Milk-sisters,

"Your" step-daughters,[11]

"Your" wives' mothers,

Two sisters simultaneously,

Own sons' ex-wives.

This is basically *Torah* (and, apparently, still relevant). Minus: "However, bygones are bygones. God is very forgiving and protecting" (4:23).

Married women, too, are unlawful, unless they are concubinized as prisoners of war (4:24).

So God prescribes for you. Lawful for you, beyond all that, is that you may seek, using your wealth, in wedlock...Such wives as you enjoy thereby... (p.104)	This is God's command to you. Women other than these are lawful for you to acquire with your wealth. Pay their marriage money in return for making use of them. (4:24)

Women are commodities per order of God. If you cannot afford to marry faithful free women, you may marry your faithful concubines. If they practice prostitution after marriage, one half of the penalty for free women is applied to them (4:25).

Islam is an easy religion: "God wants to lighten your burden, because man is created weak" (4:28).

"Do not exchange and acquire property other than by way of commerce based on mutual agreement" (4:29). Otherwise, you go to hell. "If you avoid big sins, we will overlook your little sins" (4:31). Islam is a tolerant religion.

Do not covet that whereby God in bounty has preferred one of you above another. (p.105)	Do not envy (covetously desire), others' God-given superiorities. (4:32)

Reminiscent of *New Testament*'s "differential gifts of grace," this injunction, which assumes inequalities between human beings in general, is immediately complemented by gender-inequality:

Men are the managers of the affairs of women for that God has preferred in bounty one of them over another, and for that they have expended of their property. Righteous women are therefore obedient...And those you fear may be rebellious admonish; banish them to their couches, and beat them...God is All-high, All-great. (pp.105-106)	Since God has made some human beings superior to others and since they spend from their possessions, men are women's administrators and protectors. Therefore, righteous women are obedient...Give advice to those women whom you worry would rebel, leave them alone in their beds, and (if they don't reform) beat them...God is high and great. (4:34)

A perfect mechanics of inequality and hierarchy of men-men and men-women. All-encompassing and cumulative. Natural (Godly) superiority → greater wealth→ greater power and divinely legitimate authority to rule and dominate the inferior ones (most men and all women) who should obey/submit and not rebel. Women are beatable per order of God, and on pretext of suspected mischief and before the fact. Preemptive disciplinary punishment.

Some moral rules (4:36-37), deriving from the Ten Commandments:

• Worship God

- Treat well: parents, relatives, neighbors, poor, friends, travelers, slaves, concubines, servants
- Do not: brag, be stingy

Do not behave like "Saturday-men" (4:47): those Jews who do not observe the Sabbath.

Abraham is reaffirmed as the first prophet to whose descendants was given the Book (4:54).

O believers, obey God, and obey the Messenger and those in authority among you. (p.109)	Ye, believers! Obey God. Obey the Prophet. Obey your governors. (4:59)

SUBMIT TO AUTHORITIES! In divinely legitimating worldly authorities and powers that be Islam is replicating the basic political theory of Christianity.

In case people bring their dispute to the Prophet to arbitrate but do not wholeheartedly accept his judgment, such people cannot be considered to be true believers (4: 65). This absolute authority and unquestionable legitimacy given to Muhammad, like that of Moses and Jesus, is further fortified by the following:

Whosoever obeys the Messenger, thereby obeys God. (p.112)	Whoever obeys the Prophet, obeys God. (4:80)

The "God → Prophet/Governors → men" hierarchy is hemmed in from another (again, un-Promethean and biblical) angle:

Whatever good visits thee, it is of God; whatever evil visits thee is of thyself. (p.112)	The good that accrues to you is from God. The evil that befalls you is from your self. (4:79)

Some rules concerning "holy war" ("jihad"): "Ye, believers! Be prepared for and go to war, all-out war if necessary" (4:71). "There are some among you who drag their feet in going to Jihad" (4:72). "Except for the disabled, the faithful who sit on their backs are not the same with those who make holy war in the way of God with their lives and possessions: God holds the latter superior to the former" (4:95).

Immigration ("hicret") from Mekke to Medine is obligatory for the faithful. (Cf. Exodus, the wandering and warring in the desert.)

"A believer does not have the right to kill another believer.[12] If he does so accidentally, he must free a believing slave and pay ransom to the murderee's family, unless the later waives it...If he cannot afford these...he should fast for two consecutive months in order that God accept his repentance" (4:92).

"The punishment for intentionally killing a believer is to stay eternally in hell" (4:93), in addition to retaliation in this world.

Nisâ *sura* closes with a series of Mosaic and Biblical rules after God says to Muhammed "we truthfully revealed the Book to you so that you rule among people in the manner shown to you by God" (4:105):

Slander is a big sin (4:112).

"Whoever opposes the Prophet and goes astray from the believers' way...we put him in hell" (4:115).

Satan is cursed; his followers are nominated for hell (4:118, 121).

False testimony is not to be given against parents, the rich or the poor (4:135).

"Believe God, his Prophet, the book he revealed to him, and the book(s) he had previously revealed" (4:136). And his angels.

Believers are not to mix with non-believers (4:140).

God is to bless both of the separating spouses (4:130).

The *Koran* respects the unity and continuity of the Abrahamic tradition, with its Lord, book(s), and prophets: "Those who deny God and his prophets and want to separate God and his prophets from one another and say "we believe in some but not others, and thus wish to strike a way in between faith and disbelief...These are the real infidels" (4:150-151). Such will be tormented.

Moses, the Golden Calf, Sabbath, plagues are reminded.

Jesus was not killed but gathered to God; "Every one of the peoples of the book shall certainly believe in him before dying. He, in turn, on the day of last judgment, will stand as witness to each" (4:159).

Those Jews who convert believers, take interest, encroach upon others' possessions are cursed; those Jews who convert to Islam are blessed (4:160-162).

God revealed to Muhammad as he did to Noah. Abraham, Ishmael, Isaac, Jacob, their descendants, Jesus, Job, Jorah, Aaron, and Solomon, and gave to David the Psalms (4:163.) And God "really talked to Moses" (4:164).

God is one, God is not three, he is above from having a child, Jesus is merely a prophet of God, the Messiah and the angels are but his servants (4:171-172).

And some more inheritance rules.

24. Nûr (Light, illumination, enlightenment) (Medina)

In this *sura*, which receives its name from the 35th *ayat*, further rules concerning women and gender/sexuality are prescribed. Therefore, I once interfere with the chronological order and bring this *sura* close to Nisâ *sura* along with *suras* 33, 58, 65, and 66.

Some cultic *ayats,* and then the rules for women and gender relationships.

God is "light" in the most comprehensive sense and knows everything. (See 24:35) God created all living beings from "water" (24:45). (As opposed to "dust?") Believers just say: "We heard and obeyed" (24:51). Prophet's word is God's word: "Obey God; obey the Prophet, too" (24:54).

Now, social rules:

Hundred sticks each to the adulterer and the adulteress (24:2)—if they are singles. (If married, stoning to death. Cf. Nisâ supra.)

An adulterer cannot marry women other than adulteresses and non-believers (polytheists) (24:3).

Eighty sticks to that which charges an honest woman with adultery without being able to prove it with the testimony of four witnesses (24:4). (See also 6-9.)

Bad women become bad men and vice versa; good women become good men and vice versa (24:26).

"Ye, believers! Do not enter others' homes unannounced and without salutation" (24:27).

"My Prophet! Tell faithful men not to fix their eyes on women who are unlawful for them and to protect their chastity" (24:30).

And: "Tell faithful women, too, not to eye men who are unlawful for them" (24:31).

Ayat 24:31 continues to give a long list of do's and don'ts for women. They

should not expose their (bodily) "zinet"[13] except for those parts that are visible (face, hands, and feet—feet being controversial);

should extend their head covers down to the brim of their necks;

should not stamp their feet (or walk in such a manner as) to draw attention to their (bodily) "zinet" (secret treasures of their body).

And, women should not show their "zinet" (bodies, bodily treasures) to men other than:

husbands,

fathers,

fathers-in-law,

sons,

step-sons,

brothers,

sons of brothers,

sons of sisters,

maidservants,

manservants,

servant-like persons or slaves who do not feel "lust" for family-women,

children yet "innocent of women's secret feminine characteristics" (12 categories).

What an array of men to whom women can show their bodily treasures (beyond face, hands, and feet)! How unconvincing is the "jewelry-hypothesis"[14] in the face of textual-linguistic data concerning "lust" and "innocence of women's secret feminine characteristics!" And: how incontrovertibly libertarian Islam is in the private sphere, in the intimate atmosphere of family life, of the household!

As for the public sphere, there is much futility in the present debate; veil is not commanded, but turban *is*, by the *Koran* in view of the foregoing.

Nûr *sura* cares for concubines and female slaves: "With your slaves and concubines in whom you see talent and have confidence make a "mükâtebe" (a contract of freedom in return for a price)…do not force your honest concubines into prostitution in order to acquire this world's temporary gains" (24:33).

33. Ahzâb (The Confederates)   (Medina)
(Please also Cf. Chapter V, for the rest of the *sura*.)

If a woman is one of the Prophet's wives, her shameful act is punished doubly (33:30).

"Ye, prophet's wives! You are not like those ordinary women…" (33:32). (Cf. also the hierarchization and stratification of women within their own category of woman in Chapter V, Rûm *sura*, [30:28].)

More importantly, the "lawful" quota of wives for the Prophet himself beyond the standard maximum of four wives for the ordinary faithful men (Nisa 4:3) is as follows (30:50):

wives for whom he has paid "mehir,"[15]

his concubines,

daughters of his

(both) uncles,[16]

(both) aunts,[17]

who have migrated with him,

faithful women who "donate themselves" to him if he accepts to wed them.

But: not more wives than this (lip-service to auto-limitation), as if "this" leaves anything to be desired (33:52). (Yet, compare to David's 700 wives and 300 concubines.)

And: quite a number of comforting privileges to the prophet in his dealings with wives (33:51). And all these for the "happiness" of the wives.

58. Mücâdele (The Dispute[rs])   (Medina)
Those women who discuss their husbands with the Prophet and denounce them to God are "heard by" God, and Muhammad enters between husband and wife per order of God (58:1). "Wives of those men who make "zihâr"[18] are not their mothers…No doubt they (men) are saying an unbecoming thing" (58:2). In case that the man declaring "zihar" wants to return to his wife, he should free a slave (58:3) or fast for two months or feed sixty poor (58:4) before he has intercourse.

65. Talâk (Divorce)   (Medina)
When a man wishes to divorce a woman, he should fear God and observe her periods before he divorces her with two witnesses (65:1-3). The waiting period for post-period women is 3 months; it is 9 months for pregnant women (65:4).

66. Tahrim (The Forbidding)   (Medina)

"If he (the *Prophet*) divorces you, his Lord may give him better wives than you—devoted to God, faithful, persistently obedient, repentant, worshipping, fasting, widow or virgin" (66:5). (Cf. the *New Testament*: "Obey your husband as you do your Lord.")

The treacherous wives of Noah and Lot are contrasted with that of Pharaoh and with Mary (66:10-12).

Notes

1. "Muhkem" has connotations also of firm, explicit, self-evident.

2. "Müteşabih" has connotations also of similar, indefinite, implicit, open to interpretation.

3. "Tevil" is also to explain away, to make forced interpretation, to use analogy.

4. "Religion" means obedience and punishment, nation and shariah; "Islam" means to obey and be bound, to attain liberation, there through (p. 51).

5. About his being Jewish or Christian.

6. Recall Numbers, Ch. 16 and Deuteronomy, Ch. 28.

7. *Koran* means "recite." Not "read," but "recite"—recite catechistically.

8. "Takva sahipleri."

9. Dowry is given/brought by the woman('s side); "mehir" is given by the man to the woman as the price for her.

10. Lawful: "helâl," unlawful: "haram."

11. "Unless you have formally married the mother but not yet lain with her" (4:23).

12. A fellow Israelite is replaced by a fellow Muslim believer.

13. "Zinet" means body here, but the other, more generic connotation of the word is ornament, jewelry. So, "bodily treasures" of women would be most apt. One interpretation that "zinet" here merely means expensive jewelry is not convincing. You don't normally feel "lust" for women's jewelry except in a figurative sense, anyway. Moreover, the *ayat* is using "zinet" in the context of face and hands and feet, and not with reference to expensive trinkets, rings or earrings.

14. The "jewelry-hypothesis" is over-determinedly doomed to bankruptcy in the light of further counter-evidential data contained in the *ayat* 24:60, concerning older or less attractive women: "There is no sinfulness in their taking out (some of) their dresses without exposing their zinet (to outsider men) for elder women who are not hopeful of marriage and expectant of children." Obviously, not mineral ornaments but bodily ornaments is the relevant connotation of "zinet" throughout. In other words, the essential, eternal beauty of the feminine body. Arberry, too, has "private parts" and "adornments."

15. The upper limit of 4 is not mentioned here.

16. Nieces were not lawful for ordinary believers. (Cf. 4:23 above.)

17. Nieces were not lawful for ordinary believers. (Cf. 4:23 above.)

18. "Zihâr" means saying to a wife: "You are to me like my mother's back," meaning that the husband is bored with the wife and that this is sufficient reason for the woman to become unlawful ("haram") to the man. *Koran* supposedly corrects such unfairness to women.

16

III. Suras 5-9: Mâide, En'âm, A'râf, Enfâl, Tevbe

5. Mâide (The Table)   (Medina, exc.3)

"Honor your contracts." (5:1)

"A list of lawfully huntable animals is to be announced." (5:1)

"Fear God, because his punishment is severe. (5:2) Carcass, blood, pig, etc., are not to be eaten." (5:3)

God speaks:

Today I perfected your religion for you, and I have completed My blessing upon you, and I have approved Islam for your religion. (p.128)	I completed your religion today, I concluded my blessings for you, and I chose (liked) Islam as the religion for you. (5:3)

Islam, on its own account, is the last and most perfect religion.

Honest faithful (Muslim) women as well as honest women of the book(s) are lawful for faithful men (5:5).

Rules of cleanliness for prayer (5:6).

Be truthful witnesses; be just even towards communities you hate (5:8). Islam is more Christian than Judaic here.

God was with the Israelites, but they did not keep their promise: "We cursed them because they violated their covenant, and we hardened their hearts. They changed the places of words. They also forgot a significant portion of the commands taught to them. Except for a very few of them, you see nothing but duplicity from them. All the same, forgive them and do not mind them. No doubt, God loves those who do good" (5:13).

Yahweh and Moses speaking, admonishing the Israelites for their betrayal of the absolute text. *Koran* owning the previous book(s). Very few good, many evil among the Israelites (and men in general). A more tolerant, however ambivalent, attitude towards the "other," compared to the *Old Testament*.

Christians, too, violated the Book (5:14).

Jesus Christ is not god (5:17).

"Jews and Christians said 'We are the children and the beloved of God', why then is he tormenting you because of your sins?" (5:18) "Ye, peoples of the book! Our envoy (Muhammad) came to you at a time when the succession of prophets was interrupted. He is explaining the truths to you… " (5;19).

Moses, chosen people, grumbling, Moses's complaints about the Israelites ("O, Lord! Set us and this deviant community apart," 5:25), 40-year wandering are reminded.

Cain is reproved, narrative of the Pentateuch is selectively referred to (sometimes with some gloss beyond the original text, e.g., the crow in 5:31), jealousy is disapproved (5:27-31).

Israelites' sins, especially their unrelenting "extremism" is mentioned (5:32).

"Those who war against God and his Prophet and try to create disorder on earth shall be punished by death, by hanging, by exile, or by cutting off of hands and feet diagonally… (and) great torment in the other world" (5:33).

Remember Numbers, Ch. 16 and Deuteronomy, Ch. 28.

Hands of a thief (man or woman) shall be cut off (5:38). Islam is more Judaic than Christian here.

"We revealed the *Old Testament*, which contained light and guidance to truth. Prophets devoted to God used to rule the Jews according to it" (5:44). "In the *Old Testament* we wrote for them: Life for life, eye for eye, more for more, ear for ear, tooth for tooth" (5:45). "We sent Jesus son of Mary and gave him the *New Testament*, containing light and guidance to truth, in affirmation of the *Old Testament*" (5:46).

And: "We sent you the Book (*Koran*) to affirm the previous book(s)" (5:48).

The textual lineage of the *Koran*, according to itself, is very clear. The Book means the two previous books and the third, last Book.

Who the people of the book are is not so clear:

O believers, take not Jews and Christians as friends… (p.136)	Ye, believers! Do not make friends from among Jews and Christians. (5:51)

That is, Jews and Christians are peoples of the book only, and only if they convert to Islam. The "universalism" attributed to Islam may be true in the sense of the nonexistence of ethnic discrimination (as in the *Old Testament*), but it stops there. Believers among the peoples of the book(s), who do not belong to the religion of Islam, are excluded—with sanctions, of course: from not mixing or messing up with to killing in holy war. (Which is not only an historical practice, but also a theoretical precept of the Islamic scripture, just like the Hebrew *Bible*. This is not universalism; it is unitarian religious communalism.)

Prejudice against the non-converted majority of the peoples of the book remains intact: "Majority of them are evil, but some among them are moderate" (5:66).

And, we may add, only a few of them can become good even if they convert to Islam.

A waltz of tautologies:

But had the People of the Book believed and been godfearing, We would have acquitted them of their evil deeds, and admitted them to Gardens of Bliss. (p.138)

Had the peoples of the book believed in Islam and avoided evil, we would have forgiven their past evil and have put them in heaven that abounds in blessings. (5:65)

And:

Had they performed the *Torah* and the Gospel, and what was sent down to them from their Lord, they would have eaten both what was above them, and what was beneath their feet. (p.138)

Had they correctly applied the *Old* and *New Testaments* and the *Koran* revealed by their Lord, they would have eaten both from above their heads and from below their feet [would have lived in prosperity, benefiting from the riches of the earth and of the underground]. (5:66)

So, it is as much a matter of believing in the *Koran* per se—it is only a final supplement to the *Bible*, perfecting it by way of affirmation and sublation—as a matter of correctly applying the three books, the Hebrew *Bible*, the Christian *Bible*, and the Muslim *Bible*, if you will, or the Biblical *Koran*, if you wish. This is what the *Koran* itself says. Three books in one: the Book. The problem is not with the Book; the problem is with the People(s) of the Book—with their non-compliant, deviant behavior. Please note the fact that Muslims, Christians and Jews, both preferably "ex-," are elevated—as "*the* people"—above other, non-bookish, peoples of humankind. Elitism continues; it is only that "chosenness" and "holiness" and "worthiness" is pushed one notch above in level of abstraction. It is not the chosen tribe any more but the chosen peoples, as opposed to infidels. The other(s) remain. Is this universalism?

And: Is it only the people who are faulty? Are there no faults in the Book(s)? (And: Who wrote the Book? Moses, Paul, Muhammad, and authors and redactors, of course.)

And: Are the three really the same book? (Scriptural, cooptative diplomacy may not be textual accuracy and identity.)

No trinity, but unity (5:73); Jesus's mother, despite what the Jews say, is an honorable woman (5:75).

In some ways the *Koran* identifies more with the *Old Testament*, in others with the *New Testament*. (That being its own intention, to my mind, in net balance, it resembles the former more than the latter.)

"Those Israelites who are non-believers have been cursed from the mouth of David and Jesus son of Mary. The reason for this is that they do not listen and they transgress limits" (5:78). And:

Thou wilt surely find the most hostile of men to the believers are the Jews and the idolaters; and thou wilt surely find the nearest of them in love to the believers are those who say 'We are Christians'; that, because some of them are priests and monks, and they wax not proud. (p.141)	You will find out that the worst enemies of believers are Jews and those that bring partners to God. Who are nearest to believers are those that say 'we are Christian'. For there are among them monks and priests who are not condescending (patronizing, vociferous). (5:82)

To my mind, this is very interesting and revealing in that Islam feels a greater threat of competition from Judaism precisely for the reason that it is doctrinally closer to it than it is to Christianity. Also, it seems, Islam feels that it can recruit more and more easily from the Christians.

Converts, too, are headed for heaven (5:85). (Also Cf. 5:69.)

You will not be held responsible for your accidental vows but for your conscious vows. Atonement ranges from fasting three days to feeding ten poor or freeing one slave (5:89).

"Ye, believers! Wine, gambling, idolatry, divination are Satanly unclean affairs" (5:90).

Limitations on hunting animals (5:95); fishing O.K. (5:96).

"Unclean and bad are not the same with clean and good" (5:100).

Don't ask too many questions (to Muhammad about the *Koran*) (5:101).

Limitations on animal offerings (5:103).

Don't give false testimony (5:107).

Miracles are given to Prophets by God (5:110). (Limits of prophets are reminded.)

Only God knows fully (5:110).

God is omnipotent (5:120).

6. En'âm (Cattle)   (Mecca, exc. 91-93, 151-153)

Creation story à la Genesis, destruction of sinful and ungrateful generations, day of last judgment, doomsday for unbelievers, omniscience and omnipotence of God, and descriptions of the *Koran* by God: "Had we revealed to you a book written on paper and had they held it with their hands, they would still have denied it"[1] (6:7).

Non-believers believe only in this world and reject resurrection (6:29).

And some of them there are that listen to thee, and We lay veils upon their hearts lest they understand it, and in their ears heaviness. (p.151)	In order that they (infidels) do not understand it (*Koran*) we put curtains over their hearts and weights on their ears. (6:25)

This is stronger, for example, than the *New Testament*'s "they see but not perceive, they hear but not understand" and closer to the *Old Testament*'s premeditated debilitation of men's understanding and comprehending. Hardening/sealing of hearts of the unchosen many. Blinding/deafening of the worthless multitude *so that* the chosen elect may remain few (the "remnant").

Are they infidels because they don't understand or accept or because God wants and predestines them to be so? Is this omnipotence in a perverse way? But this is the logic of Abrahamic monotheisms.

"Life in this world is but a play and entertainment. Life in the other world is certainly better for the faithful" (6:32).

"No man can change the words of God" (6:34).

"The dead will be resurrected and gathered to God" (6:36).

All animals and birds are "communities just like you" (6:38).

And those who cry lies to Our signs are deaf and dumb, dwelling in the shadows. Whomsoever God will, He leads astray, and whomsoever He will, He sets him on a straight path. (p.153)	Those who reject our *ayats* are the deaf and the mute who live in darkness. God leads astray or guides in the way of truth whomever he wishes. (6:39)

It is not that God punishes those who go astray because they are deaf and dumb; God premeditatedly makes some (most) deaf and dumb so that they go astray so that he can have the pretext to punish them.

Do they go astray or sin because they are deaf and mute (logical) or do they do so because God makes them deaf and mute and wilfully leads them astray (not very and kind)? Another implication: human beings do not have free will even to believe in the right book and to convert. It has already been decided for them by God.

Miseries and diseases sent to previous nations so that they submit (obey) (6:42). Here, not as punishment for non-compliance but as incentive for fearful compliance.

Torah, Moses, Yahweh speaking: "They should have bent their necks at least when we sent our fury upon them. But their hearts were further hardened… " (6:43).

Break their necks and bones when they are stiff-necked and hard-hearted; break their necks and bones when they are yielding and unenduring; break them any way. And who stiffens the neck and hardens the heart? Human beings themselves or God, at his prior will? (From this vicious circle, neither God nor men can emerge better off; only the authors of the books who rule men in the name of God can.)

The immense contemporary relevance of this sort of reasoning in our (still) monotheistic religious-"secular" Western civilization is nothing less than the following.

Since God *un*chooses, as he chooses, from the very beginning with the corollary that the unchosen ones are by definition guilty and therefore punishable in every severe and violent way. The modern men, too, looks at other men who err or think differently (according to any religio-cultural occasion at hand) as punishable or annihilatable violently, for it is ordained by no lesser a judge than God himself. Chosen men kill unchosen men (no "brothers" or other beloved children of God but sons of Satan); they comfortably perpetrate violence in the name of God and in their capacity as God's true children.

God knows who is worthy or not, regardless of riches and poverty (6:53).

"Men are returned to their real owner, God. Sovereign judgment belongs solely to him, and he is the fastest of reckoners" (6:62).

Do not mix or converse with nonbelievers (6:68). No rational discourse or discussion.

Abraham, Isaac, Jacob, Noah, David, Solomon, Job, Joseph, Aaron, Zaccariah, Joshua, Jesus, Elias, Ishmael, Elyesa, Jonah, Lot are mentioned. They have been given one or more of the following: prophethood, kingship, a book (6.83-86).

...and of their fathers, and of their seed, and of their brethren; and We elected them, and We guided them to a straight path. (p.159)	We gave some of their fathers or brothers superior merits (gifts of grace). We elected (chose) them and guided them in the way of truth. (6:87)

In other words, few men (the elite) more Godly, most men (the believing multitude) less Godly, the rest of mankind (unbelievers or believers of other ways) unlike him. Now, is this universalism or parochialism in the sense of unitarian religious communalism, which is anti-humanistic in the larger sense.

Jews did not recognize God properly and obey Moses properly (6:91). Now (with the *Koran*): "Your Lord's word has been completed in terms of truth and justice. There is no one to change his words. He hears, he knows" (6:115).

Sacred books are absolute texts; the (last) Book is the most absolute of them all.

Most men are worthless:

If thou obeyest the most part of those on earth they will lead thee astray from the path of God; they follow only surmise, merely conjecturing. (p.163)	If you conform to the majority on earth, they would lead you astray from God's way. They are directed by nothing but "zan" (opinion, surmise) and tell nothing but lies. (6:116)

Trust in the chosen, elite few; mistrust of ignorant and dishonest multitude. This is the Judaic-Christian-Islamic view of human nature or men in general, save for God's elect few. "God opens to Islam the hearts of those whom he wishes to lead in the way of truth; he constricts the hearts of those whom he wishes to lead astray" (6:125).

Rational will and free choice (to become a believer) or predestination predetermined by a segregationist God? Before questions such as "Are faith and reason compatible?" or "is faith reasonable" or, à la Kant, "religion within limits of reason?," must be put the question "doesn't Faith itself preempt and forbid reason in, to start with, choosing a belief, but requires, above all, "fear" of an "early-deciding" God, who is also a "fast-deciding" one on the last day.

All this is premeditated action, if not trap-setting. (I am borrowing the last phrase, too, from the *Koran*, as we shall shortly see.)

God does not destroy lands of people without prior notice (without sending prophets as warning) (6:131); God forbids killing of (female) children (6:140); eating carcass, blood, pig is forbidden; God forbade some animals to Jews not because they are unclean but because Jews were unjust (cruel) to them.

And a confession:

...for had He willed, He would have guided you all. (p.167)	Had God wished, he would have led all (human beings) in the way of truth. (6:149)

Why didn't he? (Cf. also supra.) Why isn't he as well-wishing as he is omnipotent. No manoeuver of theodicy has been able to convincingly answer such questions. Reasonless faith to the contrary notwithstanding.

A list of unlawful (unrighteous) acts (modified ten commandments) is given: Do not worship other gods, do good to your parents, do not kill your children because of poverty, avoid evil, do not kill unjustly, do not expropriate possessions of the fatherless, use honest scales, keep your promise to God (6:151-152).

Old Testament to Moses, *New Testament* to Jesus, *Koran* to Muhammad, and in Arabic so that "you couldn't say 'we didn't know' " (6:156; 6:154-157).

En'âm *sura* concludes with some more rules and articles of faith:

"Who comes into the presence of God with good (deeds), he will be rewarded tenfold; who comes with evil (deeds), he will be punished with an equal measure." (6:160)

"No doubt my prayer, my sacrifices/offerings, my life, my death, all are for my Lord God" (6:162). In other words, men *for God*, not God *for men*. It follows that men for *Prophets and Books*, not vice versa. (Cf. "Peoples *of the Book*, not the Book *of People* or Peoples' Book.) As I said above, neither people nor God form these inverted equations. Only the authors of the books who rule with them are the beneficiaries. When will "men" see that this is so? A critical analysis of the books is, perhaps, a first step.

God has Muhammad say: "He (God) has no partner. Only this was commanded to me, and I am the first of Muslims" (6:163).

What about Abraham and his 12 grandsons and the 12 apostles, whom the *Koran* had previously introduced as the first Muslims?

Finally, some testing and choosing (or first choosing and then testing, which is a non-testing): "He (God) is the one who made you successors of the earth, who made some of you superior to others in degrees in order to test you for the blessings he gave you. No doubt, your Lord punishes quickly, and he is forgiving and merciful" (6:165).

The elitist hierarchization of human beings aside, there is, in the light of the above, no real testing involved. Some (few) are made to get favor and some are made to get earmarked for sure punishment. It is not that some (most) err or sin; God has already, from the beginning, issued their contract. (Some interpretations state that the Prophet has said Jews were divided into 71 groups and all are in hell except one; and his community will be divided into 73 groups and all but one shall go to hell.) Revolutionary religions eating their own sons, and in ratios of 70/71 and 72/73. The "one" in Muhammad's community are his "ashab" (close companions)—just like, e.g., Moses and Aaron of Sons?) "Religions of salvation" saving all/most or very, very few?

7. A'raf (The Battlements) (Mecca)
Wicked nations were destroyed ("Our punishment descended upon them at night or in daytime," 7:4); day of judgment, Genesis, Satan, tree of knowledge, the fall.

"Ye, sons of Adam! We created clothing and ornamental raiments for you to cover your shameful parts" (7:26); beware the Satan so that your end will not be like your mother and father (7:27).

"There is an end to all communities/nations" (7:34). (Philosophy of history?)

Those who believe prophets who tell God's verses need not fear, those who do not will be in eternal infernal fire (7:35-36). (Cf. also 6:159.) Hell and heaven, the two parties in purgatory (7:45-46), *Koran* as the "scientifically explained book (7:52), creation in six days (7:54), destruction/annihilation of the (rest of the) tribes of Noah, *Hud, Salih*, Lot, Şuayb, of Sodom and Gomorrah, and of the Midianites. (No mention of Lot s daughters.) Plagues can be sent any time and unawares: while sleeping (7:97), while merry-making (7:98). (Cf. also the thief-like God.)

Exodus narratives and Mosaic wonders are selectively repeated; Pharaoh is reported to say "I shall cut off your hands and feet diagonally" (7:124); the 7-year famine is made to happen after Moses (7.130), but God says: "We took our revenge (from Pharaoh)" (7:136) any way; "Golden Calf," stone "tablets" of Moses, the 70 elders and the earthquake, 12 tribes, Sabbath regulations, plagues are mentioned.

And when they turned in disdain from that forbidding We said to them, 'Be you apes, miserably slinking!' (p.191)	When they (Israelites) became proud (conceited) and did not give up the things we forbade them, we said to them: "Become lowly (base) monkeys!" (7:166)

Also see the "dog" simile in 7:176.

We have created for Gehenna many jinn and men; they have hearts, but understand not with them; they have eyes, but perceive not with them; they have ears, but they hear not with them. They are like cattle; nay, rather they are further astray. Those—they are the heedless. (p.193)	We created most of djinns and men for hell. They have hearts but do not comprehend, they have eyes but do not see, they have ears but do not hear. Thus they are like animals; they are even more stupid than animals. They are the real unwary ones. (7:179)

Please also refer back to 6:165 and 6:159 for the large population of hell and note again that most men are considered to be evil, sinful, wicked, bad, *and* to be punished. Who says that religions are for "most," let alone "all"; they are for the chosen few. This is what all the Books themselves say in the Judeo-Christian-Muslim tradition, *Koran* reiterating *Old Testament's* and *New Testament's* view and end of men and heart-eye-ear discourse.

And this is—to some—the more/most universalistic religion of all. One that leaves out (or burns) "most" of human beings, or 72/73 of its own community. Penological choices are legion.

The beauty and importance of God's names is stated (7:180).

God the trapper, again: "We slowly destroy those who reject our verses and do so from a place totally unknown to/unexpected by them" (7:182).

In short, the sinful are punished in due course but suddenly and severely. No prior notice and deadline for repentance are given; the pre-chosen, if you will, sinful are directed to fall further astray, their hearts are sealed and hardened so that they will sin more, and consequently they are treated to heavier penalties.

Koran is the last station in the Abrahamic tradition: "Which word, then, shall they believe in after the *Koran*?" (7:185).

8. Enfâl (The Spoils) (Medina exc. 30-36)

> "War booty belongs to God and the Prophet. Therefore, if you are true believers, fear God and obey him and his Prophet." (8:1)

Meaning: Do not contest the Prophet's distribution of war booty.

Do not drag your feet in going to holy war (8:6), God fights for his faithful (8:12), believers should not evade war except for reasons of tactical manoeuver (8:15-16). Believers' conscience for killing in war is comforted: "In war you didn't kill them, but God killed them (enemies)" (8.17). Animal metaphor is repeated:

Surely the worst of beasts in God's sight are those that are deaf and dumb and do not understand. (p.199)	No doubt, the worst of animals in the eyes of God are the unthinking deaf and dumb (men). (8:22)

And:

If God had known any good in them He would have made them hear. (p.199)	Had Allah seen any goodness in them, he would have certainly made them to hear. (8:23)

Expendability. And tautology.

Homophobia against non-Muslim human beings repeated; pre-condemnation reiterated; the unchosen ones have no chance:

...and if He had made them hear, they would have turned away... (p.199)	Even if he had made them to hear, they would have turned their back. (8:23)

Control of minds through control of bodies is established graphically:

God stands between a man and his heart... (p.199)	God enters between the person and his heart. (8:24)

This physical proximity, as yet another intimation of omnipresence, to human beings' bodies, even to their internal organs, shall be reinforced by the celebrated phrase of "God's being nearer to people than their own jugular veins" (infra). Christianity, was "in" men; Islam, too, is in him, dividing him.

"Your possessions and sons are a matter of trial, and the big award is in the presence of God" (8:28). Promised land in this case is the other world.

God addresses the faithful: "Ye, believers! If you fear God, he gives you discretion to differentiate between good and evil, covers your crimes, and forgives you" (8:29). Fear → discretion → cover-up and forgiveness. Not, for example, discretion → love → award.

There is more. God addresses Muhammad:

And when the unbelievers were devising against thee...and God was devising; and God is the best of devisers. (p.200)	While they (nonbelievers) were lying in ambush for you...God, too, was preparing a trap for them. For God is the best of trap-setters. (8:30)

"God will separate the unclean and the pure (non-believers and believers) and heap all the unclean on top of one another and throw them into hell" (8:37).

"Make war to them until sedition is suppressed and religion totally belongs to God" (8:39). Final solution!

Distribution of spoils: "One fifth of war booty belongs to God, his Prophet, his relatives, the fatherless, the poor, the traveler" (8:41).

Reminiscent of God's share going to Aaron & Sons, 20% of war booty is to be appropriated and administered by the Prophet and his family.

God commands constant military preparedness (8:60).

Taking prisoners does not become a prophet, unless and until religion predominates in the world (8:67). So: "Ye, Prophet! Encourage the faithful to go to war. If there are to be twenty determined men among you, they will be victorious against two hundred (infidels)" (8:65).

In 8:66, God reduces the above ratio to 1 to 2.

9. Tevbe (Repentance) (Medina, exc. 128-129.)
Held by some interpretations to be a continuation of Enfâl *sura*, Tevbe is also primarily about holy war.

After a grant of respite to "müşriks" (those who reject unity and singularity of God, God of Islam, that is) (9:2), God instructs believers to kill them unless they repent (convert, that is), perform the prayer correctly, and give alms (9:5).

Holy war is waged with possessions and lives (9:20). (Note the ordering.)

"Fathers, sons, brothers, wives, relatives, possessions, commerce, houses" should not be valued more than "God, his Prophet, and holy war" (9:24).

"Jews said Uzeyr is God's son. Christians said Jesus is God's son...May God annihilate them" (9:30). "Jews made their rabbis lords and Christians made Jesus a lord" (9:31). "Ye, believers! Most of rabbis and priests unjustly appropriate people's possessions and lead them astray from God's walk. And those who heap gold and silver and not spend them in God's way: give them the news of painful torment" (9:34). "Those monies will be heated in hell's fire and their foreheads, sides and backs will be branded there with, and on that day it will be said to them: "This is the wealth you accumulated for yourselves, now feel the torment of it" (9:35).

Some opposition to religious leaders' and institutions' enriching themselves. Quite like the Gospels and unlike the Catholic church.

It is obligatory to wage holy war, except in four months out of twelve; evasion means preferring this-worldly life to the other-worldly life, which is sinful (9:36 and 39). Apparently, religious difference and peace are incompatible.

Resisting God and his Prophet sends one to hell (9:63); plagues sent to the tribes of Noah, *Ad, Semûd* are reminded (9.70); faithful men and women are promised heaven but, above all, God's favor (9:72); the weak, the poor, the sick are exempted from holy war (9:91); but the rich who drag their feet are held responsible (9:93).

Alms-giving of those who repent (and convert) is acceptable (9:104).

Mercy and rewards for faithful and repentant behavior—a conditional business transaction:

God has bought from the believers their selves and possessions against the gift of Paradise; they fight in the way of God; they kill, and are killed; that is a promise binding upon God in the *Torah*, and the Gospel, and the *Koran*; and who fulfils his covenant truer than God? So rejoice in the bargain you have made with Him... (p.220)

God has bought from the believers their possessions and lives in return for the heaven he will give them. For they make war, they kill and they die in God's way (for God). This is a true promise in the *Old Testament*, in the *New Testament*, and in the *Koran*. Who is more loyal to his promise than God? Therefore, rejoice over this exchange (transactions) you make with God. (9:111)

Do not ask for mercy for infidels (non-believers) even if they be your relatives or even still your father (9:113-114).

Another category is exempted from holy war: "It is not correct for all believers to go to war. Some of them should stay at home to cultivate their knowledge in the religious sciences and to guide (warn) their nation after the latter returns from war" (9:122).

"Since they are an uncomprehending tribe (unbelievers), God has turned their hearts away from faith" (9:127). As there are wicked individuals, there are wicked tribes—wholesale precondemnation of human groups, reminiscent of "solidarity in guilt" or collective guilt.

Tevbe *sura* closes with a Christian-like, or rather, Jesus-like verse. God speaking: "Such a Prophet has come to you within yourself that he feels very sorry for (he takes upon himself) your suffering. He is very caring, compassionate, and merciful for/to the faithful" (9:128).

Notes

1. The *Koran* was dictated by God to Muhammad either directly or through Gabriel.

IV. Suras 10-24

10. Yûnus (Jonah)   (Mecca, exc. 40, 94, 96)

Creation in six days, God's powers, heaven and hell, punishment of guilty tribes especially for treating their prophets unjustly, oneness of God, God the trap-setter:

God is swifter at devising; surely Our messengers are writing down what you are devising. (p.227)	God's trap is faster. No doubt our prophets are writing down the traps you set. (10:21)

Koran is absolute and unalterable (10:15).

People in distress pray to God, God saves them, they become ungrateful, they rejoice in their earthly blessings (power and wealth), God sends a plague suddenly at night or in day time. A surprise attack.

Righteous believers go to heaven, they are rewarded more than their good deeds; evil-doers go to hell, they are punished multiply (10:26-27). Above, it was said, proportionately. Human reason, reasoning, rational discourse, debate is outlawed again: "They abide by nothing but opinion. Opinion is no substitute for truth (science)" (10:36). "They" being "other than Muslim," and "science" being "Islamic faith."

This *Koran* could not have been forged apart from God; but it is a confirmation of what is before it, and a distinguishing of the Book, wherein is no doubt, from the Lord of all Being. (p.229)	This *Koran* is not something made up by one other than God himself. It is solely one which reaffirms its precedent and one which that explains that Book. There is no doubt in it; it is from the Lord of the universe. (10:37)

And:

Or do they say, 'Why, he has forged it'? (p.229)	Or, do they dare say he [Muhammad] made it up? (10:38)

The *Koran* and Muhammad again want to feel the authority of the *Bible* behind them. 10:41 states that the duty of Muhammad as a messenger of God's word, is but to announce and inform. (What about the holy war?)

Noah, Moses and Aaron against Pharaoh, Mosaic wonders are reminded.

Many prophets were sent to their respective communities; they rejected the prophets ("Thus we seal the hearts of those who transgress limits," 10:74); then(!) Moses and Aaron were sent to Pharaoh and his community.

We revealed to Moses and his brother, 'Take you, for your people, in Egypt certain houses; and make your houses a direction for men to pray to; and perform the prayer… (p.235)	We told Moses and his brother to prepare houses in Egypt for their community and to make these houses places for "namaz" (prayer) and to perform the prayer most properly. (10:87)

Selective repetition of the exodus narrative. *Koran* has Pharaoh, too, say:

I believe that there is no god but He in whom the Children of Israel believe; I am of those that surrender. (p.235)	I now really believe that there is no god but the God in whom Israelites believe. I, too, am a Muslim (one of the Muslims.) (10:90)

This is not only counter-factual given the original text; it is also anachronistic. But the *Koran* insists on continuity in and belonging to the Judeo-Christian-Islamic tradition. And:

So, if thou art in doubt regarding what We have sent down to thee, ask those who recite the Book before thee. (p.236)	My Prophet! If you doubt what I reveal to you, ask people who have read the Book (*Torah*) before you. (10:94)

And:

And if thy Lord had willed, whoever is in the earth would have believed…It is not for any soul to believe save by the leave of God; and He lays abomination upon those who have no understanding…But neither signs nor warnings avail a people who do not believe. (p.236)	Had your Lord willed, everybody on earth would certainly have believed…No one can believe without God's permission. He makes into heretics those who do not use their heads…Proofs and warnings are of no avail for a non-believing community. (10:99-101)

Again, what is the direction of the causal arrow? And why don't you let everyone believe, if you are a religion of salvation?

11. Hûd (Hood)   (Mecca, exc. 12, 17, 114)

| He knows what they secrete and what they publish; surely He knows all the thoughts within the breasts. (p.239) | God knows what (people) expose and hide. Because he is the one who knows the essence of hearts. (11:5) |

Omniscience of and omnipresence even within the hearts, the inner-beings, of human beings. Another variation on the theme of control by virtue of physical proximity to and penetration of bodies.

"Levh-i mahfuz" (preserved tablets, Moses's stone tablets) confirm the *Koran* (11:6).

Non-believers are skeptical, ungrateful, spoilt, and conceited (11:7-10). They "mock" the *Koran*. (Repeated sensitivity to "mockery.")

Detractors of Muhammad are defied to bring just 10 *suras* comparable to those in the *Koran* (which they cannot) (11:13). "If they can't answer you, know that this one (Book) is revealed by God's omniscience" (11:14).

Whoever cares only for worldly goods is awaited by fire in the other world (11:15-16).

Peoples of the book are different from total heretics (11:17). Yet, monotheists of the previous two books cannot escape from the holy war!

Noah and the flood are narrated at some length. Noah's 4th son[1] (?), who didn't believe, is said to be drowned (11:42).

Noah's ark lands on Mount Cûdi (not Mount Ararat) (11:44).

"Three visitors" of Abraham and the son given to his barren wife are mentioned, and Abraham is praised: "Abraham was really a good-natured, life-worn person, who had given (surrendered) himself to God" (11:75).

As recognized by all three, Judaism, Christianity, and Islam, Abraham was the first believer in monotheism.

Tribes sin, God destroys.

Lot's homosexual tribe is destroyed because they even wanted to harass God's angels (11:77-83). Lot's offering his own daughters in their stead is rendered in *Koran* in the following way: "Ye, my tribe! Here are my daughters;[2] they are cleaner for you. Fear God and don't shame me before my guests" (11:78). No qualms in the *Koran* about Lot's behavior, as is the case with the *New Testament*.

God addresses Muhammad concerning the familiar theme of the "remnant": "In the centuries before you, virtuous persons who could prevent people from corruption were not very forthcoming. But we have saved an exceptional portion (of people)…" (11:116). And yet: "Your Lord does not unjustly destroy countries whose people are good" (11:117).

But according to the book itself, narratively-factually, the ratio of good people/salvation to evil people/destruction remains lopsided at the expense of the former: Few/less against most/more is the basic balance.

As a matter of fact, the sacred book shortly says, once again: "Had your Lord wished, he would have made all human beings into one nation. But they will continue to remain in conflict" (11:118).

We leave the final word to God, addressing Muhammad:

...excepting those on whom thy Lord has mercy. To that end He created them, and perfectly is fulfilled the word of thy Lord: 'I shall assuredly fill Gehenna with jinn and men altogether.' (p.253)	However, those whom your Lord shows compassion are excepted. In fact, your Lord created them for this purpose. Your Lord's word has been vindicated: 'I swear that I shall fill hell completely with humans and djinns'. (11:119)

Koran, better than *Old Testament* and *New Testament*, explains and states the purpose of creation, that is, creation of men: To send very few to heaven and a very heavy majority to hell.

12. Yusuf (Joseph)   (Mecca, exc. 1-3)

This *sura* which is one of the few *sura*s that are named after a Biblical prophet (the others are 10. Yunus/Jonah, 11. Hûd/Hood, 14. 0brahim/Abraham, 71. Nuh/Noah) begins with the fraternal hostility between Jacob's sons. The *sura* has Joseph have a dream, and Jacob is made to say to Joseph: "My beloved child! Don't ever tell your dream to your brothers; if you do so, they would set a trap for you. For Satan is an open enemy of man" (12:5). And: "Your Lord will thus choose you...And bless you..." (12:6).

The reason for this particular choice is not given; the fact and privilege of "chosenness" (of one and or few) is axiomatically necessary for the argument.

The *sura* opens with the statements that:

We have sent it down as an Arabic *Koran*; haply you will understand. (p.254)	We revealed it as an Arabic *Koran* in order for you to understand. (12:2)
We will relate to thee the fairest of stories... (p.254)	Ye, Muhammad! In revealing this *Koran* to you, we are telling you the stories of past nations in a most beautiful (in the finest) way. (12:3)

The *sura* is about Joseph's story, told basically in *Old Testament*-like style. But why is Joseph chosen editorially for an exclusive narrative? Noah and Abraham are more readily understandable, but why Joseph? Is it because it is a success story, a story of power and wealth, a story of "from rags to riches?" Of course. Islam, very much like Judaism and the ambivalent Christianity, places great value on worldly riches as a reward for righteous behavior—diagonal messages to the contrary not-withstanding.

Joseph's tale is told in detail, with occasional glosses and embellishments that would not be supported by the letter (and spirit?) of the original text. For example:

- the mise-èn-scene of ladies' gathering in 12:31
- the gloss in 12:35
- the preaching in the prison in 12:39
- Joseph's preparing himself to Pharaoh in 12:55
- the distortion in 12:65
- the exaggeration in 12:100

The *Koran* has Jacob say: "Take my life as a Muslim" (12:101)!

God says to Muhammad: "However much you try, most of the people will not believe" (12:103). God has always sent male prophets (12:109). The historical-factual fact is verified, or perhaps rather prescribed, by the sacred text. Theory determines practice.

13. Ra'd (Thunder) (Mecca)

The very first *ayat* (verse) repeats a main theme: "These are the verses of the Book. They are the truth revealed to you by your Lord, but most of the people do not believe in them" (13:1).

Knowledge of truth is based on faith. The Book(s) do not only contain, among others, a political and moral theory but also an ontological and epistemological theory concerning the basis of our knowledge of reality.

Creation, creatures, unity and powers of God.

If obedience then reward, if disobedience then punishment; heaven and hell. More binary, Manichean oppositions and tautologies.

Heaven is described: "Features of the heaven promised to the faithful are (the following): rivers flow on its floor; its fruits and shadow are perpetual" (13:35).

The "promised land" with its rivers, milk and honey, fruits, etc., is being transferred, transplanted, projected, postponed to the world hereafter, but the structural features are quite similar. (*Torah* is more worldly than *New Testament* and *Koran* in this respect, too.)

The absoluteness and unalterability of the Book(s) is repeated:

God blots out, and He establishes whatsoever He will; and with Him is the Essence of the Book. (p.272)	God erases whatever he wishes and leaves intact whatever he wills. The original of all books is with him (in his presence). (13:39) –

The *sura* closes with the "trap" and legitimacy themes:

Those that were before them devised; but God's is the devising altogether. (p.273)	Previous generations, too, had set traps (for their prophets); whereas all traps belong to God. (13:42)

The threat is complemented by the legitimacy that the Book gives to the Prophet: God speaking, telling Muhammad to say to infidels:

God suffices as a witness between me and you, and whosoever possesses knowledge of the Book. (p.273)	Sufficient as witness between me and you is God and that one (Muhammad) which has with him the knowledge of the Book. (13:43)

Proximity to God, distance to other people, legitimacy bestowed by the knowledge of the Book, which is God's word: this is a powerful and authoritative (because power is legitimized) position indeed. A case of juxtaposition of God, Book, Prophet (the triad against the people), if not complete equation and identification of the three as in other Qoranic and Biblical situations.

But there is one trivial logical awkwardness in this spatio-sacred interrelationship: How can Muhammad be both in between two sides *and* on one of the opposite sides? He may ventriloquize textually, but can he also (perhaps miraculously) simultaneously occupy two coordinates?

14. İbrâhîm (Abraham)   (Mecca, exc. 28-29)
Only half as long as "Yusuf."
   Prophets are sent in the language of their own tribes/nations (14:4).
   Preferring this world to the other world is "perverse" (14:3).
   "God blesses only his chosen servants" (14:11).
   "Truly, man is very cruel and very ungrateful" (14:34). Very precise judgment on human nature.
   "Nothing remains secret from God on earth or in heavens" (14:38).
   Learn from the sins and punishments of previous peoples (14:45-52).

15. Hicr (El-Hijr)   (Mecca, exc. 87)
Creation, blessings, curses, mistreatment of prophets and Muhammad, story of Abraham longer here than in İbrahim , Lot, Sodom and Gomorrah.
   God speaking: "Surely we sent the *Koran*, and it will certainly be us who shall protect it" (15:9). And:

So We sent it down to the partitioners, who have broken the *Koran* into fragments…We shall surely question them all together. (p.286)	We torment those who divide *Koran* into parts. (15:90)

Absolute and indivisible text written and guarded by the infinitely wise maker and the omnipotent guardian, God.

16. NAHL (The Bee)   (Mecca, exc. 126-128)

A good example of tautology: "We did not send as prophets those to whom we did not re-veal" (16:43). It is wrong to bury newly born daughters (16:59). A very important passage which reveals God's approach to human beings:

If God should take men to task for their evildoing, He would not leave on the earth one creature that crawls; but He is deferring them to a term stated... (p.292)	Had God been intent on punishing people for their evil, he would have left no living being whatsoever on earth. But this, he is postponing to a certain period of his own discretion. (16:61)

Semantically means: he has not yet left but eventually will leave no living being on earth because all in fact deserve punishment. That is, the substantive intent or intention is not different in time 1 and time 2 (or x); "intent" pertains merely to timing. But why postpone? To prolong the torture? For most, if not all. (But here it is "all.") Homophobic in any case. (Not all or most of infidels, but "no living being.")

Following in tandem is a verse in which the same God gives kind advice to the honey-bee, pointing a picture of charming natural harmony (16:68).

Some intimation of equality (in nutrition?):

And God has preferred some of you over others in provision; but those that were preferred shall not give over their provision to that their right hands possess, so that they may be equal therein. (p.294)	God gave some of you a larger lot than others. But the former do not share their lot equally with those near them. (16:71)

That this is not "equality" but charitable inequality becomes clear immediately:

God has struck a similitude: a servant possessed by his master, having no power over anything, and one whom We have provided of Ourselves with a provision fair, and he expends of it secretly and openly. Are they equal? (p.294)	God gives the example of a powerless slave who has become the property of another man and a freeman who overtly or covertly spends (gives alms) from the nice lot we have given him. How can they possibly be equal? (16:75)

Charity is a corollary of inequality, not equality.

Surely God bids to justice and good-doing and giving to kinsmen; and He forbids indecency, dishonour, and insolence. (p.296)	God commands justice, goodness, (charity)[3] and help to relatives; he forbids wickedness,[4] evil, and injustice (oppression). (16:90)

Thus, 3 do's, 3 don'ts.
Honor contracts (16:91).
No false vows (16:94).
And:

If God had willed, He would have made you one nation; but He leads astray whom He will, and guides whom He will. (p.297)	Had God willed, he would have made you into one community, but he leads or misleads anyone he wishes. (16:95)

More predestination than free choice. More Babelization than universalism.

"Your worldly goods waste away; God's treasures endure." (16:96)

Continuity with Judaism reiterated: "What we are making unlawful to you, we had then made unlawful to the Jews. We were not unjust to them; they were unjust onto themselves" (16:118). (The Book is right, people are wrong.)

And We know very well that they say, 'Only a mortal is teaching him.' The speech of him at whom they hint is barbarous; and this is speech Arabic, manifest. (p.298)	We surely know that they say "*Koran* is taught to him (Muhammad) by a mere man." The language of the person allegedly involved is foreign, whereas this (*Koran*) is manifestly in Arabic. (16:103)

This is a refutation of the then current allegation that a Greek or Christian slave or monk was teaching the *Koran* to Muhammad. And linguistic nationalism, too?

17. İsrâ (The Night Journey)   (Mecca, exc. 26, 32-33, 57, 73-80)
In the Book he gave to Moses, God had said to Israelites: You will create disorder in the world twice and become conceited to an extreme degree (17:4).

God sent them to exile, he made them victorious again, they increased in number, wealth, and sons (17:5-6). They killed their prophets (Zacchariah, Yeremiah, Joshua) and attempted to kill Jesus.

Again, less free choice than predestination.

And every man—We have fastened to him his bird of omen upon his neck. (p.303)	We tied every man's fate onto his neck. (17:13)

No room for free will; both deeds and final destination pre-determined. (Then why postpone judgment?)

Behold, how We prefer some of them over others! And surely the world to come is greater in ranks, greater in preferment (p.304).

Look how we have made some men superior to others. Surely, the difference of degree and superiority shall be even greater in the other world (17:21).

Who says these are religions of salvation? They are religions of election of few and condemnation of most. And unequivocal declarations of inequality in the other world, too.

Some don'ts, mostly from the *Torah*:

Don't kill you children (17:31).

Don't go near adultery (17:32).

Don't murder except for a just reason (17:33).

Don't touch possessions of the fatherless (17:34).

    (girls who have not come of age)

Don't use dishonest scales (17:35).

Don't go after what you don't know about (17:36).

Don't be conceited (17:37).

Don't worship other gods (17:39).

Don't be stingy, and don't be overgenerous either (17:29).

Another wholesale punishment of all nations:

No city is there, but We shall destroy it before the Day of Resurrection, or We shall chastise it with a terrible chastisement; that is in the Book inscribed. (p.308)	Before the doomsday we shall either destroy or violently torment each and every country.[5] This is written in the preserved tablet. (17:58)

"Who is blind in this world will also be blind and further astray in the other world." (17:72)

Reminiscent of the admonishment of falterings of Moses and Aaron, God says to Muhammad: "Had we not made you patient, you were almost about to lean a little towards the others" (17:74). Continuity of the textual tradition is reiterated:

...the wont of those We sent before thee of Our Messengers; thou wilt find no change to Our wont. (p.311)	The law for the prophets we sent before you is the same as this one. You cannot find any change whatsoever in our law. (17:77)

18. Kehf (The Cave)   (Mecca, exc. 28)

Praise be to God and warn those who say "God adopted a son" (18:1-3).

[He] has sent down upon His servant the Book and has not assigned unto it any crookedness... (p.316)	He revealed to his servant (Muhammad) the truest of true books, this Book, which contains no contradiction or fault. (18:4)

God is one, he is the sole ruler, his sovereignty is indivisible (18:26). (Divine monotheistic prototype of later kingly or stately unitary sovereignty theories.)

In hell, the thirsty [greedy] will be treated to "a water like melted ore that burns faces" (18:29).

In heaven, believers will (18:31):

sit on thrones,

be ornamented with gold bracelets,

wear green clothes from brocade.

The other-worldly kingdom is modeled on this-worldly kingdoms. The heaven (and the postponed rewards of the earthly underdog) are royal, royalist, materialistic, aristocratic, and plutocratic. (Cf. Christianity's "the last to be the first.")

Still (it is said to the underdog here and now), worldly goods are temporary and unjust (18:32-43), and: "Wealth and sons are mere ornaments of this-worldly life" (18:46).

If temporary, unjust, ornamental, essentially meaningless, why promise them as good and valuable on the other, and allegedly more meaningful, side? (*Torah*, in this respect, is less hypocritical: "Prosper!" Greater possessions and more sons!)

The foregoing is not a typo, a slip, an accidental awkwardness. They are real values, and very crude materialistic values, for the Book cannot err or contradict itself as expressed many times above and as confirmed below:

How is it with this Book, that it leaves nothing behind, small and great, but it has numbered it? (p.322)	...what a book! It exhaustively enumerates everything that we have done great and small. (18:49)

And "shall do," we may add.

On human nature:

(M)an is the most disputatious of things. (p.322)	The creature who loves quarrel most is man. (18:54)

Rational and free discussion, including that about the book(s) and even among the faithful is banned. No questions allowed; believe and recite! Men are unthinking "things."

(As a logical extension), Hızır kills a boy: The parents of the boy were believers. We prevented the boy from dragging them to rebellion and ingratitude (18:80).

19. Meryem (Mary)   (Mecca, exc. 58, 71)

God gives a son, Joshua, to Zachariah s barren wife; he also gives a son to virgin Mary after Gabriel announces the good news; Jesus is a prophet from the cradle; he is not God s son; he is to mention Abraham, Isaac, Jacob, Moses, Aaron, Ishmael, and İdris as God s chosen ones (19:58).

But their descendants stopped performing the prayer ("namaz") and pursued selfish desires (19:59).

"We destroyed many generations" (19:90).

20. Tâhâ (Ta Ha)   (Mecca)

God chooses Moses, gives him Aaron as helper, Pharaoh is not convinced, plagues, contest of wonders, magicians come to believe in God and defy Pharaoh (20:72), exodus, wandering in the desert, Golden Calf, Genesis, and: "God is the true ruler/king" (20:114).

Tâhâ *sura*, which is reported to have convinced Omar to become a Muslim, approaches the end with,

Stretch not thine eyes to that We have given pairs of them to enjoy—the flower of the present life, that We may try them therein; and thy Lord's provision is better, and more enduring. (p.349)	Do not ever fix your eyes on the attractiveness of this-worldly life, which we have bestowed on some to test them. Your Lord's blessing is both more beneficial and longer-lasting. (20:131)

Do not covet worldly goods of others, "we give you your daily sustenance (subsistence)" (20:132), the *Koran* that commands this to you is itself a miracle (20:133), and ever mention the name of your Lord and ever sing your praises of him (20:130).

21. Enbiyâ (The Prophets)   (Mecca)

Unbelievers describe *ayats* as nonsensical dreams made up by Muhammad, who perhaps is a poet (21:5).

God speaking: We have not created the heavens and the earth and everything in between as a matter of play (and players) (21:16).

Abraham, Moses and Aaron, Lot, Isaac, Jacob, Noah, David, Solomon are mentioned.

Job, Ishmael, İdris, Zülkif—all good and patient persons—Janas, Zachariah, Joshua, and Mary are to be remembered. One book, not several:

We gave Moses and Aaron the Salvation and a Radiance, and a Remembrance...[6] (p.21)	We gave Moses and Aaron the Furkan.[7] (21:48)

Continuity of books and continuity of prophets and communities:

Surely this community of yours is one community, and I am your Lord; so serve Me. (p.25)	Truly, all this (prophets and their followers) are your community as one community. And I am your Lord. Therefore, serve me. (21:92)

Unity in religion and unison and order in the state:

But they split up their affair between them; all shall return to Us. (p.25)	Men have spoiled the affairs [of religion and state]. But all shall return to us. (21:93)

Even if absolute order does not obtain in this world, it shall do so in the other world. Yet:

For We have written in the Psalms, after the Remembrance, 'The earth shall be the inheritance of My righteous servants.' (p.26)	We had written in Zikir (*Torah*) and Zebur (Psalms of David) that: "My good servants will inherit the earth." (21:105)

Which one? This earth or the other earth? Plus: What about the chosen good always being the few, as opposed to the punishable "most?"

22. Hacc (The Pilgrimage)   (Mecca, exc. 19-24)

This *sura*, which maintains that the obligation of pilgrimage was initiated by Abraham (22:26), opens with fear of God and threat of death:

O men, fear your Lord! Surely, the earthquake of the Hour is a mighty thing. (p.27)	Ye, men! Fear your Lord. Because the earthquake of the doomsday is a terrible thing. (22:1)
On the day when you behold it, every suckling woman shall neglect the child she has suckled, and every pregnant woman shall deposit her burden. (p.27)	On the day you see it, all breast-feeding women shall forget their suckling child and all pregnant women shall abort their baby. (22:2)

Remember Deuteronomy, Chapter 28.

Facts of natural existence described as God's miracles, no "discussion of/about God" (22:9) allowed, punishment in hell:

They will be dressed up with fire (22:19).

Boiling water will be poured down over their heads (22:19), with which
their skin and the organs in their abdomen will be melted (22:20).

They will be beaten with iron whips (22:21).

As opposed to rewards in heaven (22:23):

They will be adorned with gold bracelets and pearls.

Their dress will be silken.

Rules of and offerings in pilgrimage specified, nations destroyed, God vs. Satan, "preserved tablets" (levh-i mahfuz).[8]

God at the beginning-throughout-at the end:

It is He who gave you life, then He shall make you dead, then He shall give you life. Surely man is ungrateful. (p.35)	He is the one who gave you life, who will give death to you, and who shall then resurrect you. Really, man is very ungrateful. (22:66)

And:

He has chosen you, and has laid on you no impediment in your religion, being the creed of your father Abraham; He named you Muslims aforetime and in this. (p.36)	He chose you. He imposed no burden on you as regards religion like in the religion of your father Abraham...He gave you the name of Muslims in this book [*Koran*] as well as in the previous ones. (22:78)

Islam is an easier religion, and it portrays Abraham's creed as such, in implicit distinction to the ritualistic Judaism and Christianity.

Five Commandments again:

O men, bow you down and prostrate yourselves, and serve your Lord, and do good; haply so you shall prosper. (p.36)	Ye, believers! Bow down, prostrate yourselves, worship your Lord, and do good, so that you may be saved. (22:77)

Fear → believe → obey → be righteous → and PROSPER! Happiness and salvation more often than not identified with prosperity.

23. Mü'Minûn (The Believers)   (Mecca)

Prayer, alms-giving, chastity, proper sexual relations, honoring oaths (23:1-10). Those who observe these first ten verses go to heaven.

Natural things described as supernatural blessings.

Unbelieving generations destroyed. Those who had said that Noah was a "mad person" (23:25) drowned.

...whenever its Messengers came to a nation they cried him lies, so We caused some of them to follow others, and We made them as but tales; so away with a people who do not believe! (p.40)	Every time they rejected our prophets we destroyed them one after another...From now on, any nation that does not believe, go to hell! (23:44)

Division of nations into communities in conflict is derided:

Surely this community of yours is one community, and I am your Lord; so fear Me. (p.41)	No doubt, all these people are one community, and I am your Lord. So, fear me (and yourselves from my anger). (23:52)

Religious unitarianism and totalitarianism. One, undivided, Islamic community of the faithful. Peoples of the book(s) becoming the People of The Book. Fear → believe → obey. If not, perish.

Still:

Or did they not recognize their Messenger and so denied him? Or do they say, 'He is bedeviled?' (p.42)	Are they, then rejecting their Prophet (Muhammad) because they have not yet recognized him? Or are they saying that there is madness in him? (23:69-70)

And, an indication of the purpose of creation:

What, did you think that We created you only for sport, and that you would not be returned to Us? (p.45)	Do you think that we created you for nothing and really will not summon you back into our presence? (23:115)
Then high exalted be God, the King, the True. There is no god but He, the Lord of the noble Throne. (p.45)	Allah is is most exalted. He is the absolute true. There is no god but him. He is the owner [lord] of the high throne. (23:116)

Islam, thus, is no less royalist than Judeo-Christianity.

24. Nûr

See Chapter 2 supra, ff. *sura* 4.

Notes
1. *Bible* mentions only three sons of Noah: Ham, Shem, Japtheth.

2. One interpretation has it that "my daughters" means not his own daughters but, in the generic sense, the girls of his tribe. Whatever the merit of such a stance and interpretation ethically, compare its textual validity with Genesis 19.

3. İhsan.

4. Fahşa, including lying, slander, adultery.

5. Destruction (helâk) means ordinary death; torment (azap) means murder or various calamities.

6. From hereon, page references are to Arberry, vol. II.

7. "Furkan" means that which separates the true from false, good from evil, right from wrong. In the *Koran*, this word is used for celestial books. In fact, one of the names of *Koran* is "Furkan," which is also the name of a *sura* (no. 25).

8. Stone tablets of Moses, the source of the whole *Bible* and the *Koran*.

18

V. SURAS 25-56

25. Furkân (Salvation, "That which separates the true from the false.") (Mecca, exc. 68-70)
God is sovereign, has no children, has no partner in power and wealth, creates and gives order to everything, determines destinies (25:1-2). God in the beginning, God in human history, God at the end (future). They say:

'This is naught but a calumny he has forged, and other folk have helped him to it.'…Fairy-tales of the ancients that he has had written down, so that they are recited to him at the dawn and in the evening. (p.56)

Koran is nothing but a lie made up by Muhammad. Another group has helped him in this respect…These verses are tales of yore recited to him day and night by others whom he has had written down. (25:4-5)

Koran is directly put into Muhammad's mouth without any human mediation.

Punishment and torment is not for once; it is perpetual (25:14). Denial of prophets and ensuing plagues are repeated. God speaks to Muhammad:

Or deemest thou that most of them hear or understand? They are but as the cattle; nay, they are further astray from the way. (p.60)

Do you at all think that most of them will truly listen or reason? No, they are like animals; they are even more deviant in their ways. (25:44)

Most human beings are animal-like or are lowlier beasts. This is *Koran's* estimate of human nature and worth. And:

If We had willed, We would have raised up in every city a warner. So obey not the unbelievers, but struggle with them thereby mightily. (p.60)

My Prophet! Had we willed we would certainly have sent a prophet to every country…But we gave the mission of warning all nations to you. (25:51-52)

Muhammad is the last and most authoritative prophet of Abrahamic monotheism; both holy war and persuasion(!); God sends him "only as a warner and a messenger of the good news" (25:56); still, the unrepenting non-Muslims "…are mocking [him] by saying: Is he the one whom God has sent as a prophet?" (25:41)

26. Şuarâ (The Poets)   (Mecca, exc. 224-227)
Muhammad is not a poet, nor is *Koran* poetry, as the detractors say. (It is not literature; it is solid scientific truth.) God's unity, his miracles, Pharaoh's magicians' believing in Moses' and Aaron's Lord, diagonal cutting off of hands and feet, exodus…

Noah saying(!) "Fear God and obey me" (26:110), his brothers replying "How can we believe you while people of low status are submitting to you?" (26:111). (Recruitment appeal to the dispossessed.)

God grants "flocks, sons, vineyards, streams" (26:132-134). (Note the ordering.)

"Do not create disorder in the world by subversive acts" (26:183).

On the authenticity and the lineage of the *Koran*: God revealed the *Koran* to Muhammad's heart in Arabic via Gabriel, the (essence and principles of) *Koran* was already there in the previous (true) books, this is proved by the fact that Israelite teachers of the law already knew it (26:192-197).

Although the poetical merits of the *Koran* is universally praised and acclaimed, the Book is not (sheer) poetry, for:

And the poets—the perverse follow them; hast thou not seen how they wander in every valley and how they say that which they do not. (p.75)

…only the perverse follow poets…who wander aimlessly in every valley and tell things which they don't really do. (26:224-226)

Koran, by its own fiat, is not metaphor, allegory, or myth. Unlike the *Old Testament* and the *New Testament*, it is pure scientific truth.

27. Neml (The Ants)   (Mecca)
Wonders given to Moses and David and Solomon (all three mighty and wealthy rulers).

Infidels say: Those are the same threats made to our ancestors; God replies: Tell them to travel around the world and see the end of sinners (27:68-69).

Concerning Israelites:

Surely this *Koran* relates to the Children of Israel most of that concerning which they are at variance. (p.83)

Truly, this *Koran* explains to Israelites many of the things they disagreed on. (27:76)

The same claim put forth by Christianity.

28. Kasas (The Story)   (Mecca, exc. 52-55)

Moses' story. Two textual problems: (1) It was not Pharaoh's wife (28:9) but his daughter who saved Moses; (2) the stories of Moses and Jacob are somewhat intermingled (confused) (28:26-27).

Some more textual lineage: "After destroying first generations, we gave to Moses that Book (*Torah*)" (28:43). And: "My Prophet! Tell them: If you are honest, bring me a book from God that is truer than these two (*Torah* and *Koran*)" (28:49).

Understandably and explicably, Muhammad sees the *Old Testament*, rather than the *New Testament*, as the stronger and more authoritative source (both rival and closer). "Those to whom we gave a book before the *Koran* will believe in the *Koran*, too" (28:52).

And: "They will also say: 'We were essentially Muslims before' " (28:53).

Some more on good and evil, reward and punishment:

How many a city We have destroyed that flourished in insolent ease. (p.92)	We have destroyed so many countries spoilt by their wealth (prosperity). (28:58)

The sin is not prosperity per se, but becoming spoilt and stiff-necked because of prosperity and wealth. (Note: not indifference to the poor, but insolence against God is involved. Still, there is the Christian breeze of "the poor shall inherit the earth" [which?].) As a matter of fact, the rest of the verse is as follows:

Those are their dwelling-places, undwelt in after them, except a little; Ourselves are the inheritors. (p.92)	See! Here are their lands. They have been scarcely inhabitable. We have become the inheritors. (28:58)

Muslims replacing (displacing, too?) Jews. No social class dimension, only religious-ethnic change of places.

Ambivalent or not so un-ambivalent?:

What, is he to whom We have promised a fair promise, and he receives it, like him to whom We have given the enjoyment of the present life, then he on the Resurrection Day shall be of those that are arraigned? (pp.92-93)	Is a person to whom we made and fulfilled a good promise the some as a person to whom we only gave the temporary interests and pleasures of this world?—and who will be brought before us on the doomsday (for torment)? (28:61)

"Your Lord creates and chooses men as he wishes. They have no right of choice" (28:68). No freedom of choice.

The Lord also commands: "Pray for the other world, but don't forget to ask for your worldly lot, either" (28:77).

Without "transgressing limits," of course. Not in getting richer, wealthier, more prosperous; but, depending on these, in becoming "stiff-necked" against God and his prophets and his ministers (priests, clergy, ulema, etc.). For:

Now Korah was of the people of Moses; he became insolent to them, for We had given him treasures such that the very keys of them were too heavy a burden for a company of men endowed with strength. (p.94)	Korah was from the tribe of Moses but had transgressed limits (rebelled). We had given such treasures to him that a strong and sturdy company of men could scarcely carry (even) his keys. (28:76)

And:

When his people said to him, 'Do not exult; God loves not those that exult'... (p.94)	His tribe had told him: "Don't become spoilt! Know that God does not love the conceited" (28:76).[1]

True, Aaron & Sons, Inc. was very rich. But:

(1) Korah had gone not against his tribe, but against Moses and Aaron.

(2) It was Moses and Aaron who had accused the tribal leaders of "having gone too far" ("transgressing limits") against themselves and, therefore, God. (Cf. Numbers, Ch. 16.) So, beware *Koran*'s glosses over or distortions of its original source, *Torah*; but more importantly, note that the bone of contention here is not *much money* but *weak faith*. (And remember money may have no nationality, but it does have its religion.)

I should make haste to add, however, that the matter is not that clear-cut, and that there is a tension between riches and something. But what is, precisely, that something?

In 28:78, the *Koran* has Korah say: "This (wealth) was given to me thanks to my own science" and in 28:79, the *Koran* states that the people coveted Korah's riches. Wrong: a faithful Jew may, and certainly does, want God—ordained riches, but not the wealth of his neighbor. In other words, Jews can, and do, want riches as their God commands: PROSPER!

In 28:80, the *Koran* ambiguously counterposes worldly goods to God's rewards to the faithful, to whom science is also given.

In fact, what is counterposed is not riches vs. poverty or money vs. science—the second terms being superior in value; it is money *with* the right faith vs. money with the *wrong* faith. Plus, science, too, derives from and follows in the wake of faith—preferably to be crowned with money in this world (in the case of the actually "chosen" few); if not, to be postponed (not to be replaced by something different) to the other world (in the case of the allegedly chosen multitude). In this sense, the matter is quite clear cut: The rich are not necessarily guilty or unfavored; if they pass the test of faith, all the better for them. The capitalist spirit or spiritual capitalism does not have to wait Protestantism; it is already here in the Book(s)—perhaps a little more ambivalently so in the Gospels. (Cf. supra, Part II.)

29. Ankebût (The Spider)   (Mecca)
Stories and lessons of prophets, destruction of kings and nations, torment forthcoming in due course of time but suddenly...

Illiterateness of Muhammad: "Prior to this (*Koran*), you could neither read or write" (29:48). (Proof of the necessity of revelation.)

30. Rûm (The Greeks, "Byzantians")   (Mecca, exc. 17)
Christian Byzantians (one of the peoples of the book) are favored against the Zoroastrian Iranians.

Repetitions...

"Don't be one of those groups who divide their religion...and brag about their own" (30:32). Unity of and homogeneity within Islam. One God, one religion, one monotheism, one community, one book, one prophet, one kind of believer, one interpretation, and so forth. "Universalism" of monopoly, "universalism" of the parochial. Islam is also totalitarian, if not so much as Christianity is. A very important and interesting argument for the unity of (the Muslim) God, with crucial implications for Islam's philosophy of man, society, and politics.

Slavery is justified on the basis of natural inequality:

("Byzantians")He has struck for you a similitude from yourselves; do you have, among that your right hands own, associates in what We have provided for you so that you are equal in regard to it, you fearing them as you fear each other? (p.107)	God is giving you (men) an example from yourself: Do you have among your slaves who are your property any partners who are equal to you—any partners who you would reckon as you reckon each other? (30:28)

This attitude or conceptualization very neatly shows the hierarchy that is inescapably constructed once you start positing a god, especially the God, over men. The social hierarchy of free men → slaves is conveniently legitimized and buttressed by the supernatural divine hierarchy of God → men, smoothly unfolding in the descending order of God → freemen → slave. Onto this basic skeleton you can easily fit in other intercalations: God → prophets → priests → men of the tribe → (men of other nations) → women → maidservants → concubines → slave girls. (Play with slight nuances and locations depending on the particular context, historical and cultural. Insert temporary hired aliens, etc., into the proper slot, e.g., foreign workers in Germany: Italians, Greeks, Turks, Africans, and so forth.)

You can, of course, put all nations on a vertical scale, as it is done in this *sura*: Arabs → Greeks → Persians.

This is one of the main, axiomatic functions (and purposes) of (all) religion: to hierarchize human beings, to legitimize the domination of some (few) over others (most) and of *both* over women. The keyword and vortical concept here is less "religion" than "God."

31. Lokman (Lokman)   (Mecca, exc. 27-29)

Though all the trees in the earth were pens, and the sea—seven seas after it to replenish it, yet would the Words of God not be spent. (p.115)	Words of God could not be exhausted (by writing) even if all the earth's trees became pens and the seas, multiplied by sevenfold, became ink. (31:27)

Surely, this is not poetry; but it is poetical, indeed.

32. Secde (Prostration)   (Mecca, exc. 18-20)

33. Ahzâb (The Confederates)   (Medina)
(See also supra, Chapter II, ff. *sura* 4.)
    Men and women are to be awarded if they are (33:35):
    Muslim,
    Faithful,
    Honest,
    Patient,
    Modest,
    Alms-giving,
    Fasting,
    Chaste.
"Muhammad...is the last of prophets" (33:40). "Truly, man is very unjust and ignorant" (33:72). Human nature. (For verses 30, 32, 50, 52, 53, which predominantly concern women, please see Chapter 2.)

34. Sebe (Sheba)   (Mecca, exc. 6)
Praise of David and Solomon (34:10-14). "We gave superiority to David" (34:10). Superiority meaning prophethood, book (Psalms), power, and wealth. David and Solomon, the wealthy king-prophets of the *Bible* are among the favorite prophets of the *Koran*.
    Criticism of and threat to wealthy and conceited notables of communities; faith better than possessions and sons (34:34-37), meaning: Be righteous and prosper! And: Wealth of the unfaithful is not legitimate, but riches of the faithful are legitimate—in fact, a sign or proof of "election."

35. Fâtir (The Angels)   (Mecca)
Repetitions; descriptions of hell and heaven (gold, silver, silk).

36. Yâsin (Ya Sin)   (Mecca)
Accepted as the "heart" of *Koran*.

"Whether you warn them or not, it is the same for them; they don't believe" (36:10).
"You can warn only those who obey the *Koran* and fear God" (36:11). It is either a foregone
conclusion or futile. Muhammad's burden is not too heavy. No argumentative and persuasive effort is called for. Predestination, not free choice. And:

We have not taught him poetry; it is not seemly for him. It is only a Remembrance and a Clear *Koran*. (p.148)	We didn't teach poetry to the Prophet. In fact, that wouldn't have become him. What he says is solely an advice revealed by God and a crystal clear *Koran*. (36:69)

37. Sâffât (The Rangers)   (Mecca)
"They" "mock" God's miracles (37:12,14); they say "Are we going to abandon our gods for
the sake of a mad poet?" (37:36).
     Hell, heaven; some features of the latter (37:41-49):
     A clean, delicious drink that does not make one drunk.
     Companions with large eyes that direct their beautiful look only to the favored ones.
     All-white companions like an egg that hasn't seen the light of day.[2]
Prophets, Lot (incest never mentioned), salutation to all prophets, praise be to God.

38. Sâd (Sad)   (Mecca)
Mighty and wealthy prophets David and Solomon are praised, who were also just and in
control of their desires and whims (esp. 35:26).
     Solomon says:

Lo, I have loved the love of good things *better than* the remembrance of my Lord... (p.160)	Truly, I harbored the love of wealth in or-der to remember my Lord (in remem-brance of my Lord). (38:32-33)[3]

(Cf. *supra* as regards money and faith, or holy wealth.)

39. Zümer (The Companies)   (Mecca, exc. 53-55)
"Watch out, pure religion is only that of Allah" (39:3), "God is one and overpowering"
(39:4), "I (Muhammad) was ordered to become the first Muslim" (39:12) (what about the
previous ones?), "Real owners of reason are the faithful" (39:18), warning and forgiveness
only before and until the *Koran* and none after once rejecting it (39:59).

God has sent down the fairest discourse as a Book, consimilar in its oft-repeated, whereat shiver the skins of those who fear their Lord. (p.168)

God revealed the most beautiful word in the form of a Book (*Koran*), one which is internally consistent and readable over and over again without causing boredom. Under the impact of this Book, those who fear their Lord shiver, and their bodies and hearts warm up and relax by this recitation. (39:23)

RECITE in FEAR AND TREMBLING. And Warm Up(!)

40. Mü'Min (The Believer)[4]   (Mecca, exc. 56-57)

"Except for infidels, no one contests God's verses." (40:4)

"God knows the treacherous look of the eye and what the heart hides." (40:19)

Moses & Aaron and Pharaoh; a member of Pharaoh's family becoming a closet Muslim; description of infidels.

Those who dispute concerning the signs of God, without any authority come to them, very hateful is that in the sight of God and the believers; so God sets a seal on every heart proud, arrogant. (p.179)

Those who contest God's verses without having any proof revealed to them are received with great hatred in the sight of God and his faithful. God seals off the heart of every presumptuous thug. (40:35)

Religions do business with hate, labeling, and defamation as their stock in trade. If God hates, men can, and will, hate, too. What is easier than to hate other human beings if God himself hates them?

And:

So when their Messengers brought them the clear signs, they rejoiced in what knowledge they had, and were encompassed by that they mocked at. (p.184)

When prophets brought them self-evident (divine) knowledge, they trusted in their own (human) knowledge and mocked it. And that which they mocked immediately strangled them. (40:83)

It would be too late for unbelievers to believe after they see God's torment.

"No prophet, on his own, can bring any verse without God's permission." (40:78)

Authority or validity-claim of messengers and their verses should be based on God's delegation of power of logos.[5]

41. Fussilet (Distinguished)   (Mecca)

This is a book explained (revealed) in verses in Arabic for a nation who comprehends. It brings good news and it warns (41:3-4).

"For a nation who knows," suggest both a positive circularity and a negative futility. The latter as regards "they"/"those" who do not "listen" (41:4), whose hearts are sealed (41:5), whose ears are closed (41:5). If the mission of the messenger and the function of the message is not to open up minds, hearts, eyes, ears, what is it? Those (we) who already know, readily believe; those (they) who cannot ever know, do not believe!

"The punishment for the enemies of God (and Muhammad) is fire. They will eternally stay in hell as the penalty for having rejected our verses" (41:28).

Nature is the miracle, and the proof, of God; e.g.: "Night and day, sun and moon are among his *ayats* (verses, proofs, miracles)" (41:37).

Human beings are stiff-necked and ungrateful by nature: "When we give man a blessing, his disregards and avoids us. But when he experiences an evil, he begs and implores" (41:51).

Too late! No way! Not even next time!

42. Şûra (Counsel)   (Mecca, exc. 23-26)

Fear (of) God, fear (of) the Prophet, fear (of) the Book; the Trinity of Fear: and we gave you such an Arabic *Koran* so that you may frighten them with the day of judgement (42:7).

Fear is the basis of faith, faith is the basis of reason, ergo: fear is the basis of reason. (How could have Kierkegaard soundly reasoned in "fear and trembling?")

Abraham → Moses → Jesus → Muhammad. Unity of God.

Some ambiguous consolation for the poor: "Who wants the gains of the other world, we increase his gains. Who wants the profits (kâr) of this world, we give him, too, some worldly things, but he would have no lot in the other world" (42:20).

Do not covet the riches of others in this world and console yourself with the penalty to be given to others in the other world. Is this not something like "reverse coveteousness," for the bone of contention remains, above all, material well-beings in both worlds. Let alone questioning the value and meaning of material goods (Islam is as materialistic as Judaism), it is just that the location of inequality in the two spaces is being reversed.

Not only does God not give equal lot (nasip) to men in life, he does not feel the compassion to give them at least equal sustenance (rizk):

Had God expanded His provision to His servants, they would have been insolent in the earth; but He sends down in measure whatsoever He will. (p.195)	Had God given his servants abundant sustenance, they would have transgressed limits (rebelled) on earth. But he diminishes sustenance to a degree he wills. (42:27)

That is, the multitude would have asked for more and become aggressive and stiff-necked (whereas Solomon, supra, wanted wealth to be a better believer). So they should remain fastidious and grateful and obedient and even, perhaps, under-nourished to such a degree as to be without energy to be active. (Just enough nutrition to be able to go to work the next morning.)

God is omnipotent, omnipresent, omniscient; he is a friend and he is the punisher; he forgives and he crushes (42:28-34); all your miseries are the result of your own deeds (42:30); do not question or discuss our verses (42:35).

Implication (or one of possible implications): Poverty and servitude is what you deserve; wealth and domination is proof of your "chosenness."

It is, presumably, the latter believers who

...answer their Lord...their affair being counsel between them, and they expend of that We have provided them. (p.196)	...conduct their affairs by way of consultation among themselves. They also spend from the sustenance (rızık) we give them. (42:38)

The wealthy ruling elite govern with a consultative assembly, also charitably giving alms from their sustenance (rızık), not lot (nasip). (Cf. that zekât, the 1/40 to be given to the poor, is from income (current sustenance?) and not from wealth (accumulated riches.)

"They" (the mutually consulting elite) avoid big sins and shameful behavior (42:37), "they" help each other when they encounter injustice (42:39). Solidarity of the elite. But mainly against whom? The unjust? But, who are the "unjust?" The uncharitable rich? ("There is torment for those who treat men unjustly and those who transgress limits on earth...[the elite?] Whoever behaves patiently and with forgiveness, he is to be lauded [the underdog?]" (42:42-43).

Quite ambivalent, indeed. I shall here stretch one of the possible logical extensions. It may well be, in view of supra, that the poor multitude are being invited to endurance and obedience to the powers that be (Cf. "submit to authorities") and are being warned against any act of uprising, rebellion, going too far (Cf. Numbers, Ch. 16), or transgressing limits in this sense. "Taşkınlık" (excess) or, here more relevantly, insolence, after all, become more the multitude than the elite.

Another internal evidence for this interpretation: immediately following "patience, endurance, forgiveness" (42:43) and their opposite, "deviance" (42:44) (= non-endurance and contestation of law [letter/verse/word]) and order, that is, disorder, sedition, rebellion, resistance, comes in close tail in verse 42:45:

Surely the losers are they who lose themselves and their families on the Day of Resurrection. (p.197)	They, in being thrown into the fire...are the (unjust) ones who shall be the losers on the doomsday, themselves and their families. (42:45)

Remember Korah's rebellion.

It was not Moses, Aaron & Sons, and the ruling Israelite elite, and it is not Muhammad, his companions, and the ruling Muslim elite (Cf. the 72/73 supra) who were/will be thrown into fire and down into the belly of the earth with their households and "little ones," as in Numbers, Chapter 16. It was and will be the rebellious, disobedient, un-submitting people or some popular leader who did not endure the economic hardships and questioned the political "lording it over" of the powers that be.

Conceedably the threat in question may have more generic implications of no practical consequence, but that the real veiled threat is directed to those who question the worldly status quo is more plausible textually-logically and more probable empirio-historically.

43. Zuhruf (Ornaments) (Mecca)

The Arabic *Koran* is "an exalted book full of wisdom and is contained in the Main Book we have here with us" (43:4).

Whenever prophets and books were sent to a country, the wealthy rejected them (43:23), and now they ask if this *Koran* could not have been sent to a great (wealthy) man (43:31)? Muhammad's populism in the Meccan years of formation was to be attenuated in his Medinaen years of consolidation in parallel with the aggrandizement of his wealth, status, and power. Again some more ambivalent, or diagonal, or cris-cross, message:

What, is it they who divide the mercy of thy Lord? We have divided between them their livelihood in the present life, and raised some of them above others in rank, that some of them *may take others in servitude*; and the mercy of thy Lord is better than that they amass. (p.201)

Are they (the wealthy) the ones who distribute Lord's blessings? It is we who distributed men's sustenance in the worldly life. We made some of them superior in degree to others so that some have the others do the work. Your Lord's mercy is better than that they accumulate. (43:32)

The higher the rank, the higher the livelihood and possessions. The lower the rank, the lower the latter. Is this egalitarianism or outright, unscrupulous inegalitarianism? The last sentence is but an awkward catch.

And some more precious metal: "Had there been no danger of men's becoming a single community united in disbelief, we would have made unbelievers' houses' ceilings and stairs from silver" (43:34).

Their "doors" and "seats," too. A discourse in which inequality and silver shine.

44. Duhân (Smoke) (Mecca)

In heaven, the faithful will be "espoused to large-eyed houris (very beautiful girls)" (44:54). Remember that the *Koran*, too, addresses men and that, here, "large-eyes" belong to women.

45. Câsiye (Hobbling)   (Mecca)

"No doubt, for the faithful there are many signs on earth and in the heavens" (45:3). (*Ayat,* here, means proof, evidence, sign, wonder, miracle. That is, nature, all creation is a miracle.) (Then, and since God wills and makes everything, is all evil a miracle, too?)

Koran forbids agnosticism, too: "You have said that we do not know what doomsday is; we think that it is but a conjecture; we have no definite knowledge of it" (45:32). Is that so?

"The thing they mocked will besiege them." (45:33).

46. Ahkaf (The Sand-Dunes)   (Mecca)

Torah narratives and lessons are repeated. Much tautology, as well.

47. Muhammad (Muhammad)   (Medina)

When you meet the unbelievers, smite their necks, then, when you have made wide slaughter among them, tie fast the bonds; then set them free, either by grace or ransom... (p.220)	When you encounter (in war) infidels, behead them. Tie prisoners tightly. When the war is over, free them with or without ransom. (47:4)

This is more *Torah* than Gospel.

There are in heaven rivers of:

water,

milk,

wine,

honey (47:15).

"Milk and honey" of the "promised land." God curses, deafens, blinds, seals hearts (47:23-24). Don't be stingy: "God is rich; you are poor" (47:38).

48. Fetih (Victory/Conquest)   (Medina)

Old and *New Testaments* are affirmed; *Koran* leans more on the former rather than the latter.

49. Hucurât (Apartments/Rooms/Chambers)   (Medina)

"Ye, believers! Don't get in front of God and his Prophet" (49:1). The two proximate; the rest distant. (Not trinity but duplication. Or duplicity?)

"Ye, believers! Don't raise your voice above that of the Prophet" (49:2). Know thy station; thou should not go too far.

50. Kaf (Qaf)   (Mecca)

God speaking:

We are nearer to him than the jugular vein. (p.234)	We are closer to man than his jugular vein. (50:16)

Physical proximity, full of intimations—and intimacies—of impending, and then, sudden death. Admittedly, this is more powerful and frightening than the Christian God's and Prophet-Son's being "in" men, for the simple reason that its associations are more bloody.

And: "There is not one word said by men that goes unrecorded by an angel who observes from close" (50:18).

Close monitoring, constant surveillance, and control of bodies and acts from close range. Monitoring, recording, punishing to assure belief, obedience, and helplessness in the hands of God and his officers.

And: "Give advice with the *Koran* to those who are afraid of my threat" (50:45).

Supra it was "frighten with this *Koran*"; here it is "give advice with the *Koran*," not withstanding the "threat," threat of death, typically lurking behind.

51. Zâriyât (The Scatterers)   (Mecca)
Abraham, Moses, Pharaoh, repetitions.

52. Tûr (The Mount/Mount Tûr)   (Mecca)
The Book was given to Moses on Mount Tûr. The book was written on fine leather (52:1-2). (Stone tablets?)

In heaven:

abundant fruit and meat (52:22);

heavenly wine—no nonsense and no sin (52:23);

pearl-like youths serving (52:24).

Creation, not evolution: Have they been created without a creator? Or, are they themselves creators (52:35)?

53. Necm (The Star)   (Mecca, exc. 32)
"He is none other but what he has revealed" (53:4). God's word becomes God, God is word. ("I am who I am?") Gabriel came near Muhammad and God revealed (53:8-11).

"These idols are nothing but names given by you and your forefathers." *Koran* is not names, but truth itself. Similarly, opinion is inferior to knowledge (of truth) (53:28) which comes with faith.

54. Kamer (The Moon)   (Mecca)

55. Rahmân (The All-Merciful)   (Mecca)
Natural facts are made into miraculous creations.

56. Vâkia (The Terror/Doomsday)   (Mecca)
On the day of last judgment, those on the right to heaven, those on the left to hell (56:8-9).

In heaven:

wine that does not derange and give headache (56:19),

cherry and banana trees (56:28-29),

elongated shadows (5:30),

cascading waters (56:31),

houris, newly and totally differently created, who are devoted to their companions and who are virgins of the same age (with their men) (56:35-37).

And no promises to women.

God omnipotent, man powerless creature: "And what do you say to the water you drink? Is it you who brought it down from the clouds or is it us?" (56:68-69)

Notes

1. *Diyanet* exposition, p. 393, is full of textual errors and dubious factual claims: (1) It makes Korah Moses' paternal cousin(?); (2) It says that Korah at first believed in Moses but then, because of his greed and jealousy he became a hypocrite(?); (3) It says that Korah rebelled against Israelites as an agent of Pharaoh (?); (4) It makes Korah = filthy rich(?) and vociferous about his wealth and science (?); (5) It says that Korah was an expert chemist and businessman(?). Now, all this is being more royalist than the king and more old-testamentlike than the *Old Testament* itself: (1) Numbers, Ch. 16 does not hint at his being a cousin of Moses; we know that he was Esau's son; (2) Korah did not become a hypocrite or unbeliever; he criticized Moses and Aaron on grounds of a truer interpretation of God's Word; (3) The bit about Pharaoh is both counter factual and anachronistic; (4) The *Old Testament* does not hint at his being a very rich men; in fact, he was criticizing Moses and Aaron's lording over both politically and economically; (5) There is in the *Old Testament* no intimation of his being a chemist or businessman. All the same, *Koran* vindicates the *Old Testament* as regards Chapter 16: OBEY OR PERISH!

2. (Cf. The Turkish saying "white woman trade.")

3. Although my (*Diyanet*) version has "in order to," I think Arberry's "better than" is correct.

4. Arberry has the erroneous plural here. "The Believers" was the 23rd *sura*. This is "The Believer" in the singular.

5. *Diyanet*, p. 475 states that the Koran mentions 25 prophets whereas in the *tefsirs* it is reported that God has sent 124,000 prophets.

19

VI. Suras 57-114

57. Hadîd (Iron) (Medina)

"God is first, last, self-evident, inconceivable. He is all-knowing" (57:3). "He is azîz, wise" (57:1). "He is the sovereign of the heavens and the earth. He resurrects and kills. He is all-powerful" (57:2). "Know that the life in this world is but a play, an entertainment, an ornament, a bragging among yourselves, and but a desire for more possessions and children" (57:20), Noah, Abraham, others, and Jesus. "As for the priesthood they made up, we didn't write that. They found it to win the favor of God. But they didn't properly comply with it, either" (57:27).

58. Mücâdele (The Disputer(s)) (Medina)
Please see Chapter II, ff. *Sura* 4.

59. Haşr (The Mustering) (Medina)
Concerning booty from conquered lands: "Take whatever the Prophet gives you and avoid whatever he forbids to you" (59:7). And fear God:

If We had sent down this *Koran* upon a mountain, thou wouldst have seen it humbled, split out of the fear of God. (p.270)	Had we revealed this *Koran* to a mountain, you would have surely seen it fall into pieces because of fear of God. (59:21)

Who are *you* to contest God (and Muhammad)? He overwhelms and crushes even mountains. So, fear him.

60. Mümtehine (The Woman Tested) (Medina)
Holy war; marrying faithful women who take refuge in you; …

61. Saf(f) (The Ranks) (Medina)
Jesus affirmed the *Old Testament* and announced the coming of a prophet named Ahmed. "Ye, believers! Shall I show you the trade (ticaret) that will save you from painful torment?

Believe in God and his Prophet, and wage holy war in God's walk with your possessions and lives" (61:10-11). What a discourse: Trade, commerce, bargain, transactions, etc.

"In that case, he forgives your sins and…sends you to heaven…This is the greatest salvation" (61:12). War is profitable: "There is another thing you will like: Help from God and an imminent conquest" (61:13).

62. Cum'a (Congregation) ("Friday")   (Medina)

"God has sent the Prophet to all (believing) peoples who have not yet joined the faithful." (62:3)

The condition of the Jews who do not comply with the *Old Testament* is like that of the "donkey who is carrying many volumes of books" (62:5).

The faithful should quit shopping and trading when they hear the call to prayer (62:9).

63. Münâfikûn (The Hypocrites)   (Medina)

64. Teğâbün (Mutual Fraud)   (Medina)
"God created the heavens and the earth properly. He shaped you, and shaped well" (64:3). (Cf. "God saw that all was good.")

65. Talâk (Divorce)   (Medina)
Please see Chapter 2, ff. *sura* 4.

66. Tahrîm   (Medina)
Please see Chapter 2, ff. *sura* 4.

67. Mülk (The Kingdom)   Mecca)
Guards of hell say to the sinful: "Hasn't a frightening prophet come to you?" (67:8) They reply: "Had we listened and used our reason, we wouldn't be among the prisoners of this firey hell" (67:10).

Too late! And:

"You shall soon know what my threat means" (67:17).
Threat → fear → faith → "reason." Otherwise, hell!

68. Kalem (The Pen)   (Mecca)

69. Hâkka (The Indubitable)   (Mecca)
Plagues to unbelieving, disobedient nations; torment does not end with death.

Those who don't believe in God (69:33) and feed the poor (69:34) will be caught with their hands tied to their necks (69:30) and thrown into the fire (69:31) on the tip of a long chain. The *Koran* is not the word of a poet or a diviner (69:41 and 42); it is revealed by the Lord (69:43); it is "Absolute knowledge itself" (69:51).

70. Meâric (The Stairways) (Mecca)

Hell is a flaming fire; it burns and peels skins (of the head and body) (70:15-16). It summons those who heap wealth (70:17-18).

"Truly man is created very ambitious and impatient...He complains and whines when evil touches him...He becomes stingy when he is given opportunity." (70:19-21)

Ecce homo! According to the Book(s). But, here, is it "is" or "is created?"

But those who pray, give alms, believe in the day of judgment, fear God, remain chaste, honor commitments, testify honestly shall go to heaven (70:24-35). The others shall get out of their tombs and go to hell (70:43-44).

71. Nûh (Noah) (Mecca)

72. Cinn (The Jinn) (Mecca)

73. Müzzemmil (Enwrapped) (Mecca, exc. 10-11,20)

Covering of Muhammad when he shivered and quivered upon seeing Gabriel.

74. Müddessir (Shrouded) ("The covered one") (Mecca)

Nonbelievers are likened to "wild donkeys who are frightened by and escape from the lion" (74:49-51).

75. Kiyâme(t) (The Resurrection) ("Doomsday") (Mecca)

76. İnsân (Man) (Medina)

Creation, testing, hell and heaven. In hell: chains, iron (locks) rings, flaming fire (76:4).

In heaven:

heavenly wine (76:5-6),

silk (76:12),

moderate climate (76:13) (neither burning heat, nor freezing cold),

shadow and fruits of heavenly trees (76:14),

heavenly wine served by youth (sâki) in silver vessels and crystal goblets, in transparent cups that are silken-white (76:15-16),

immortal, young and pearl-like manservants (76:19),

many blessings and great kingdom (76:20),

green silken dresses and silver bracelets (76:21).

The name of the *sura* is "insan" (man, human being; his awards in heaven are royal.) Not much, or anything, for women.

77. Mürselât (The Loosed Ones) (Mecca)

"Each flame in hell is like a yellow camel." (77:33)

78. Nebe' (The Tiding)　　　　　　　　　　　　　　　　　　　(Mecca)

"Hell is in lying in ambush." (78:21-22) In heaven: gardens, vineyards, heavenly drinks, and young "girls whose breasts have burst like buds" (78:31-34). Islam's penchant for fresh maidens.

79. Nâzi'at (The Pluckers)　　　　　　　　　　　　　　　　　(Mecca)

80. Abese (He Frowned)　　　　　　　　　　　　　　　　　　(Mecca)

Human nature:

Perish Man! How unthankful he is. (p.324)	May he vanish! How ungrateful man is. (80:17)
Of what did He create him? (p.324)	Why did God create him? (80:18)

To give life to him (80:19-20), to take away his life (80:21), to resurrect him (80:22), and to reward some (few) (80:38-39) and to punish some (most) (80:40-42), for: "Man did not obey God's commands" (80:23).

So, a better answer would be: To fear, to believe, to faithfully "reason"—all of this to submit to domination by other men.

81. Tekvîr (The Darkening)　　　　　　　　　　　　　　　　(Mecca)

God speaking (to men):

...but will you shall not, unless God wills. (p.327)	You cannot will unless the Lord Allah wills. (81:29)

Free will? Free choice? No! Not even faith or works. Faith or no faith—upon God's will.

82. İnfitâr (The Splitting)　　　　　　　　　　　　　　　　　(Mecca)

83. Mutaffifîn (The Stinters)　　　　　　　　　　　　　　　　(Mecca)

84. İnsikak (The Rending)　　　　　　　　　　　　　　　　　(Mecca)

85. Bürûc (The Constellations)　　　　　　　　　　　　　　　(Mecca)

86. Târik (The Night-Star)　　　　　　　　　　　　　　　　　(Mecca)

Man is created from water; *Koran* is the true book; God is the best trapper.

87. A'lâ (The Most High)　　　　　　　　　　　　　　　　　　(Mecca)

God is creator, regulator, destroyer. Beginning, middle, end. God-fearing men to be saved; same words in the previous books of Abraham(!) and Moses.

88. Ğâşiye (The Enveloper)　　　　　　　　　　　　　　　　　(Mecca)

89. Fecr (The Dawn)　　　　　　　　　　　　　　　　　　　(Mecca)

90. Beled (The Land)   (Mecca)

91. Şems (The Sun)   (Mecca)

92. Leyl (The Night)   (Mecca)

93. Duhâ (The Forenoon)   (Mecca)

"Has the Lord not found you fatherless and sheltered you? Has he not found you
poor and made you rich?" (93:6, 8)

Be chosen and prosper! Plus, don't oppress the fatherless or ever scold the poor (93:9).

94. İnşirah (The Expanding) ("Relief")   (Mecca)
In your every free moment, worship and think of your Lord.

95. Tîn (The Fig)   (Mecca)

By the fig and the olive and the Mount Si-   I swear to olives, figs, Mount Sinai, and
nai and this land secure! We indeed cre-   this secure city that we created man in the
ated Man in the fairest stature then We   most beautiful manner. Then we debased
restored him the lowest of the low. (p.344)   him below the lowliest. (95:1-5)

Why?

96. Alak (The Blood-Clot)   (Mecca)
First 5 verses of this sûre, are the first verses of the *Koran*.

97. Kadir (Power)   (Mecca)
The *Koran* was revealed on the Kadir night.

98. Beyyine (The Clear Sign)   (Medina)

99. Zilzal (The Earthquake)   (Medina)

100. Âdiyat (The Chargers)   (Mecca)

101. Kâria (The Clatterer)   (Mecca)

102. Tekâsür (Rivalry) ("Plentitude" and bragging therewith)   (Mecca)

103. Asr (Afternoon)("Century")   (Mecca)

104. Hümeze (The Backbiter)   (Mecca)

105. Fîl (The Elephant)   (Mecca)
Birds dropping hot baked clay on the enemy forces and their elephants. (Harbinger of the
atom bomb.)

106. Kureys (Koraish)   (Mecca)

107. Maûn (Charity) (Mecca)
Charity to the orphan and the needy.

108. Kevser (Abundance) (Mecca)

109. Kâfirûn (The Unbelievers) (Mecca)
"Your religion unto you; my religion unto me."

110. Nasr (Help) (Medina)

111. Tebbet (Perish) (Mecca)
A wealthy but faithless man and his wife are cursed: May both his hands dry up. May his wife, too, go to hell as a carrier of firewood and with a rope on her neck made of palm fiber.

112. İhlâs (Sincere Religion) (Mecca)

113. Felak (Daybreak) (Medina)

114. Nâs (Men) (Medina)
The last *sura* of the *Koran*, en-Nâs, means men; that is, it is on human beings. I quote it here is full, from Arberry (Vol II, p. 36):

> In the Name of God, the Merciful, the Compassionate
> Say: 'I take refuge with the Lord of men,
> the King of men,
> the God of men,
> from the evil of the slinking whisperer
> who whispers in the breasts of men
> of jinn and men.'

Is there any human being, human agent, human person here, any more than there is in previous testaments or, for that matter, in *sura* 76 Ýnsan (man, human being) above?

The Book(s) are not on human beings; they are on God(s), King(s), Prophet(s). And on the subjection of human beings thereto. Truly, woman and men are for the Law, not the Law for women and men.

The *Old Testament* was much history and law; the *New Testament* was less history and some law (some semi-original doctrinal contributions); the *Koran* is thus even less history and more law (few semi-original doctrinal contributions) in the sense of recitation and catechism of some rules. This can also be seen from the latter's text (and mine), *surâs* ever getting shorter and shorter and content-lighter toward the end, anticlimaxing in Nâs.

CONCLUDING NOTES

The texts I have analyzed are so rich in material and suggestive of ideas and problems that I cannot here attempt to summarize what I have said in the body of the work. So I shall offer only some of the possible conclusions—after I repeat several limitations of the study.

This is not scholarship but criticism. It is not theologically informed but non- and anti-theological. It is not Biblical or Koranic criticism but a critique of the *Bible* and the *Koran* from an anti-theistic standpoint. I may be seen as a barbarian "terrible simplificateur," but the immense yet simple problem posed by this modern/ancient civilization is itself so terrible that I have no qualms in this respect.

I do not take any literary liberties with these sacred texts, which are deadly serious; I, too, am painstakingly, and painfully, serious with them. I do not refine or deepen many a theme which merit more pages, separate articles, even books; I try to make an initial statement of the case in its stark wholeness. I trod mainways and do not enter into innumerable, rich byways. I emphasize continuities, similarities, and essentials, rather than discontinuities, differences, and details at lower levels of abstraction. Refinements can come later and, indeed, should be brought by others.

I don't argue with secondary sources. I don't go into any other complementary and integral sacred texts of these religions other than their core canonical doctrinal Books. And I am not concerned here with these religions' internal divisions, derivatives, theological controversies and interpretations that have developed over time and across space. I deal with their main Books that all sects and denominations of which consider as canonical and binding. In other words, I confine myself to, or focus on, the center of the circles, not on the outlying circles of the system of concentric circles. Historical and minor doctrinal variations of institutional religion and their practices—or malpractices—do not concern me here; I look at the basic doctrine "as if" that were the only one that has been pristinely put into practice. We know that that is not the case, but we also know, and should admit, that the core doctrine is a parameter or *does* bracket a certain range beyond which no historical-doctrinal variation can stray (much). In other words, and in Freud's rich phrase, I do not tackle the "narcissism of minor differences," in this case narcissism of minor religious and theological differences.

Finally, this is a critical study on/of Western monotheism, but in no way does it absolve, let alone endorse, other religions and ideas and conceptualizations of god(s). What I say about these monotheistic religions is generally valid for all theisms (including deism, pantheism, polytheism) as a genus; monotheism, to my mind, is but a particular species of that genus—and its logical extreme, I may add. Differences among the members of this category or taxonomy are matters of degree, not of kind, in my scheme of things.

Politics, Morality, Religion

There are quite a number of varieties of scientific political theory as there are numerous definitions of its subject matter, politics. But most can conveniently be grouped under two main headings: power politics theories and anti-power politics theories.

For some, these are mutually exclusive, and for still some others, the former is *the* scientific kind of political theory. Analysis and interpretation of "who gets what, when, how," or of "authoritative allocation of resources," or of "monopolistic use of force," or of " 'power' as a quantity to be acquired, aggrandized, struggled for," to cite a few prominent examples of this approach—in short, interpretation of relations of domination as they historically (and, therefore, "normally") exist in the world—is accepted as the proper task for the political theorist. He or she studies the "is" and does not concern oneself with the "ought" and other "possible" political arrangements and relations. Such are generally positivistic, empiricist, elitist, proceduralist, hierarchical, status-quo-apologetic, ideologically (overtly or covertly) conservative (and conservative-liberal), and purportedly value-free theories.

For some, however, these two groups of theories of politics—of power politics and anti-power politics—are but complementary, the former being the analytic prerequisite of the latter, or being the necessary but not sufficient condition of full theoretical political analysis: in other words being a half-way station in full theoretical practice. The concern for the "ought" and the "possible," according to this approach, is not only necessary for changing the world by ethical choice and political practice, scientific and otherwise, but also crucial for a better and fuller understanding and explaining the "is," the existing state of affairs itself. For politics is organically interrelated with morals, moral rules, basic human values, fundamental social goods, ideal and material, and distribution and sharing thereof. "Power" is but an instrument, not a goal of purposive political human action. It is not to be idealized, fetishized, reified, striven for; on the contrary, it is to be reduced, abrogated, and, at the least, to be divided and equally shared by all human beings. Therefore, on this account, mature political theory has to be normative in the final analysis and philosophically and ethically critical of the moral values and bases of political orders and relations that perpetuate inegalitarian and unjust social arrangements. Just as the end of politics is to correct unjust political relations, the vocation of political theory is to criticize and change incorrect definitions and perceptions of politics itself.

It follows (a) that political theory and moral theory, like politics and morals, are substantively intertwined making any political theory pretending to amorality a contradiction in terms and (b) that any adequate political theory has to be normative political theory in the final analysis, after and beyond being also, initially, an empirical-realistic one (in distinction to being solely a crude empiricist "real-politiker" one). Political theory and practice, be it individual or collective, involve first and foremost ethical choices and actions based thereupon (not to be confused with sheer moralism, arbitrary or voluntaristic).

Nowhere is this kinship relationship clearer than that obtains between the political theory and moral theory of great religions in general, and those of the Western monotheist religions in particular. The political theory of early human societies are embedded in, if not coterminous with, their theology, and the triadic Western monotheism (Judaism, Christianity, and Islam) is a monument par excellence to this relationship, where the moral theory of the theology is the premise of the political theory or, at a second glance, the moral component is the handmaiden of the political component.

From the mono-God at the helm, or at the apex of the system, issues in Western monotheism are a religio-moral and social order that necessitates a distinct brand of politics and sovereignty; or, a certain form of political theory and order creates/uses for its legitimation a religio-moral theory, on the vortex of which is put the arch axiomatic *idea* of mono-God. The circuit is closed; the system feeds itself back. Western monotheism has the most powerful religio-political theory and ideology, compared to other Eastern and previous Mesopotemian religions and civilizations.

The idea of the omnipresent, omnipotent, omniscient, etc., God, the he-mono-God, is the distinctive doctrinal achievement of Western civilization in creating and heretofore sustaining inegalitarian and unjust social-political orders, which other religions try to achieve in other ways.

Monotheistic Political Theory

Once a grand creator (and inquisitor) is posited as above everything human and natural, present at the beginning (creation) and in the middle (history, this world) and at the end (other world, future), all else smoothly follow. This idea of the mono-God, this immaculate conceptualization of the idealistic strain of the human mind, is the distinguishing trademark of monotheistic Western civilization.

In distinction to the more pluralistic *and* coed gods and deities of other great or lesser polytheistic religions, the Middle Eastern/Western religions have come up with the idea of an absolutely sovereign, absolutist he-God, from which emanate or derive profound implications for an undemocratic, geometrically perfect hierarchical, pyramidal political order. Eastern religions, too, notably the Hindu triad, for example, have their hierarchy among their deities;[1] but doctrinally and analytically, Western monotheism is singularly efficient in its achievement of creating an epistemological, moral, and political theory of perfect hierarchy, like Pythagoras' triangles.

The moment a first and most high creator is accepted, at least three crucial hierarchies and systems of inequality ensue: (1) a mono-causal reductive (and unscientific) epistemology about nature, material and human; (2) a moral or spiritual inferiority and worthlessness of human beings and human agency in general, along with an internal hierarchy of worth among human beings (major prophets, minor prophets, chosen men, unchosen men, more gifted ones, less gifted ones, women, slaves, etc.); (3) an inegalitarian, undemocratic political order of all sorts, from theocratic monarchy to elitist procedural democracy, be it based on Western Christian liberalism or "Eastern" Islamic varieties of political theory, intermediate forms notwithstanding.

With the possible exception of certain versions of Renaissance humanism, Enlightenment rationalism and certain brands of "Jesusism" (such as in Dostoevsky and Kazantzakis), Western Civilization, owing to its still predominant monotheism, is anti-humanistic, inhuman, even homophobic. Attempts at anthropomorphizing god or holifying man cannot humanize religion; the *idea* of God itself is anti-human to start with, and it de-humanizes and sub-humanizes human beings.

The compact of social contract theories are enacted between unequal men but at least *among men*; the covenants of Western monotheism are *dictated to men,* under duress and in fear of death, by God (and his prophets). Fear → believe → obey → become holy → prosper. Or else perish/die.

Monotheism is predicated on absolute power—indivisible, inalterable, incontrovertible. Power rests with God (and his prophets and rulers). If in polytheism distribution of power is feudal, that is, the higher god(s) is primus inter pares among lesser deities; in monotheism, God is one and only. The unity—unity of God itself (Christian trinity notwithstanding) and unity of God and men (e.g., corpus dei)—of power in monotheism is like the overpowering sovereignty in absolute monarchy. From yet another point of view, the greater anthropomorphism in polytheism and paganism is to be contrasted with the distanciation of God and men in Western monotheism. God is dangerously close but also qualitatively different. He—capital H—is not made in the image of man.

The Abrahamic Triad

All three are Near Eastern/Western religions in their point of origination, in their prophets, in their books and basic ideas. They constitute a triad, or a trilogy. It is a trinity within unity. *Old Testament* and *New Testament* explain *Koran*; *Koran* holds a retrospective projector on the unfoldable potentialities of the *Bible*.

Neither Moses nor Jesus is a European or North Atlantic oracle; they are, like Muhammad, semitic Middle Eastern personages. All are Abraham's seed; Muhammad, at least on his own account, is not even a step-child.

In their basic ideas, all three Books have more in common and represent a continuity that outweigh their differences at lower levels of abstraction and detail. While the *Old Testa-*

ment is the source of all and the *New Testament* a partial immanent critique thereof, *Koran* claims to be the last and definitive chapter of the same big book. It is, in fact, an eclectic and not too original offshoot of the previous two, inheriting its basic vices therefrom. In that sense, it is more innocent and less bloody, or rather less responsible for the doctrinal and historical misdeeds of Western monotheism, whose tone and precedents had been already firmly set by the earlier two. None renounces the basic vices of its predecessors. *Koran* is the least ritualistic and burdensome of the three.

Love, compassion, mercy, respect come later, if at all; all three are based on fear and threat of death and are covenanted under duress.

All are Manichean, binary oppositional, exclusionary, anti-human in general and inhuman especially towards non-believers. All three debase human beings, including their own faithful—Judaism, Christianity, Islam in descending order.

All are homicidal, but the *New Testament* and the *Koran*, are not infanticidal like the *Old Testament*.

None is universalistic in the proper sense of the term; all are but religious-unitarian and communal-parochial. *Old Testament* is also ethnic-tribally exclusionary; *New Testament* and *Koran* not so. But neither Christianity nor Islam can have a legitimate claim to universalism beyond non-ethnic-tribalism as regards potential adherents. Just: repent and live, or repent or perish.

All are totalitarian. Islam is not at all more totalitarian than Christianity, for example, which with its corpus dei and corpus christi is much more so. That the Christian countries have democratized more(?) in the course of time than Islamic countries is the mark less of religious-doctrinal factors than of other historical economic-social-political factors, such as class struggles. Doctrinally Christianity and the *New Testament* are much more totalitarian than Islam and the *Koran*. Attribution of false causality should cease.

All are inegalitarian, oppressive, and violent within (*New Testament*'s greater vagaries notwithstanding) and belligerent outwardly. Islamic "jihad" is but the less delinquent child of Judeo-Christianity's "wars of the Lord" and "crusades," *and* "Revelation."

None is seriously secularizable beyond a measure of laicism. And, again, doctrinally, Islam is not less secularizable or more unsecularizable than Christianity. Misplaced causality should be avoided here as well.

The harms of religion are not historical accidents or malpractices of institutional religion; they emanate from the books, the doctrine, the moral and political theory thereof.

In fact, the *Koran* basically builds upon the *Bible*; if Judeo-Christianity falls on epistemological, ethical, and political grounds, Islam does, too, being a direct descendant of the former. By the same token, if Judeo-Christianity can stand to moral-political (and logical) scrutiny, Islam can fare even better because it is later, derivative, softer, easier, etc.

In one sense, *Old Testament* is more secular than *New Testament* and *Koran* in that there is no afterlife and other world. Blessings and, much more abundantly, curses are in this world. In another sense, *Old Testament* and *Koran* are more secular than Christianity because they are more this-worldly (Cf. women, money).

All treat women as inferior. *Old Testament* and *Koran* like women; *New Testament* is outright misogynist. All are written by men, taught and enforced by men, addressed to men. They serve to legitimize domination of few men over most men and domination of all men over all women. There is no benefit to accrue from religion even to a few women. The Books give even to the dominated men the whole dominion of women as their patrimony; they give women nothing but their chains.

God is father, prophets are sons, believers are brothers(!). There is no female deity in Western monotheism, no female prophetesses or priests. Women are dispossessed even of their feminine reproductive function; they are barren and sterile; they often give birth to "worthy" children (= sons) upon God's opening up their wombs (extreme case is Virgin Mary). God, or authors thereof, hit two birds with one stone: Woman is defertilized at the same time as man is made impotent to beget highly chosen sons (extreme case is Jesus' carpenter father).

In all three, God is both close to and distant from man. Threateningly omnipresent and hovering above, but at the same time very dissimilar and in that sense far away. That he is more "within" man in Christianity is perhaps more frightening. (To the minor differences between the three in this respect I will not go into here again; the reader may go back to the texts.)

All require total submission and surrender to God, his prophets, his books, his rulers. In this sense, "muslim"—he who has surrendered—is not very original in Islam. In fact, Muhammad does not repeatedly say for nothing in the *Koran* that Abraham, Moses, etc. were the first "muslims." Christianity and Islam are very Judaic in essentials; Islam is very Judeo-Christian in basics. The three are but "great schisms" in the Abrahamic monotheist tradition.

All three are inegalitarian in their economics. They present charity and almsgiving as social justice and as legitimation of wealth. They all pay lip-service to the temporariness of worldly riches as good recruitment policy for gaining constituencies from among the poor and needy and at the same time preach fastidiousness and resignation in this world in return for fictitious gains (of the worldly kind) in the other. They all prohibit and penalize social unrest and rebellion against the wealthy and the mighty rulers of this world. Submit or perish! The promised land and prosperity of the *Old Testament* becomes the promised after-life of the *New Testament* and the *Koran*—"prosperity" being a quintessential value and meaning of human life—here and there.

All are divisive and exclusionary of some portion of humankind. They "Babelize" human beings and persistently destroy "others," favoring only "the remnant."

It is quite illogical for the Jews and the Christians not to recognize Islam and the *Koran*; Muhammad is more logically consistent in his ecumenicalism. After all, *Koran* is indeed the last statement of Abrahamic monotheism, incorporating and superseding the previous two in exemplary Hegelian sublation.

The *Koran* gets its relative merits from the *New Testament*, which is a weak internal critique of the *Old Testament*, and its vices from the *Old Testament*, to which it regresses more instead of progressing beyond the *New Testament*.

Very importantly, the *Koran* and the *New Testament* adopt the cosmology, epistemology, and ontology of the *Old Testament* and do not repudiate or disown its basic morals, philosophy of man, and inegalitarian social-political theory, however different their cultic tenets may be. Both adopt *Old Testament*'s creationist and genealogical stories and its grand narrative with local, contemporary additions.

In their philosophy of history, *New Testament* and *Koran* are linear-eschatological, whereas *Old Testament* is cyclical (exile and return). History is mainly told by *Old Testament*; the more we proceed through *New Testament* to *Koran*, history diminishes, repetition and catechism increases.

The three are so alike in their essentials that their perennial in-fighting should be explained less by doctrinal differences than historical/cultural/ethnic/political differences. Perhaps, the crucial thing on which they agree and collectively depart from is their assumption about the baseness and worthlessness of human beings. Humankind's alleged sinfulness is but a euphemism or pretext for subduing and penalizing majority of men and all of women. Christianity may seem less militant in this respect and more loving and compassionate, but it is not really so. Just like its God being more anthropomorphic and therefore nearer, its being seemingly less humiliatory toward human beings results in better public relations but not less punishment (remember Revelation), and in greater schizophrenia.

All three can compete for the grand prize in mortal statistics, both (obviously) historically and (not so obviously) doctrinally. None can compete with Sophocles in Antigone: "Of all the many wondrous things, nothing is more wondrous than man."

Rudimentary (Good) or Bad Morality

The moral-political theory of Abrahamic monotheism can be conveniently summed up by improvising on the 10 Commandments:

the first 4: mono-God rules;[2]

the other 6: social-moral rules;[3]

the 11th political rule: SUBMIT[4] OR PERISH!

(Implied in the 3rd: "...jealous God, punishing the children for sin of the fathers to the third and fourth generation of those who hate me...")

Let us skip the first 4C's as axiomatic for the faithful and the theologian. And let us assume for the moment that the other 6 are rudimentary and good social-moral rules. But let us also remember the several other sets of commandments in the Book(s) of the "peoples of the Book," the Book(s) of the "God-fearing peoples."

The 5 Commandments:
>
> Fear
>
> Believe
>
> Obey (submit, surrender) [5]
>
> Be holy
>
> Prosper or PERISH!

The 2 Commandments:
>
> Repent or PERISH! (Repent and live!)
>
> Submit or PERISH! (Disobey and die!)

The 1 Commandment:
>
> FEAR!

The composite basic political rule:
>
> FEAR—SUBMIT—LIVE! or else: DIE!

Let us for a moment not problematize the fact that the peoples of the Book have not been perfectly consistent in applying these rules, the fact that there are in the Books many more moral rules that are not even rudimentary good rules but outright unethical rules or represent bad morality, the fact that even the good rudimentary ones concern the tribal or faithful "neighbor" but not all human beings, and so forth. And let us just ponder the simple, parsimonious, elegant architecture and mechanics of the foregoing psychological-moral-political theory of the Book(s) of the peoples of the Book.

> Fear and submit to live and prosper!

Conversely:
>
> Suffer and die if you don't fear and submit!

I won't go on. Just remember, for example, Numbers, Chapter 16 (politics of death) or Deuteronomy, Chapter 28 (psychology of fear) or Revelation or the "submit to authorities" of the Romans or any similar *ayat*.

An already worthless, devalued creature is frightened to death and further debased into undignified submission. Men deprived of self-respect show no respect for other men and slaughter "others" in the name of God. The chosen few prosper and subdue the ungifted majority; the latter are mollified with the promise of getting even later by exchanging places with the former. (Cf. the "first and last" in the *New Testament*.) Certain values of bad morality are not abrogated but reinforced and sustained.

Contemporary Relevance of Religion and God

Religion in general and Western monotheism in particular are not obsolete things, or passé historical episodes, or ancient mythologies. They are in certain crucial ways, overt or covert, direct and indirect, part and parcel of contemporary life and reality; influencing and determining other parts of that reality. Theocratic states, divine kings, ruler-prophets, state churches, etc., may not be the norm today, though there are still very thick residues. Religion as ideology, as underlying moral and political theory is still very much around.

It would take a plump volume to enumerate and demonstrate in contemporary life the numerous ways in which religion, if not as institutional religion, but as epistemological moral-political "grund" theory and, emphatically, the idea of god, continue to shape and condition everyday life in Western (and Eastern) civilization, as "living and active" factors, beyond being strong residues of 2500-3000 years of cultural socialization.

I will randomly point to some. In many countries there is still an official state religion. In many "secular/laicist" countries who do not have that, religion underlies many moral, social, political practices as the "grund norm" of legitimacy.

In the constitutions of 7 or 8 states of the United States disbelief in God is still considered a crime. Jordan may not be a theocracy like Iran, but its prince, succeeding his father the king, takes an oath by the *Koran* to uphold the constitution in 1998. The United States may not be a theocracy like Vatican, but its Congress has a chaplain and its president ends his public speeches with a "God bless you." The mighty American dollar bills are adorned with a "In God We Trust."[6] The supposedly "laborite" prime minister of England quotes from the "Corintheans" in his speech during the royal-religious rituals upon Princess Diana's death. It may not any more be wholly a world of kingships and state-churches, but it is still a world of inegalitarian, however popular, political regimes, religion being the mainstay of legitimation for the former.

Christian Serbians are decimating Muslim Bosnians with greater religious fervor than an ethnic-nationalistic one; Hindus are oppressing Sikhs and Muslims; the latter doing the same to others in other localities; in fact, religious communalism lurks behind many nationalisms. (Which is the lesser evil, or is there a lesser evil?) *And*, less easily discernable even in ethnically and religiously more homogenous societies, many domestic inequalities, domination and exploitation, continue to be legitimated and rationalized by the fundamental religious belief that some human beings are "nearer to God," and therefore worthier, than others.

But more important is the fact that, however secular or secularized we may be, we still believe in God, his Word and Books, as "secular/laicist" Christians or Muslims, even if we do not any more believe in his religious institutions and clergies. In other words, we have not yet come a seriously long way from Protestantism.

And these Book(s) and those Words always preach worthlessness (sinfulness) of the many, chosenness (giftedness) of the few. In short, inequality among human beings, which aximotically derives from the hierarchy of (superhuman) God → (supermen) prophets → more gifted man-believers → less gifted man-believers → women → manslaves → maidslaves → "others" (nonbelievers or believers of other religions).

This has not changed. Not only historical religious wars and massacres were not accidental or did not result from malpractices or abuses of religion, but contemporary ethnic-religious conflict and homicide continue to take place in the name of God and religion—both conducted militantly or condoned by passive but not disapproving spectators. Domestic inequalities and injustices, too, continue to derive from and be legitimated by this divine-human hierarchy of religions.

I generally use, even when narrating, the present tense because I do not treat these three great religions and their main sacred books as historical phenomena but view them as persisting moral and ideological systems in which the Word of God is still "alive and active." For most of us these "Law Books" are not only historical grand narratives but also contemporary, current normative texts. Of the grandest and absolutist sort. They not only narrate past religio-cultural stories; they continue to regulate present day norms, moral and political, in divers direct and mediated ways, in profound and fundamental respects. So I use "is," rather than "was."

Any argument to the effect of my having de-contextualized or a-historicized religions and religious rules, I consider ill-founded. Religions are not just the content of bygone historical periods; they are still the basic precepts, presuppositions of today. Today is the context. Or rather, the context is the last 2500-3000 years—encompassing our age as well. Some rules of these books may have faded out and away, but who can sanely and in good faith deny the fact that many people still believe in God and in his words which tell that some people are more chosen, holier, worthier, "set apart" than others so that they shall be mightier and wealthier than the latter, although the latter, too, may be equally "God-fearing" (and God-believing) people. Religious presuppositions do still shape our belief in the spiritual inequality of human beings with the attendant, or resultant, legitimation of our inegalitarian and discriminatory anti-humanistic social, political, economic, and international orders and relations.

Not only the statesmen and the citizenry of Western civilization have not yet significantly secularized, Western political theory itself is still under heavy spell of theism, or monotheism.

Doctrinal religion, if not institutional religion, and the idea of God have constrained, even constricted, the greatest minds in political theory in their reach for more humanistic, democratic, egalitarian, and just ordering of interpersonal relations among human beings. Take the very recent theories of justice. None has proceeded further than justice as legal equity or justice as procedural fairness or justice as impartiality (toward the rich and the poor alike), because they are all under the yoke of Christian "charity" and Godly ordained spiritual inequality of human beings.

One last remark concerning the present contextuality of religion and God: God is in the beginning (epistemology and ontology) creating men and nature and society; God is in the middle (morals and politics) regulating and sanctioning our existence in this world; *and*—with the *New Testament* and *Koran*—God is in the end, or rather in the future, too (psychology of fear and illusion). How can such a thing, which is not only in the past but also very much in the present *and*, moreover, shall be in the future—a future which, in turn, also shapes our present—be said to be *not* quite relevant any more, today?

Theism, Deism, Agnosticism, Atheism

Many see a linear progress in mankind's transition from magic through polytheistic to monotheistic religion. Frazer calls magic a "dupe." But how are the miracles, wonders, etc., of monotheism qualitatively different from that? And how is a mono-God superior to a crowded pantheon of antropomorphic gods and goddesses, other than providing a more absolute sovereignty and hierarchy—and a patriarchal one? With its peace—hating, war—loving ethos?

Polytheism or paganism may be more pluralistic and less totalitarian than monotheism, but the basic structure and dynamics of Godly and, then, manly hierarchy are still at work. Besides, a critical reading of Hesiod and Plato shows how ready the idealistic streak in ancient Greeks was for a monotheistic quantum jump. Pantheism and mysticism, too, are forms of theism in the final analysis. There may be differences in degree as regards their worldly implications, but the moment you postulate a God, you start to differentiate between human beings as to their unequal worth (not individual differences) in interpersonal relations, namely social and political, and economic, relations.

Deism and agnosticism are also adopted as more "secular" and "rational" positions. Surely, they are cuter gestures, at once with less pernicious effects in life; but they are not logically stronger or ethically irreproachable positions, either. Deism, too, is a form of theism, in which God, as the perfect and perfectionist creator, is present at the beginning but does not show up in the middle or at the end, as does the mono-God of Abrahamic monotheism—notably more so in Christianity and Islam than in Judaism. But the basic structure and dynamics of the "doctrine of God and man" are still operative. Even if his God does not constantly interfere in human history and will not eternally interfere with human future, the deist still believes in the correct formative power of his God and remains oblivious or indifferent to the workings of monotheism—not institutionally, perhaps, but as to the plethora of legitimations of inequality and injustice in this world. And he or she is under the illusion, that his/her God is independent of the idea of the God of monotheistic religions. No, genetically and conceptually, that God, too, derives from the God of monotheism.

In general, god and religion are complementary; there is no religion without god and there is no god without religion. God is religion's axiom; religion is god's prop. In particular, the mono-God of Abrahamic tradition *is* the God of the Western deist—if she or he cares more to probe into it.

The agnostic, again culpable for his/her obliviousness and indifference to worldly inequality and injustice, seems at a first glance to be on sounder ground at least logically. I beg to differ. The matter, as it is conveniently put, is not the parallel impossibility of proving or disproving the existence of God. Existence of God cannot be and has not been proven in any logical or empirical manner, except for the believers' and theologians' nonscientific and psychopathological manouevres of rationalization, not too different from Frazer's magical "dupe." That non-existence of God has not been and cannot be proven, either, is not a symmetrically legitimate or logically equally valid claim. There is no reasonable need to prove the nonexistence of something which is known to be a figment of idealistic human imagination. That is a social-cultural symbolic construction, with no basis in material reality. It "exists" in culture not in nature. To prove the non-existence of something non-existent is absurd. The burden of proof is irrelevant here.

What I have said concerning deists I can repeat concerning those who profess to have a "personal God" and to have had a "religious experience." Religion and God are so grave matters in their adverse consequences for many human beings that no one should have the luxury of differentiating between the "public sphere" and the "private sphere" here.

The Necessity—But not Sufficiency—of Atheism

Atheism is a stand-offish position as well. It wouldn't be if many human crimes were not committed in the name of religion and God. Religious atrocities are not historical accidents or unfortunate results of misuse or abuse of the Book(s); they are doctrinally commanded and condoned. Similarly, inegalitarian and unjust practices within religious communities are commanded and legitimated doctrinally. What is called for is an anti-theist position which would emphasize that religion and the idea of God are not simply innocent, however illogical, private affairs of individuals; they have immense and grave consequences for the majority of human beings.

They are extremely functional for creating and sustaining unjust, inegalitarian human societies. Political and economic inequalities are based on the spiritual inequality of human beings, ambivalent disclaimers, especially in Christianity, to the contrary notwithstanding.

Atheism in itself is not a sufficient condition of egalitarian and just society either; it is just a necessary condition. There have been illustrious atheists from David Hume to Antony Flew, who are conservatives in their political theory. Freud, too, is merely an epistemological and philosophical atheist; his social theory is elitist and conservative. He is a pacificist and a critic of civilization, but his pessimistic view of human nature (ironically much influenced by Judaism) arrests his otherwise critical thought. Bertrand Russell accepted the title of "Lord." Theism is not the only route to elitism.

Relatedly, philosophical and praxiological anti-theism, too, is only a midway station on the way to constructive, egalitarian moral and social-political theory which should base itself on the worth of human beings in general and on the equal worth and therefore overall equality of all human beings in particular.

Religion (and the idea of God) cannot be personalized, privatized, modernized, secularized, rationalized, reformed, humanized—given these Books and "this Law." They are more religions and books of damnation than salvation, cursings than blessings, hate than love, cruelty than compassion, bad morals than good morality, undemocratic politics than a democratic one—both for the "other" and for the less worthy brethren.

They debase and deprive majority of men and all women. They deceive the mild and the meek with false promises of bad values. They silence and oppress the questioning and the dignified as rebellious and stiff-necked.

They preach hypocritical equality but they condone slavery and hierarchy; they hypo-critically criticize worldly riches and they make prosperity both as a criterion of chosenness and success in this world and as fictitious compensation in the other world. Their ambivalences, ambiguities, vagaries, inconsistencies, diagonal messages are but fakes and re-cruitment policy as well as oppressive containment. The "spirit of capitalism" is inaugu-rated by them; they propagate "spiritual capitalism" and "holy wealth." "Two masters"—Money and God—*are* worshipped in Christianity, too. "Last here, first there," is not only delusion and deluding, it is based on the same materialistic, egoistic, unjust value categories.

Religions dehumanize and infantilize human beings. They make them "fish" and "vi-pers" and "child"; they make men "virgin women," too. They make human beings schizo-phrenic and death-obsessed instead of whole and lively.

More pernicious than institutional-historical religion is the idea of God and his Word or Book. For that absolute, unquestionable text or law of the superhuman, supernatural en-tity or construct totally precludes respect for one's self and therefore for other fellow human beings and citizens. It makes human beings subhuman. The more you revere the God (or a god) and his prophets, the less you respect other members of your species. The more you put in God, in Marx's telling phrase, the less human you become, and the more inhuman you become toward other human beings, I may add.

God and his few men "Babelize" and hierarchize human communities; they stand in the way of creating a humanistic and egalitarian polity and morality. To get rid of communal strife, violence, injustice, and murder, it is necessary to get rid of religion and the idea of a discriminating God. (Religious exclusionism and aggression is a precedent for all eth-nic-national-tribal atrocities. The modern "nation-state" is no more humanitarian than the traditional religious community save for a measure of secularism and laicism domestically.)

If God is superhuman, man becomes subhuman, and most men more so than others. If the righteous man is conceived as a hearty but thoughtless believer or faithful, the normal human being becomes worthless and reasonless.

If contextualizing religion historically and sociologically means whitewashing the "Law," the political and moral theory of these Books, I am not for it. It is the greatest folly, error, and malaise of human cultural and political history, invented by few men, imposed on most men and all women. Three millennia ago and for three millennia, in the case of monotheism. Human beings are socialized into it, frightened and threatened by it, eventu-ally internalizing it as a good thing. If not persuasion, then coercion. If not ideology, than power-politics. Power-politics of fear and death, including homicide, if not infanticide. Psychology of fear (Cf. Ch. 28) and politics of murder (Cf. Ch. 16). FEAR → BELIEVE →

OBEY → BE HOLY (only some/few of you, that is the "REMNANT"). That is: SUBMIT OR PERISH!

What for? TO PROSPER! (Here *and* there; "last and first," same in both places.)

It is not a matter of good books/religions having been misapplied or abused in history. Though that is part of the story in the sense that excesses have of course occurred, the problem is that such excesses are not historical deviations from the books but they are inspired and dictated by the very doctrine contained in those books. It is not true that even religions/books have been ineffectual in curbing historical evil, let alone inspiring real goodness; it is the case that religions/books have aggravated, if not outright created bad morality and politics, from infanticide, genocide to subjection of all women, oppression of most men, and so forth. Textual-doctrinal evidence has, I think, been amply provided in the present study.

Although it has not been my business in this study to deal with the more interesting and the crucial question of "How, then, many people could have believed and still continue to believe in the goodness of these books?" I shall proffer one plausible answer. They did not read them fully and carefully. To the extent that they read them or listened to them in part, they were under duress to believe that these books/words were good ones. In fear and trembling, under threat of death (of their children, too), exposed to psychological warfare, they were forced to countersign an invalid covenant. FEAR AND BELIEVE. SUBMIT OR PERISH. These are the basic commandments of Western monotheistic religions.

Fear is a part of human mature. But courage is, too. A psychological (and social) need for morality is also a part of human nature. But not religious morality or faith. There are still, at this hour of human history, some philosophers and scientists, some sociobiologists, who try to advance a case for religious morality or religious belief, to the effect that the need for religion is in human genes or the "idea" of God (at least a personal one) and the "fact" of religious experience are genetically embedded. All this is sheer scientistic theology. It is misplaced causality; it is attribution of causal determinative power to certain effects of certain historical-cultural factors.

"Philosophy of religion" is a misnomer, though it exists historically. What is real is not necessarily rational. Logically, it is a contradiction in terms. Philosophy asks, reasons, argues; religion prohibits questioning, commands faithful belief, recites. Philosophy calls men to learning and knowledge; religion, from Genesis onward, says "thou shalt not know." It says to men: God knows, you don't know. Who are you to know? And who are you to question God's (and his prophets' and his rulers') word, wisdom, government, etc.?

Theodicy is a redundant and futile occupation. Religion and the idea of God(s) are the direct source and cause and legitimator and occluder of most of the evil in this world. Many social and political injustices, many cultural and psychological malaises persist not despite religion and god but because of them. They are not only opiates but also stimuli for inequality among human beings and for the murder of the "other" "brother"—filial or otherwise. If not Cain *vs.* Abel or Jacob *vs.* Esau or Shem *vs.* Ham (*and* Canaan) or Absalom *vs.* Ammon any more, it is, through Paul *vs.* Greeks or Luther *vs.* Catholics, still brethren *vs.* heathen or John *vs.* Ahmad or Bill *vs.* Dick or Hassan *vs.* Hussein, ad infinitum.

The principal, not archetypal but cultural or rather religio-cultural, principle remains the same: The other brothers are not equally worthy different entities; they are relatively worthless entities alien to the allegedly superior self. Nothing short of narcissism with a bonus: not only self-loving solipsizm but also other-hating xenophobia. Identities (individual or collective) based on the negation of other human beings, at the expense thereof.

It is bad moral and political theory for the multitude (who are afraid because they are frightened) but very functional for the chosen few; Western monotheism, first but not least, is a very cunning and serviceable economic ideology for that same chosen few. It legitimizes their holy wealth within the framework of a Godly hierarchical architecture built on the essential(istic) spiritual inequality of human beings.

Of the four great atheists, Freud over-psychologized religion overlooking this inegalitarian aspect of it due to his ironically faulty understanding of human nature and of the nature of society. Darwin let matters go at something like the following: If the misery of some of our human brothers is the work of God I have nothing to say, but if it is our doing shame on us. Marx and Engels, much ahead of the former two in their critique of religion, over-sociologized religion as part of the superstructure along with politics, law, ideology, and as subject to change with determinative changes in the economic base. Yet they underestimated the staying power and resilience of religion. True, much change has taken place in the political, legal, ideological departments of the superstructure due to changes in the mode of production and developments in the forces of production, but no proportionate change has been forthcoming not only in the religious department from slavery to feudalism to capitalism and to late-capitalism, but also in basic relations of production, namely private property and maximization of worldly riches. Save for a brief, and ambivalent, period in the history of the Christian church, the monotheistic Western Civilization (500 BC–2000 AD) has been worshipping "two masters," Money and God, commanded by this "Book of Law" that has been regulating unequal "relations of worth" between human beings.

I said that this is criticism. Embedded in every critique is an implicit alternative proposal, which at the next stage can be developed into a positively elaborated constructive theory (which is also already antecedent to that critique). Mine should be readily recognizable: Difference is not inequality; it is richness. Inequality is not an attribute of human beings; it is an historically contingent, culturally manufactured, social aspect of the nature of interpersonal relations of human beings. Equality in all its dimensions—legal, political, economic, *and* spiritual—is the sine qua non of the freedom and full development of human beings: equality and, only then, freedom of each for the full development of all *and* equality and freedom of all for the full development of each!

Religion and God stand in the way of equality of opportunity, not to mention equality of conditions, for which each and every woman and man is entitled by her or his "birthright."

And they stand in the way not only of the unchosen, non-remnant multitude, but also of the remaining, treasured few by depriving the latter, too, from reasonable, just, meaningful, natural, and normal human lives and human flourishing. The whole ontology, epistemology, morality, political theory of the Western civilization, with all their fundamental concepts and values should be reconceptualized and revalued.

A naturalistic humanism would suffice. A scientifically grounded moral and political theory based on an egalitarian, non-theistic human psychology and biological anthropology would do the trick. There is nothing in monotheistic religion that is a logical, or has been an historical, prerequisite of our present rudimentary-good moral and political theory. It is the other way around. Monotheistic religion has arrested and preempted the development of our political and moral theory.

If, or when, religion is seriously humanized, it would cease to be religion; that category will have been abrogated.

Notes

1. I am not implying that more polytheistic religions are not authoritarian—all religions and ideas—belief systems of god(s) have their own devices for that; I am simply saying that Western monotheism is one particular example of the doctrinal perfection of this conceptual construction of worldly hierarchy based on divine hierarchy. I would be among the last to sympathize, for example, with Hesiod's *Theogony* or Plato's hierarchies, or with Hinduism which sustains the deplorable caste system, or the pre-monotheistic Mesopotemian religions from which the former has borrowed a lot and/but to which it has added a lot in a new configuration. That the pantheon is more pluralistic and co-ed does not alter the basic mechanics of hierarchy that emanates from the very idea of god(s).

2. God, no other gods, punishment of generations, no misuse of the name.

3. No dishonoring of parents, no murder, no adultery, no theft, no false testimony, no coveting of neighbor's possessions.

4. To God, his prophets, his worldly rulers.

5. To God, his prophets, his worldly rulers.

6. Remember: Fear God, believe and obey him, be holy and prosper. And, not but, see also the Gospels' "You cannot serve two masters, God and Money." Don't forget that in this God-believing America, a huge continent of natural resources with a relatively small population, about ¼th of the populace is chronically under "poverty line."

FURTHER READING

Alter, Robert and Frank Kermode, eds., *The Literary Guide to the Bible*. (Cambridge: Harvard Uuiversity Press, 1987)

Angeles, Peter A., ed., *Critiques of God: Making the Case Against Belief in God*. (New York: Prometheus Books, 1997)

Arberry, A.J., *The Holy Koran*. (London: George Allen and Unwin, 1953)

Arberry, Arthur John, *The Koran Interpreted*. (London: George Allen and Unwin Ltd., 1955), 2 volumes.

Armstrong, Karen, *A History of God*. (New York: Ballantine Books, 1993)

Asad, Talal, *Genealogies of Religion*. (Baltimore: Johns Hopkins University Press, 1993)

Campbell, Colin, *Toward a Sociology of Irreligion*. (London: Macmillan, 1971)

Delaney, Carol, *Abraham On Trial: The Social Legacy of Biblical Myth*. (Princeton: Princeton University Press, 1998)

Delaney, Carol, *The Seed and the Soil*. (Berkeley: University of California Press, 1991)

Dods, Marcus, *The Bible: Its Origin and Nature*. (Edinburgh: T. and T. Clark, 1905)

Eisler, Riane, *The Chalice and the Blade*. (San Francisco: Harper and Row, 1988)

Ferré, Frederick and Rita H. Mataragnon, eds., *God and Global Justice*. (New York: Paragon House, 1985)

Flew, Antony, *Atheistic Humanism*. (Buffalo: Prometheus Books, 1993)

Flint, Robert, *Anti-Theistic Theories*. (Edinburgh: William Blackwood and Sons, 1880)

Freud, Sigmund, *The Future of an Illusion*. (New York: Anchor Books, 1964)

Gibb, H. A. R., *Mohammedanism*. (London: Oxford University Press, 1969)

Gilson, Etienne, *God and Philosophy*. (New Haven: Yale University Press, 1969)

Gora, *Positive Atheism*. (Vijayawada: Atheist Centre, 1972)

Holyoake, Jacob, *The Principles of Secularism*. (London: Book Store, 282, Strand, 1870)

International Bible Society, *The Holy Bible: New International Version*. (USA: Zondervan Corporation, 1984)

Jomier, Jacques, *The Bible and the Koran*. (New York: Desclee Co., 1964)

Kinsley, David, *Hindu Goddesses*. (Berkeley: University of California Press, 1986)

Leach, Edmund, *Genesis as Myth and Other Essays*. (London: Jonathan Cape, 1969)

Mann, Scott. *Heart of a Heartless World: Religion as Ideology*. (Montreal: Black Rose Books, 1999)

Marx, Karl, *The Economic and Philosophic Manuscripts of 1844.* (New York: International Publishers, 1964)

Marx, Karl and Frederick Engels, *The German Ideology.* (New York: International Publishers, 1970)

McLachlan, H. *The Religious Opinions of Milton, Locke and Newton.* (New York: Russell and Russell, 1972)

Miles, Jack, *God: A Biography.* (New York: Vintage Books, 1996)

Newell, William Lloyd, *The Secular Magi.* (Maryland: University Press of America, 1995)

Nielsen, Kai, *Philosophy and Atheism.* (Buffalo: Prometheus Books, 1985.

Pals, Daniel L., *Seven Theories of Religion.* (New York: Oxford University Press, 1996)

Parrinder, Geoffrey, *World Religions.* (New York: Barnes and Noble, 1983)

Schwartz, Regina M., *The Curse of Cain: The Violent Legacy of Monotheism.* (Chicago: Chicago University Press, 1997)

Sharma, Arvind, *Our Religions.* (San Francisco: Harper, 1993)

Shelley, Percy Bysshe, *The Necessity of Atheism and Other Essays.* (Buffalo: Prometheus Books, 1993)

Smart, J.J.C. and J.J. Haldane, *Atheism and Theism.* (Oxford: Blackwell Publishers, 1996)

Smart, Ninian, *Religion and the Western Mind.* (New York: State University of New York Press, 1987)

Smith, Henry Preserved, *The Bible and Islam.* (New York: Arno Press, 1973)

Turner, Bryan S., *Religion and Social Theory.* (London: Sage Publications, 1994)

Ward, Harry F. *Our Economic Morality and the Ethic of Jesus.* (New York: Macmillan, 1929)

Wilkins, W.J., *Hindu Mythology.* (New Delhi: Heritage Publishers, 1991)

Wilson, Edmund, *The Scrolls from the Dead Sea.* (New York: Meridian Books, 1959)

Yoder, John H., *The Politics of Jesus.* (Michigan: William B. Eerdmans Publishing Company, 1972)

ALSO PUBLISHED by BLACK ROSE BOOKS

winner of the 2001 Robinson Book Prize for excellence in Communication Studies

ISLAMIC PERIL

Media and Global Violence, updated edition

Karim H. Karim

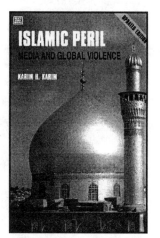

Islamic Peril explores the lack of historical and cultural understanding in the mass media as it studies coverage of conflicts involving Muslims in the Middle East, the Caucasus,
the Balkans, and the West, and demonstrates the resilience of
core European images of Muslims that have continued to recur in depictions of Islam for over a millennium.

> If the importance of this kind of scholarship was evident
> prior to the events of September 11th, such work has
> taken on added urgency since that time.
> —*Canadian Journal of Communication*

Karim should be applauded for his excellent analysis. A timely book…that makes a
very important contribution. —*Middle East Journal*

An important addition to the critical literature. —*Choice*

A valuable book that should take its place among the serious works that enlighten.
—Edward S. Herman, *SAIS Review*

Karim's *Islamic Peril*…updates and substantially extends Edward Said's *Covering Islam*. —*Journal of Communication*

Islamic Peril's message has taken on a more forceful sense of relevance and urgency
in the aftermath of September 11th and the crashes that literally shook the world.
—*Media*

An intellectually engaging book offering insightful and constructive suggestions.
Must reading. —Baha Abu-Laban, Professor Emeritus, University of Alberta

This book challenges conventional ideas and deserves to be widely read.
—Martin Shaw, International Relations & Politics, University of Sussex

KARIM H. KARIM, Ph.D., is an assistant professor at the School of Journalism and Communication, Carleton University in Ottawa. Prior to teaching, he worked as a journalist for
the Rome-based Inter Press Service, and for the Luxembourg-based *Compass News Features*.

224 pages, bibliography, index, *with a new Introduction and Afterword*
Paperback ISBN: 1-55164-226-3 $26.99
Hardcover ISBN: 1-55164-227-1 $55.99

WOMEN AND RELIGION
Fatmagül Berktay

While taking women's subjectivities and their reasons for their taking to religion into account, this book focuses mainly on the *functions* of religion, the way it relates to women; its contribution to gender differences; and the status of women within it, particularly the relationship between gender on the one hand, and power and social control on the other, and within this context, the meanings attributed to the female body. Undertaken as well, is an exposition of contemporary Fundamentalism in both its Protestant and Islamic variants (in America and Iran).

FATMAGÜL BERKTAY is an associate professor with the Department of Philosophy, and teaches feminist theory at the Women's Research Center, both of the University of Istanbul, Turkey. She is a political scientist; translator; and publicist active in the women's movement in Turkey; and, has published many articles both in Turkey and abroad. She is a contributor to *Being a Women, Living and Writing*.

240 pages, bibliography, index
Paperback ISBN: 1-55164-102-X $24.99
Hardcover ISBN: 1-55164-103-8 $53.99

HEART OF A HEARTLESS WORLD
Religion as Ideology
Scott Mann

A comprehensive, accessible exploration of religious thinking from stone age times through to the modern world, *Heart of a Heartless World* traces the origin and development of religion in economic and political life, and its lasting influence on both the individual and the family. Topics covered include the religious beliefs of hunter-gathers, shamanism, goddess worship in Neolithic times, religion and ecology, religion and the origin of the State, Jesus as magician or social revolutionary, the psychology and the politics of celibacy, and the mythico-religious dimensions of modern physics.

SCOTT MANN has taught philosophy and social theory at the universities of Sussex, Sydney and Western Sydney. He was a lecturer and director of the Center for Liberal and General Studies at the University of New South Wales, and is currently teaching in the University of Western Sydney. His previous book was *Psychoanalysis and Society: An Introduction*.

400 pages, bibliography, index
Paperback ISBN: 1-55164-126-7 $24.99
Hardcover ISBN: 1-55164-127-5 $53.99

a definitive and enlightening study of a complex set of explosive relationships which may, in the end, determine the future of our world

FATEFUL TRIANGLE

The United States, Israel and the Palestinians

Noam Chomsky

Foreword by Edward Said, Updated Edition

Since its original publication in 1983, Chomsky's seminal tome on Mid-East politics has become a classic in the fields of political science and Mid-East affairs. For its tenth printing, Chomsky has written a new introduction, and added a foreword by Edward Said. This new, updated edition highlights the book's lasting relevance, and should be a treasure for fans of the first edition, and an eye-opener for those new to the work.

> Disturbing, provocative. When Chomsky takes on the complexities of Israel and the cauldron of Middle East politics, you can expect controversy. —*Montreal Gazette*

> Chomsky's tough-minded analysis raises difficult, painful questions for Israel. —*Globe and Mail*

> Chomsky's unrelenting tone paints a frightening picture. —*Maclean's*

> A must read for anyone following the still tangling mess that is today's Middle East. —*The Financial Post*

> A devastating collection. —*Library Journal*

> A monumental work. —*Choice*

> Powerful and thoroughly documented. —*The Progressive*

> This is a jeremiad in the prophetic tradition, an awesome work of latter-day forensic scholarship by a radical critic of America and Israel. —*The Boston Globe*

A world renowned author, linguist, radical philosopher, and outspoken critic of the mass media and U.S. foreign policy, NOAM CHOMSKY is Institute Professor of the Department of Linguistics and Philosophy at MIT. For an overview on the life of America's most famous dissident, see the companion book to the critically acclaimed video documentary *Manufacturing Consent: Noam Chomsky and the Media* (Black Rose Books).

485 pages, extensive annotation, bibliography, index
Paperback ISBN: 1-55164-160-7 $28.99
Hardcover ISBN: 1-55164-161-5 $57.99

send for a free catalogue of all our titles
BLACK ROSE BOOKS
C.P. 1258, Succ. Place du Parc
Montréal, Québec
H2X 4A7 Canada
or visit our web site at: http://www.web.net/blackrosebooks

to order books
In Canada: (phone) 1-800-565-9523 (fax) 1-800-221-9985
email: utpbooks@utpress.utoronto.ca

In United States: (phone) 1-800-283-3572 (fax) 1-651-917-6406

In UK & Europe: (phone) London 44 (0)20 8986-4854 (fax) 44 (0)20 8533-5821
email: order@centralbooks.com

Printed by the workers of
MARC VEILLEUX IMPRIMEUR INC.
Boucherville, Québec
for Black Rose Books Ltd.